MW01595372

ISBN: 9781314562088


Published by:
HardPress Publishing
8345 NW 66TH ST #2561
MIAMI FL 33166-2626

Email: info@hardpress.net
Web: http://www.hardpress.net

[redacted]

[redacted]

# THE VOICE OF AFRICA

## VOL. II.

Woman of Ifë.

Nupe-Woman.

Tuareg of Asben.

Gober Man.

SOUDANESE TYPES
(from oil and water colour sketches by Carl Arriens.)

# THE VOICE OF AFRICA

BEING AN ACCOUNT OF THE TRAVELS OF THE GERMAN INNER
AFRICAN EXPLORATION EXPEDITION IN THE YEARS 1910—1912

BY
## LEO FROBENIUS

IN TWO VOLS.

WITH
SEVENTY PLATES, INCLUDING
TWO COLOURED FRONTISPIECES
TWO HUNDRED ILLUSTRATIONS IN THE TEXT
FROM PHOTOGRAPHS AND DRAWINGS
FOUR MAPS AND TABLES

TRANSLATED BY RUDOLF BLIND

VOL. II.

LONDON: HUTCHINSON & CO.
PATERNOSTER ROW
1913

# CONTENTS

## VOL. II.

# ILLUSTRATIONS

## VOL. II.

vii

## MAPS

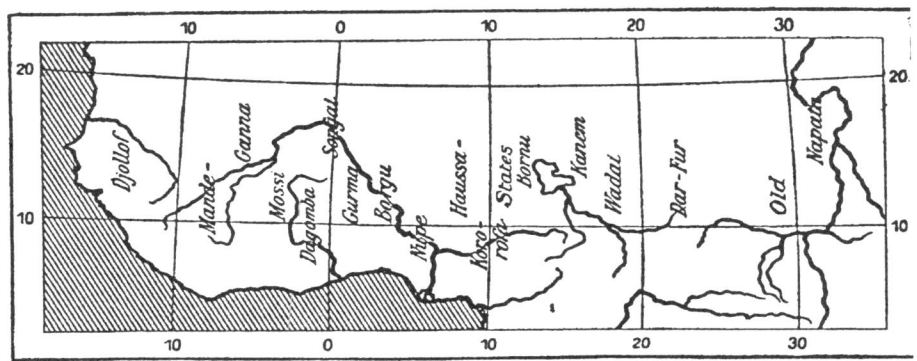

The most important older States of the Soudan.

*( Drawn under the direction of Dr. M. Groll.)*

## CHAPTER XVI

### THE SPECTACLES OF ISLAM

Different Soudanese races; State-building races and "disruptive" tribes—Islam; its origin and influence on the Soudan—The meaning of the "spectacles" of Islam—Division of the following chapters.

THE investigation of ancient civilizations and the existence of an ancient cultured nation on the West Coast of Africa occupied the first portion of this work. We will now proceed to the actual Interior and it will be my endeavour to supply material for properly judging the so-called Soudan and the state of its culture.

The Arabs gave this country the name of " the Soudan." It means and is the land of the blacks, and thus these first words demonstrate the influence of the people who brought the religion of the Prophet into the Continent, a religion which, as many believe, introduced the higher civilization to " poor negroes " and gave them the opportunity of higher development! The Arab, who first pronounced the word " Soudan," *i.e.*, the black's country, must have come from the North. It stretches from the Southern edge of the mighty Great Desert, which is inhabited by fairer-complexioned races, from the Nile away to Senegambia. Geographically considered, it represents the equation of the tropical South with the burning waste lands of the North in this Continent, and is not, therefore, uniform in character, but contains evidences of transitional qualities in the north very similar to the desert districts for which "Sahel" is the most fitting name, and towards the South has the characteristic landscapes and other attributes peculiar to the tropical Western or Southern regions. The Soudan can scarcely be said to be beautiful in the proper sense of the word. Its general aspect is flat, and its uniform plains of clay soil are signalized by annually recurrent bush fires, debilitated vegetation and sparsely distributed acclivities. Its rivers and streams are shallow and sandy, dry up almost entirely when the rainy season is over, and give the population far less water than the millions of wells which have been hacked out and driven into the earth.

Two completely different types of nation dwell in the Soudan. By "type" I do not here mean to indicate generalized racial peculiarities, but signs of civilization. The extremes of both these types are so pronounced as to be without parallel in Europe, and I call these peoples or tribes respectively "statebuilders" and "disrupters." For the Soudan, going from east to west, is composed of a great series of "powerful" kingdoms (in the African sense of the word), namely: Nubia or Napata, Darfour, Wadai, Bornu-Kanem, the Houssa states, Kororofa, Nupé, Borgu, Gurma, Mossi, Songai, the Mande state and Joloff. Their distinctive quality is that a State-building, dominant race dwells in capitals varying in size, which command the traderoutes of more or less length and the commercial centres, while more or less different kinds of petty tribes, having nothing to do with politics and being actually peasants whose quite different languages prevent their completely understanding the ruling races, live on the plains; who scarcely ever profess Mahommedanism, but very primitive religions and whom their exploitation by the governing nation drains dry. These small tribes I call "disruptive." They represent the second type. As already stated, it is impossible to imagine a greater contrast than actually exists between them while frequently living in close contiguity. The "state-builders" dispose of all the adjuncts to power, such as government offices, troops of cavalry, embassies and bazaars; the "disrupters" are without towns, live together only in small settlements and chiefly in places as difficult of access as possible, such as mountain declivities, forests and swamps. The "state-builders" are always rich in their clothing, while the "disrupters" cover their nakedness to the best of their ability. Everywhere the former are the effective momentum, the driving force and the possessors of commercial monopoly, while the latter are mostly the hoers of the soil and employed in domestic industry, only go to market to sell their agricultural produce and are universally in the most wretched dependence, even when they are held in fear on account of their warlike prowess, which is not infrequent. The difference is especially typical when the material of speech is compared. All the constructors of states speak a widely distributed tongue but little differentiated by dialect. The resources of language of the "disrupters," however, change so greatly from place to place that none but a few women can understand their neighbours. While it is possible with a command of four languages, viz.: Mande, Houssa, Fulbe and Arabic, to hold easy converse with all city-dwellers from the mouth of the Senegal up to Abyssinia, one is compelled, for example, in the Niger-bend, the South Houssa country, or in Adamawa to use a different and fresh mode of speech daily in travelling through the settlements of the "disrupters."

It has, however, been customary in Europe to judge of the historical development of the cultural importance of the Soudan by the character of these state-forming nations. It is a common practice to assume the existence of a higher form of civilization among these alone, to consider them alone worthy of notice and to observe the population of those countries from the standpoint adopted by themselves. But, as a rule, one not only fails to stop short at this intrinsically unjustifiable mode of investigation, but aggravates the wrong thus done by listening to these ruling and state-forming races as the *a priori* mouthpieces of Islam, and paying no attention at all to the unorthodox builders of states, although there still are "heathens" even among the nations of the "policy-creating" type! This critical attitude is quite intelligible and explained by the fact that within the last eight centuries Islam itself was adopted by a great number of these aggregations and this influenced their own judgment of the state of affairs. As, now, explorers in general are inclined to get into touch with the upper strata and adherents of Islam, and, since the Mahommedans, as I shall directly show, are ambitious to be everywhere considered the prime originators of culture, the explanation of this presents no difficulty.

Now it is, however, easy to establish considerable distinctions among the Soudanese "state-constructors," with whom alone I shall be principally concerned in the following pages, because a separate volume treats of the "disruptive tribes" in the scientific edition. Speaking ethnologically, we may at once assume— although, naturally, the soundness of the assumption needs proof —that these "disrupters" represent an older form of civilization. But even among the "state-formers" themselves we may at once easily recognize two different types which conform to the historical development and find their expression in two clearly visible streams of tendency. There is a little map in the text (v. p. 449) intended to show these movements pictorially. On the one side we see the northerly and westerly streams advancing, carried along by the Mandes, Fulbes, Moroccans, Songai and Djerma pushing southwards. On the other side there is plainly a movement undertaken by the Mossi, the Nupé, the So and the Napata people. The first, according to its historical growth, we differentiate as the Western, the second as the Eastern group. It is the former which brought Islam into the Soudan, the other which represents an older strain of civilization among the formers of states (v. sketch map facing p. 496).

Popular judgment has hitherto been based on the knowledge acquired of the Southern races, which was the material offered in the Mahommedan group of the West. It is, then, most highly important for us to be clear about the quality of this light of Islam, and what is the meaning in general of Islam in Africa. For, without this preliminary elucidation, a proper account of Soudanese life on the whole and the experiences of an Expedition in the great cities of the Mahommedan Soudan will be impossible.

\*　\*　\*　\*　\*　\*　\*　\*　\*

The question before us is, what did Islam's migration with regard to the Soudan imply ? What were its form and the direction of its influence ?

Islam appeared with its panoply of war in the Soudan only after a great part of its inhabitants had already joined the Mahommedan faith. The Arabian migration, which bore the Crescent aloft after the Hedjira (A.D. 622) through Northern Africa and Egypt towards the lands of the Cross, never reached the Soudan. Islam recruited adherents there only after that tremendous upheaval of nations in which the growing might of the Fatimid dynasty shattered the North. And then Islam came in, not with alarms and excursions, but crept its way in through the back doors of Soudanese palaces in the comfortable slippers of Inner African commercial life, which was already thousands of years old.

Now, it must be borne in mind that Islam arose in a nation whose culture was meagre and that its founder was a man so poorly educated as to be unable to distinguish between Judaism and Christianity. It was only after conflict and contact with superior peoples like the Persians, and especially the later Hellenes, that Islam acquired a most remarkably higher development and intellectual depth. Then, too, its continued growth was hindered in Asia, because, on the one hand, lacking its adoption by some great and magnetic personality which could bring to it converts, it evaporated in far more civilized Persia, and, on the other, fell into the hands of the Turkish tribes who were now for the first time appearing upon the scenes in a very primitive way.

The African Soudan gained nothing whatever from the high state of development of Islam which was specially influenced by later Hellenism and not a little furthered by the Zoroasterism emanating from Persia. It is not at all improbable that in former days, and even in quite modern times, it always produced a few eminent intellects in the Soudan, nay, it even survived the institution of universities and high schools, but never in its later growth penetrated the real heart of Negro Africa. The Soudanese accepted it in its original form, namely, as a comparatively primitive religion poor in culture. But not only so !

Islam, particularly in the form in which it reached the Soudan, lacked the vigorous strength which bore it onward across the soil of North Africa, based on the state-building idea of a race migration. The impetus of this race-dislocation, which made the Mediterranean countries tremble and gave Islam the tremendous power of its infancy, never got as far as, or even near, the Soudan. And for this reason Islam could only show a tendency to gain in power where it found a soil congenial to its growth. Wherever Islamism exists in the Soudan it is underpinned by older civilizations, the height of which must not be undervalued. Let us remember this! The question as to whether Islam represents a growth in the sense of spreading culture and depth of thought is not, however, so easy of solution.

Yet the general underestimation of this older civilization is an established fact, and its existence is that which I have undertaken to establish in this portion of my book. It is true that the more ancient culture had to some degree outgrown itself before the appearance of Islam which fertilized it anew, and true also that it was stimulated to a resistance which brought about renewed expression of its reassembled forces. This is of quite special importance for the verdict to be passed on the power of self-development of the so-called " negro " nations. For not only among laymen, but in expert circles as well, it was hitherto believed that it was Islam which had not only given the negro the greater part of his higher culture, but also that it was the best lever for raising the negro race to a higher level to-day. This view has even induced various great nations not to oppose Islam in the Soudanese colonies in the African Interior— against which nothing can at present be effective—but even to further its spread in every way. And thus several Colonial powers have decided to go so far as to defray the cost of building large new mosques. But this enterprise is full of danger, not only because the ever increasing number of believers in the Prophet may some day rise up against the Christian European rule à la Mahdi on the Nile—a danger which I consider less— but rather because the Islamite morale and ethics must in the long run harm the blacks of Africa, at least in the form in which it there appears. For Islam carries with it two distinct ideas throughout the Soudan: in the first place, it says that all Mahommedans are higher beings than the "infidels" and thus repels the unbelieving, more industrious peoples. Secondly, it also brings in its train the fatalistic creed, or the view that it is right to square the serious problems of life with the practice of a little ritual observance, to natives of already sufficiently phlegmatic disposition.

I certainly do not wish to dispute the fact that Islam gave the dusky Africans a few things, although some of these are of doubtful origin. We will take an illustration or two: There is, for example, a certain dignity arising out of the richer clothing and out of praying in common, which is inherent in the Oriental poise. But the Soudanese dress is pre-Islamitic; they had the prayers in another form before and their gestures cannot be other than inherited from an immemorial past, since the heathen tribes in the remotest districts have them too. Nay, I would even go so far as to maintain that the garb which preceded the advent of pre-Mahommedan civilization was more becoming, and assert that the Islamite got his clothing from no higher inspiration than the negro. He also brought a simple, easily intelligible love of law and love of order with him. But familiarity with the heathen tribes of Africa soon teaches one that the negro has such a genius for knotty points of law and adroit management of things involving legal questions as to make it difficult to see what advantage a Mahommedan Cadi's decision can be to him. It is stated that Islam founded the great Soudanese empires and thereby furthered social ideas and means of communication. If we go piecemeal through the records written in Arabic, we always find Arabians set down at the head of the older dynastic rulers of mighty kingdoms, but we also discover that these had already attained the full growth of their ascendancy at the moment of their rulers' conversion to the Crescent. Another assertion is that the Moslem developed the commerce and improved the highways of trade. If, however, we go through the chronicles we discover that when the Mahommedan merchants came to the Soudan about A.D. 1000, they already found a well-arranged system of commerce established everywhere, and entered the great cities on roads splendidly built for traffic. It is, therefore, easily proved from chronicles written in Arabic that Islam was only effective in fact as a fertilizer and stimulant. The essential point is the resuscitative and invigorative concentration of negro power in the service of a new era and a Moslem propaganda, as well as the reaction thereby produced.

This is all the summary in brief of what long years of study showed to be good in the Islamic movement. I failed to find any evidence that fostering the Mahommedan spirit in our modern colonial endeavours to speed up the strength of the Soudanese nations and to make them more useful in the work of the world, can possibly be favourable to day. On the contrary, the Islamite influence seems to make all its adherents into traders and capitalists, but also to enslave all the " heathen " to an ever increasing degree and degrade them to lower classes of labour, which is as dangerous a thing as can be. For the true interests of commerce can finally be further developed by our own intelligent merchants, since all negro nations are dealers by nature ; but the fact that the small infidel negro tribes, who are the real tillers of the soil and forces of production, should be fretted, oppressed and extruded, chased from their workshops, and penned in territorially in their habitations (as I saw in Adamawa in particular)— I say that to suffer this to go on, would simply be a policy fraught with danger to ourselves.

But by this I do not wish to cut into the question whether it is not our business to oppose the fatalism of the Crescent with the feeling of duty implied in the thought of the Cross, or whether this is not our own civilization's appointed task. And I am not even thinking of baptism, but only of education as we understand it.

Of great and serious import also for arriving at a conclusion on this point, is the question whether I am not right in saying that the Moslem movement has done nothing but revivify forces which are slumbering only, and also right in maintaining that, even before the advent of Mahommedanism, forms of civilization of equal value and significance must have been operative in the Soudan.

To settle this query, I must again place in the foreground the fact that up to the present the Soudan has been looked at more or less through the grey spectacles of Islam.

\*    \*    \*    \*    \*    \*    \*    \*

When, in the beginning and middle of last century, the first celebrated European explorers were travelling through the Soudan, Mahommedanism was regarded in quite a different light from to-day. At that time the view still taken was that it stood for an independent, great upward movement in the civilization of mankind. The fact that the most significant thing in Islam was by no means its religion, but the mighty migration of culture which in Islam only made use of the unifying power of religious impulse, had not been recognized. There was no clear perception then of Islam's originally being comparatively a very primitive religion and, at bottom, no more than an Orientalization of the great beliefs of antiquity, of Judaism and Christianity, slightly tinted with the colours of late Hellenic and Persian culture. The productive power of the Crescent was still an article of faith; the African-Moslem historical descriptions were thought to be truthful. The explorers of that period spoke Arabic, lived under one tent on equal terms with their Arabian hosts and were delighted to meet with men of considerable education among them; and, as they constantly travelled more or less in the cavalcade of these followers of the Prophet, they perpetually saw all things and all men, all history and all heathen tribes, through the glasses of an Islam diluted with Africanism. In those days there were no travellers who would have taken the trouble to raise the question whether the wicked heathen, who were very disinclined to pay tribute and hand over slaves to their ostentatious Mahommedan potentates, might not in their hearts retain a memory of an older civilization which was all their own in spite of the primitive fashion of their garments. And still less could it enter their heads that in these countries Islam was actually no other than a re-christened but more ancient and equally developed culture. It is extraordinarily typical of the then condition of things that travellers coming from the West, like Mungo Park and Binger, lived in the dwellings of the Mahommedans and not in the courts of the princes of heathendom. Everything heathenish was at that period regarded as being culturally poverty-stricken and of no account.

What these travellers saw and noted was seen and set down coloured by the tinted spectacles of Islam. If I now ask that they be finally laid aside, it is certain that our eyes will first have to be accustomed to the new method of looking at things and that at first they will perceive only a flickering, unsteady and dim light in which forms will be lacking in firmness of outline. We shall have to learn how to see. The part to come of this work is an attempt to teach others the way in which I slowly managed to shake off the trammels of historical prejudice, and this ought also to help the reader to do likewise.

The subject to be treated in this half of the book is the life under pre-Mahommedan civilization. The arrangement of the material must be made clear at the outset, and I will therefore confide its entire scheme to the reader.

The first part of four chapters contains an account of these countries' method of living: I shall guide him on the pilgrimage along the high roads between cities; he shall come with me into the court of a king; observe the activities of the mart; listen to popular talk on business and the occurrences in the life of each day, and will gain the impression that existence in the Soudan is remarkably full and instinct with vitality.

The second part has three chapters, the first of which is taken up with a historical epic of the fight fought by Islam against the Infidel in the central lands of the Mande; the second one shows the influence exercised by the Libyans upon Soudanese culture by juxtaposed variations of a particularly significant legend; and the third tells the story of the revolt of the mighty heathen Powers of the West against the reaction of the stream from the East against the Islamitic advance.

Then, in the third part, we shall be occupied with the philosophies of the nations flowing eastwards, as they appeared in pre-Mahommedan heathendom; that is to say, we shall see the glorious gods of ages primeval at work in the first; the legendary love of an ancient and most remarkable cult in the second; and then find the meaning and origin of this religion in the third chapter.

ˎ And, finally, the fourth part will describe the downfall of a nation of heathens, the decay of a great national heathen force before the onset of Islam, but which, when victorious, can itself achieve no more than to carry on the whole system of civilized politics possessed by the heathen it conquered. We shall go on to show that even before the advent of Islam along the path of the stream from the East, the Soudanese had already owned a civilization which of its kind had grown into a noble and magnificent power in the formation of states.

The reader may find some of the matter in the course of these narratives unentertaining, and if he does, perchance the beginnings and ends of each chapter will interest him the more. I am fully aware that this book is not exactly light literature, but so far it is in general the best hitherto offered to help the public in coming to a judgment about the Soudan based on accounts of its culture as recorded in history, and I believe that this work will possess some permanent value of its own by its inclusion of documentary evidence which bears on the development of Soudanese civilization.

I venture, then, to ask the reader to follow the marvellous machinery of Soudanese life and the singular, partly mystical, partly fantastic, partly racy and also partly unassuming stories of my pre-Mahommedan, heathenish blacks. I can assure him that if he will but stick to the road in this pilgrimage, his guerdon will not be withheld.

Masked dancer before our compound in Mokwa.   The dancer is the Ello-Gara.
*(Drawn by Carl Arriens.)*

# CHAPTER XVII

## MOKWA, SEEN IN THE LIGHT OF ANCIENT STORY AND FROM THE CARAVAN ROAD

*Treats of all which can be heard and seen in an ancient Soudanese provincial town lying on an antique caravan route.*

IN describing my travels I had got as far as the results of the *contretemps* at Ifé. All that is now over. What I must here set down is idyllic. Let us take a peep into the jolly, happy, peaceful life which runs its course in the small provincial town of Mokwa in Nupéland.

Mokwa! Who ever heard of it? This place is never mentioned in universal history. And I greatly doubt whether its name can be found in any geographical index. Who then can be expected to know this Mokwa, situate north of the Niger, away from the railway being built between Yebba and Zungeru? To tell you what and where it is, I shall have to go a long way back—right away back to that old, eleventh century Arabian traveller, Señor El Bekri, who informs us that there was a mighty kingdom called Ed-Denden, on the Lower Niger, which excluded all Arabians, because its people and its culture were self-contained. Ed-Denden was a complexus of civilizations of

which the old Nupé Empire was part, to whose exploration
we devoted ourselves from the middle of January to the middle
of June, 1911, in Mokwa, Bida and Lokoja, and with whose
nature and significance I desire to acquaint the reader in much
the same way as I myself entered this peculiar world—from
mid-January, 1911, in the little country town of Mokwa.

The active life of Nupéland in general, and Mokwa in
particular, is full of marvels! Before me lies the history of
Nupé, a history wide and deep and full of meaning. I can
travel back into the thirteenth century; I have gathered such a
mass of records, writings and traditions that I can also trace back
the love of humanity for historical research in this other corner
of the world no less than other travellers in the neighbouring
kingdoms of Central Africa before me. And all that the old
Arabian said, with a few words about the ancient empire in the
statutes of the tenth century, corresponds with my own notes of
the history of 1275 B.C. until the Fulbe dynasty was victorious
in the previous century. The people which created this Nupean
Empire and gave it strength and constitution, were a nation rich
in culture and in power. Those who, long before the tenth
century, fashioned and inspired it with vitality must have been
deep thinkers with well developed brains, bearers of a higher
nature and a nobler culture. It need not at once be objected
that I cannot probably prove that this was so. For in the
following pages I will say something to the point.

There is before me, as I write, quite a block of this Nupé
Kingdom's history, a row of documents, legends, and ritual
songs. And the town of Mokwa is not mentioned in a single
one. I shall be asked why, since I must have known this from
my previous explorations, I, notwithstanding, went to this tiny
Nupé town to begin my studies and lay the foundations of my
Nupean ethnography there. Why, precisely, to this unhistoric
site ?

The question is but natural! I am uncertain at this
moment whether I am well advised to refer once more to the
system which, as the years ran on, I found so well adapted for
getting into closer touch with the native mind. Let me accentuate
this principle again: Never set foot upon a central point in

Africa without due preparation. And this must be explained as follows:

When gathering information necessary and essential for my exploration of Timbuktu, both as to its localities and people, I got the most important and lucid statements in Bamako from persons who had come from Timbuktu and were prevented by social reasons from going back again. They then spoke of all they knew without the least fear of their fellow-citizens. It was in Timbuktu where I obtained a full description of Ifé and its temples as well as of its inhabitants, and in other Soudanese towns from slaves who never again could hope to see their native homes. They knew full well that none could bring them, the exiles, the social outcasts and the lost, to book for having given away some ancient and secret tradition.

I could bring many examples to prove that only those who have been expelled, are far from home, have run away, become slaves and been purchased and have no real home in Africa, are those who, at a distance, will give any information sufficiently useful to put one on the proper track. In a place itself every man fears every other man. There the terror of public opinion squats beside every saucepan; there the spectre of the Zoon Politikon leers round the corner at every ethnologist. This is why I made most of my inquiries about Nupéland in general among the homeless Nupeans in Wagadugu and Ibadan and about the best city for exploration purposes in the countries between Timbuktu and Sansanne Mangu as early as 1908. I chose Mokwa as the starting point of the Research Expedition because its ancient independence had been least affected by the modern Nupé-Fulbe State; because it is under the rule of the last native-born prince; and because I might there hope to gain the best information about the older, the old, and the new kingdom, and thus of Gbarra, Rabba and Bida. In a word, Mokwa had remained a spectator for centuries of the history of Nupéland wherever its despots may have set up their dynastic throne.

So I went into a corner in a quarter where the riot of the modern African metropolitan town could not disturb me while hunting. And I fished with assiduity. Ought I not to

The old Lilli in Mokwa.
(Drawn by Carl Arriens.)

endeavour to give the reader a sketch of the old, full-coloured and magnificent pictures which here met my eyes in the twilight of legends of old ?  Indeed, one's hearing has got to be strained to catch the melody of these marvellous stories, for it was first played very, very long ago; it is but a slight, slight echo only to be caught in the whispering trees, primevally old, which stand round the wells of a bygone day and the markets of old. All such delicate tones are whelmed in the clash and the din of the hundreds and thousands of throats which make up the orchestra of a modern Soudanese city.  Here alone, in the emptiest corner, in the most cloistered solitude, the last dying fall comes whispering over the grass of the plains.

To expect to hear such things as these in a metropolis would be much about the same thing as to listen for a Robin Hood echo in London, a Parsifal chanson in Paris, or a Kyffhäuser ballad in Berlin.  Old recorded things and new happenings, learning and wealth and the dazzling palaces of kings may be found in these great hives; but folk-song, folk-feeling, and folk-wisdom are swept away from the space round the throne in the commercial turmoil of the modern world.  There is no folk-wisdom left in London, Paris, Berlin—or Bida.  This is what took me to Mokwa, and, settling down there in front of the ancient market-hall, I listened all day and all night to the trees which rustled above me.

    &ast;     &ast;     &ast;     &ast;     &ast;     &ast;     &ast;     &ast;

The old fairy song of the Nupé sounds something like this: Nothing is known of the ancient Arabian, El Bekri, in Mokwa and Bokani, and years cannot be added up in these places, but the list of the kings who are dead and now of the second dynasty is remembered; this list was chanted in song " in the days before Islam " at their funeral festivals; the singers called upon each of the mighty protectors and extendors of the realm by name, told him the number of years and of months his reign had endured, and blood fell in drops upon his tomb and title.  All one has to do is, add up the years of their reigns together, and arrive at the foundation of the penultimate dynasty in the year A.D. 1275.  And what preceded this ?

The real world of faërie was before that year of 1275. In this particular year, viz.: one thousand two hundred and seventy-five, the Yorubans came into the land from the South, annihilated the ancient Empire stock, and—the only good thing they did—fostered the new dynasty, which, at first, blossomed modestly in the south-west until it attained its victorious growth. What, then, was it the Yorubans destroyed?

No name of a country or Empire is preserved. No place is mentioned. The Fulbe troubles of the last hundred years drove all this out of people's memories. All they know is this: Once upon a time there was a vast, vast Empire; its ruler did not live in Nupé, for Nupé was only a province of it. But that was a very, very great while ago, and it was broken up long before the Yoruban incursion. The Emperor lived at a very great distance, so far away that no Nupé, except those who took him the tribute, had ever seen him. This took such a long time that the messengers of two successive years, if they travelled with speed, would meet exactly half way on their journey, one company on the way thither and the other on its way home. Then they were able to exchange the writings (the Nupé says "books," and is able to say that these "books" were bound in hard ivory cases). For, on each such occasion the Great King sent his viceroys letters containing his exact commands. They said how much tin, silver, bronze, cut stones and other treasure, was to be sent to the Great King.

The old story says that the Great King at that time also commanded that rings of glass from Nupé should be sent to him. But history may perhaps be wrong. For it does not seem impossible that the art of producing glasswork of this special kind may have reached the South from the East just at that time and have been acquired by the people coming from the Great King's country who had immigrated into the South. At least, so I suggest. Why should we expect a fairy tale to be always true?

When the envoys sent to the Great King took their departure, many people joined them, for they wished to take advantage of the opportunity to cross the wilderness with some protection, do some trading on the way and gather riches for themselves. And many of them yearned to see the monarch if even only once in all their lives; for this sufficed to make them particularly noted and enviable persons for everyone at home. When the vast Empire fell to pieces, the Mahommedans came, and many pious Nupé folk afterwards made the pilgrimage to Mecca. But the stream of people was never so full as that which flowed towards the Great King of old.

His city and castle and wealth must have been wonderful indeed! The city lay by a great water in which there was neither crocodile, nor serpent, nor river-horse, which so easily and so often overturns fishing boats on the Niger. On the water there were only great ships with wings.—With wings?—Yes, with wings! like a crane, or a pelican, or some other bird. The town rose up at the edge of the water, and its houses and walls were built of Sui-Lantana (red jasper) stone. And the roofs of these stone houses were not made of straw and of leaves, but of Chinkall (a sort of home-made bronze). They were chased in the same way the Nupés to-day hammer their water jars and food dishes, their various basins and ewers. But the Nupés were said to be filled with pride that the people of the Great King's city should have learnt this craft from themselves, who, in their turn, had acquired the art from Ata-Igara (*i.e.*, the Atagara of Ida).—Here I think the tale makes a blunder: it wants to mislead us; for, even if the supply of bronze may perhaps have come from the South, the greater part of the shapes and the patterns chased on them came from the East or from that very kingdom. But again I ask: Why shouldn't a mistake find its way into a fairy tale? Especially when it is so very, very old and nought but the gentlest of whispers in the leaves of the trees?

In this marvellous city, built of red stone and brown bronze on the water with no beasts of prey, but with boats which had wings, lived the King—the Great King! This King had no dogs like other princes. When he went forth, lions went by his side. He went neither on foot, it is certain, nor did he ride, but was carried in a great, long basket, covered with cloth and coloured leather. Round about him gambolled his horsemen, all in padded armour, each of them with a mighty spear; many, many great princes went in procession behind him.

When there was a truly great festival the women were carried behind him in baskets like his. Only, his first wife was not so carried; she was young and strong; she rode like a man on a strong steed which was white.

A great red cloth canopy, with a handle of gold, was carried above the King and each of his wives. At his Court none but himself and his spouses were allowed to have such precious things as these above their heads. But, because the viceroys in Nupé could do the same as the King, the Nupé folk in this way learnt to know the King's canopy.

This great, Great King reigned for many, many years and much longer than Edegi (Edegi, however, ruled for 68 years!), and as long as he lived, Nupés of distinction longed to be able to make one pilgrimage to this city—grandfather, father, son, grandson, from generation to generation, and this for many hundreds of years. The Nupés grew wealthy. They sent much vast treasure to the great Royal City and, in return, received many things which were strange and new. But it all came to a sudden end.

The Great King, after wielding the sceptre for many hundreds of years, grew old. Then he quarrelled with his younger brethren. There was a war. All nations began to wage war until the Great King died. Now he was one of Issa's sons, and therefore those who afterwards came from Mecca hated him and his followers. It was the children of Mahommed who destroyed the remaining portion of the ancient Lantana city. The road was interrupted; nobody could get there any more. Since that time the Nupé have not wandered on the broad ways that lead to the ancient town.

The man who told me this legend in Mokwa was old and not exactly very intelligent. He was a feeble dotard and at first I gave not much heed to his little story. And who can swiftly find his way through the hundreds of legends which are written out fairly in the course of his travels? Very frequently, and all too easily, one learns to value what is most important only when it has slipped away unnoticed. And I only got to grasp the meaning of this legend, which I regarded as a mere attempt to reconstruct a civilization, when the first MS. of the

Edegi story had been translated for me. It contained a statement to the effect that this some five-hundred-year-old ruler had spared all those who prayed to him for mercy " for Issa's sake."

For Issa's sake! And at the end of my fairy story of the hoary-headed king there are these words : " He was a son of Issa, and therefore those who came from Mecca hated him and the memory in which he was held."

Now, in Northern Africa, Issa is the name of Jesus Christ!

The Cross looms up before us. Athwart the myth of Nupé, the glorious pomp of old Byzantium sends its rays across to us. —Whither do you, who read this, think the road will lead ?—I say no more. We must get accustomed to the thought and ponder it. I follow here the single path of duty. He who is led by a guide is entitled to know the road and its end in the mind of this guide at the start. But the guide should not, at first, paint the part of the journey to be next undertaken in colours too bright, or the neophyte may be disillusioned on the road. Such is the guide's obligation.

And by this I want it to be understood right at the beginning that, after having lain at the market-place of Mokwa with my comrades for a few weeks, I had an impulse towards a great new goal of my wandering. I came away out of the Yoruba lands of the Atlantic and pushed on with my explorations to the North and the East, but I also wished to declare why it is always, and here in especial, desirable to try to catch the voices of the Past as they fleet by in whispers in dreamy seclusion before plunging into the deafening whirlpool of the more strenuous, more vitalizing and flourishing life of the Present.

\*     \*     \*     \*     \*     \*     \*     \*

Mokwa! Arrived there: 14th January, 1911. Departed thence: 16th March, 1911.

At last, the rattle of the railway, the swarms of trouser-wearing " niggers " of alcohol-sodden Ibadan lie at our backs; behind us, at last, the hateful impressions made by the end of December. When on entering Mokwa with our complement of carriers about noon, I saw its sociable market-place in the shade of gigantic, magnificent trees, and arrived at the compound of old Lilli, the " mayor of the village," formerly agnate of princes, now vassal to Fulbe, I felt immeasurably at ease and breathed an air of such irresistible good fellowship and comfort in this sleepy little country town that I gave myself up to it.

Old Lilli is one of the best known and most popular chieftains of Northern Nigeria. One scarcely knows why, when one sees this quiet, retiring, almost pitiable, tallish man, of no superiority as to mind, but whose amiable smile seems always to show an inclination to say : " Do, for the love of God, let me sit here in peace and quiet with my drop of beer in a corner apart. I assure you, I don't want to meddle with history or the fate of the Government." A harmless, friendly kind of person, whose popularity is due to the hard knocks Destiny dealt him.

And now, in presenting my first friend in Nupéland, I have to think of that awful scourge, the Fulbe invasion. As late as the middle of last century, the scions of the Fulbe priest, Dando, had so set the Nupean princes against each other by fomenting dissension that they began to mangle and rend themselves just like wild beasts. The offspring of Dando looked on and enjoyed the natives' stupidity. Then came the times when they, in fact, were the rulers, but in which the oppressed Nupeans revolted, now here, now there, and once in Mokwa as well. Then all the old people were removed from there and sent to Bida. The Emir of Bida butchered four of the most eminent men, made a sort of table and set up their heads on its four corners. The Lilli stood before it, bound with thongs to a tree. The degradation of the Mokwa rebels was meant to be seen by all the market folk, and everybody saw the violation of this old man's dignity. When the four heads had rotted, old Lilli was set free and all the Mokwa people were hunted forth into Houssaland. Then, a few years later, came the English and brought the Fulbes to justice for their atrocious cruelty and, after that, the old Mokwans were recalled and reinstated.

Old Lilli's popularity dates from that time. Everybody knows that he is very gentle, so gentle, indeed, that not even the brutal Fulbe despots dared to cut off his whitening head. So he became beloved, but lost the greatest part of his revenue.

Before then he had owned many dependent peasants, slaves and wives. He had farms and well-filled barns. Much cloth was woven for him and he went abroad robed in the finest dresses. Not only had he goats and sheep and cattle, but fertile farm-lands and cleanly compounds were his principal possessions. It has all gone. He can scarcely call a single thing his own; some-times he is even anxious about his beer and so is always a little embarrassed, a little worried and a little depressed when he comes into contact with " big people."

Dear old Lilli came towards us across the market-place. I at once felt: " This man is frightened by our foreign looks!" Old Lilli had made his first acquaintance with the Fulbes as his foes. They had robbed him of his native country and his all. Then came the English, who must have been his friends, for they had restored old Lilli to his native place and his paternal roof; but, as he often told me when we had made fast friends, he had also had to accept the missionaries, those missionaries who had taken away from him and his people their greatest pleasure, namely, the ceremonial of the mask and burned the masks, saying that they were evil and of the Devil. And now, quite suddenly and unannounced, there came a German expedition, and as nobody had been concerned " to make a good reputation for us " in advance, the population, and old Lilli too, were terror-stricken, perplexed, and somewhat subdued, all which things were, *more Africano*, concealed as far as might be, but could not be kept entirely secret.

To my rescue, then! ye best of companions of my African wanderings! Come, ye " nods and becks and wreathed smiles," come!—Who will give thee cause of offence, O venerable Lilli ? Which of us, old man, will do thee a hurt ?—And so he soon came round. Fear and embarrassment fled from the faces of himself and suite. One Daima, a singular person of ancient princely descent, cunning and sly, reticent and calculating, and, in the Northern sense, not quite sincere, but with the sincerest affection for Lilli, had come to my help on the very first day. This Daima's friendship for Lilli was so strong and affectionate that he had given up a very high Court position he once held at Bida to gratify it, and when I left Mokwa he at first came on with me to Bida, then to Lokoja up the River Benue. Directly he saw us he had at once formed an opinion which did equal credit to his understanding and grasp of the situation.

Daima took Bida, my man, aside and talked to him in flattering speeches, instructive conversational skirmishings, playing the listening game in the true African roundabout fashion; he made up his mind, retired with Lilli for a very few minutes, and then the perplexed old gentleman asked us whether we would like to share his African house, saying he no longer had large compounds and houses like others, but that the space of which he still was master might, perhaps, do for us all, with a little good-will on the part of us both.

This was the way in which we took possession of our little corner of dreamland in Mokwa.

\*     \*     \*     \*     \*     \*     \*     \*

The red earth on which Mokwa is built lies about the sources of a stream which runs through a gorge and empties into the Niger near the old capital of Rabba, about two hours' march to the south. Mokwa lies on a plateau at the head of this valley on red, brilliantly red earth. This and the big, lofty, dome-shaped ant-hills, its situation at the river-head on a fertile table-land are its distinctive characteristics. The parching Harmattan wind blew its greasy dust and ash clouds over the barren, burnt up, horribly desolate tableland, whistled and buffeted and roared around the tall old giant trees which grace the market-place, the site of the ancient "castle ruins," and the southern parts of the town; then it roared along its accustomed path from East to West and tore across the Mokwa vale and forest without affecting them. It can paint the trees and roofs of the town, the plain and the plateau brown and cover them with sticky sand, but it sweeps across the unharmed vale unharming. It cannot injure this luxuriance, this plenitude of Nature's power. Every leaflet which it colours yellow to-day, to-morrow finds a hundred verdant substitutes, and every evening a sultry, moisture-laden steam arises, which, like the breath of Gods, in spite of the harsh and drying Burner of the Plains, revives the ears of corn and farmlands and all the wards of Mokwa town, laves them and gives them strength to fight against the might of the suffocating wind which blows with every dawn.

How often we went down in this valley towards the evening, when most of the day's work was over, bathed in its dewy moisture, and went back so refreshed that many a further hour could be spent in studying Nupéland. I have still some more to say about this vale.

The plan of Mokwa is peculiar. A vast rectangular wall and ditch now in ruins includes not only the little country town itself, with all its " garden suburbs," carefully whitewashed indigo dye works, deep clay pits, forges and spinning sheds, slaughter houses and granaries; no, these crumbling ramparts of defence surround the camping ground of caravans; the valley head both broad and deep; the wells and springs; a goodly portion of the valley basin; and a few square miles of farmlands to the west and otherwards. It is erroneous to suppose that the enclosing wall was ever filled with a compact and uniform mass of civic dwellings. Mokwa once was no doubt larger than it is; it never, however, took up all the space within its defensive lines, but was always the central point of farms and vale and well-sites.

The market occupies the middle of the town, and is the tradesman who supplied me with the food wherewith I satisfied my ethnological appetite in Mokwa. We live, then, reasonably enough near this market in a queer, tumble-down compound of some five-and-twenty huts, one half of which the Expedition occupies, while Lilli and his family dwell in the other. All day long I live in the twenty-feet-wide hut which runs across the compound. When the great exit-door is open to the front, I can see everything that happens on the market square beneath the ancient trees, and at its back can always gaze upon the little courtyard where we take our afternoon siesta. My " katamba," as this hut is called, is broad and spacious, filled with constantly changing ethnological " stuff," such as coffers, mask-dresses, photographic apparatus, and boxes which serve as manuscript and book cases. My katamba is not beautiful. It is even ugly and smeary, for, daily, the wicked Harmattan blows its greasy soot in from the plains, no matter whether the gate be shut or open, for it will gnaw at the uneven old clay walls, force its way, disgustingly importunate, through some cracks in the ceiling, and then pour down a shower of dust, cobwebs, mouse-dirt and vermin, always evilly intent, of course, upon disfiguring my nice, clean, white manuscript.

Yet it is an old and dreamy nest in which I sit, a hidden fairy-corner whence to spy out the track which ancient history took. Small wonder if the house whose secrets are being so craftily unlocked is shaken and sheds its filth in wrath upon the curiosity-monger! But be it said that this is only its passive resistance. For if I go suddenly at night into the katamba with a light, hundreds of cockroaches scuttle rustlingly asunder, rats scamper off, and once I persuaded an abominable scorpion to come out from under my manuscript chest.—I never could understand how Martius could sleep soundly in this hole afterwards, and took precious good care to hunt up all such bedfellows in my own sleeping-room, from which that wicked fellow, Akelle, tried to steal my cash-box.—The proper place for such creatures as bugs, etc., is an old and dreamy corner. And, moreover, was I not myself a sort of spider, hidden away at one end of my web, on the eager lookout for some specially longed-for dainty to come into my net, to be wrapped round afterwards and then sucked dry? Was not this katamba my spider's corner from which I looked from dawn to dusk upon the market square? And was it not in Mokwa that the most luscious titbits fell into the trap, when they, the pilgrim-wanderers in the Soudan and leaders of the caravans, who knew the ways and countries, thought they were crossing some little harmless market-place? Yea—"harmless!"

I rub my hands and smirk when I remember many a noble capture as my eye is caught by well-filled books of manuscript. Let me try now to paint the ethnological fly-trap I set up on Mokwa's market-place.

\*     \*     \*     \*     \*     \*     \*     \*

Anyone wishing to get to Atlantic Yorubaland, famed far and wide as being rich beyond all measure, from the northern districts of Mid-Soudan, which breed enormous flocks of sheep and herds of cattle, or from that singular country, Asben, in the Sahara, or from the desert-cities, Gadames, Moursonk, Ghat, or, finally, from the Osmanli coastlands, say from Tarabulus (Tripoli), can take many roads to Ilorin-town, viâ Sokoto, viâ Katsena-Kano, and Bornu-Bautshi; but he will always have to cross the Niger either at Rabba or at Yebba, and then through Mokwa go he must, because all the other younger or older baiting stations with "good accommodation for man and beast," have been destroyed for far around.

Now, every one of these caravans, which, day in day out, during the dry season, arrive here, camp here from day to day and daily hence depart, takes its way across the market square of Mokwa. Each such caravan pitches its camp on one of the two Songos stretching east and west of the valley head with many wells. Every single member of them comes every morning and evening, and mostly about noonday too, once at least to this square of commerce under the ancient trees in front of my "spider's corner." What was it not that passed before it in that space of time? Here there were wealthy Houssa merchants on splendid steeds in gorgeous trappings, women from Kano, with neatly knotted loads upon their heads and robed in the ample tobés worn by men. Here were the lean, black Busu-Songai from Adrar, with leathern aprons round their loins, and heavy-laden asses, water skins and iron bells, black-skinned men with features of Northern cut, sun-dried, haggard Sons of the Wilderness! Here were the Tuaregs with the "litham," or scarf, and an indescribable dignity of manner. Here were the Ringi, mostly a cavalcade of men, with a few women whose nakedness was only clothed with leaves, a primitive people from the Houssa lands, always ready to have the early simplicity of their dress, the curves of their buttocks and their manner of dancing at home, shown, inspected, paid for and laughed at in business haunts. Here were pilgrims to Mecca and folks from out of Egypt. And what was my joy at once more seeing a man whom I knew and who had come from Ulled-djellal, a South Algerian oasis, and with whom I had struck up acquaintance a twelve-month since in the town where he was born. Picture our mutual surprise!

Of a truth, North Africa is not so impenetrably vast, and
even to day the stream flows backwards and forwards between
Byzantium and Atlantis, although the over-population of the
Coast has drained some of it away.

Most assuredly! Mokwa was a good catch, not to say trick,
and my katamba peep-hole gave me an opportunity for watching
out of which I made very good use. And full preparation had
been made. My satellites stood outside and heard my every call
and whistle. Many a stranger was stopped by a good-natured
word or for a snap-shot. But more especially we had our
laboratories working, working on a system.

From my own part of the compound, a zigzag road led first
to the camp of those stalwart soldiers of science, Arriens and
Martius, and then to the interpreters' quarters under Bida's
inspectorship. If there was a more than usually interesting
individual worth knowing, whom I could not catch hold of
through my own impatience or my want of skill, he was
submitted to the pencil and brush of Carl Arriens, the artist.
Many a typical fellow was made as immortal in colour and form
as the hurry of sketching allowed.

We were living, indeed, at a milestone on the high road of
antiquity, and all our doing and being was measured accordingly.

At five o'clock in the morning the market women shouted
their invitation to the wayfarers to take a sup of their splendid
porridge before they continued the journey, and each one
screamed out that her own was the best. This call, which I
also heard in the same tone and cadence in other Nupéland
cities, was exactly the same in sound and production as the
offers to sell of the women of Italy. In France and in Belgium
the call is thinner and seems more petulant. When I heard this
clamour ringing in the square, I jumped out of bed. I often
went and looked at the picture outside. There was a mighty tree
which had fallen down in front of our compound, whose great
limbs stretched out in all directions. The bark of its trunk had
long since gone, and it was smooth and black—how long a time
it may have lain there! How many travellers, coming up from
the Songo below, had set their loads down on it in the grey
light of dawn to take a last cup of the excellent, famous dish

(meal soup) of the Mokwa women, before they went their ways. This smooth, black colour of the " tree of rest " is a tribute to the ladies of Mokwa, for, were their sup of meal broth not so good, this colour would not here be seen.

From six to eleven in the morning is given up to work. Then Martius sallies out with his satellites to survey and make plans of the compounds, houses, stables, barns, corn-bins and mosques; then the painter Arriens sits unruffled at his easel; then I assemble my old people, distribute kola (Guru-nuts) among them, and we talk of the river of humanity running over the great roads, of the peaceful life of the Mokwa burghers whom the stranger only sees upon the streets, the mart, the Songo, but never, never in his own four walls.

The market tide increases towards noon. Now come the great herds of long-horned beeves; riders on over-driven horses round them up and guide them in. Flocks of long-legged sheep and goats, shepherded by women carrying well-packed loads upon their heads. Then ring the iron bells of Busus astride on asses; then the Ringi women rattle their gourds. And many a wandering musician with lute or flute will quickly try his luck at our " castle gate " in hopes that the " noble lords " within may gratify him with a trifle. I never to my knowledge let one of these depart in disappointment. For these living journals brought me many a bit of news of more importance than all the columns of a European local leaflet.

In the Songos things begin to hum. From many sides the travellers begin to congregate. Curious little caves are built of sacks and shocks of straw, with a backbone of a donkey's saddle and a carrying pole or two; the flocks are watered and driven out to graze; the horses tethered and fires set alight. Then men and women saunter back up to the market and gloat upon the dishes which the Mokwa women, red with rouge, are selling; they haggle a lot and buy a little. But into the compounds and the houses of the old Mokwa folk they never set a foot unless there happens to be some particularly wise and educated traveller, who will go to the Great Mallem of Mokwa, whose reputation as a learned man is known abroad and to whom one likes to do honour and bring a salutation from a friend or piece of news, or perhaps, to get a letter written by one of his disciples, and many a penny finds its way like this into the pouch of some venerable pillar of the Church.

Yet still more enchanting are the pictures ˎoffered by this caravan-life when night comes on and darkness reigns. The flames of many camp and cooking fires shoot up on every hand between the little shelters; many Rebeccas, brown, yellow and red of skin, bring water from the wells below; the cattle are driven together by all the people; smouldering fires are set a-going between them, so that the hobbled beasts may be kept as free as may be from the stinging scourge of swarming little flies; the men and women lie all around; asses bray and oxen low; the fumes of oil and burning wood float up into the starlit winter sky. Above, the clear and shining vault of splendour; fantastic silhouettes and shadow-play below.

How many a time I let the charm of all these pictures sink into my soul! The order of their sequence never varied. At four o'clock, when all the store of sounds I heard became oppressive, I took my gun or rifle on my shoulder and went down with my comrades into the river glades. Wild pigeons, a monkey, guinea-fowl, and many another such " small deer " of the woods as well, found their way into the stew-pot. (Yes, indeed, monkey, too!) We liked to go into this primeval growth through swamps and tangled lianas. The air was heavy with the glorious scent of water, woods and moss. It was always a refreshing bath which Nature made. Then we went up and crossed the Songo, and this was just the time when this constant flux of folks both to and fro appeared so very striking, here beneath the star-strewn, splendid dome of sky, where the shadows and the silhouettes were strangely mingled in the camp-fire's glare.

When we were able to tear ourselves away from this scene, had got home and supped in haste, there were still two hours of work in front of us. My interpreters would bring me some stranger selected on the caravan route, or some ancient settler in the land of Nupé, who might have something worth relating about old times and customs, or, maybe, a legend. And it was in an hour such as this that my old Bokani friend, a none too brilliant fellow, but feeble and somewhat senile, who had come over to the funeral of a member of the Lilli's family, told me the story of the old, nay, very ancient kingdom, of which this distant province also was a part; the story of the far-off water, the roofs of bronze, the extinction of Issa's posterity, of that Issa so hated by the Mecca pilgrims; the story of the pilgrimages to the red stone city and of the streaming populations which then went back and forth.

Whence did he get this tale? Was it not probable that this treasure had been handed down along the road on which from days of old the black Busus, the leaf-decked Ringi women, the Kano traders and the princes and professors of Tarabulus had gone a-travelling? I thought so, and put no great value on the song.

But I jibbed when the name of Issa reappeared in the Edegi myth, when everywhere, on articles antique and modern, the cross of Issa, the cross of Jesus the Christ, the Byzantine crucifix, met my eyes; on the ferry-boats of the Nile, on gourds, on box-lids, on saddles; but, more especially, when my acquaintance with my Nupé friend had ripened, and from his hidden chest all sorts of marvellous vanities came forth: old book-covers, chased bronze work, cut beads. Then I saw that this people were wealthy, rich in their inheritance. And yet they had not got it on the highway, not from the fashionable caravans from Tarabulus, Adrar, Aïr and Houssa. No—all these things were here, as the ancient heirlooms of this land itself, the heritage of an age which had really and actually been. And they not only hold it as a dead estate; they have it in their ancient art, but not in Mokwa, not in this peaceful corner of the great highway. As we shall see.

Like all the wanderers of this region, I too, naturally, saw nothing but the high road, the caravan route; for the Nupés closed their doors against me, too, as they do to every other stranger. It was only afterwards I saw the treasure of their souls. Both the inward legacy and the caravan road were widely separated in the course of time, because none but the foes of Issa, the children of Mecca, travelled into this country by this route after the Great Empire had had its day, whereas the Nupés had never entirely fallen away from Issa, and the heritage of the Great King's ancient empire had become flesh of their flesh and bone of their bone.

They barred their gates when a son of Mecca passed along the great highroad; they put everything antique and precious out of sight. And so it came to pass that the stream of caravans flowed on without, however, having any further connection with the things which lay concealed within the storehouse of ancient Nupean culture through which it ran.

Ah, how I loathe those sons of Mecca, who have torn to tatters, suppressed, choked and annihilated so much between Byzantium and Atlantis!

Sham duel in Mokwa market-square. The seconds to the right and left.

*( Drawn by Carl Arriens.)*

# CHAPTER XVIII

## THE NUPÉ-FULBES : OLYMPIC GAMES AND RELIGIOUS HOLIDAYS IN MOKWA

Arrival and reception of the Fulbe Prince—Joy of the Nupé Elders at the revival of the ancient sports and mask-ceremonial—Our sorrow at leaving Mokwa.

EVERY morning the old Lilli, with Daima and other notables, came quietly and in a friendly way to ask how we were, to listen to my wishes and to have a chat. The Elders threw themselves down, touched the ground with their foreheads, murmured all sorts of greetings and, as is their custom, bobbed a curtsey whenever possible. In this country ceremony is hereditary and correct behaviour is held in high esteem. We shared the monarchy during the fortnight with the old Lilli, and, apart from the caravan traffic, it was a very peaceful time indeed. It was very pleasant to be able to live alone, for this enabled us to overcome the shyness and timidity of the Nupeans easily, which would not have been practicable with all the " right honourables " on the spot. For the old Lilli was no longer really the Lord of the place.

One fine morning, about eleven, the sound of drums and admiring cheers is heard from far away. A crowd arrives with a lot of baggage, not a bit like the goods of travelling merchants or like caravanners. Then the women clear a space in the market square, which they never do when a caravan arrives, and messengers run to and fro.

The Benno! The great Fulbe Prince, the Ruler of the Province, the Lord of Mokwa Town is about to arrive! The excitement is terrific. A brace of messengers also come to me, are formally presented and announce the forthcoming visit.

O Mokwa! quiet little provincial corner, how canst thou give up thy repose? Whither has fled thy peace! Mokwa and its people does not huddle in a frightened cluster as does the poultry yard when the shadow of the kite falls upon it suddenly. Oh, indeed, no! This is not terror! It is the other way about; it wakes up, it struts, it preens itself and puts on its Sunday suit. They all behave alike, the ancient head of the town, the broken Lilli, the scions of an ancient princely stock who live here in exile, the comfortable farmers and those who live upon the fame of ancient clanship and not upon what they own or earn. It is very, very strange! These Fulbes broke the power of the olden princely houses in all the countryside; they hounded on the folk to civil war; they ruined much which Lilli and his family possessed and robbed them of the rest; all these people enjoy only what these thieves of state and land and men left them through whim or accident or ignorance; yet, for all that, they all put on their robes of state in a certain spirit of elation with evident pleasure the moment the representative of this race graciously deigns to enter the gates of the town, welcome him joyfully and meet him without any grudge. It is just as if they would say: " Behold, such a splendid fellow as this stands for the nation which destroyed all we possessed and stole it away! See, is it not delightful to sacrifice everything to such a master as this? Ought I not to be proud that such a magnificent people robbed my own family of its all ? "

It seems incredible! Yet the negro thinks in this way, this breed of slaves, these multiplying beasts for sacrifice in human history. It is repugnant and painful always to experience this want of pride and proper self-consciousness, this abasement and this readiness to place one's neck beneath another's heel. And

Wrestlers in Mokwa.
*(Photo by Leo Frobenius.)*

The seconds plucking the locked duellists asunder.

on this day in Mokwa, the old Lilli and his Elders made a very painful impression! They had told me only the day before how the Fulbes had hunted them, exterminated them, butchered them with infinite cruelties in the market-places, driven off their fathers and brothers into slavery; and to-day a member of this band of murderers and robbers comes along whose fingers are still clammy with the blood of innumerable atrocities, and—they feel honoured, if you please, when he so much as approaches them. Thus the "niggerized" Nupés! In other ways I like them well enough, but I feel urged to go on painting this detestable feature, so that it may be seen in its befitting aspect.

But now for the other one! There is not very long to wait. The great drums come nearer and nearer. A squadron of horsemen comes galloping and halts in front of the katamba. They dismount. A tall slender person is helped from the saddle and, accompanied by the others, walks up to my front door. They all come in.

The salutations are done with. The Benno lets me know by his interpreter: "He had been at the Emir's in Bida, to his quarters; he had heard that I had come to Mokwa; Mokwa was his provincial capital; he had made a journey to greet me in his city of Mokwa, for there was nobody here to look after me." (What disrespect of the old Lilli!) "He was proud to be able to place himself at my disposal now; I only need say what I wanted; the Emir of Bida sent me greetings; he expected to see me; but he (the Benno) desired me not to go there until he himself had the opportunity of showing us the esteem in which he held us."

I was able to observe him as he spoke in the measured accents which beseem a prince, with dignity and ample gesture and compare him with the pictures of the Fulbes whom I got to know so well in the West. He stood the comparison with other princely thieves of his breed well, and I liked the look of him. He was a tall, lithe-limbed figure, grey bearded, aristocratic of feature. Sitting there, dressed, with his huge white turban on his head and the litham, or scarf, of fine material hanging down, he might well look less than his age. When I saw him afterwards in *négligé*, rushing in to us during an outbreak of fire in our camp (started by the carelessness of one of his own policemen), it was evident that he was, in fact, very greatly advanced in years. But his fine set of teeth, his hearty laugh, his bright, steady eye, his ceremonious but never humble gestures gave him a princely air, made him sympathetic and by those qualities alone appear a being far removed from the crowd of negroes surrounding him.

Henceforth the picture presented by life in Mokwa was changed at a blow. The Benno sent us some ducks, a turkey, and fresh lemons immediately after arrival, accompanied by a message regretting he had no farms in this neighbourhood or he would have sent us something finer. But our people got great bowls of wheat porridge with stewed chickens. Every morning he either came in person or by proxy, and not a day passed without eggs, poultry, pigeons, lemons, game, guinea-fowl, or ducks, etc., being sent over from his compound to ours. And when his mango trees were bearing their first crop of fruit he was polite enough to share the first consignment with us and when I left I had to make the Benno handsome presents in order to equal the value in money only of the gifts he had made me.

This naturally put the dear old Lilli's power still further in the shade. He was now very little better than a good-natured landlord in his dressing-gown, felt slippers and smoking-cap, who wishes his lodger " good-morning." Ah, the dear old boy ! In his heart of hearts he was jolly glad that he was quit of representing authority. And he said very pleasantly : " If there's anything you want, just mention it to the Benno ; he can manage much better than I do ; the people obey him, but not me ! "

The daily life of the old Lilli was very considerably altered with regard to one thing. Higher up than his and, therefore, also, my compound, there was a " Masalatshee," or small mosque, or at all events the new masonry of it. Directly the Benno had come, the estimable Lilli said his daily prayers there in the forms prescribed. This greatly astonished me and I asked him one day when chatting after the discussion of the past history and peculiarities of the Nupés at the usual meeting of the Elders : " But, Lilli, I have only just noticed that you are a Mahommedan ! " The old man, indignantly : " What's that ?  I, a Mahommedan ?

I, a Moslem ? " Myself: " Of course; don't you bow down
regularly every day ? " He : " That does not make me a
Mahommedan ! I only do it to please this Benno ! He likes to
see it ! Besides, it's just as good a Kuti " (the Nupé " Kuti " is
the same as the Yoruban " Orisha ") " as all the others ! But a
Mahommedan, never ! Not one of those who make the salaam
with me in the Masalatshee is Alfa." (Yoruban for Islamite.)
" Not one ! " The old chap was quite angry that I should take him
for an Alfa. That was a Kuti in his eyes, something holy, like
his old heathen mask-dances, like his skin wallet and his amulets,
and—the Cross of the Christian !

Very well, then—and so this Masalatshee-Kuti pleased the
Benno and his folk ! This was most significant. The Benno and
his nation, the Fulbes, were feared more than anything else.
I saw another charming little scene, shortly before I left in
March, bearing on this point. On the eve of our departure ' I
assembled the Fulbe with the Benno, and then the Nupé with
the Lilli. They all received presents. They all made a pretty
farewell speech. The Benno's will be found elsewhere, but there
may here be room for a few of the Lilli's words, viz.: " He
was grateful; his people were grateful; we had only done good;
we had allowed them to dance with masks, which the other
whites (the missionaries) had forbidden them and burnt. We had
also, by our presence, protected them from the Benno. The
young people had been able to work on their own fields; they
had not, as in other years, been compelled to till only in the
Benno's fields at this season. But, more than all that, they, the
old folk of Mokwa, had been able to drink their durra beer in the
old way without paying attention to the Benno. Not one of
the Benno's police (Dogari) had dared to break their beer jugs.
And he himself, the Lilli, had once been able to drink a great
deal of beer." (As a matter of fact he used to get pretty well
fuddled at times.) " They were thankful for this ! We were
good, kind people ! "

This confession of a grateful soul reveals a bottomless depth of
primitiveness. It is original peasanthood which mentions forced
labour and guzzling in the same breath. It is one of the
frankest admissions ever made by a negro. Yet in one point this

speech, taken in conjunction with all the circumstances, ought to enlighten us with regard to the position of the ruling Fulbes and the conquered Nupés. Here speaks the "Tyrannis," the heavy pressure which the one party brings ‿to bear, the indifference with which the other submits, and still, when greeting his despot, proudly carries the stigma: "See what a powerful Lord I have! See how strong he is at the moment he conquers me!"

Tyrants the Fulbes are. But they ‚are also great organizers. I have already given an account, in the description of my travels in Massina and elsewhere, how these specimens of the Fulbe tribe in particular (those whom I met then were of the same stock) were masters of directing and arranging things, just as these people give quickly, unconditionally, freely, parcel out and systematize on broad lines. While the savage is haggling about the egg, the Fulbe has given away the hen that laid it. While the former is wasting his substance in family quarrels, the other consolidates his power by spreading his net over vast districts.

It cannot be denied that order reigned in Mokwa even before the arrival of the Benno. But directly he turned up with his catchpoles, and his Alkali, or Fulbe scholar, etc., the heart of the town began to beat more strongly. The market square and main streets were swept painfully clean every morning, the stands in and about the market itself were more properly arranged as to goods, while up till then they had been pretty higgledy-piggledy: the Songo was regularly supplied with straw, wood, and so on and so on. And in particular a thief was caught every day or two, while before this complaints had been rife about Houssa "area sneaks" without one ever being so. When one of these beauties was actually collared, the Benno held a Court of Justice. The Alkali opened a law book, read out the appropriate sections, and then the chaps with the bright red turbans (the Dogari) gave the criminal the number of prescribed lashes. In fact the government was excellent and I was delighted with this simple administration of the law and official summary punishment. Of course, now and again the proceedings are somewhat too vigorous. But, as a general thing, the governing spirit was first-rate and cheerfully accepted by the Nupés.

This was how I got my insight into the conditions prevailing in this modern coalition of the Nupé-Fulbe tribes.

\*　　\*　　\*　　\*　　\*　　\*　　\*　　\*

This Benno was a polite and extremely obliging person. He was indeed a prince without his equal among all the Fulbe rulers I afterwards got to know. Not even the Emir, whose power was enormous; not Nokoji, by everybody said to be the wealthiest; not Saba, not a single one of the Emir's brothers and sons was such a prince as this Benno. All the others were either petty or great curmudgeons, malicious pedlars of trifles and scandalmongers. But Benno was royal in grain.

I had only to hint that I might like to go for a ride for the horses to be at my door. I had only to say that Arriens wanted a lemon and a messenger went off to Bida to get some. I let fall a word about kola nuts, or Labodji, which, strange to say, are cultivated in Nupéland. Four sturdy fellows went off, wrapped mats round great branches thick with the pods to protect them from the glowing rays of the winter sun, and fetched them along. No matter what I might mention, the Benno would get it. He was a Chief desirous of honouring his guest in every possible way.

One day I said to the old Lilli: "Are there no more games for the youngsters? Don't you people any longer know anything at all about the curious Eko-Cheche? Have you forgotten everything?" He shook his old head: "When I was a lad," said he, "I was an Eko-Cheche player; I was very good at the sport. I grew old. The Fulbes came. They smashed our Eko-Cheche drums. Since then it is played no more in Mokwa. If our own children and lads want a game they go to Bokani. There they have the old drums still."

I said to the Benno: "I should like to see this Eko-Cheche. But they haven't got the right kind of drums in this place. They've got them in Bokani." He laughed: "What," said he, "thou hast not yet seen the Eko-Cheche? O! but thou must see it. Thou wilt laugh! The drummers shall be here in three days' time."

Eko-Cheche, the merriest of all the sports I saw in Africa!
The Jap has his jiu-jitsu; the Britisher his boxing; the Nupé his
Eko-Cheche—the same sport as the ancient Olympians; wrestling,
to wit. But it requires a special drum and a peculiar rhythm.
The swarthy West Africans love a special drum and a special
beat for every form of movement. And so the drums must be
fetched from Bokani for this great wrestling match, the Eko-
Cheche. And from Bokani come the drums. Full of excitement,
the Lilli comes to me at night: " The drums are here!"

The next day dawns. The young men have come along
from all the country compounds. When the Eko-Cheche calls,
the hoes are thrown aside. The best seconds have come from
Bokani. Folk have come even from far-off Yebba. Much beer
has been brewed in Rabba, is brought in by the back door
in large pitchers in the daytime and poured into little gourds
in the evening. The news of a big Eko-Cheche has been spread
in the Songo too. Two oxen have been slaughtered. Not a
single caravan has moved on.

At noon, then, the drummers need not beat their summons
long. They sit upon the tree-trunks worn smooth and black by
all the caravanners who have sat there before them. The crowd
hurries up. The squatting market-women are pushed into a
corner. Mats are spread. There is a large circle of closely
packed humanity. Our tables and chairs are brought out and put
into position facing the orchestra and then the dignitaries take
their places all around.

But it is not easy to begin with so much gentry on the
ground. The drummers beat an invitation for quite a while in
vain. Impatient cries begin to rend the air. The two seconds
go through a saltatory performance, little sham manœuvres,
threatening actions, each one showing what his principal, who
has not yet turned up, would do if he were in his place.
That, too, is ineffective. Now the ancient Lilli gets on his
legs; goes across the square to the young men. He has
had quite a little drop of beer by now. His voice is raised:
" Boys," says he, " do not put us oldsters to shame! Off with
your coats, tuck up your loin-cloths high. Show us your
arms. The Alfa champions want a bout with my young men

Let them not see your fathers shamed. When we old men were young the masters of the ceremonies had to beat us back with sticks when we pressed too eagerly about the drums to give our challenges. Prove that we veterans have reason to be proud of you!"

Hello! That's done it! Bravo! my dear old Lilli! The blood of thine ancient manhood still in thy veins runs warm! One can see it. And now the Lilli and all the Nupé Elders of Mokwa, Rabba, Yebba and Bokani are no longer conscious of their modern oppressors, those Fulbe! This is their very own Eko-Cheche! Their very own national sport in which they can openly and gladly take a hand. Forward, my lads, then!

Agreed! One lad has doffed his holiday clothes. He tightens his apron behind him. He goes to the drum. He bows forward. By touching it, he takes his place on the ground as a wrestler, throws himself back, bends forward once more and again touches the drum-skin three separate times. Then he prances around, his fist in the air, all over the place. His "pals" cheer him on. His example excites them. Another now throws off his ample tobé. He, too, bends low to the drum. He, also, runs round the ring.

Meantime, the two seconds arrange the affair. This Eko-Cheche is not a mere wild, unregulated jumping or knocking about. Not at all. It is a sport with its clear and definite rules. Woe to him who should break them. He gets a bad time of it and is for ever excluded from a share in the game. Two parallel lines are marked out as far apart as a good man can jump, somewhere about the width of a northern Mensur.* And each combatant puts his left foot on the end of the line in the Eko-Cheche too, standing behind, and without overstepping it. The seconds stand on their principals' lefts. They give them the signal to begin. The champions leap forwards, meet in the centre of the diagonal, hold out their fists, and then they leap back.

Go!

Yet—remember! This is neither a fencing-saloon in the North nor a sacred Olympian arena. This is Africa, the land

* TRANSLATOR'S NOTE.—Fencing ground of the German student.

where they hesitate. The word here is not " go," but " tease and go on teasing." And so, Messieurs the contestants jump and manœuvre, cut grimaces the reverse of Olympic and go dancing about, trying to make the lookers-on, the opponent and seconds laugh—not a bit like the heroes of old ; they mock and gibe at each other—for " it is their nature to." They skip and jump and hop and then—flop! one of them is round the other's neck. A few blows fall—whack! Or they lift one another up in a hold, or one of them gets a kick delivered with inconceivable cleverness in the mouth with the sole of the foot. Suddenly they are both men made of india-rubber, all elasticity, going at it for all they are worth.

Now the drums whir quicker; the crowd cheers jubilantly; the seconds hop with delight until the blows are too hard, the wrestling grips too tight and the kicks beyond registration, and then—well, then comes the real fun of the whole business. The seconds fling their arms round the bodies from the rear of each of their interlocked principals, tear them asunder, and each one of them carries off his kicking, crab-like, struggling protégé back to his corner. And then the duellists are surrounded by their backers, congratulated with thumps and cheers. Then it goes on as before, until one of them is thrown, or having had enough of it, leaves the ground. And then the crowd shouts louder and more madly than ever.

The games are now in full swing. Now the wrestlers throng forward, quite tiny fellows and full-grown men; but it is not considered *comme il faut* for the actual heads of houses. Time runs on. There will be no moon to-night. Then great fires of straw are lighted and as it is growing a bit cool now it is also as well to get warm inside. So the beer pot goes round the circle. The drums rattle. The shadows of the wrestlers slip across the square in the blaze of the fires of straw.

\*       \*       \*       \*       \*       \*       \*       \*

I said to the old Lilli on another day: " You once told me about the days of old when the great Spirit, the Great Father, Dako-Boea, wandered among you. You told me that you had

Duko-Baca dances on the market place in Mokwa.

( Photo by L. v. Frobenius. )

even seen him and honoured him here in Mokwa; that he came to judge the wicked, educate the children and reward the good. Can't I see the Dako-Boea once, too? Won't you, who say you are my friends, satisfy this wish of mine?" And the old Lilli and the other Elders were sitting before me in my katamba. The Ancient shook his palsied head, saying: "We had the Dako-Boea here once, it is true; but the white folk came; they talked about Issa and then took our Dako-Boea away and burnt him. Since that happened we have no longer dared to speak to our Great Father.—The Gushi has him—he lives a long way off. The old Gushi is dead. The young Gushi would willingly show him. But he is at a distance.—Ah! I would fain see him myself once more, the Father Boea; but I cannot. If only the young Gushi could be persuaded to show him?"

So I said to the Benno: "I should like to see the Dako-Boea. Thou knowest, the English missionaries burned him in this city. But the Gushi over there has got him. Couldst not thou send and have him brought hither?" The Benno's answer was: "The Gushi lives on the edge of my province. I will send for him. But ·it will take a long time. Thou shalt see him, but thou must forgive me if I cannot call him hither any sooner. He is at a great distance and the Gushi must ·first communicate with the Dako-Boea."

Envoys depart. The Lilli comes and thanks me. He says: "Now I shall once more be allowed to gaze upon the Dako-Boea. My brother died recently and did not set eyes on him again. We thank you. All the people will forgather to see the Dako-Boea."—It is pathetic the way these men, so stricken in years, hang on to something which is older than themselves. They furbish up everything as though for a very great festival.

It was as if Mokwa were suddenly to assume the mantle of its youthful bloom again. People came from everywhere; from far and wide; friends and relations swarmed into every compound. Every town which no longer possessed the holy thing and dared not reinstate it, sent its surviving priest of the Dako-Boea. From every quarter came those who had been instructed by the Great Father. They all wanted to see their "Sacred Sire" once more. They all wanted to make sure that the "white man" wished to

revive the old customs, which the red and white people, Fulbes
and missionaries, had destroyed and forbidden.

When I bid the Eko-Cheche rise up again for the first time,
folk came to Mokwa in their hundreds. But when the Dako-
Boea danced, I think there must have been assembled some
thousands of men and women and children. The fleshers
slaughtered oxen, sheep and goats; beer was brewed in every
village farm. Beer was brought from Rabba, Kutigi and Tatabu,
places where there was still sufficient grain. I had deprecated
being visited because I always had a lot to do, besides being ill.
But crowds of callers went in and out of the Benno's gates.
The worthy ruler looked very merry because everyone brought
him some little gift to keep him in good temper. He smirked
when he came to me in those days, and frankly said he was the
gainer by the restoration of the old arrangements I had procured.
And he also presented me with a couple of turkeys and a very
handsome old silk-embroidered robe.

The day, the great day, came. The people had arrived the
night before. There was a great to-do. Drums and iron bells
sounded all over the place. I had fixed the first solemn act for
ten, the second for three o'clock, as being the best for photography. We had to wait from ten to eleven until the " Holy
Father " was dressed. There was some disorder in the morning
and it was after midday before the wild confusion produced by
the convergent streams from everywhere was reduced to something like organized order. It was only then that the massed
crowds took on an air of solemnity.

And now, in order to make what happened here in Mokwa
intelligible, I must dilate a little on the true inwardness of this
ceremonial.—All these West African religious services are not
significant by reason of their more or less coarse, bizarre, fantastic
and clumsily primitive externals, but their characteristic quality is
to be found in the ancient traditions and the world of inner
ideas and feelings to which they owe their preservation. The
thought of reverential remembrance is embodied in this Dako-
Boea of the Nupés. When Egedi, the founder of the young
Empire, came into the country some 475 years ago, the Dako-
Boea, a mask of several yards in height, stood upon his canoe.

When Gushi, the original Gushi, one of the oldest rulers of the land, died, his corpse vanished and the mask referred to rose up where it had lain.—Or the associated idea of growth into manhood, the unfolding of masculinity out of the neutrality of childhood: When the man-child is not far from puberty, the Boea one day seizes and swallows it, runs about with it in his belly for months or years in the forest, and then throws it forth again. Then the youth returns to his home as a respectable citizen.—Or, possibly, the protective armour of the *suprema lex* of nations, the preservation of the race: Suppose some evil person makes himself obnoxious by magical machinations such as sorcery. Nobody would dare to attack such a fearful thing as a wizard who goes about at night like a vampire. The Dako-Boea is abroad. In his eyes all prowlers by night are feeble in spite of their sorcerer's cunning. He finds them, and terrible, indeed, are his judgments.

Some such national deity as the Dako-Boea stands at the head of every social-religious institution. Its presence alone is an effective shield against abuses of strength; its mere existence means peace and security. The Gods set up of old by secret societies and nations in their time have played an enormous part in civilization.

Now, what was it we actually saw?

Firstly, profound emotion, a real stirring of the spectators' feelings. It was, as I take it, the expression of memories of days gone by when these tribal Gods of the South Nupé peoples were their all in all, power and protection, a sign and a tradition. I agree that these dark-skinned races have not the same strength of love and sincerity which is born and nursed in the gloomy woods of the North, among fields of golden corn, beneath roofs of tile or shingle and in the midst of meadows green and bright with flowers which bloom in the spring. I concede that their thoughts and feelings have not been whipped into action by centuries of contrast between the light of the day and the gloom of the night, of summer and winter, by the " to be or not to be " of intellectual existence. They are all children of an ever luxuriant, ever generous Mother Nature, never late with the youth of the year. They grow as Nature grows. They know neither the meaning of limitation of power in its highest sense, nor of slackness in wrestling for sublimer possessions. And, therefore, they are ignorant also of that highest happiness of the Northern races: affection and loyalty and communal solidarity. Were this not so, they would know how to intensify the sanctity of their religion and defend it. But they do not do this. They let themselves be robbed of it and allow others to forbid them. No St. Boniface is needed to cut down their oaks. Some missionary may come along and commit to the flames the God of their nation. They give him up without lifting a hand to defend him. But when they once again see him their hearts are stirred to the depths, and they remember that he was their saviour, their strength, their sign and tradition of old.

But what now was there in it ? What was this " Holy Father " of theirs ? For us it meant little more than a fantastic, several yards high column of cloth which now rose, now fell. This stuff mask danced along with another one like it, originally female. Only when the wind caught and fluttered the ribbons at its upper edge was there something more essential to be observed in this ritual dance.—But those who danced round about these gigantic figures were altogether different. The priests carried long palm-leaf ribs and tripped busily about their " holy father " with ceremonial stride. They covered him with leaves when he lowered his top before the people, they followed when he danced towards them.

So exalted were some of the elderly people that they danced towards the sacred symbol with a singularly measured tread and performed a counter-dance with the giant who paced opposite to them with friendly motions. But it was singularly and irresistibly affecting to watch a group of women gradually gathering about the black and polished tree-trunk so often mentioned. They sang their devotional chants in chorus and in time. They clapped their hands together, either when they lay upon their knees or when they raised their arms aloft. One of them always danced up and down in front of the singing line. There was one woman with an unusually developed bust. All the others were either very old or very young, and, like the male ceremonial dancers, had divested themselves of their upper bodies' clothing. All these women prayed to the mighty Dako-Boea that they might be blessed with babies, some because they were anticipating speedy marriage, others because the married state had long been unfruitful, and a few did so, too, although they were well past the usual child-bearing age.

The proceedings visibly took a strong hold of these women and other lookers-on. Particularly the old Lilli. He never got tired of pacing up to the great masque every now and again, and then everybody's joy was always very great. The Fulbes did not put in an appearance, and therefore the people had the fullest licence to practise their customs in the old free fashion. As the sun was going down I pointed out to the old Lilli that the time for salaaming in the Masalatshee close by was at hand. And the old heathen only grinned. He made a most improper and unmistakable gesture in the Mosque's direction.—Let his excuse for this be that he had got very near the bottom of the first big beer jar.

More conversions to Islam were nipped in the bud that evening in Mokwa than in the ordinary course of things would come into flower there in a twelve-month. I will not mention the beer pots which were brought over brimful from Rabba, Kutigi, Tatabu and other places where there was still some grain left. The people gave themselves up to jollity and gladness, once more inspired by the return of their ancient God, until the " wee sma' hours."

I received a many-headed deputation next morning with a petition! They begged me to grant them permission also to carry out this ritual when I should be among them no longer. My reply to this was that I was as much a stranger among them as a man from Tarabulus or a Busu, but that I would prefer their request to the White Lords of this province, Captain Hopkinson and Mr. Edwards; as far as I knew the mission could not very well prevent them.—I brought this petition to the notice of the Resident and subsequently of the Governor.

\* \* \* \* \* \* \* \*

Days of farewell.

Such as we are accustomed always to say " Good-bye " after feeling at home, making friends and finding out what was wanted for the work in hand. Why was it harder for me to leave this place than others ? Why could I not strangle the desire within me to stay a fortnight longer in Mokwa ?

Such as we are accustomed to be hailed as strangers with no knowledge of things alike by the white man and the black. I was the first ethnologist to go to the Interior of Africa, and up to date only a few have followed me there. Who, then, was likely to understand what we wanted ? But always, when one of our sort arrives, pitches his camp and settles down to work, comes the great real task of my vocation—namely, to make friends, excite interest, get collaborators—and especially among the black members of the civic community.

Such as we are accustomed everywhere to meet with opposition, unintelligible to us of the utilitarian school of thought, and see in that the most dangerous rocks of our voyage. And just at the time when I was leaving Ibadan and Ilifé I had Mokwa in my eye.

Is it a wonder, then, that I rejoiced doubly in being able to give myself up to the quiet idyll in store for us at Mokwa ? Is it matter for surprise that doubly dear to me were these people who allowed me to feel that my own way of treating them eventually allowed me to know them and what they had in their hearts, when the ill-feeling based on the prejudice of others left us to ourselves ? And I was thrice happy in Mokwa because I was able to provide simple, natural folk once more with a few happy hours of traditional enjoyment, hours of pleasure of which unfeeling or unintelligent persons, fanaticism or superciliousness had deprived them.

I was glad to hear the hearty expressions of friendship which all the people of Mokwa extended to us when taking our leave of them. Many a charming word was uttered in the final speeches. A little of what the Lilli said has been given above. But what the Benno gave forth may here be repeated. The old Fulbe prince received the present I gave him, was silent for a space, and then said :

" Thou wishest now to go hence with thy two brothers. To-morrow thou wilt say ' farewell ' and travel to the great Emir in Bida.   In Bida there are those who have great possessions and all that I can give thee is as naught to that which is in the power of these to give thee.   But thou hast made us rich gifts.   Much money didst thou bring to Mokwa and didst spend it with both thy hands.   Ye played with our little ones and were always friendly with our womenkind.   Ye made the old men happy and let the young ones make sport for them.   We ourselves can give you nothing.   But the eye of Allah watches over all.   None of the Mokwans will forget ye ! "

And what " Godspeeds " fell upon our ears and what a mass of people met our eyes when we rode out from Mokwa !

Kakatchi or trumpeters of the Emir of Bida.
*(Drawn by Carl Arriens.)*

# CHAPTER XIX

### OUR ENTRY INTO THE CAPITAL OF BIDA

Describes how all the vitality of the ruined countryside is drained off and concentrated in the Metropolis, where we had a splendid reception and discovered what a great Soudanese mart can offer in jewellery, dress, fat stock, manufactured goods, foodstuffs, and the like.

THE continent of Africa has many beautiful countries by the shores of the sea, on its river banks, in its hilly districts and mountain heights. Nupé, whose character of austerity is its particular charm, is one of these. At this season, the end of winter, when the dry season's heat has withered all things up and even burnt off the grass in all directions, it is difficult to see the real source of the reputation for fertility which this country of extensive plains enjoys. Wide stretches of this prairie-land, yellowish grey, brownish red and muddy green in tint; barely covered, distorted trees, whose trunks are begrimed with soot and twisted by prairie-fires; grey and red ant-hills rising here and there above the level surface. There are the wearisome West African patches of plain from a mile and a half to six miles in extent, but cut up by splendid, towering walls of verdure, where oil-bearing palms and parkias, cotton-wood trees and samias are crowded together. The ground falls away, and, along the course of a brook, mighty bamboo palms and lianas,

400

The Nupe and Fulbe princes say good-bye in Mokwa.

(Opposite Text colony.)

[Facing p. 70.]

majestic trees whose trunks are wreathed with flowering creepers almost to their summits; brilliant butterflies flit in and out and round about, and the glimmer of sun-spots dancing in the woods laughs all the more gaily in contrast with the aching brightness of the traversed plain.

And after crossing swamp and stream, the farmlands meet the eye, not now at winter's close rejoicing in productive opulence, but, none the less, well tilled, long furrowed, carefully divided, park-like with their ornamental clumps of azaleas, parkias, bombaciæ, kigelias, fig-trees, and other spreading timber, beneath whose shade the country people stand together in their intervals of labour for a rest. The pointed cones of the farm compounds rising above the cultivated fields glitter in the distance and a few horsemen, the farmer and his brothers or his sons, race across the furrows on our approach to give us greeting or to offer goodwill gifts.

A moment's halt and a little talk about the country, the season and past times, and then the column marches on for a space through tilth and parkland and then, by slight inclines, up to the scorched and scorching prairie. Now, although the roving sight may search in vain for some pleasant spot beneath the blazing sun on which to rest; although Nature, stricken and dead through the blasting heat of the Harmattan wind, can offer nothing pleasing to the eye, the memory of the oasis just left behind and a glance from the topmost ridge of the swelling prairie we are crossing toward the grey-green, deeper line of woodland, reminds us that a further strip of forest lies ahead and that this country, too, can boast of beauties of its own.

The Lord who rules this land to-day and fills it with his own remorseless breath is hard and has no flesh upon him. The pitiless destroyer, Death, is Overlord of Nupéland. He is the Conqueror in that vast tract of those far-stretching levels, and with an almightiness which broke all resistance, forced what little life was left back into the valleys where the rivers run. For some five score years he slew and wiped them out, laid waste and sent them into exile. He overran the wretched country of the Nupés with all a ruthless despot's might and drove them into corners of the forests and the streams.

Ride but a while aside from the narrow path and your horse will tread upon the fallen fences of farms which once were flourishing; at times his hoof will catch on fallen walls; the earth around is deeply gashed where men took out the clay with which to build their dwellings and their village walls; cones of earth rise up among the bushes—ancient wells; and then, again, your mounts crush up the broken fragments of old pottery into bits still smaller. Death has been busy with his sickle here for centuries. This is Death's kingdom and that which mankind brought within its rule under the banner of the laughing God of Life in the struggle of a thousand years, Death's chilly skeleton made its own within a hundred's space. Where, formerly, thousands of comfortable beings strode happily across the fields they tended with so much care and sought the noisy marts of neighbouring towns, returning thence to their reposeful farmstead hearths, the form of the Destroyer spreads his length, and, where his bony finger touched the soil, it yields no ears of corn for harvest, there is no sound of children's laughter and human life is banned from settlement.

Alas, how long before the grizzly Victor shall be driven from this land again? Where are they, strong enough to scare away the horrid foe to life, to tear his deadening hand from off the earth, and, smiling, overcome him with the hoe and corn for seed, laughing offspring and the warmth of homes? Where?

I looked around me in this country and saw many things. But among the people I never met Our Lady of Hope. There were two women, certainly, whom I frequently saw: one in the company of the old aboriginal Nupés, namely, My Lady Patience. She wore an old and dirty robe and always bowed her head submissively when in the presence of a man; the lovely, lofty Lady Patience has been turned into an apathetic wench among the black West Africans. Then, too, I saw another, the companion of the modern rulers of the land, garbed in the raiment of to-day, who beckoned right and left to Greatness and to Power, and kept a book in which to register the names of those whom she desired to please, while pointing out with pride such names as these: Riches and Honour, Favour and Might. She herself was My Lady Arrogance. I turned over many pages bound in the volume of the Nupé heart, but failed to find on a single one the fair name of Mistress Hope inscribed.

This country's fate creeps on its way to-day. Life and the work to be done in it vegetates but miserably in the nooks of the brooks with their beautiful belts. But the heart of the land beats strongly in Bida, its capital. It draws the blood to itself in long passages and ejects it again in extended channels, but the arteries only connect great living centres, Bida and Ilorin and Kano and Saria and Bautshi. None of these arteries opens into the plain, upon the burnt-up prairies of Nupé, the "abomination of desolation" under the heel of the tyrant named "Death."—No. I did not meet My Lady Hope in Nupéland.

\*     \*     \*     \*     \*     \*     \*     \*

We are nearing the great capital's gates. We need only to cross the river Kaduna to-morrow to be within Bida's metropolitan area, whose agricultural district extends roughly for about fifteen or eighteen miles. And this evening the Nokoji, the last Emir's son, has been sent on to meet us by the one now in power. This grandee is going to entertain us hospitably on his princely estate and forward us on our journey in the morning.

Now we are at the fields of Egbago, our host's possessions on the Kaduna. The single trees spread their mighty crowns over the straight running furrows with a more luxuriant foliage than elsewhere; the yellow dwellings and outhouses and garners are cleaner and better arranged; cattle graze on the slopes of a neighbouring hill. This noble, Nokoji, must be a personage of great wealth.

Then the dry ground reverberates. Drums are beaten. We can hear the neighing of horses. Brilliantly red cloths dart among the trees. To the right and to the left of us, there is a sound of hoofs trampling over "brake, bush and briar." Wildly, defiantly, it surges towards us. Above the red, princely cloths flaunting in front of them, are Nokoji and his suite. They all spring from their saddles. They all bow low with the deepest respect, yet with dignity. The Fullani and his troop prostrate themselves on the ground. The Emir's salutation is offered again and again. Then: " Mount. To the saddle !" is the word. We sit up in the stirrups, surrounded by the heaving, half-hidden figures and excited steeds. The horsemen are fresh. Then we, too, will try a more rapid pace, since crawling along with the baggage all day has made us tired enough. So up and away !

Ha ! what a joy to tear and crash and break one's way through the bushes, over the stones, between the tree-stems and over the ditches. Hurrah ! How the clumsy old Nupé hats flew off our heads ! Never mind, let the sword-bearer behind pick them up. Hurrah ! How we cut through the evening air, how the branches and twigs both sides of us whipped us ! My own man, Bida, catching the right spirit of the situation, blew a blast on his bugle and galloping hard, we, knee to knee with the proud nobles of Fulbe, while the notes of the bugle are flung on the air, entered Egbago. It was a whim ; it was impulse ; it happened spontaneously ; it was born of the joy of being so close to one's mark.

What reason had I to think that this might seem an omen to our hosts ? Ah, thou angel of accident, whose hand so often lay upon the bridle over mine, this time thou didst indeed direct it happily ! I only heard the reason long afterwards. Nokoji's father was once the Emir. In his time a wise Alfa had prophesied : " When horsemen come out of the West who beat the sons of the Emir in a race on their arrival, then the end of the house of Maliki and the beginning of new greatness are at hand." I only heard this saying from Nokoji himself some weeks later on, but we were really welcomed by this family as though we were princes from the moment we saw them. I can trace many of my little successes to this incident. Therefore, " Fortune, I thank thee ! "

All the arrangements at Egbago were on the most splendid scale. Spacious huts and courtyards and high mettled horses everywhere. Next day there would be no difficulty in the substitution of some of my staff's weakly nags. I also for the first time here saw the magnificent, white, broad pewter dishes on which the fragrant meals for our people were served. I could not believe at the time that African skill could produce things

such as these. We, personally, were generously presented with
turkeys, rams, pigeons, wonderfully woven coloured mats, and so
on. When I added up my contra-gifts very carefully calculated
in value, Nokoji was about £4 to the good. This clouded me
with care. Everybody assured me: "The Great Emir of Bida
will give you still handsomer presents every day!"—Alas, and
woe is me! How could my little "money-cat" bear it? How
was I to suspect that a lucky (that is, lucky for me) fate had
created the greediest miser of all the Fulbe nobility in the
person of the Great Emir, Mamadu?

March the 9th!

I always heard in song and story of the erstwhile prosperity,
the olden greatness and the ancient wealth of Nupéland in the
long, last weeks of my stay. The Elders had told me of the
farmlands of miles in extent, which had girdled every city of the
many, many hundred towns, and that everywhere one such agricultural circle touched its neighbour. I can still see an old
blind man who got up while the recital was going on and
pointed all round the horizon with his hand saying: "Farm-
land was everywhere. There was no shelter for elephants or
flocks of antelopes because our hunters drew every river glade.
Towns both great and small covered the face of the land and
thousands of people gathered in their market squares. Folks from
Ilorin came to us to purchase grain and clothing. They came
from Kano and did the like. Oxen were slaughtered daily in
all the markets, and every evening the elderly drank their beer.
No man went hungry, but all men worked. The men went to
the farms and laboured. The women went to the market and
toiled. All the people in the Soudan said: 'The Nupetchi are
the richest of all mankind.' Thus our fathers before us spake to
us old men. But then came the Fulbe as Monafiki" (instigators,
traitors, cheats) "into the land. Our young men were sold into
slavery. Our women dragged into their camps. Nothing but
grass now grew on the farms. The apes stole the last ears of
maize. The looms fell to pieces. The towns were wasted with
fire. Foreign thieves built their nests in the farmsteads. The
Fulbe slaughtered our beeves. They struck off the heads of
our Kings and set them on boards in the markets. Our smiths

were only allowed to make handcuffs for the wrists of our fathers when they were driven away."

I always had to think of this old, blind fellow standing erect and upright in my house, with hand pointing round the horizon as he painted the riches of Nupé, whenever I rode over the prairie ridges in the country and my horse trod on the potsherds, stumbled over pieces of wall and shied at the waterless wells.

March the 9th.

Now we had crossed the Kaduna and entered the farmlands and jurisdiction of that city in which those " Vandals of the nineteenth century" had gathered together everything they had been able to tear from this country's quivering trunk! Was it strange that these farmlands round the capital had been brought to a splendid condition by the hands of the former natives who now were enslaved ? But could it be a pleasure to see peasant compounds and granaries, well ordered hamlets and well tended herds on all sides here only ? What could it be but pain to me, whose mind was still full of the misery which hung over the rest of the land to benefit this one spot on its surface ? Does it not all tend to show that thousands of towns were razed to the earth in order to build up a new one ?

The sentiments I felt for the Fulbes and their metropolis, Bida, were not very friendly and neither the extreme politeness with which, now here, now there, a troop of horsemen galloped up with greeting, nor the ovation of the constant addition to our train could avail to soothe my ruffled feelings. The only thing of any comfort to me would have been the substitution of a higher civilization for the one so extensively destroyed.

The swollen staff of the expedition reached the rising ground above Bida. Below me lay the city. I stopped to let the picture sink into my mind. A rather low, battlemented mud wall of a vast irregular square enclosed a considerable amount of ground, through whose centre ran several green-edged brooks, and the quarters of the town decorated with great trees but separated from each other by little ornamental gardens extended far in all directions. The first impression which the city made was favourable, because of the meticulous cleanliness and the orderly

arrangement of its extremely cheerful, long-drawn " High Street."
Yet again : how much more monumental, taken altogether, is the
effect produced by the dirty and clumsily laid-out towns on the
fringe of the Sahara, like Timbuktu or Sansanding, or even the
little towns of Kumi. And Bida as it stands is an absolutely
young city. One perceives it on the very first day; at least one
thinks so, and, at all events, I thought so. But I quickly
changed my mind : only its dress is new and " Fulbish."

Our entry even was peculiar !

Shortly after we had passed the gate, some of the Emir's
envoys met us on the broad street, greeted us in his name,
expressed his regret at not being well enough to come in person,
but he was sending the successor to the throne and his brothers to
welcome us, who would arrive directly. Would we be pleased
to tarry a little ?—And so it was : very soon a train of about
fifty richly-clad nobles on magnificent horses came along, amid
the blare of trumpets and the beat of drums. They all dismounted, prostrated themselves, did us the greatest reverence.
The heir-apparent made a fine speech, in which he praised the
town's good fortune in being allowed to honour us to-day,
alluded to us as " Germans " (!) and " warriors " (!) and offered us
generous hospitality.—Having replied by the mouth of my Bida,
the gentry allowed themselves to be lifted into their saddles.
Then the drums began anew to rattle and the ever swelling
retinue went down the wide and cleanly road.

All around us were the signs of varied and vigorous life.
Really fine horses, richly caparisoned with gold and silver embroidered trappings, carried noblemen in magnificent flowing robes
introduced by the Arabian merchants trading with the Mediterranean. Scarlet cloaks from the Orient, silks from Tunis, em-
broideries from Bornu and the far East. The backs of the
saddles were covered with delicately patterned silken covers native
to Morocco. For the first time I saw the wonderful trumpets,
although in the Emir's absence they were not blown to-day.

Everywhere along the broad way along which we went
slowly and with dignity towards the Palace, there were beautiful
trees and markets where life was now beginning to stir just
about three o'clock. Here the road was bordered by the massive

walls of princely compounds, there by the gates of important quarters, here again by low machicolated walls, behind which were claypits and gushing springs.   When I saw this form of architecture getting more distinct and varied, the suspicion struck me for the first time that Bida might well have been built and developed at the behest of the Fulbes, but that it could not possibly be a genuine Fulbe city, because all these features were familiar to me as the elements of ancient Nupean buildings in a degenerate form which contained nothing essentially Fulbesque.   And the suspicion ripened into the idea that the possibly not yet extinct Nupean civilization might still be alive under cover of the Conquest; nay, more—might have to-day attained the height of its bloom.   And I trembled with the pleasant anticipation of perhaps being able to find what I thought was hopelessly lost.

We continued our way.   Pedestrians and riders thronged about us.   The horsemen got down, saluted and joined us.   The others stayed where they were, bowed to the earth.   We came to a new square, on the left of which a great wall connected vast entrance halls.   This was the ruling Emir's palace.   I told Bida, to the great joy of the crowd, to give them his best on the bugle.   We entered the huge hall with its painted ceiling, went across that and a courtyard and found ourselves in a long narrow veranda facing the Emir Mamadu, who advanced a step or two and offered his hand.   He fell back groaning on his pillows.   We were each of us given a chair; the whole lot of nobles lay for a long time on their stomachs near the wall—and then remained reverently squatting on their hams.   Very tall Dogari (policemen) in glaring red vesture stood about between them.   The spokesman knelt by the side of the Emir.

It may be as well to say so here and at once.   The Emir Mamadu is diseased from top to toe—a spongy, sly, greedy and artful mass of black-skinned human flesh, with swollen sensual lips, cunning eyes and always sweaty hands.   As a youth, the worst Fulbe slave-raider; in his predecessor's time, the vilest intriguer (who worked up his direct forerunner Bubakari to rebel against the English and so gained his succession to the throne), he is to-day a half used-up debauchee who is paying the bill for his salacious adventures and his unbridled gluttonies by an envenomed carcass.

This ultra-noble Emir with the purple past greeted us most amiably, at once mentioned some golden jewellery he had heard I possessed and handed us over to our domestic host, a far more sympathetic Nupé grandee, the Chief Chamberlain of the Emir's court.

The drums rattled again; the trumpets blew; the horses stamped; everybody climbed into the saddle and conducted us to our own quarters close to the huge palace of the powerful Maliki clan. Here a great crowd had assembled, and our guide drove away the women poultry-dealers who began to gather for the evening market, which he at first did none too gently.

To my great relief our host was not a Fulbe, but the Tsoadja, a wealthy Nupé of high rank, who is said to have exercised great influence, especially before the Fulbes got into the seats of the mighty. He gave us up the largest part of his compound, so that each of us had his own set of rooms and a courtyard and plenty of room both for his work and his play. I myself was inordinately pleased at occupying one of the real old Nupé castellated houses, which could not in fact resist the onslaught of the elements in the first thunder-storm of the next few days, but whose age-greyed walls, gloomy side rooms and veranda, so completely satisfied my idea of a genuine antique little fortress in the Nupé style.

The grandees got their *congé*. We gave the separate house-boys the necessary instructions. We rested awhile till dusk set in and then followed the crowd that surged towards us over the high castle wall of our quarter. We got free of it and the first astonishing glimpse of the market of Bida filled me with amazement.

\*    \*    \*    \*    \*    \*    \*    \*

One of my boyhood's memories is a very large oil painting of some Italian All Souls' Day in the house of a family we knew. There were a great many little lights everywhere under a deep blue night sky. Everywhere flattish hills, between which people in curious head-gear wandered about and amused themselves. It showed a group of Italian ladies, lighted up by the little flames in the foreground, who, strangely enough, could not contain themselves for laughing in one corner of the picture, and in the other there were some Neapolitan-looking chaps sitting down and eating stolidly from a basket. This group was, of course, also lighted by the little flames.

I could not help thinking of this deeply azure, flame-illumined picture when I set my eyes for the first time on the evening market at Bida in the shimmer of light. It has a fairy-like quality; it seems to have grown out of some complete picture of a child's imagination. And I know I kept on saying to myself: " This is like the Arabian Nights! This is like the Thousand and One Nights! " And the impression has never faded, for all that I was able to enjoy the scene every following evening.

The eye at once recognizes the long line of people keeping to both sides of the gangway and the disposition of the booths in the enormous press of humans and animals; one distinguishes between the Dsukoko trending to the left and the broad Lotshita extending far to the right. One sees the human river flowing along the more than thirty-yard-wide Lotshita road, along the huge wall of the Maliki-Karra (a palace in Nupé is Karra; in Houssa, Katanga; in Yoruba, Igbarra), between the rows of lamps of the women squatting here beside heaps of stuffs and articles of food, and pouring between the Mosque and the rear of the Maliki Palace into the opening leading to the Dsukoko market until the streams run in the opposite direction late at night.—The eye is immediately conscious of great regulation of the traffic and yet surprised at the number and variety of the figures composing it.

A singular thing about the Bida market is that its greatest activity begins at or before dusk. I could not think why this was so at first. Why are the markets everywhere else held in the day-time and not also here ?—The answer is simple enough: Bida is an industrial city, and, next to Kano, the largest in Africa and, in many respects, as Kano people assured me, very much its superior. Everyone works at his trade in Bida in the quarters assigned to his guild from early morn to dewy eve Then there is only time to clean oneself and go to market.

We all, of course, know that when the sun rises on a great

Late Katamba (passage house or dendi-editoci) in Bida.
*(Photo by L. Johnson.)*

city of Europe, the apprentice sets out for his master's workshop; works all day long at his appointed place at the job set him; goes on with it after breakfast and dinner-time; knocks off about dusk and thinks this nothing but natural and as it ought to be; do we not? What else should we think at home about a regular artisan, lawyer's clerk, shop assistant, or whatever he may be? Very well, then! And it is for all the world the same thing in Bida, that curious capital of Nupéland. Now, that sounds only like a fairy-tale, but would in reality be the commonest prose but for the fact that masters and 'prentices, clerks and merchants, barbers, and the many, many women especially, would look so very different. I have cudgelled my brains how best to stimulate the reader's imagination by a comparison. If this involved nothing but describing the market-life, the allusion to the Arabian Nights and the sights of great Bagdad, so vivid from our childish days, were quite simple and a matter of course. But with regard to Bida such a comparison applies only to a part of its activities. The essential particulars of daily life, the busy pursuit of craftsmanship which also goes on in the bazaar itself, are all the more markedly characteristic of Bida, because they recall and compel us to think of the manner of life of our own mediæval guilds.

If now, on this ninth day of March, I am to conduct you out of our Tsoadja lodgings into the turmoil of industry in the mart, if I should squeeze you into the eddies made by the lounging, chaffering, hunched-up and by-standing thousands, a vision of a lazy, good-for-nothing, sleepy and indifferent negro society would be the reverse of reality. The true picture is one of people who have toiled very hard all the day through. Many of them have been hard at it in the workshops of their guilds. They have washed off the coal-smears, the oil-stains and stone-dust, shaken the shavings off from their nether garments and combed the cotton-flakes out of their curls. Then they have put on a fine, large, gaily-embroidered coat, and now they saunter bazaarwards.

Most of them have arranged the goods they have finished. Women come and take them away in their baskets, quite systematically. The wives of the workers in wood in the Esoa-baji sit in a long row on the Dsukoko, selling clay-stampers, stools, pick-handles, wooden pestles and mortars, and so on. Then comes a row of straw and matting plaiters, and over there many lads have gathered round a large square space filled with embroidered pockets for the tobé. Such things as these are not produced by associations, but are the work of young people of good birth who belong to small guilds or may want a little pocket-money. So each one has brought his bit of stitched rag and exposed it. Most of these are in varying stages of completion and consequently vary in value. The lad works at it by day, offers it for sale at night and many a purchaser finishes the embroidery himself.

Leaving these stands, we come to the goat and sheep market, or Esoa-ningi. Here there are gathered by far the most striking figures of the whole place; very tall and slim Busu and Adrar with lithams and dirty clothes, aristocratic Houssa lords, and as buyers the most respected persons of the city with their usual retinue. There are also the most beautiful beasts. Firstly, the Belemi, or long-legged sheep of the Soudan with Ammon-curved horns whose points are frequently pared to prevent their growth piercing their eyes. Then the Arara, also long-legged Soudanese whose corkscrew horns stick out horizontally. I measured one pair which was thirty-four and three-quarter inches from tip to tip. The upper class Nupé is fond of keeping a fine Belemi or Arara, which will follow its owner like a dog. I noted this curious and, possibly, extremely ancient custom amongst the feudal lords of Malinkeland on the upper Milo. Next to these magnificent sheep, there was the short-legged, " turnspitty " breed of Yoruba,* highly esteemed as roast mutton on account of its flavour and fat. The goats are the long-legged Urias of Houssaland and the " dachshund " Bikunji breed of Yoruba.

I often stood here trying to find an explanation of the singular phenomenon that all the sheep, goats, oxen, dogs and men on the Soudan plateau are long-limbed, slender, thin and tough, while in the West African swamp- Coast- and forest-lands one everywhere finds bow-legged goats and sheep with long, cylindrical bodies, short, thick-set dogs, bow-legged cattle, and amongst the older human tribes chiefly compactly-built people, with thick lower limbs and strongly developed, broad chests.

* Here called Kerro or Korro.

The idea is inadmissible that this may be accidental. Some powerful law must here be at work.

To get to the Lotshita, to the right of our compound, the Dsukoko has to be crossed. From the Esoa-ningi to the Esoa-bi, exactly opposite our own doorway, there is a broad road called Esoa-da, lined on both sides with traders, all of whom have shovelled up a little flat mound of sand for exposing their treasures for sale. Everything outlandish, as well as some products of Bida and the neighbourhood, are to be got in the Esoa-da. I shall never forget one man with whom I haggled for many a stone-bead, whose sand-stand offered everything of this kind spread out on sheets of paper. He had the stone bracelet of the Tuareg and the Tommo of the Homburi hills; he sold glass beads from Egypt and Wadai tomb-jewellery; from him one could get glass imitations of old African seals and stone ear-pegs from Ilorin. There was always a crowd of his friends about him who chattered and stared and admired, but never, by any chance, bought. These starers, however, were his advertisers or touts, for in Africa also everyone looks over the shoulders of a mass of people so as not to miss what is going on.

He was the "boss" dealer in the Esoa-da. But the little sand tables of the smaller genii of commerce were packed together in great numbers. Here sulphuret of lead to brighten the eye, civet, Kano daggers, Sahara salt, and especially paper from Egypt were on sale. These paper merchants sat and stood around, calling loudly upon the Mallems to come and write their beautiful letters and vied with each other in pompous obeisances to the literati walking about in search of what they wanted.

Crossing the Esoa-da one arrived at the Esoa-bi, where the trade was in kola nuts, and which lay midway between the Maliki palace corner and our Tsoadja compound. Every evening I bought my little bag of nuts to offer to such of my numerous friends in the city I was certain to meet on the Lotshita.

Then, when I saw my friends had made use of the last gleam of day to grab this or the other old bead on the Esoa-da, we strolled slowly down the broad Lotshita and enjoyed the sight of the jolly life of the market and the wonderful figures looking doubly fantastic in the flickering of many little lights.

A wide street follows the wall of the Maliki-Karra to the jugular vein of the city. Here squat the women and little girls who at this season sell mango-plums and limes, at others pisangs, oranges, etc., as well as ground-nut oil and ghee. They don't only squat, do these little ladies, but the younger ones have got up and invite one shrilly to come buy their wares. And how strange! What before had struck me in Mokwa struck me still more in Bida, namely, that, shutting my eyes and listening to the noise and the shouting, I could mark no great difference between these calls and those on the Cannebière in Marseilles and the great market-place of Florence. No doubt, the mixture of gongs and bells of the tramways, the commands of the Carabinieri, the blaring of newspaper names is not heard! Yet apart from this—and Arriens had to agree—the quality of the tone, the tuneful vibration, these "ah" and "oh" sounds here echoed the not, it is true, always melodious but always characteristic market cries of French and Italian women.

The Kola merchants' market faces our compound's gateway looking Dsukokowards, but we face the poultry market when we turn towards the Lotshita. Poultry! When one of us ordinary mortals talks of a chicken or chickens, he is apt to cut a comical figure in the eyes of the Nupés. As if they were just plain barn-door fowl! Great Scott! How simple, indeed! First of all there is the bristle-feathered rooster, the tsokun-lua, then the curly one, the tsokua-bigbi. Nobody knows where they come from; they are rare and treasured as curiosities; no one could tell me their original home. All other chicken are called biji or bishi and distinguished by colour, such as white or allaji; or edson, darker, but rather more light than dark; or gilla, tawny; or tutumbirri, black and white and red; or gunguro, red; or juko, black; or kwaro, speckled, and, lastly, the biji-kwai, which has a green back to its head and a green neck. This biji-kwai is never selected for sacrifice. It does not effect its object. Besides these there are a great many turkeys, but ducks are less plentiful (the duck is the favourite bird of the Benue people) and curiously enough apparently no pigeons, although these are plentiful in Bida. This part of the market, close to the cookery and food department, is open the longest and the sellers of their stuffs or beads or other goods to advantage will go to the poultry section to take their housekeepers a chicken or pullet. For, as will presently be seen, in Bida they are mightily fond of a good mouthful. The good Bidanese are belly-worshippers.

We, however, thread our way through the bustling crowd from the Dsukoko to the central and main point of the Lotshita. Here the flood of folk divides. On the right is the Esoa-dilali, a passage doubly lined with clothes dealers. Here the master-tailors spread their best tobés, and rolled or tied them up neatly in piles at their sides. One of them gets up, unfolds a tobé with a great flourish, stands as though crucified with the robe on his out-stretched arms. The folks stop, criticize the cut, examine the embroidery, count the seams and dozens of loungers enjoy the work of art, until at length up comes an intending buyer. And then, what bargaining begins! Not loudly or obtrusively, nor meanly or stingily, but slowly, deliberately, solemnly ; indifferent statement of price and dignified refusal with the simple word " Barka." When, however, the would-be buyer gets up on his last offer and moves away, the seller often rises to his feet and follows him, saying, " Take it." That is the way we do business in Bida town.

Next to this is the Esao-de, the market of the women-dealers in stuffs. Since, sad to say, a good many dresses are now made of European material, their baskets contain plenty of poor Manchester goods and some cloth woven in the interior from European yarns. But, for all that, dealers with great bales of home-spuns come daily in from the Bunu district in the South, an outlying province of the Yoruban territory. The larger portion of the beautiful stuffs used by the Nupé ladies comes from there, and although they themselves can manage the handloom, their own producing power is a mere fleabite to the enormous output of Kabba and Bunu. The merchant from out yonder hands over his wares to a woman. Here these saleswomen sit and every passer-by is at liberty to plunge a hand into the basket and unfold piece after piece. Now the good dames of Nupé are just as difficult to please in their choice as our own wives, sisters and mothers at home, but (dare I say so ?) in one respect just a wee bit more amiable. The careful shopper herself folds up the piece again!

Turning still more to the left as far as the corner of Maliki-Karra, along whose wall the stream of kola, poultry, dress and cloth marketers carried us, we first come to Esoa-masaga, the glassware square, and then right round the corner to Esoa-ba, the place for bamboo and building material. The former naturally fascinates us more keenly. Is it not peculiarly interesting to everyone to hear that rings and beads of glass are manufactured in a town in the heart of Africa? And if the most superficial, European idea that nothing but its own beer and gin bottles are used in the process has lasted long enough, the fact alone is sufficient to warrant a moment's delay and make us make up our minds to pursue the subject somewhat more fully to-morrow.

Meanwhile the mantle of night has fallen. All the booths and industrial products have been cleared away. Now, the high-statured Nupé women, erect in their flowing robes and veils, bearing on their heads their beautiful baskets, pass by, not without letting a glance full of curiosity fall on us through their face-veils; now, the dealers in goats and sheep, with their more or less unwilling flocks, move in front of us; now, all who have nothing better to do, saunter up and down the great street in front of the Maliki palace and which intersects the Lotshita. The Esoa-bonkuru, side by side with the Esoa-malufa, the hat-mart, runs along this thoroughfare devoted to scandal and gossip.

He alone, and only he, who has studied the Esoa-bonkuru, the sale-place of vegetarian gourmets, and the Esoa-mozotchi, the rendezvous of delighters in flesh-meats, only he, I say, knows the high grade of Bidanese culture, if there be any truth in the French proverb that a nation's civilization may be measured by its bill of fare. I have studied this question attentively, and, boldly assuming the truth of this saying, I can firmly maintain that the Nupés must be heroes and Colossi of culture. For, kindly be so good as to turn your nose that way! Is that not a whiff like the finest confectioner's? Come into the light of a few little oil-lamps, strung like a pearl chain with hundreds of links in and about the Esoa-bonkuru and the Esoa-mofotchi. Look at those thin brown cakes smelling like gingerbread. They are crisp, but to my taste a little too spicy, worse luck ! Massas, Kulli-Kulli, a preparation of oil and pepper and all kinds of aromatics, and like the massas made of ground ground-nuts, are still more luscious. But almost still more toothsome and sweet to the smell are Bonkurra, a Bida speciality, bean cakes and karra, or meal dumplings, which from their bath of boiling oil leer at the glutton. These are delicacies of the primest and costliest kind ; but the coarser, long-shaped bean-buns called Jenkaraga, and the yam fritters, baked, like everything else, in oil, would not appeal to us in vain but for over-seasoning with red pepper. Directly peppery dishes are cooked in oil, they acquire a pungency which makes them as good as uneatable, at all events to us, although I was always able to detect the fine under-flavour of the food. And that is why I preferred the simpler messes, like Enjibotchi, a dish of rice with a most delicious sauce, or Ekoa, a durra porridge, cooked à la Yoruba, or Sambu, yes, Sambu and Furra, two maize flour foods which can be flavoured to taste with their appropriate sauces made to perfection in Bida.

It will be well to give our sense of smell a short holiday before leaving the vegetarian restaurant to prepare it for encountering the domain of the master-butchers and cooks. Not to put too fine a point upon it, this quarter " hums," not, that is, the long row of roast meat and stewpot-stands, but the " slaughteries." Unless particularly strong measures, quite practicable, I fancy, in large towns, are taken by a European administration, an African " abattoir," where beasts are killed in the morning and the meat and hides left in the sun all day, without a soul thinking of cleaning in the evening, cannot possibly smell sweet. As is well known, the carrion vultures serve as street and market-scavengers in this part of Africa, where they hop and stalk about by dozens and dozens round these butchering stations in the large towns, sitting around hunched up on the trees and roofs of the little shade huts. These creatures are, of course, in a sense, a boon, because they remove the worst animal offal and, it is stated, some of the fæcal matter. They enjoy the protection of man, and sometimes do not move out of the passer-by's way. When a sheep or goat is killed in some compound, the vultures' keen sense of smell soon brings them along and in a very few moments they ornament the tops of the surrounding roofs.

They do not croak, but make their presence known by the thud of their wings as they settle. And yet anyone with a passable nose at once knows them, for they stink at about thirty or forty yards off, and one can easily imagine the effect on the air of the company of from eighty to one hundred such carrion birds at every killing-place in the morning. I think their existence very unsanitary. For these carcass-devourers are so impudent as to come within a knife's length of the cutter-up and he need only turn away for a second to sharpen his blade for some of these filthy birds to meddle in his work with the hooked beak and claws wherewith they have been raking about in some mass of corruption a moment ago. But a trifle like this is nothing to the honest African butcher; he just moves his hand to scare away the importunate biped, which hops a little further off, and then gets on with his job.

Since, also, these disgusting creatures naturally keep near the butchery as much as possible during the day and roost in the trees overnight to be up and about in the early morning for their share of their favourite human industry, one can easily imagine the penetrating stench they exhale and the extraordinary quantity of their unstinted excrement.

Thus, these abominable butchers' assistants are not great contributors to the olfactory amenities of the place, surely malodorous enough without them in the rays of a Central African sun, and, therefore, let us get over this threshold to the flesh-pots of Bida with all possible speed, so as to keep what little appetite the description of these things may have left us.

But perish prejudice! The fare I must now dish up is delicate, although a European palate and eye may have to acquire a taste for it. Meat is mostly an adjunct to the satisfying porridge of the worthy West African. But in such a "glutton's corner" as Bida, where general prosperity and even unusual wealth is the lot of all respectable fellows and a great many strangers, there must be folks, desires and opportunities for reversing the formula, and reducing the porridge to a side dish to the roast. After all, it is not surprising! All agricultural

The Emperor comes.
*Photograph by A. J. Lewis.*

populations are more addicted to a vegetarian food staple, while the sluggish and inactive townsfolk prefer smaller and more concentrated rations of meat.

That being so, let us squat down before the celebrated cook who has set up her stall at the corner of the Esoa-mofotchi. There are two mighty pots in front of this culinary artist, and no less than three little oil lamps whose wicks are smouldering and giving off oil fumes, which the edge of our hunger prevents us observing. I hold out my shilling (two thousand cowries would also be currency, but unduly prolong the transaction). The "cordon bleu" looks at it disdainfully, pitches it under the lid of a neighbouring basket, where its tinkle betrays the existence of a whole tribe of its family relations! Now, she takes a cloth from her lap, and lo! there's a baby sleeping as yet, but it would at once wake up and cry if mammy were to be absorbed in her business of selling. A wise mother makes her arrangements. So she takes one of her swelling and generally expansive breasts and puts the little mite to it. The peace of Europe is assured. The sound of lusty sucking strikes the ear and mother grabs the ladle.

And then, fully conscious of the incomparable excellence of the goods which it is her pride to offer to starving humanity, the superb craftswoman, certain of victory, lifts off the lid and plunges the ladle deep. A steam of thick soup of pleasing fragrance assails the nostril. Then she seizes a clean clay bowl, which she fills up slowly with the equivalent of a shilling or two thousand cowrie shells; very slowly, for it is a difficult thing to do. It is difficult to say what this mess does not contain. Anyhow, plenty of beef as well as some pieces of goat or of mutton. First of all we see some entrail, then a strip of lung, then a joint of a tail, then some bits of the muzzle, then, at last, liver fat, pettitoe, belly, etc. The artiste, however, takes care. The shilling or its value in shell money entitles us to a bit of all these good things and, as she has a reputation worth keeping, she does not lose patience, but fishes about till the basin is half full. Yet wait a while! Patience! There's something else belongs to this dish, whose name is Atchia-Kara. When the spoon has been well tapped, wiped clean with the finger and put back on the first lid, the mistress-cook takes the

other cover off, and with another spoon fetches from the second
pot a thick, gluey, green sauce and some pieces of thoroughly
soaked yam, which is poured over my Atchia-Kara for gravy.

We can now rise, eat it up near by and give back the
bowl or, as our credit in the market is good, take it away to
taste it in secret and not before witnesses, and then return the
basin. For a great many spectators gazing at the steaming dish
of the " upper ten " are here jammed together. Their hands
jingle the cash in their pockets, and many a thoughtless person is
turning over in his mind whether he ought to " blue " all this
money in a single evening on which he can easily live, although
modestly, lodging included, for ten days in Bida.

Delicacies done in another way are sold close to this stall,
in part still more appreciated, and partly prepared for travellers
intending to leave Bida next day and wanting to take a Lucullan
repast in their portmanteau. One of these luxuries is Killishi.
Slices of meat are well rubbed for some days in succession with
oil and spices and laid in the sun all the time. This kind of
sun-dried meat is in great favour and its Soja variety most of
all. The very best cuts are taken for Soja, which is first roasted
and then rubbed with aromatic herbs, etc.

Perhaps I have now said enough of the debauches of Bida
market to enable an idea to be formed of the number of good
things which might here tickle the jaded palate. We will, then,
leave the market with its little flames and turn to the other side.

What is there still to be seen ? The market-place in front of
the Maliki castle gate, the Esoa-malufa, where everyone sells the
home-made, world-famous Nupé hats of straw; the Esoa-wo, where
the trade is in all kinds of calabashes, is just as much deserted
now as the Esoa-tochibe, or drug-stand, which is in full swing
next to our own house, and where many old women sell
herb and root simples and dried berries in baskets big and
little, so that there is probably not a single " ill that flesh is
heir to," from the cradle to the grave, for which a herbal cure
would not be offered here. At this hour of the night all these
places are empty. Only the stands for the refreshment of the
inner man have lights. Only here is there some life and some
traffic, the rattle of cowrie shells and something doing; here alone.

The Emir of Nupé's progress in the main street of Bida.

(*Drawn by Carl Arriens.*)

# CHAPTER XX

## THE SPLENDOUR OF BIDA

*Describes how the Fulbes grew to be what they to-day are in Nupé, and assumed its ancient civilization; what this brings to ripeness in the land's metropolis, and the eloquence of the essential meaning of this development of culture.*

A PANORAMA of brilliant pictures passes before our gaze in the court-life of the Emir of Nupé. This potentate is a Fulbe, one of the great rulers of the Houssa country. The historical events which resulted in the elevation of this singular Nupé nation among the dominant powers in these regions will be more fully set forth in a following chapter. In this one a few of the main features of the growth of this special Fulbe race will be portrayed. I personally got to know the many varieties of this remarkable people, whose habitat is between Senegambia and the Nile, and from 1907 to 1912 I was in a position to study its affiliated tribes in Senegambia, Guinea, Timbuktu, Masina, in Mossiland, in Togo and Yoruba, in Adamawa and Kordofan, but more especially in Nupé proper, so that scarcely any historical transformation is more intelligible than that of the Fulbes and the Fulbification (to coin a word) of the Soudan.

In considering the Fulbe tribes, two eminently distinct types must be kept strictly apart in one's mind, namely, the emigrant

421

and the returning types. These were frequently dissolved in each other, and the ingredients of the mixture are difficult of individual recognition, but, having once noticed the diversity, the investigator is able to distinguish the elements of their fusion in many places. I call the emigrant Fulbes the remains of that migration of peoples which at some prehistoric epoch led them from some part of Eastern Africa towards the West. At that time they were a pastoral race. While the bulk of the wanderers reached the Upper Niger up to Senegambia, some portions of it broke off and remained on the road, which was a long road, as, for example, the Simili in Mossiland, a few tribes in Futa-Jalon and the original Bororo in Adamawa. These detached fragments of the migration are partly preserved in their particular purity and partly intermixed with the back flow of the Fulbes, and have even forgotten their traditions. An illustration of this are the Bororo in German Adamawa, who were reinforced from Bornu and the Kanodi districts and are to-day given to declaring that they are a comparatively recent immigrating tribe. But the Bororo I became acquainted with in Laro told me that this branch of the Adamawa-Fulbe had been settled in the land longer than could be remembered and had come, not from the West, but from the East at a very remote period.

The emigrating and returning Fulbe have one thing in common, namely, complete correspondence of temperament, emphasized by an extreme fanaticism, which is differentiated only by the line of its direction. The Fulbe idiosyncrasy was based on one solitary principle, the effort, namely, to keep unsullied purity of blood. They were "breeders" in every field of their proved activity; wherever they might be, their emigrants never took up agriculture, but cattle raising only. When they migrated, they drove along their herds of Eastern hump-backed cattle. But in the countries on their way there were already two breeds of beeves, one of them uncommonly like our European stock, while the other short-legged and generally dwarfish variety seems so singularly suited to West Africa, where apparently all animals, goats, sheep, dogs, horses, cattle and also men, develop short, thick-set legs. The air of Western Africa tends to the production of bow-legged things. Now the Fulbes came upon these two strains on their road. But they took particular care on their passage not to let their own hump-backed stock breed with the native strain. They regard the purity of their cattle as almost sacred, and I often found that their old bulls received an amount of attention almost approaching to religious adoration and that to touch them was forbidden. This fact, on the one hand, pointed to an East African origin, and, on the other, might be regarded as a proof that their fanatic disposition impelled them to insist upon racial blue-bloodedness among themselves no less than among their cattle.

The interests of the emigrant Fulbes' spiritual life were concentrated in their whole-souled observance of keeping the strain undefiled. Generally speaking, they had no particular religious or political bias (none of the emigrant Fulbe tribes had adopted Islam before the return of its brothers); their one and only concern was, at any price, to maintain all their blood kin against the negro races. In the East I nowhere noticed that the departing Fulbes had attained to any political organization as ordinarily understood. As already stated, they only recognized the principle of upholding their own race, the conservation of whose purity was their principal preoccupation.

Now, the power of fanaticism of the returning Fulbes is typically the same, but does not comprise the question of race purity to the same extent as the pursuit of religious ideas combined with active political organization. According to all the historical records, there would seem to have been a great turning point in the development of Fulbe-dom when its wanderings came to an end and they had settled on the Upper Niger in the country lying between the ancient Ganna Empire and the Yolof district. Here there had been towns from very early days, far-reaching civic institutions of no mean order and political systems to whose jurisdiction the immigrating Fulbes became subject. They met with new forms and conditions of life and, more especially, came into contact with fair-skinned races, all kinds of Moors and Berbers, Arabians and Desert tribes. In these circumstances, the racial backbone began to sag. Just as the Fulbe regard the light-coloured European as the same in race, so they also looked upon the North-Western nations as akin in blood and of equal birth. But in mixing their blood with these, as they had never done before with blacks, this quality of fanaticism lost ground, it lost its title and significance in the domain of race distinction. There is many a tradition of the marriage of Fulbe maidens with the light-complexioned supporters of old Mahommedan culture.

But at the moment when the migrating Fulbe established a closer connection with the fairer tribes and, hurrying to embrace the advancing Crescent, entered into familiar relations with the religious zealots of the Prophet in the North-West, at that very instant their fanatical insistence on the necessity of keeping their own race pure was quite obviously diverted into the channel of the Mahommedan religion and world-empire. And with all the characteristic ardour of this singular people, the Fulbes turned away from the problem of race and towards the new range of ideas.

This is the only explanation offered in the material available for the extraordinary transformation of Fulbe nature. With it it lost its old ideal. Islam is the foe of all race preservation principles. It knows only the Faithful and the Infidel. And henceforward the Fulbe only intermarried with the daughters of the "Orthodox." The vigour of his fanaticism drove him from the steppes into the towns, in which the mosques and priestly seminaries, the universities and propagandists of the new belief were situate. The whole environment of Fulbe existence was thus changed at one fell swoop; for they now took part in a politically organized scheme. The lands between the Deltas of the Niger and the Senegal were peopled from very early times by nations divided into castes: lords, vassals, players, smiths, etc. It is a distinguishing badge of the Fulbes that, when they first appear in the light of their dawning history, there is no " shepherd " caste upon their record, but that they always appear as the " masters."

The processes of dislocation and transformation must in their case have run their course as silently as in most of those known to us in the world's history. And as far as there is any documentary evidence, into some of which we shall presently inquire, this, too, is in harmony with the nature and traits of Fulbe history. The chapter dealing with the fall of the Edegi dynasty will inform us of its successive steps. Here, however, I only propose to deal with the results of the metamorphosis of the Fulbe nature. The martial Fulbes, who had wandered in most peaceably in the guise of shepherds, appear, after a short interval, as the zealous champions of Islam and then as Kings. The principle of maintaining racial purity retires behind that of defending the Crescent flag and Islam domination. As soon as the Fulbe grasp the reins of government, they take into their harems all kinds of women, both dark and fair. Religion and family-rank alone now kick the beam. The Fulbe child is a black child.

The results of these proceedings for some one hundred and fifty years lie before us. The Fulbe, divided into castes on native lines, themselves acquired a swarthy hue by intermixture with the aboriginal negro races already mingled with the Berber blood. The original type of the immigrating Fulbe is now only represented in a few districts of Senegambia on the Bani and elsewhere, but the type of those who were on the way back is fully developed.

The latter then set out on their world-historical mission. They began their retreat as the Prophet's "hot gospellers," conquerors and organizers. It is easy to see how this came about. All the western tribes in Senegambia and the Upper Niger had already adopted Mahommedanism. This ground offered them no field for their proselytizing zeal. So they invaded the heathen lands to the East, to plunder, enslave and rule them as was their Islamite "duty" and "right." At first they overwhelmed Massina, the land south-eastward of Timbuktu, and then began their work in the Houssa countries at the turn of the nineteenth century.

Their active influence starts in the province of Gobir, continues in Ilorin, Nupé, etc., and is everywhere identical. Osman-dan-Fodie appears in 1800 as the Mallem, the fanatical preacher of Islam in Gobir. This person gets many adherents and followers on the quiet. He disturbs the unity and good feeling of the leading houses by intrigues and trickery, is held in more and more honour as being the King's trusted counsellor, and then he strikes his blow. It is a sudden effervescence. Gobir, Gando,

Sokoto fall to him; he breaks the resistance of Katsena and submissive Kano thus becomes the centre of Mid-Soudanese commerce and industry.

From this kernel of power the Fulbe victors extend their operations to the South and South-east. A few lands, politically unorganized, are taken by storm, others with an older civilization, independent political power and strong determination to live, are, according to time-honoured precept, occupied " for the benefit " of the inhabitants. Nupé was one of the latter, which was unquestionably lashed more than the rest·by the scourge of the retiring Fulbe. An innocuous personality, the famous sage, Mallem Dando, settled there quietly with his sons and a small number of followers.

About the middle of last century Nupéland was, according to the African standard of comparison, still extremely rich and powerful, but even at this early period that monster, Discord, had reared its head in the bosom of the royal house. Disputes as to the succession, so common in old African kingdoms and satisfactorily arranged by a vigorous African people unless decomposing acids are injected from the outside, had weakened the influence of the nobility and the royal family. But misfortune from abroad was also simultaneously carried into poor Nupéland. And this was the Mallem Dando, the leader of the wave of retiring Fulbe imperceptibly pressing onwards. With an amount of diplomatic skill it would be hard to equal, this astute fellow managed to hound on the members of the former dynasty against each other. Now he supported first these, then those; now he sent his " peacemaking " sons first hither, then thither; and, finally, when the desired confusion had come to a head, he invited an embassy from Gando which was already everywhere an object of fear. This was the way in which the Fulbe Emir of Gando was installed as arbitrator and matters were so arranged that they turned out to his, the Mallem's, greatest advantage.

The real dance of Death, however, only tore across the face of the land on the death of the father and the official nomination of one of the fanatical Mallem's sons as king. Once more the ancient valour of the sire Edegi pulled itself together in his offspring. Once more a Nupé prince upheld his claim and sent

Industrial Life in Bida.   Pl. I.

Scenes in the great night market in Bida.
*(of kolá-nut sellers.)*

the Fulbe packing. Yet this victory only put things off a while; the Fulbe sat around the land like hyenas on the scent of prey and that last knightly ruler of the royal Nupean race had scarcely drawn his last breath when the baiting and the raiding began anew. The mounting wave was breaking into surf which swallowed up the land by pieces. Thousands of Nupés were slaughtered in great baths of blood; hundreds of towns were burnt to ashes. The heads of the "ringleaders" found guilty were set up to view in the market squares. The women who, as was their wont of old, went to the assistance of their fighting men, were raped in public by these wielders of the Fulbe sword and torch.

For here, once more, as in each, of their retreating waves, the Fulbe were only the dancing crown of white foam on the crest, but dragged in their wake the entire mass of the uncontrolled, exasperated and unfettered black, oozing slime of brutal negrodom. The Fulbe were but the leading minds; the weight of the fist was that of the military captains of mercenary hordes, who rightly expected to fish in these troubled waters.

And thus it was also here in Nupéland by no means difficult to understand that one day these Fulbes would find their own weapons wrested from, and turned against, themselves. The war of extermination ended in the Fulbes having to fight their own victorious General and nothing but their tremendous diplomatic skill succeeded in inducing the last remnants of Nupé nobility, deceived as to the true origin of the long and bloody internecine strife, to take up arms against the last great commander and help them to victory.

The decisive battles were fought in the neighbourhood of Bida. Thus the new Emirship was created in Bida and the Nupé nobles did homage.

\*　　\*　　\*　　\*　　\*　　\*　　\*　　\*

The backwash of the Fulbes had come to rest in a new nest; the old chief cities of the land had been laid waste. And now its new rulers built their new seat with all the pomp they could imagine. All the nobles were summoned into Bida. They were compelled to build their palaces in Bida, and the Fulbe had their own mighty castles erected in the Nupean style. The craftsmen and the artists were assembled in Bida, and thus arose that strange place, the " Fulbe city," into which we made our entry on 9th of March, 1911.

I had really expected to find a genuine " Fulbe city." But Bida had absolutely nothing characteristic of the central Fulbe type which was so familiar to me from my knowledge of the Western lands. Everything in each compound, in each palace, of every piece of cloth, every dress, even down to every part of the armed equipment, was totally different. More, I scarcely heard a word of Fulbe in Bida, which caused me great surprise at first.

And yet it can all be easily accounted for. In the long butchery which went on for close upon a century the Nupés were assuredly the losers, but the Fulbes had in the course of generations acquired all the culture of, and many things more peculiar to, this nation which had so magnificently resisted them. They had been conquered by the Fulbe, whose individual civilization was dissipated on coming into contact with the Nupé people. How often may this process not have been repeated on this globe— when Mongolian and Manchurian tribes invaded China the fertile ; when neighbouring barbarians swarmed into the regions of the Euphrates and the Tigris or the plains of India—how often ?

And that is why one sees no Fulbe houses in Bida, but palaces in the style of the old Nupé rulers; that is the reason for the court ceremonial being not Fulbe, but based on the Nupean mode of life. That is why Bida is not, as it was so often said to be, a new city with a new civilization. The culture of this country is ancient and has only changed its home. Its history, which is well worth study, tells us that each of its erstwhile rulers had his own town. We know that the capital of Nupéland was changed four times within the last hundred years. If ever there was a metropolis which retained every possible trace of ancient culture and always possessed a name and reputation for primitive magnificence, beyond all doubt that city was Gbarra ; but the Fulbes laid it waste so thoroughly that nothing but its ruins and its slag remain, while the conquerors were clever enough to lead captive to their own city the venerable guild of workers in glass whose only home had been Gbarra.

In planning their towns in Nupéland, firstly in Rabba, then in the alleged " foundation " of Bida (Bida was, in fact, a very ancient but unimportant provincial town), the Fulbes gave evidence of something of the faculty possessed by the great lordly houses of the Renaissance. They attracted all the brains, all the intellectual forces, all the artistic ability of the country to the capital. They crushed the land itself beneath an iron heel, were the greatest barbarians in their foreign relations, and amongst themselves chary with neither poison nor the poignard's point. But they robbed the broad countryside, declining far and wide, of all its higher culture and amassed everything which redounded to their own pomp and glory and the reputation of their own race, everything which could contribute to the splendour of their own town. Under the influence of the treasures of culture they had themselves amassed, they then had to pay for them by the loss of their own individuality and become the guardians of a reinvigorated Nupean civilization rooted in its former ruin. The country homes were laid low, but the light of the new capital shot its rays more brightly and dazzlingly aloft than any previous site of culture of more recent days in the land where the Nupés dwell.

Such is Bida!

\*     \*     \*     \*     \*     \*     \*     \*

The Fulbe, however, did not behave like other conquerors by force of arms, stealing a statue here, an obelisk there and a picture elsewhere, setting them up at home and saying: " See what great diffusers of civilization we be! All the lands must acknowledge our might and deliver up to us the glories of their art! Lo, such is our greatness! " This was not the Fulbean way. They did not attract the products, but the forces which were productive.

I often rode and wandered on foot through the quarters of the town where glassware, stone beads, chased metal vessels, moulded bowls, carvings and other goods were manufactured, and now that I wish to take the reader there, I must first remind him of the only comparative example in recent times with which I am personally familiar, namely, the industrial life in Tunis and other Mediterranean towns. In these far-off cities of this inland ocean I found that all the trades were dwelling together as guilds, or corporate bodies. In Africa they are called the " sooks." On going through a passage in the industrial parts of the city we find one street devoted solely to leather goods; another with nothing but sieves; a third where only silks are woven; then a street given up to smith's work; and yet another where the paper-makers live. These are the celebrated " sooks."

There is one difference only between Tunis and Bida in the arrangements. In the former the workshop and place of sale are one and the same; one buys direct from the actual craftsman. In Bida there is a division of labour. In certain parts of it, called Ephu, the industrials are gathered, but the trade is whole-sale only and single articles are not sold. The goods are sold in the Esoas, as before described.

The Ephu-massaga interested me most as the place where the glassware is produced which goes all over the Soudan, and some of which I also found on the Senegal as well as on the Nile, on the Gold Coast and at a merchant's who had come from Dakkar down to the Congo.

\*　　\*　　\*　　\*　　\*　　\*　　\*　　\*

The moment one sets foot in the craftsmen's quarters of the city of Bida one is in another world. This is no longer that " dark Africa, the homeland of the care-free, indifferent negro," who works how, when and where his humour or inclination may take or make him. The land so richly endowed by Nature as to yield all necessary food for man and beast if only gently tickled with a hoe, is left behind us. One is face to face with men who have advanced to the highest point to which culture has attained, namely, voluntary labour. And not as individuals, but as associations of industrial workers, who do not " earn " their daily crust with the plough and mattock, but work for wages that have been agreed beforehand for to-day, to-morrow, for weeks and months and year by year, on lines prescribed.

It is a fact, which I cannot but repeat, that the Africans are the most industrious of all " natural " nations, for the great majority of them are an agricultural race who spend a few months yearly in scratching the surface of their Mother Earth and spend the rest of it recovering comfortably from their exertions.

It is also true that the Africans are skilled in many handicrafts and that they are beautiful plaiters, weavers and hut builders. They are good workers in iron, potters and wood carvers and no despicable producers of articles made of leather and fells. Taken broadly, all these things are not the result of organized labour. This, in the main, holds good for nearly the whole of black Africa and only a very small fraction of African handiwork is made by trained and professional craftsmen. The small artist in African industry spreads the pleasure in his work over a long spell of time; does a little to it to-day; lays it aside for a week; picks it up again and, if he has lost delight in going on with it, will use it unfinished, only half decorated, its handle only half shaped, using it continually until it wears out and never is completed. The African peasant craftsman's creations are the sport of his temper and moods.

It is certainly true that the majority of the West African agricultural nations have graduated in the bitterest school of the world, namely, slavery. But if the African had paid for his apprenticeship only by temporarily sacrificing his manhood, this would have been a sufficiently sad business, yet still seem worth while if it had been the sole fee for his instruction in the art of working. There is, however, another side to the question which makes me regard this road to learning as being very depressing and unprofitable. There are two forms of labour essentially different in their aspect, expression and reaction on man. I mean the field worker's, who, taken altogether, compels the soil to produce values, and the artisan's, in whose activities the man himself is valued by what he creates. Now, the form taken by Soudanese slavery, the lowest form of enslavement, has more or less only brought its victims to extending their field labour, but not to developing their handicraft or independent production. And this is the most fundamental distinction between the slavery of to-day which seems to have been changed by the influence of Islam, and the slavery of classic antiquity.

The wisest and ablest settlers of the Old World, namely, the Romans, that singular nation whose greatest and most individual genius lay in the peaceable and warlike development of statesmanship, attained (if the broad features of their total achievement may be taken into account) their supremacy in colonization by subjecting the people they conquered to forced labour in the sense of compulsory production. The Roman only took the interest of the work of the conquered, whereas the Arab took the principal or capital, everything that was earned, the entire " Ego " which every man puts into his own work. The Roman subject and the Roman slave could find joy in the possession of his " real self," joy in its further growth; the productivity of these essentials, individual exchange and power of creative interchange, was raised. The Arabian subject and Arabian slave was robbed of these and, consequently, lost his productivity.

I may be thought to have lost sight of my Bida glassware and to be pursuing some irrelevant idea. No; I am on the road to my Massaga friends, but to know the whole extent of this peculiar guild's effectiveness, I think it very necessary to realize the essence of the African's work, its correspondence to his natural disposition, its transformation in the course of history, and, perhaps, how it illustrates the efficiency of this Bida guild in a very special way. For eventually the real charm of our excursion lies in the general survey of the actual facts: perspective and horizon, vista and look-round are the watchwords of our wanderings.

And so from the great city of Bida I look out towards the Congo and to Senegambia, to Liberia and Timbuktu, to Algeria and Tunis and I see the old negro children with their honest simple field work and occasionally capricious play with handicraft. In later days I see the stunted, blunted, degraded slaves, joyless, rightless, defenceless, busy beneath the lash of Arab culture; but in the Past I see the furthering, fostering, elevating incentive to productive work in the organized civilization of the classic ages.

And I ask myself two questions: Can then, the negro only

be compelled to greater productivity by the lash, by deprivation of manhood and robbery of his rights ? Are there, at the commencement of this new era, no proofs that the colonial ideas of antiquity which found their way to the nations of Interior Africa ran free before the Arabian butchery ?

We have now reached the brook which divides our quarter of the town from the Massaga's, the workers in glass. We ride through the banana grove. Up there, under the spreading canopy of leaves, lies the first Massaga workshop. We had so frequently heard such a lot of the wonderful arts of these people that at last they seemed to be legendary. We should undoubtedly see something perfectly marvellous. The network of secrecy with which they know how to surround themselves is so close, has so grown into a veil of quite unexpected surprises as a matter of course, that we cannot possibly prevent ourselves looking out for something tremendously expressive.

But then I say to myself: "Is this not Africa, the Continent of disillusionment; the Continent where the reverse of the expected always happens; the Continent certainly rich in results which must be toiled for, and never fall into one's open mouth; is this not Africa, where all great, ancient and lofty things are wrapped in shabby tatters which must be stripped off rag by rag before its soul be reached; is this not the abiding place of lies ? "

Well, then, what actually met our eyes was once more unadulterated Africa. It was growing dusk when we saw the Massaga for the first time. There were a few compounds in the wan evening light of the discolouring Harmattan, quite ordinary houses with the typical conical roofs, which looked even grimier and more tumbledown than those in " our " part of the town. I cannot imagine what gave me the idea that this remarkable and (for Negro Africa) unique guild must show something quite out of the common in its architectural features. And as to the dun sootiness and blackened roofs, I entirely forgot for an instant that labour neither wears its holiday robes anywhere in the world, nor that the hives of industry in European cities do not show us palatial fronts, although they produce the means by which the genial " captain of industry " acquires a noble villa and the skilled worker a comfortable home.

Grey and colourless. Until we came to a house with many doors. And there the scarlet glow from a sunken fire-pot. Around it sat the workers with their rods of iron on which the rings of lovely glass were twirled above the glare; there in the background the bellows wheezed; there on the floor lay finished bright-hued goods; here rings of plain glass were being turned and gaily patterned. And this busy, moving picture, full of tints 'stuck so fiery off, indeed' from its background; the work-folk went on so assiduously with their employment; the glass of rainbow hue glittered so gaily amidst the uninterrupted hammering and rocking and smelting and turning, that I might well say my first glimpse of this Massaga industry gave me one of those rare moments in Africa which were free from disappointment.

And this impression grew still stronger. For presently the guild-master, who months ago had been informed of the coming visit of the foreigners, stepped up to us, robed in a coat of many colours, and said: The real working-day was over now, the men had already worked the number of hours agreed, but some of them wanted to earn a little money for themselves in overtime.

What was this?

Definite working hours?

Agreed wages?

Overtime?

Own account?

The bellows roared in the background. The heat glowed white in the crucible; the tinkling sound of glass broken off when being weighed; the twisting-up of the whirling, thickening rings—limited working hours; a wage agreed; overtime; and own account. One workshop ranged behind another and over all a worthy master of the guild—there could be no doubt at all but that here there was a well preserved, living instance of a momentous past, which, taken bye and large, was foreign to negrodom in general.

After that, Martius and I often visited our Massaga friends and he could study all the details of ring and bead production to his heart's content. At last there was only a single secret left: the mystery of the Massaga themselves. We are, of course, not the first who have seen or heard of the Bida glass industry,

Glass-workers (Massage) in Bida.

(Study in oils by Carl Arriens.)

although apparently so far nobody has sufficiently studied its details *in situ*. But whence the Massagas got the glass, had always remained an open question for my predecessors in this department of research. The accounts gathered from a native in Adamawa by that careful observer, Passarge, seem nearer the truth than most, but even he was unable to settle the question as to its place of origin. The Englishmen I had previously asked about it simply said that the glass used was taken from whisky and castor-oil bottles.

This view fits, inasmuch as the manufacture does, as a matter of fact, depend on the employment of European glass which comes into Bida from all sides. But I regard it as a successful result of my own research to be able now to state that the Massaga themselves to-day make black and yellow glass. The basis of the inquiry, then, is not whether the material is imported, but fundamental knowledge of its method of production. And, therefore, the quite superficial, but, also, quite common, verdict that the Massaga glass work is fed by imported European raw material, falls to the ground. It is on all fours with the problem of the origin of West African bronzes. Naturally, getting to the bottom of trade secrets is none too easy and our friend, the Massaga Master, made it no easier, but, at last, the European method, conscious of its aim, once more hit the mark and the explorer can once more gleefully throw the question, " Well, what do you say to that ? " into the teeth of the sceptical stay-at-homes who refuse to believe that the Moors had any connection whatever with the ancient epoch of civilizations in the North and East and would fain trace everything higher to modern European influences.

This explanation will seem much more satisfactory to those who consider the externals of culture of greater significance than the internal intellectual tendencies at work in it and the explanation found in the existing guild system by Martius and myself. And, for all that, this presents a fully developed economic institution which may, perhaps, have its only equal in " Moorish " lands. As a rule, at the head of every industry in the Houssa states and, maybe, still more frequently in Bida, there is a guild-master. As all handicrafts are more or less hereditary in the same family and since guild membership to a certain degree means economic association, the guild-master is also not unseldom the banker or employer of all the confederates or even the occupants of the workshops. Among the Massagas everyone works for himself and gains his own livelihood through him. Every workshop consisting of five men has to furnish a stated output per diem, receives its measured quantity of raw material and has to deliver the finished articles day by day. When the labourer's task is over, the confederation is allowed to use the place for its own benefit and what it then earns is paid for in cash on the nail and shared among the five.

In this fashion, a closely circumscribed activity of economic life is manifest round these crucibles glowing at white-heat in such a completely ripened form as to point to an undoubtedly far-reaching historical origin.

How? Old, well-established industry, an old matured economic system, incorporated in the bone and muscle of the general body of culture! How can that in any way tally with what I said above about the forms which labour takes among the Aethiops and Moors? Well, do but step into the workshops of Bida where rings of glass are swung to and fro; or where they polish chalcedonyx, agate and cornelian; or where the busy smiths engrave all kinds of cans and cups and urns; or where the carvers carve and weavers weave, and so on; and then, having looked at all this strenuous toil and interrelation of work and workers, you needs must know that here there can be, on the one hand, neither the playing at work of the Moor nor the botching of Mahommedan slave-labour on the other. This is a nobler and intenser form, whose birth must be looked for, in the North, among the subtle, statesmanlike, colonial politicians or, in the Orient East, in ancient and ripe civilizations.

It is, of course, true that the guild-craftsmen have to do their daily task in full, but they have their honoured position, their sufficient income; can change their place of employment; are entitled to work overtime in their master's workshop to add to their earnings and keep what they so earn; belong, in a word, to a class, a social stratum, which I had only found among the Mande, namely, the Ooloosu, the serfs, who are similarly tied to their master's compound, to the village of the commune, but are still lords of themselves when their weekly quantum of work has been done. These, it is true, are mostly peasants, but weavers as well. They are altogether different from Mahommedan slaves. And there also, in the West, they date from eras and cultures which are pre-Islamitic.

These things, then, are still visible monuments of a recordless time—that is to say, a time preceding Islam. They are social arrangements handed down from the Edegi period, whose meaning will be clear from the chapter on Byzantine Moors. Here we see that the exquisite achievements of the negro when a free man may solve the problem of how he can be led by skilful economic pressure to higher forms of agricultural and industrial production.

And this also is one of the maggots in the brain which worry us in the coming dawn when we recross the brook and banana grove which divide the quarter of the town where the Massagas dwell from that in which " we " live.

\* \* \* \* \* \* \* \*

I often shook my head in the first days of our stay in Bida, saying: " However shall we finish all our necessary studies in the short time at our disposal ? " Arriens and his easel went from one workshop to the other, for every one of these wonderful art industries was to be set down on canvas. And yet he was often stopped from going when some gorgeous display of the Emir's brought splendour of colour and Oriental feeling into our quarter, or when a favourable light invited the laying in of an architectural drawing, or when the Kanos brought the grotesque horsemen in their padded armour, and so on. Martius every morning went to the glass smelters, bronze smiths, bead polishers, tin workers, wood carvers, so that at last he could give all the things their names in Nupé quite learnedly and yet he had to seize every opportunity of surveying every compound when its lordly owner had gone into the country with his harem. I say nothing of all that was to be noted in my head and recorded by my pen in the expedition's archives; but I often jumped out of bed because the idea that something might be insufficiently thought out and poorly explained made me spend many an hour at my desk and fix up a programme to facilitate and expedite the labours of the coming day.

I was now tarrying in a city where good behaviour and manners were taken to be the special marks of the higher culture. This was a nuisance. As soon as I was busy with my clean copying from six to seven a.m., and my interpreter, with the " daily reporters," had arrived, the interruptions would begin. First of all, my host and his sons would come in ; he was the Emir's major-domo wanting to know whether I had had a good night, was comfortable in my compound or desired anything. He mostly lingered with the reporters until it was time for him to go to the Emir's daily levée so as to listen to a few more of the questions I put to them. For the subjects we were interested in were the principal theme of conversation at the Court in those days.

So I ploughed through the first inevitable misunderstandings with the reporters up to some historical or industrial or poetic problem and just in the thick of it, along came the Sowia, the finest lady in Bida, with her handmaidens, brought me water, asked me about my sleep, did I want anything ? Then she took her gift, disturbed me a few minutes more by giving her orders in the courtyard and allowed me to bring back the reporters to the matter in hand.

Of course, we soon got into our stride after leaping the second lot of misunderstanding hurdles, and might make quite sure that one of the very high officials, some provincial noble or one of the Emir's princely friends, would darken the porch of my front court, sit down on mats laid ready at the gateway, curtsey repeatedly, utter many salutations in Nupé, Houssa or Fulfulde, ask had I slept well, what I thought of the city, and whether I had all I wanted. But one could never in any case assume that his Excellency or Serene Highness would quickly and silently bring his interruption to an end. On the contrary, what usually happened was that their Excellencies would go over all the items of salutation again with my host, and at last—*horribile dictu*—tell him " something new." Oh ! but what a nuisance this " new " was. Once one of these gentry wanted to look at my books, another time at the locks of my trunks, and then especially at my guns, telescopes, etc. These morning calls were more like a sport of which I was the victim, and would, so far, have evoked the loathing of every S. P. C. A. It was in a measure obligatory, for as soon as it was over the ruler held his morning audience and I strongly suspect the noble Mamadu of closing it with some such words as: " Very interesting; yes, very—these German fellows. You, Smith (meaning Mamadu), were very amusing to-day; let Jones (meaning Usman) go over to-morrow and be shown something else for us to talk about! "

The good Emir must have said something very like this, for a different disturber of the peace turned up every morning and the gentlemen were absolutely indefatigable in finding new subjects of interest. Wouldn't I show them the whip with which we Germans—a vile calumny, by the way—were said to keep our people in order* ; couldn't I let them see a picture of the German Emperor. I was glad to have a photograph of him in a magnificent helmet, which the Nupés always assured me was a Bulke (armed horseman's helmet), and I never denied it. What interested them most of all was the difference between the Germans and the English. They often said that the latter only sent whites to Bautshi to look for tin, but never people like ourselves who were concerned with the people themselves. When we got to this stage I always put down my pen, for now came the crucial questions : Why did we buy collections; what did we do with them in Europe ; why did Mr. Arriens paint pictures, why did Mr. Martius want to see all the tools and their uses, etc., etc. Then we always got aground on His Excellency Bode (of the Berlin Museum), who has obviously got a very great reputation in Bida and Nupéland. I had to tell them of the Emperor's great interest in museums, and happened to mention (because they could most easily grasp this) the Kaiser-Friederich Museum and its paintings, and the " Stamboul " Sultan's great architectural donation. This consumed them with curiosity, and they wanted to know whether the objects from Bida would be placed in the same hall as the Stamboul Sultan's gift. All I

* AUTHOR'S NOTE.—I must remark that not anything like the number of lashes is given in the German colonies of West Africa as the Alkalis give in British Nigeria.

could tell them was that it depended on His Excellency Bode.
So that's all right, and now Bode has a big name in Inner Africa
as well.

I have dwelt a long while on this entertainment. But the
indulgent reader's patience has not been put to the test anything like my own was every day. The worst of it was that
whenever I tried to get anything out of these noble gentlemen
of interest to myself, it was promptly and firmly refused. For
the object of these visits was to take away the wherewithal to
amuse His Highness the Emir. The most curious part of it
is that during the whole of the time I always observed two very
remarkable things. Firstly, on no occasion whatever did one of
these Nupé noblemen ever ask a foolish question. On the contrary, they knew how to keep to the subject and to make none
but the most carefully considered and pertinent inquiries.
Secondly, they never asked about women. But when they wanted
to know whether as many blind people sat about in our streets
as in their own and what was done with them, I told them of
our European Homes for the Blind and kindred institutions, and
how the highest in the land led the way. I touched upon the
part our own Empress took in the care of the sick. At once
they were all visibly embarrassed. I asked my interpreter what
was the matter. The Nupé noble's answer was: "*He* had not
begun to talk about one of the German Emperor's wives." He
wanted to deprecate any imputation of tactlessness which might
be brought home to him afterwards.

At the close of this interesting but work-hindering interpellation
the visitors, my host, the retinue, and a row of less honourable
gentlemen who had meanwhile assembled in the courtyard, broke
up and betook themselves to the audience, where everything they
had gleaned from myself was served up piping hot as the *pièce
de résistance* at the morning reception.

But is there anyone simple enough to believe that I could
now work in peace ? Ah, yes! if I had been able to shut my
door forthwith. Yet I could only afford to do this after having
worked in Bida for a considerable time and the folk's fear lest I
might ask about " secret things " had been dispelled. But in the
early part of the day the benefit of closed doors was not to be

mine, and between nine o'clock and noon I had many a caller;
either a messenger from the King with some milk (one shilling
for about a pint and a half), or a guild-master, or a man from
foreign parts picked up by one of my myrmidons to be examined.
And every man Jack of them wanted to know had I slept well,
how I liked Bida, and was there anything they could get me.

\*     \*     \*     \*     \*     \*     \*     \*

Of course, all this was a very serious hindrance, yet when I
shut myself up after lunch in my corner and pieced together
the fragments of tradition which had filtered through the
general noisy talk of the morning, and compared them with what
I heard in Mokwa and from the Elders summoned from Bokani,
I at last managed to get increasing light and, in the twilight of
popular legends, perceive the ground plan and dimensions of a
great past of which the glass-workers', jewellers', and bronze-
chasers' guilds were the antediluvian survivals.

And then I used to go either alone or with my comrades to
look up the bronze-men and the jewel-men late in the afternoon
in their lairs.

If ever the suspicion or scent of an ancient epoch of culture
could grow into conviction it must have been here, where articles
were wrought out of imported brass rods and miserable sheet
iron, the better specimens of which no one could straightway
say' were mere " negro stuff." There is no doubt that the
importation of " cheap and nasty" European metal has been
followed by obvious deterioration of technical excellence. Many,
nay, all the pieces sent to market are not made out of cast iron
at all to-day, and most of them, in fact, are merely tin and
solder. It is a sad business. But we were lucky enough to find
a clever old master-smith who forged some old shapes with old
patterns from bar iron for Martius, while Arriens sat in the corner
opposite and fixed this master craft, which soon will surely belong
to the things of the past, in a very successful painting. The dusk
of approaching night is, alas! beginning to settle on this industrial
art, and who can say if there be anyone to resuscitate it from
the lethargy creeping over it ? Even the remaining masters of
the craft are incapable of producing work of the same quality

as the older, which is so thin as to have suffered much damage. But we were particularly fortunate afterwards in being able to secure a few really old specimens, the property of an ancient Kano Emir family, dating from the best period of the Edegi dynasty in Gbarro, which had been given by a King at the Nupean Empire's height to an aged Emir of Katsena and transferred by his decadent descendants to the collateral issue of Kano's royal house.

Yet this again is characteristic of the knowledge of values and the historical sense of this highly cultured Houssa, Nupé and Yoruba nobility. All houses of long lineage have preserved a mass of treasured things; in one, ancient textiles; in another, ancient armour or swords; ancient MSS. in a third; and in yet another, imperial paraphernalia or chased bronzes or old bead ornaments. And for the most part traditions, real knowledge of their descent from generation to generation and proofs of old culture and family connections are bound up with these precious possessions. But it is all stored away in the lumber-room, decays and is, in fact, no longer of real value in anybody's eyes. The cleverer the owners, the more they are inclined to part with such things as these if adequately paid for and I hope the English Government may soon send out a capable, clever explorer with a well-stocked purse, to rescue these treasures for science's sake from silent, unnecessary, and certain, oblivion.

Bead ornaments have a place among these valuables. The city of Bida's coat of arms might well bear a crown with three peaks: glass smelting, bronze chasing and bead cutting have all attained summits of which even peoples of a higher civilization would have a right to be proud. If ever I bitterly deplored our want of means it was in those days in Bida when I went through the stone bead market and the workshops of the stone polishers, and at last I parted with my own poor savings in order to bring to Europe a decent collection of these gems of pre-historic times.

Now, if one of this book's readers casts a glance at these stones exhibited in Europe, he may remember that some of these are the traces of our extended travels through the least known parts of Africa, and that some are wrinkled and hoary with

Workshop of bronze chasers in Bida.

incalculable years, while others are as clear-eyed as a child.
Full well I know that I was right to spend the pennies I had
saved to buy these lovely things; for they are speaking stones,
and our own day will profit by ventilating the secret of their
existence after a silence of some thousand years.

What this may mean I will most gladly explain.

Having gone from one end to the other of the long wall of
Nokoji-Maliki Palace, from the stalls of those dealers who bring
the substance of the stone beads to Bida, one arrives at the
market stand occupied by the women-sellers of the finished beads,
and has, so to speak, passed through the space of time between
the wrinkled skin of eld and the shining eyes of youth, emerging
from the " Fountain of Regeneration " of Nupéland. Oh, the
marvellous riches which the saunterer between the rows of dealers
who market the material for the bead cutter's skill, can gather
together with only a keen eye and a plenteous purse. Here
are pieces thick and thin of that peculiar Sui-stone from which
Yoruba jewellers cut their beads and ear-pegs, those beads which
were so highly prized and honoured in the days of old as "red
corals." Here, too, are the deep red stones so much esteemed,
dredged from the Katagum stream, because the stones for rings
and seals and diadems are cut from them. Here, too, are those
things we would rather not see, namely, the white porcelain tower
rings brought from Europe, which the Bida jewellers cleverly
re-fashion into flat ones and whose fragments they know how to
polish into new little forms; then the better agate tower rings,
which have no other value than transformation material, and here
and there—oh, horror! Bohemian beads of glass with old Egyptian
on one, and on the other side new Arabic signs. Add: "Made
in Austria!" The sight of this makes an ethnologist's back one
goose-skin and his only possible consolation for such a bizarre
exhibition is the dealer's explanation that these rings were brought
from Cairo, via Darfur and Wadai, and that they are worth as
much as five shillings each! (Naturally, so long as they are
rarities from abroad! If any one put a hundred on the market
to-morrow the price would at once slump down to a penny.)
And then again there are broad green and yellow rings from
Bamako and Dakkar, via Wagadugu. A jolly scene took place with

one of these traders with whom I was chatting, who recognized me. He was one of the sightseers who had listened at Christmas time, 1907, to the ditty of the intoxicated singer Korongo, and everyone had laughed when he parodied Korongo's inspired pantomime.

And in this way the bead trade of Bida brings this Continent's furthest East and West together. The fact amazed me from the first. I was struck with deepest awe on discovering the connection between the stone beads forming the bulk of the market material, bought from choice and remodelled by the Nupé jewellers, and the stones described above as wrinkled with hoary antiquity.

I was repeatedly told the sad old story that all the curious stone, rock and dolmen graves in the North had been ruthlessly broken open and rifled for precious stones and beads, not only by Tuaregs in Timbuktu, Tommos in Homburi highlands, Borganas in Gurma, but also by Showjas in Algeria and Kairoans in Tunis. I only saw genuine old and, so to say, pedigree beads once for an instant in the market of Litshena in South Algeria and when I asked where they came from they were so swiftly snatched from sight that I only got a hurried impression.

But here now, in Bida-mart, Great Heaven, what masses of them ! Beads from the tombs of the hill country of Asben, some from the district north of Wadai, others again from Adrar. And the finest thing of all was that I was fortunate enough to enlist very trustworthy reporters, namely, bead dealers, in my service.

The method so energetically started soon bore splendid fruit, especially as I also sent to Kano and bought some particularly famous old trinkets. Now the bead polishers began to rummage their stores. And when it was known that I wanted not only specimens of shining, newly recut and polished Bida work, but preferred those from the North just as they came, the wealthy heads of the guild opened their jars of material and poured out a perfectly mad medley of old glass beads from Yoruban graves, Asben agates, Egyptian beads, and cornelians from Tibesti and Adrar. And then my heart was again most moved by those forms which in days of old had been brought from the Sahara into Nupéland, reburied here, and again restored to daylight. Yes, these are my stones with tongues which speak.

Some, however, are not taken from graves and these I prize most highly. The old Tuaregs who were my companions as teachers and translators for months, told me they were no longer found in graves, but always in places near the former site of a cemetery obliterated by the desert sands. The shape of the stones and their exterior at once proved the truth of the old fellows' statement. The sand blast had corroded the softer layers of the agate quite regularly, in the same way in which experiments were recently made to decorate furniture with patterns in relief. Of course, it does not take long to eat out the softer portions of wood by the action of sand at high wind pressure. But what periods of time must not the Saharan dune-sand have first required to expose the rock graves, eat them away and then " etch " the softer strata of the exposed agates so as to leave finally only the hard quartz veins as old-age furrows ? What tremendous eras ?

But day in day out, hundreds of workmen sit crowded in the workshops cutting facets on the cylindrical beads of the Past, polishing and stringing them on red thread, so that those gems which once were worn by Libyan Kings in eras beyond our present standard of computation, now sparkle rejuvenated with their glittering surfaces like twinkling eyes upon the lovely necks of Nupé coquettes. The furrows are smoothed and the beauty of youth reappears.

This fountain of stones and stone beads must have welled almost from time everlasting. Antiquity knew of these stones from North Africa and the Carthaginians or, as the Greek historians called them, Chalcedonians, put them into circulation. And so the species of gem known as Chalcedonian was not only of great repute in the days that are gone, but we name them chalcedonyx to-day as a monument to the fact.

Now, as this road from North Africa bequeathed a name to our language, so a heritage of old Libyan art was also borne on the bosom of the same stream of culture to the Nupé cutters of beads, who, far as they were from the quarries, no longer triumphed in calling new forms into life, but only in removing the ridges of age from antique memorials and restoring the pristine splendour of the days of their youth.

This, too, the stones with the tongues in the city of Bida told me.

\*    \*    \*    \*    \*    \*    \*    \*

The pictures and happenings of these regions are many and marvellous if we only keep our eyes open as they unroll before us. And if one is adept in the half-Indian art of laying one's ear to the ground and hearing what moves in spaces and times afar off; if the old people be persuaded to dream waking, to sing the ever beautiful song of their youth and their past; if one can rid oneself of the dust of everyday life and bustle with a brisk and lively mind, then the vision of these countries' and these peoples' once great and ancient history assumes reality; that which once we learnt from the Halicarnassian, Herodotus, or Diodorus of Siculus and which seemed to us and our fathers of old before us as a fairy-tale told to amuse; that which we never believed because of its remoteness and thought must have perished, even if it ever existed, together with antiquity's final inheritance, Byzantium the Marvellous —all this still lives and breathes, and is still the infallible truth.

List, oh, list! The trumpets! Hark, oh, hark! The drums! The King comes forth, he takes the morning air. In every quarter of the town the horses' trappings tinkle. From every side the flying riders come in flowing robes. Then, along his capital's main road, the mighty ruler comes. His train is glorious in colour and motley of hue. Before him stride his constables in bright red turbans and vermilion cloaks and swords to clear his path, and then the trumpet-blasts and beat of kettle drums resound. And after them, in billowing robes, his nobles on their prancing palfreys. In their midst, the Potentate himself upon a snow-white steed; calm, full of dignity, and, as the East demands, gazing impassively on all around. A canopy of heavy silk, which came across the land of Egypt, is held above his head. And, last of all, the crowd, the criers and the heralds, who unceasingly proclaim abroad the fame of this great Prince.

Is it a scene from Persia in its olden days? Or a Fata Morgana from the glorious lands of the East?

And then! A lady riding all alone amongst the men! A woman in the severely Islamite ritual train of the king? This is the moment! Bow low and listen, like the Indian, to the sounds which run along the earth from afar. Hear'st thou the distant voices whispering of princesses who still rule the smaller towns in secret? Hear'st thou them talking of the one chief spouse whose sole prerogative it is to slay the first animal for sacrifice in all men's sight to-day? When the ear has grown accustomed to the delicate tones which reach it out of the distant Past or in the mysterious customs of a nation, syllables such as Isadshi-Koseshi will fall upon it. Should the Fulbe Elders be asked their meaning they will grow confused and bite their lips. And they will but very rarely say that, though as valiant warriors they never feared to face the Nupé men, they often took to flight before the charge of the Isadshi-Koseshi, the armoured, warlike Nupé women!

What! Did women train their horses for the fray like Amazons of old in any but the lands of legendary lore?

Or again: Four great officers of State are forfeit to the monarch both in life and death and are his sexless instruments to-day, but—is the ear still pressed upon the ground?—these high and mighty nobles were yet his bondsmen, privileged to enjoy whatever they desired to possess. They were his master of the household, his master of the horse, his cup-bearer and his chamberlain or lord-in-waiting. But an unholy fate hung over the heads of those who in days of old filled posts as high as these: they accompanied the Emperor in his grave!

Yet stay! This is West Africa and what I hear rustling over the ground cannot be true. For what are the statements in Herodotus? When the Scythians laid their King to rest they buried with him his cup-bearer, his cook, his equerry, his herald, one of his concubines and a body servant! Are we to be told that a custom prevalent in Scythia, two thousand years ago and more, is still alive in Africa to-day?

Yet let the sceptic hold his peace. Let him regard with awe the mighty driving force inherent in the Past; let him give heed to the holy voices rushing through the Temple of Science; let him be modestly silent, for on every side the great globe itself and human custom whisper in our hearing the splendid epics of a splendid Past, the poem of related cultures! One need not learn to listen in Bida only.

Tread, O Teuton, into the banquet halls of thine own Imperial house, and there behold the four who in stately pomp accompanied Byzantium's Emperor and his daughter to the Court of Otto I.: the server, the butler, the marshal, the lord-chamberlain. Here is the connecting link! Here on this side is a small twig of the great tree of history whose growth can be traced to its original root between Asia and Europe; but over there its other, and possibly stronger, branch is less easily seen, because of the foliage and tendrils, and because—O misery! the tropical, rank, suffocating tangle of liana embraces and hides it.

Therefore, then: Those who have eyes to see with can, here, find plenty to see. He who has ears to hear with can, here, listen to the breath of the Past rustling across vast plains in the customs and souls of the nations.

And so, if the smooth stones sparkle and glisten to-day, renewed and regenerate on the beautiful necks of the women of Nupé, they were impressed with the wrinkles of age but a short time ago. Not even almost a century of the devastations and destructions of a war with the Fulbes succeeded in quenching the vigour of this civilization, welling up from its soil like a perpetual fountain of youth; and so many, ah! so many were recalled to life as to compel us to see here especially the constant reincarnation of ever new forms and offshoots of culture from similar germs, before whose venerable greatness we must bow our heads.

Learn thou to hear and to see before desiring to enter the Temple of Universal History; its portals are closed to the deaf and the blind.

And remember: It was but yesterday that this land's present rulers came from the North-west with Islam; but that the East is the home of its culture's glory and strength. Remember also its persistent vitality was such that even the Mahommedan Fulbes failed to add anything to increase, or so much as come near to, its splendour, and only succeeded in making their own what surpassed them in greatness and age.

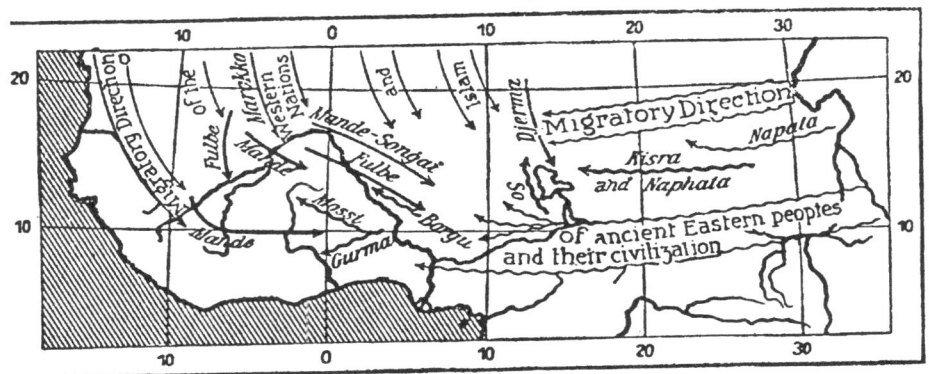

Chart of opposing streams of civilization in the Soudan.
*(Constructed under the direction of Dr. M. Groll.)*

# CHAPTER XXI

## AN HISTORICAL POEM

### (The Mandes or Mandingoes.)

The historical records of the Soudan—The Song of the Emir Diarra, called Sunjatta—The Traore youths kill the wild Koba, win the virgin-prize and bring her to their king—His marriage to Sugulunkurmang—Sanjatta is born but not recognized—The feast of adolescence—Sanjatta has to fly to Mema—His life in exile and recall when the Susus lay Mande waste—He conquers the Susu and other nations—The pronounced pre-Islamite features of the Sunjatta legend and its connection with Libya.

IT seems to me, however, that we have dallied far too long within this old patrician edifice of Bida, and make our life and work, our wandering and sight-seeing far too comfortable. Bida is only one among a hundred large-sized towns and Nupé-land a mere fragment of the vast tracts of country in the Soudan. It is one nook where various kinds of relics of an ancient culture and splendour are found stored away, and yet we stand only on one spot of that mighty plain which lies spread out between the Red Sea and the Atlantic Ocean, called the Soudan. For him who wishes to obtain some knowledge of a thousand years of history and a decent slice of an entire Continent, the horizon is too restricted.

Let us then doff the enchanted robe which the fairy-tale of

Mokwa and the lust of the eye have thrown over us in Bida. Out into the open! Fetch out the records!

The Soudanese plain stretches in seemingly endless monotony into the far, far distance, but its documentary history, in perfectly marvellous records, towers like mountains in front of us. In some of these, some bard sings of the might of the kings of old, in others some priest invokes by name the spirits of sires deceased. The weird and eloquent ghosts of a strange religion, whom the kings of the past called their gods, appear in this mystical twilight, and, cheek by jowl with these, a follower of the Prophet Mahommed sits in a crumbling ruin, in the light of a flickering oil-lamp, ready to tell us the story, culled from old chronicles written in Arabic, of the migrations of nations and the course of the streams of humanity. No, in sober truth, there is no time for day-dreaming in Bida, where gathering the acts of the past from a mountain of deeds is our business.

We saw, now, how a Mahommedan race swept over the old heathendom in modern times and how the ancient heathen decked out his new master with his own rich ornament of finer culture. Now for another picture. I turn the books of history backwards and study the pages on which are written those legends and times beyond, when Islam broke into and dominated the Soudan. The scene is set in the district between the Niger-bend and the Senegal; the time the thirteenth century. Those who supply the matter are the ancient bards who used to sing before the king's throne of the glory of the past and his forbears, as was their wont in heathen days.

Arabian travellers have furnished us with an account of those lands' condition in that far-off time (about A.D. 1000-1200). Mighty realms: Ganna on the edge of the Desert in the North, Mandigoland between the Niger and Senegal in the South, Djolof in the West on the Senegal, and Songai on the Niger in the East, were flourishing when the first Islamite traders came into the land. Here and there in the great cities there were small districts where these merchants assembled. But the religion of the Prophet only gained a greater number of converts after the year one thousand A.D. and only became a ruling power when a man from the country of Mema of the tribe of the

Tungarra or Diarra (the name varies according to the different languages, Gara or Garra, Sara or Sarra, Diara or Diarra, Tungara or Tungarra, or also Vangara or Uangara), founded the great kingdom of the Malinke as its Emir, or Malé. The Mema country lies on a western branch of the Niger and to the south-west of Timbuktu. The first Malé was of kin to the then feeble ruling family of the Songai and that of the Mande. These events occurred about 1235; the head and founder of the first very powerful state was the Maré (or Emir) Sunjatta or the Maré Diarra. The records say but little about him, but the bards, whose song I now reproduce, say a great deal more. It brings the primitive heathen story and recorded history most vividly to life. The episodes of the foundation of the earliest great Mahommedan power are graphically portrayed in this heathen epic.

## 1.—THE KOBA

The Turre or Diara's land is called Sangara. Twelve men and one woman dwelt therein. Each man had a village of his own. All twelve brothers abused the sister, although they had one father, and one mother had borne them all. And so the sister changed herself into one of the Koba, or horse-antelopes, which are no more to be found. This Koba killed a man in every village every day. Her tail was made of the purest gold.

A hunter went upon the chase to kill the Koba. He scoured the land. All day long he ranged, but could not slay the Koba. Then two more huntsmen with bows and arrows went out upon the trail. They both said: "One of us can chase the beast, and the other can then shoot it." Horses were as yet unknown, and one always had to go on foot. Horses were called "Domwe." The two huntsmen could not come up with the Koba. Then at last three hunters set out to kill it. Each of the huntsmen came from a different village. Now, when these three set out they came upon the Koba. But each attacked it singly, so that one by one they were compelled to seek the safety of the bush and never more returned.

Then folks began to murmur: "This is no common Koba.

This is no Bush-Koba!" The Dodugu (or ruler) Niamorodiote
said: "He who shall slay the Koba may choose the loveliest or
the one who pleaseth him the best of all the girls in the twelve
villages and marry her!" There were many girls in the land.
Now, Niamorodiote had a daughter, who, it is true, was young,
but her body was covered with boils and festering sores. The
name of this girl was Sugulunkurmang. She was ugly beyond
belief.

Now in those days women were very dear or difficult to get.
Therefore the offer of a girl whom one could choose oneself was
very tempting. So, then, two brothers, Damba Masowlomba
(the elder) and Damba Sowlandi (the younger), the two uncles
of the Traore, went forth on the enterprise. At first, of course,
they asked the Kengebugurilala (the sand oracle) how the Koba
could be captured. The answer was: "There lives an ancient
woman in the bush near by who never speaks a good word and
reviles all who come her way. She is the only person who can
teach one the way. Her abuse must never be returned. Then
the old hag will tell one how to kill the Koba. Afterwards
you must not take the most beautiful maiden in the twelve
villages, but choose her who is covered with boils."

The two Traore travelled and searched for the crone in all
the land. They came into the bush where she was sojourning,
looking for firewood. The two huntsmen said: "Good-day!"
The crone replied: "Get out of my sight." The hunters said:
"We have come to help thee look for wood." Said she: "Ye
were not here when I was looking for it yesterday. Make haste
away from here to-day." The hunters took no notice, but went
on picking up wood and carried it behind her. The old hag
said: "Very well, now that ye have touched the wood I no
longer want it. Get ye hence out of my sight! Out of my
sight! Get hence!" The hunters took no notice and followed
her. They came to a hut in the forest and asked: "Is this
thy house?" The old woman gave no reply. She went inside.
Then the hunters laid down the wood upon the ground and
went.

The two Traore went unto the Dodugu Niamorodiote. They
said: "We have heard thy proclamation and are come to make

Bead-cutters' workshop in Bida.
(*Scale to suit by Carl Arriens*)

[*Facing p. 132*]

a trial of slaying the Koba." Niamorodiote spake: "It is well: then ye may sleep here. In sooth, ye have but little likelihood of bringing this adventure to a happy issue. Hither have many hunters come, but none could slay the Koba. This Koba is not like unto any other which man hath ever seen. It hath a tail of gold. A huntsman once went forth to slay it. Then two hunters went forth to slay it. Then three hunters went forth to slay it, but all three were forced to flee in different directions and disappeared within the bush. Now ye be both the last of your line; if ye, too, die, your house is broken up. I warn ye, lest your mother's house break up. For ye will not bring to pass the thing ye would."

A large calabash with rice and flesh-meat was prepared for the two Traore that night. Damba Masowlomba said: "Let us take the woman a portion of our food." Damba Sowlandi said: "Mine elder brother, she will not take it." The other answered him: "So be it; we may at least show her the food and our good-will towards her. If so be she take it not, she takes it not. But we will use our endeavour." The younger said: "Thou sayest well." Then with rice and meat they sallied forth and went into the bush to the old woman. They knocked upon the door and called: "Good-evening, mother!" The old woman answered: "What wilt thou, there, outside?" Damba Masowlomba replied: "Dodugu Niamorodiote hath given us rice with seasoning. We be come to give thee of it if thou wilt receive it at our hands." The old woman answered them with: "Kanibukenkenkan N'tafe!" (Surely a word of very filthy abuse, for I could not get a translation.) "I will not. There is no flesh for me in all the countryside. All my flesh food is mushrooms." Damba Masowlomba said: "I know it, but we would fain give thee a gift because thou art old." The old woman said: "Lay ye the mess upon the wood and get ye gone. Away!" The brethren did so and went their ways.

Then the Traore got some milk. The elder brother said; "We will take the ancient woman a portion of our milk." Damba Sowlandi said: "She will not take it, but give us hard words only." Damba Masowlomba said: "Let us make trial.

The word of the Kengebugurilala was this : " Her words of shame must not be answered so : then will the old wench tell us the manner of slaying the Koba." The younger brother replied : " True is the word thou speakest." The brethren took the milk to the old woman.

On the third day the old woman called the two Traore hunters, saying : " Just ye come hither ! " They went to her. The beldame said : " I will give ye my life ! " The Traore said : " We be not come to seek thy life." The crone spake thus : " What else, then, is it ye would ? " The hunters said : " We came to beg thee to give us thy aid in chasing the Koba." Then the old woman laughed, saying : " Know ye, then, I myself am the Koba ? But ye have brought me gifts and I have reviled ye. Ye answered me not in like manner, but showed me more kindness. If people do good, good should be done to them. Ye have given me much and now I will aid ye in hunting the Koba. I changed myself into a Koba with every dawn because my twelve brethren always treated me vilely. My brothers have all the good things, villages, slaves and riches ; but they gave me not one single slave to bring me water or wood for my hearth. This is the reason I changed myself every morning into a Koba and killed a man in every village of each of my twelve brethren. Then I came back to my bush and again took human shape. If then ye would still kill the Koba, learn that her skin is impervious to iron unless there be a red thread wound around the arrow shaft. Provide ye, therefore, with a sleave of red cotton thread and bind ye cotton threads " (Gendakalla) " on to your arrows. Say, did ye know this ? " The Traore brethren made answer : " Nay, this was unknown to us."

The old woman furthermore said : " If now ye shoot at the Koba and hit her, ye yet will not be able to flee fast enough from the rage of her death agony. Take ye, therefore, three stones which have served as a hearth for a cook-pot. When the Koba pursues ye, throw ye the stones to the rear. Then a hill will grow up which the Koba will have to surmount. The Koba will again overtake ye. Take ye an egg, and throw it behind ye. It will turn into land of swamp through which the Koba can only wade slowly.—Now am I weary. My labours are over.

I desire to sleep. But ye must arise betimes in the morning and hie ye to that bush. There will ye meet with the Koba." The brothers returned.

Very early next morning they set out. They took with them three stones which had lain round the fire of a hearth and an egg. They bound cotton threads round their arrows. With these things they went to the bush which the old woman had shown them. Damba Sowlandi first saw the Koba; he caught his brother by the arm, whispering: "There, there is the Koba!" The elder said: "It is true." So they slowly and cautiously crept on their knees towards the Koba. They came quite close to it. Damba Masowlomba laid one of the arrows ornamented with thread to the ground and sped it. It struck the Koba. The Koba leaped up. Both the brothers fled into the bush. The Koba ran round the wood, snuffing up the scent with its nostrils, then followed the track of the brothers.

The Traore ran fast, but the Koba ever got nearer them. Then the brothers threw the three stones and a mighty hill rose up between them and the Koba. They fled onwards. The Koba ran up one side of the mountain and down the other towards the two brothers. Once more it was nearly up to them. Damba Sowlandi cried: "Throw thou the egg!" and the elder brother threw the egg behind him. A huge morass was formed between the hunters and the Koba. The brothers continued their flight. The Koba could only pursue them very slowly in the mud. The younger looked back and cried: "O elder brother of me, the Koba hath fallen!" They stopped and the elder Traore said: "It is truth! It hath fallen. Yet we will not go thither at once; for the Koba might not yet be quite dead." They waited a while. Then they went thither and cut off the golden tail of the Koba. The elder brother put it in his shoulder-sack and they returned to the town.

The Traore went to the Dodugu Niamorodiote. Damba Masowlomba said: "We have killed something in the bush. Call together all the people of the villages. We will show it and question them whether this be not the Koba which has wrought so much evil for so many years." Dodugu Niamorodiote said: "I will not call the people together, who are all at work in the fields, away from their toil for naught.  Belike ye have slain some other kind of beast.  For the Koba was much too cunning for that ye were able to kill it."  The hunters said : "We demand of thee that thou call the people together, or we will not show the Koba.  If so be we have not slain the right Koba, we must depart without our guerdon."  Thereupon the Dodugu caused all the people from the twelve villages to be called together, and, when they were gathered, thus spake Damba Sowlandi : "Elder brother mine, the people are come.  Arise." Damba Masowlomba rose up and said : "Hand unto me the wallet."  The younger brother gave him the shoulder-sack.  The elder Traore dragged forth the tail of gold, held it aloft in the air and called out : "What is this ?"  Then all the people shouted : "That is the quite great thing.  That is the Koba ! We are saved in peace once more, and henceforth free from care. No longer need we fear that the Koba will snatch people from the villages every day.  These two brethren have taken away the bane from the land.  That is the great thing !"

## 2.—Sugulunkurmang

Dodugu Niamorodiote caused all the young maidens of the land to assemble.  He said : "The two Traore shall choose a maiden !"  All the maidens came.  When Sugulunkurmang would also have gone up, Niamorodiote, her father, said unto her : "Stay where thou art.  With thy boils and festering sores thou art all too ugly."  Before this happened the Diarra and the Traore had been united and friendly, yet now they began to revile one another.  The manner of it was thus :

The brothers went along the row of maidens and looked upon them.  The elder spake : "The Kengebugurilala has declared : Ye may not take the most beautiful maiden of the twelve villages, but ye must choose the maiden covered with boils. Such an one is not amongst these."  The elder Traore asked the King : "Are all the maidens of the land, in very deed, now here ?"  Dodugu Niamorodiote said : "Yea, verily, all except Sugulunkurmang.  She tarries within the house, because she is too ugly."  The brethren asked : "Why hath she tarried within the house ? " The people answered : " By reason that she hath too many blains and boils." The Traore said : " She, surely, will be the right one." Thereupon the people laughed. They conducted Sugulunkurmang. She was very ugly. Damba Masowlomba came from the right and placed his left arm round her neck. Damba Sowlandi came from the left and placed his right arm round her neck, and the Traore said : " This is the right one ! " Then the Diarra shouted : " Oh, ye blockheads ! Ye do not know the good and beautiful things ! Ye leave the beautiful maidens and choose the ugliest one. Oh, ye fools ! Ye blockheads ! " But the Traore said : " Oh, foolish people, how know ye what will be good afterwards, how know ye what is right for times to come ? " Thus, for the first time, the Diarra and the Traore reviled each other and since then have done the like until our days.

The Traore went thence together with Sugulunkurmang.

They took Sugulunkurmang to Farkuma Kakenji, the King of Mandeland, who gave them another woman in her place. In the evening Damba Masowlomba said to the maiden : " Girl, make a fire in thy chamber." Sugulunkurmang said : " I am afeared." He asked : " What fearest thou ? " She replied : " I am afeared." The hunter said : " Ah ! now wilt thou have a princely mate. Thou needst no longer feel afraid." Sugulunkurmang went in to him. Farkuma lay with her. Sugulunkurmang immediately conceived. Now the King's first wife was also big with child, but the ruler was as yet without a son.

### 3.—Sunjatta's Birth

At that time there were Subaga mussu Kononto (nine sorceresses) in Mande, and their names were:

1.—Sititi, she was the leader.

2.—Sototo, she was her assistant.

3.—Djalimussu tumbumannia, who sings the song to the dead.

4.—Muruni-pempete, who cuts off the head with a knife.

5.—Sumussu sungana Niamorodiote, the able sorceress of power who is below Sototo in rank.

6.—Dagäni Kubaga, who washes out the little magic cauldron.

7.—Djinbi djamba, who brings news at night-time and must be the first to say everything.

8.—Miniamba, who lies down like a snake in the path to bite those in the leg who are condemned by the Sumussu.

9.—Kulutugubaga, who has power to restore broken arms, heal up flesh wounds and bring the dead to life again.

Now, when Sugulunkurmang was in child-bed, Djalimussu tumbumannia was present with the women. The babe cried four times. All babes cry once when they come into the world, but Sugulunkurmang's child cried four times. At the fourth cry, the nine women fell down dead and the babe's mother came near unto death. The king heard the clamour and asked: "What happens in the village?" Some old people went thither and looked into the hut. They went back and said: "A woman has become a mother. The child cries so that nine old women died and the mother also nearly perisheth." The King said: "Nyete ma ninyoro yatayi." ("Such a thing have I never seen!") Now, because the king gave the babe no other name, it was called Sunjatta.

Now, when the child was born and a little strength had come again to the mother, she spake unto Djalimussu tumbumannia: "Go thou unto the King and say unto him that I have borne him his first man-child." Djalimussu tumbumannia set forth upon the way. She came unto the King at the hour when he was eating. In those old days the Mande ate only rice. The Subaga offered the then customary salutation, saying: "Konkondogosso!" The King answered with the salutation which was then the custom, saying: "Tantumberre! Come, eat with me!" Djalimussu tumbumannia sat down by the King's side to eat. But she quite forgot to deliver the message while she was eating.

On the same day, but some hours later, the King's first wife also bore him a babe. The mother of this prince summoned Muruni-pempete and said unto her: "Go to the King and announce to him that I have presented him with a son." Muruni-pempete went forth. She came to the King as he was sitting at meat. She said: "Konkondogosso!" The King

Bronze-chasing Work.   Pl. I.

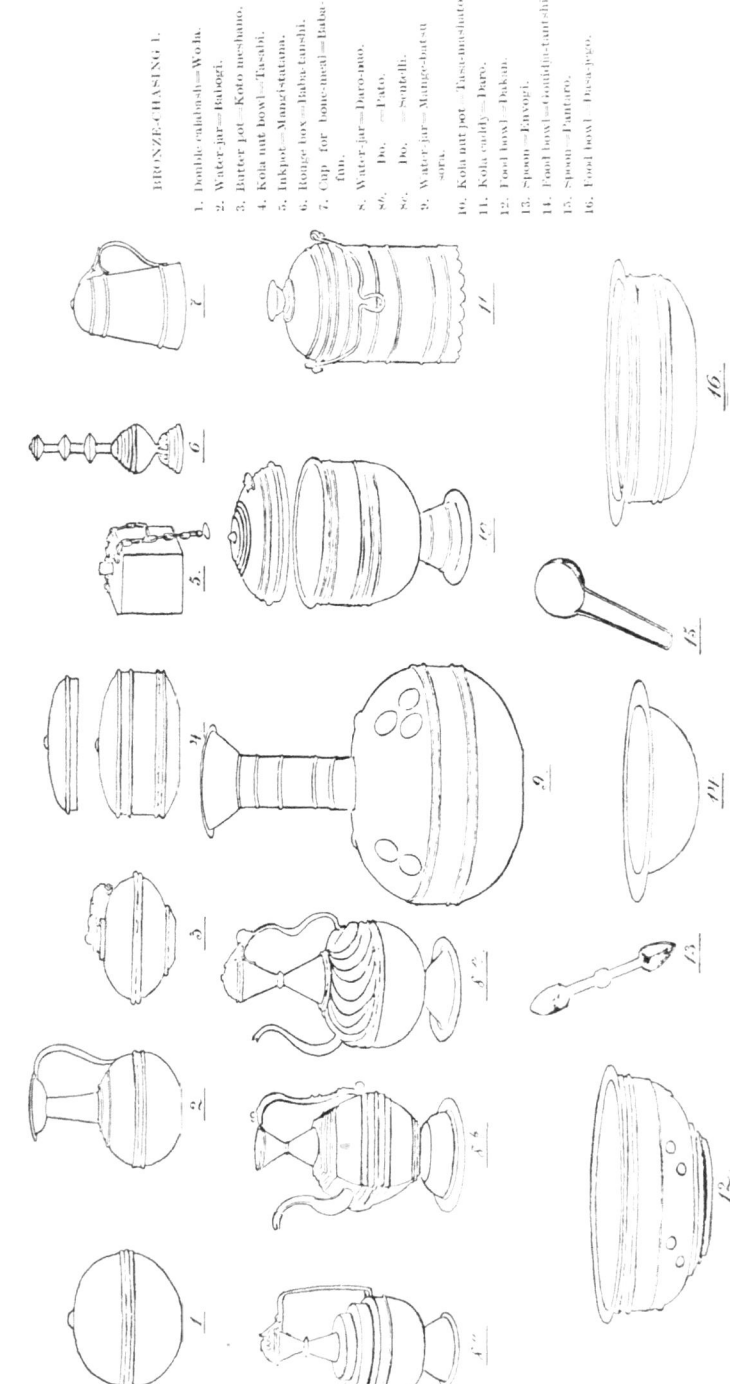

BRONZE-CHASING I.

1. Bottle valuta do=Wola.
2. Water jar=Balogi.
3. Butter pot=Koto meshano.
4. Kola nut bowl=Tasobi.
5. Inkpot=Manti-tatano.
6. Bouge box=Baba tanchi.
7. Cup for bone-dust=Baba fun.
8. Water-jar=Duro-mio.
8c.   Do.   =Fato.
8c.   Do.   =Sentelli.
9. Water-jar=Mange-dut-ei sota.
10. Kola nut pot=Tasa-meslato.
11. Kola caddy=Duro.
12. Food bowl=Pakin.
13. Spoon=Enyogi.
14. Food bowl=Toditije-tanchi.
15. Spoon=Pantufe.
16. Food bowl=Desa-pezo.

[Facing p. 439.

replied: "Tantumberre! Come hither and eat with me!" The Subaga said: "Whoso is swift of foot should be swift of tongue as well. Thy first wife bade me come to tell thee that she hath given thee a son." The King spake: "I am rejoiced!" But Djalimussu tumbumannia arose and said: "And I too have a message to deliver thee. Alas! that I should have quite forgotten, while I ate, to execute my mission. Thy wife Sugulunkurmang sent me to tell thee that she had given thee thy first man-child. This man-child is the firstborn." Then said the King: "Thou comest now too late. He is the elder whose birth was first announced to me!" The child of the King's first wife was named Massa Dangaratuma. The King spake: "Massa Dangaratuma is my eldest son." But that was not the truth, for the firstborn was Sunjatta.

## 4.—THE CIRCUMCISION OF SUNJATTA

The children grew up together. Sunjatta was weak upon his feet, but Massa Dangaratuma was well grown and hearty. Sunjatta always lay upon the ground while Massa Dangaratuma soon learnt to walk. When they were grown bigger, each of them bought himself a dog. Massa Dangaratuma called his Dindofollobiulukorote (the first born, but not the elder). Sunjatta called his Sobekonssante (well grown, but failing when called upon). When they ate, they gave their dogs a portion of their food. Sobekonssante was swift; he not only gulped down his own meat quickly but also snatched some away from Dindofollobiulukorote. Massa Dangaratuma said to Sunjatta: "If thy dog does this again, I shall kill it. I shall kill it!" Sunjatta said: "If thou shouldst do this thing, I will adventure something the noise of which shall run through all Mandingoland!" Massa Dangaratuma said: "What dost thou say? I shall be the King and thou art naught!" He sought for a heavy club and laid it by his side. When the meal was served at eve, Sobekonssante again devoured his own food and the other dog's portion too. Then Massa Dangaratuma took the club and slew him. Now Sunjatta was weak upon his legs (such children are called Nammara), and so remained squatting for many years upon the ground. But he was very strong in his body. He caught his brother by the heel and squeezed it until the bone was well nigh crushed and, in his fright and terror, he voided his excrement. He squeezed the heel very hard until Djalimussu tumbumannia came up and said: "Let go thy brother's heel!" Then Sunjatta loosed it.

Sunjatta's mother begged her neighbour thus: "Give me of the leaves of thy Sira (monkey bread-fruit tree)!" The other woman in her anger said: "I will give thee some to-day, but never again. Thy son is older than mine; bid him climb the Sira tree and risk his neck and bones in climbing. My son seeks for me. Why doth thy Sunjatta always slip about the ground?" Outside Sunjatta heard that his mother was quarrelling with someone and he asked: "What sayest thou to the other woman?" Sugulunkurmang said: "It is naught, but only about some Sira leaves for which I begged my neighbour." Sunjatta said: "Are there no smiths in Mande, then? Hath my father no smiths?" His mother said: "Yea, thy father hath smiths." Then Sunjatta answered: "Now let them make an iron staff whereby I may raise myself up." The Numu (smiths) built seven Ganso (smelting furnaces) to smelt the iron for a mighty staff. They forged the staff and brought it unto Sunjatta. He took the staff and broke it in his finger like a reed. He said: "This is no help to me. Are there no proper smiths in Mande?" The people said: "Yea, such smiths there are." Sunjatta said: "Then bid them make a fitting staff for me, for this one cannot bear me up." Then the Numu built seventeen Ganso to smelt the iron for the staff. They forged the staff and brought it to Sunjatta. When he pressed it against the earth, it bent into the shape of a bow. He threw this staff away, saying: "Now, at last, do bring me something decent. Such a thing as that cannot profit me." When the smiths heard this, they built twenty-seven Ganso to make the iron of them all into one single staff. They forged the staff and many people carried it. It was as thick as a tree-trunk. Sunjatta leaned himself upon it; he wished to raise himself. But the staff was not quite strong enough and bent a little. Then Sunjatta called: "Quick, mother, come help me!" So he supported himself on the left on his mother's shoulder and on the right upon the staff of iron. His mother lifted up her voice rejoicing and sang: "To-day is a day of gladness, the like of which the God of Goodness hath never bestowed upon me."

In those days there was but one very great Sira tree in all Mande. Whoever swallowed a pip of the fruit of this tree became King of Mandingoland. Sunjatta went to the tree with his people. Many had already tried to get one of its fruits by hurling up cudgels at it. But none could throw sufficiently far. Now, instead of a cudgel, Sunjatta picked up a man. He seized him by the legs and as he did so one of the poor wretch's legs was broken. Balla-Fasege-Kuate, a very old bard (from whom even many singers of to-day derive their descent), was standing under this tree. The song he sang was: "Sinkate Namara Konate!" ("Leg-breaker Namara Konate!") Thus Sunjatta received one of his names. The man so thrown up struck against a fruit, broke it off and hurled it down. Thereupon he fell down himself upon the ground and broke an arm, so that Balla-Fasege-Kuate's song was: "Bulukati Namara Konate!" ("Arm-breaker Namara Konate!"), which became another name of Sunjatta's. When the fruit fell down, Sunjatta was not, as others had been, content to swallow only one of the seeds gifted with power to grant the kingship, but gulped down the whole fruit as it was, thus hindering the birth of any rival to his might. And then he seized the whole gigantic tree, plucked it out of the ground as another would have torn up a little plant, carried it into the town and planted it within his mother's compound. He said: "Till now, my mother had to beg of others to get leaves from off a Sira tree. Now others desiring Sira leaves shall have to come to the mother who bore me." He left the tree to grow in the compound of his mother.

His father heard him and said: "Haha! Sunjatta has arrived at man's estate and now one may set about his circumcision." Now, the custom then was to invest the first child circumcised in solemn ritual with the Kongoton (cap) and the Muruffe Durruki (mantle of red cloth). But the Kongoton and Muruffe were so heavy that he upon whom they were placed would have been pressed to death by their weight, and, therefore, one was content to put the cloak three times about his shoulders and thrice to

hold above his head the Kongoton decorated with three hundred
and thirty-three heads of doves (Tubani) and three hundred and
thirty-three heads of the crested crane (Koma). So the Muruffe
Durruki was held above him once and then removed; twice, and
removed once more, when Sunjatta cried: " Now -let it swiftly
fall upon my shoulders, or something evil will befall Mandingoland ! " It was allowed to fall and the mantle which had
weighed down others was rent a little on Sunjatta's shoulders, so
mighty was he in stature. The cap, Kongoton, was held above
his head once and removed; twice and again removed; Sunjatta
cried: " Now place it swiftly on my brow or evil hap will come
to Mandeland ! " It was placed upon his head, and the cap,
which had crushed all others, was rent asunder on his head,
for it was too small, too delicate; so mighty was Sunjatta's
head. Then they circumcised Sunjatta, clothed like this.

## 5.—THE FLIGHT OF SUNJATTA

Three years had run their course since Sunjatta's circumcision.
Once, when Djalimussu tumbumannia was on a journey, the remaining eight Subagas changed Sunjatta into a Turani (bull) at
the request of his relatives. Then they led the young steer forth
and struck off his head; they put him to death; they divided
him; into nine parts they made him. Each one took her
portion, and the ninth, which was Djalimussu tumbumannia's
share, they kept and gave to the Subaga (protecting Sunjatta)
on her return. Djalimussu tumbumannia took her share and
asked: " What kind of flesh is this ? " The other Subagas
answered : " This is the flesh of Sunjatta, the son of Sugulunkurmang, whom we changed into a Turani and then divided." Djalimussu tumbumannia said : " What has more meat, a young
Turani or nine full-grown bush-buffalo ? " The eight Subaga
made reply: " Nine full-grown bush-buffalo have more meat ! "
Djalimussu tumbumannia's word was: " It is well; to-morrow
bring unto me all the bones and sinews of your portions, and I
will give each one of ye a full-grown bush-buffalo in exchange
therefor." Thus it was done; next morn all the bone and sinew
parts were brought together and the Turani was put together

again. It was a youthful steer once more. Djalimussu tumbu-mannia struck it on the tail and again it was Sunjatta. Djali-mussu tumbumannia said to him: "Run swiftly hence! Tarry not! Go out from Mandeland! I must conceal the young snake lest men should slay it and rob it of its life so young!"

Sunjatta got ready for a journey with his mother and caused a man he knew to ask the Kengebugurilala, the sand oracle, to divine his fate. The oracle replied: "Before thou arrivest where thou wouldst thou wilt thrice be stirred to wrath. Yet, if thou let not thine anger overcome thee, thou shalt be King of Mandeland. Get hence and hide thee now in Mema-land. Then Sunjatta girt his loins and departed thence. He took with him his mother, Sugulunkurmang, his little sister Killi-killimadjumasuko, and his younger brother Simbombatanganjati, who was a great strong man. With these three he fled and went forth from Mandeland.

He fled along the road the oracle had prophesied, and at first came into the land of Dabo, in which all men said " Dabo " for " Good-day to ye," and whose ruler's name was Kissima Dabo. The Dabo people had three different kinds of Bashi (sacred things). Chief of these were the " Do," beverages like Dolo (beer made of durra), of different strengths. Some could only drink the beers which were a month old, others those which had been brewed five weeks, and others those as much as ten years old. These people, however, were very strong and when they drank it they grew weary and drunken. The second Bashi was called Tulu Kavuli Faga Kono, which was a great jar in which much oil was boiled. Now, whoever would take an oath, would take a ring from his arm, throw it into the boiling oil and take it out again with his naked arm. He who had falsely sworn had his flesh burnt from the bone by the boiling oil. But he who had spoken the truth drew forth his arm unscathed. The third holy thing was the Bashi Binje of seven double doors, set up before a tree of the Bamanju kind (i.e., a banana tree). The oath was taken before those doors. He who had truly sworn could drive his arrow through two—yea, through three doors. But the arrow of him who had sworn to a lie could not even pierce the wood of the first.

The people of Dabo saw Sunjatta and his companions coming from afar. They said: "What is this? Here is a stranger, let us give him the Do which hath aged for a month." They gave it to Sunjatta to measure his strength. Sunjatta took the beaker and at once handed it on to Killikillimadjumasuko, saying: "This may be good for a small little maiden. As for me, I esteem it as naught." The sister took hold of the cup, put it to her lips and then flung beaker and beverage away. She said: "Faugh, this is dirty water, but not something to drink!" The people of Dabo said: "We will give them Do of two years' age." They gave it to Sunjatta. He put it to his lips and said: "This is what we give to our little children. Let my sister taste that." The drink was offered to Killikillimadjumasuko. The maiden drank a sup of it, then flung both cup and drink away, saying: "This is not good. The Dabo women do not know how beer should be brewed." The Dabo people said: "Then let them try the Do of ten years old." They offered a little bowlful to Sunjatta. He tried it and said: "That may just do for the women, but it is no good to men. Give Killikillimadjumasuko the draught!" The draught was given to the girl. Killikillimadjumasuko put the bowl to her lips, drained it and said: "It is not good. But if there be nothing better, if the women of Dabo cannot brew better than this, it may just serve as a wherewithal to slacken one's drouth. So let the great jar be brought to me." Then the people fetched the great jar with the ten-year-old Do and the girl drank it to the dregs so that her thirst might be quenched.

The people of Dabo said: "These folk are strong folk. Let this man try the Tulu Kavuli Faga Kono. Fetch it hither!" The people brought the oil jar. Sunjatta drew the ring off his arm, hurled it into the seething oil and said: "N'jatta, N'jatta ninkanja, N'jatta Namara! That am I. While yet I lay in the womb of my mother, a bird in the bush may have caused her a fear. That was no fault of mine. My mother may then have felt fear when she heard the roar of a lion. That I cannot tell. Then she may have been afraid of a Djima (evil spirit). Of that I know not. That is no part of my oath. When the thunder rolled, when her father found fault with her, she may

Pattern of chased bronze work.   1. Kambali with borders (fan-shaped; bitchidanji, or cat's foot; circular; lemusungi=lemon pip).   2. Kambali (koko, or little leaf).   3 and 8. Kambali (clamissa=leopard spots).   4 and 6. Kambali with borders and Egba-bié=snail shell. 5. (a) Leiaji (b) Eku doko=horse hoof.   7. Kambali gowosá (gowosá=many dogs).   9. Egba-bié= snail shell.   10. Tchiré-bako=mouse belly; small border, Djami-bagi=horse trappings.

have been frightened and I do not include these things within the oath I swear. But since I knew my right from my left hand, I have never been afraid. So let the oath I now make be this: May all the skin and flesh be burnt from off mine arm if I swear false. But if I speak the truth, may my arm remain as it is." He plunged his hand in the bubbling liquid and drew it forth. Every part of it was free from injury; only one tiny hair was burnt. At this the Dabo people laughed. When the people laughed, Sunjatta grew grim and furious. But his sister took him aside, saying: "The Kengebugurilala said this: 'But if thou let not thine anger overcome thee, thou shalt be King of Mandeland.' Be on thy guard, therefore. Why didst thou not tell me beforehand what was thine intent. I am but a weakly maid, a woman-child, but I can do great things." (For the girl was a mistress of potent magic craft.) Then, do thou tell me always first what thou wouldst do, and I will help thee." Sunjatta said: "Then will I swear again." Sunjatta went and repeated his oath. His sister was standing at his side. He plunged his hand into the boiling oil and drew it forth again. The tiny hair, which had been burnt before, was now restored.

And now the Dabo people brought forth the Binje. They set the seven doors up before the banana tree, and said: "Sunjatta, take thy bow and arrows and shoot upon the seven doors." Then called he his sister, and unto her he said: "Killikillimadjumasuko, behold, I am about to shoot upon these seven doors." So she came. The people said unto him: "If thy blood be pure, if thou be thy royal father's son, thou canst shoot upon these doors with mind at ease, for then thy barb will pierce two doors or even three. But if this be not so, it will not penetrate a single one." Sunjatta placed the arrow in the sinewed bow and spake: "If my blood hath been defiled, then may this arrow turn and slay me!" He sped it: the shaft flew forward and not only forced its way through all the seven doors, but even pierced with all its weight the tree root before which the planks had stood and made the tree to fall. Then Kissima Dabo, the King of Daboland, cried out aloud and thereupon the tree stood up again erect where it had grown. Sunjatti cried aloud: the tree fell down once more. They both cried out aloud, and then one half of it fell down and the other half stood up. And thus it is to-day. All banana trees in time crash down.

But now the people of Dabo said: " This is a brave and mighty man," and they showed him the way to Memaland.

This is the first portion of the myth of Sunjatta, which goes on to describe his conquest, the Saga of the first Emir Diarra, whose mother was of the Diarra stock. It follows, then, that he did not derive his name from the paternal line (as the Islamite tradition would have demanded), but, as was the Libyan custom, from his mother's side. And thus the period in which the Mahommedan power reached its zenith is focussed in the heathen Libyan manner of name-giving. This gives the clearest indications of cultural relativity. The legend states that when the Emir had established his Empire, he adopted the title Koi-ta. Now, this means no more than the son or dependent of the King, and the only name of that ancient Niger people the Songai's King is Kei or Koi, and, as the venerable Leo Africanus informs us, that nation's ruling family was Libyan in origin.

The nomenclature and the line of succession are Libyan. The dynastic title is Libyan. The basic idea of the Epos will be proved to be originally Libyan, and the latter fact is of the greatest importance, because it is desirable to determine the way in which Islam insinuated itself into the Soudan by following the lines, the methods of acquiring influence and the political intentions adopted by a pre-Mahommedan civilization, and also to prove that Islam was never in itself a force capable of invigorating, transforming or re-creating a previously existing standard of culture.

Libyan at prayer.

*(Drawn by Fritz Nansen.)*

# CHAPTER XXII

### THE FIGHT WITH THE DRAGON

*(From accounts furnished by Libyans of the Sahara.)*

The Dragon-fight legends of the Dagombas—The Niger tribes—The ancient and modern Libyans —The Houssas—The same among the peoples who migrated Eastwards and Westwards.

THE historical poem of Sunjatta just dealt with has shown us that it is a poetized tradition of Mali Diarra or, rather, of the Emir Diarra the First, a figure well vouched for in history, which tells us that he conquered the heathen Susu King Sumanguru and founded the veritable Emirate, or so-called " Mali Empire." It was made clear that this Diarra came from the North and also that the union or confluence of ancient heathen streams of influence is represented in this legend.

Now, the whole tale begins by describing the combat of the Traore heroes with the Koba Antelope, a most miraculous kind of female horned animal, which represents a woman who has been changed by the power of sorcery. The meaning of this woman, so to say, " an All-Mother," must be discussed elsewhere. Here it is only necessary to mention that some versions of the Sunjatta legend distinctly say that one side of the primeval beast was of gold and the other of silver. The gold tail is a fact always insisted upon. The conqueror has to cut it off and produce it as a token of victory. I call the entire content of these leading ideas, this tale of a hero who overcomes a terrible beast which ravages and oppresses the countryside, "The Fight with the Dragon." Here in the Soudan its substitute is a Koba antelope, in other parts a bush cow. The origin and dissemination of this Saga is of special interest, and I therefore go aside from the actual Mande territory in search of parallel stories whose meaning and form may furnish a possible clue to the place whence the legend arose.

I will take the reader to Dagombaland, to Yendi in fact, a town in German North-western Togo. Its inhabitants are an extraordinary mixture of races whose entire civilization proves the confluence of characteristics peculiar not only to the individual cultures of the West Coast and thus to the nearest coast-country of Ashanti, but also to the tribes in the further West and, lastly, to the Mossi-Gurma group, who came from the East. This Mossi-Gurma cluster of tribes extends from the central Niger-bend up to the eastern flank of the Niger. Now let us hear the story of the origin of their kingdom's foundation as told by the Yendis.

1. Traditional history of the Dagomba.—There was an old woman whose name was Malé. She was athirst. Torse, a fair-haired hunter, came to her abode. He also was athirst, turned to the old woman and asked for water. She said: "We are here in the place Nyalmajinga. All we who are in Nyalmajinga are thirsty. We cannot get any water, because there is a great Buffalo at the pool." The hunter Torse said: "Give me a calabash. I will go and bring some water."

The people gave him a calabash. He took it and went to the pool. He wanted to fill it. The buffalo heard the noise and rushed at the hunter. Torse, the hunter, took an arrow, laid it to his bow and shot it into the buffalo's heart. The beast fell down dead. Then Torse drew water. Then he took his axe and hewed off the buffalo's right horn; it was of silver. He hewed off the left horn; it was of gold. He cut off the buffalo's tail.

Then he went on the road back and came to the woman's house. He left enough with the old woman for her to drink. She asked

him : " Whence didst thou get the water ? " Torse made answer :
" I slew the buffalo." Then he drew from his wallet the horns
and the tail of the buffalo. When the old woman saw them her heart
grew white with joy. She gave her children and grandchildren
calabashes so that they might drum upon them. The King of
Bingo (Bingo is the name of the old Gurman kingdom), Muley
Malna, heard this and summoned the old woman. He asked her :
" Why dost thou let the drums be beaten and why do the people
dance ? " Malé answered him : " A white hunter called Torse hath
arrived ; he hath killed the buffalo by the pool." The King said :
" Thou hast nothing thyself and yet wouldst take the stranger
in ? " He caused Torse to be called before him and said to his
Tumpteré, *i.e.*, the captain of the riders : " Take Torse into
thy house."

Torse abode four days in the Tumpteré's house. Then he
said : " O King, I will now return. I crave a boon. Amongst
thy daughters there is one who hath no legs. Give her to me to
wife." The King said : " I have many children and beautiful
daughters. And wilt thou have none but her who hath no feet ? "
Torse said : " Her and none other ! " He took the girl Gulyen (?)
Wobega on his shoulders and carried her off. He went with her
to the old woman to take farewell of her and said : " I am going
home." The old woman said : " Did Malna give thee no escort ? "

The hunter said : " I did not ask him." Then he departed
thence.

The aged woman took her two young sons and said : " There
goes Torse away from here. Follow unseen until he gets home
so that ye may know his home and the road that leads there." The
youths followed Torse till the sun went down. When the sun
had set he cleared a place in the bush and set Wobega down in it.
Then he took bow and arrow, went on the chase and killed a
Palbua, which is the name given by the Dagomba to a little
antelope ; he struck a fire (with flint), broiled the meat and
they ate.

Next morning he carried his wife Wobega further. The youths
constantly followed him at his heels unnoticed. Torse carried his
wife ever further, and so at last they came to a mountain cave in
which the hunter lived. The cave (toward the North-east) is said

to have been beyond the land of Gurma. But no man now knows where the district was and the place itself is known less still.

There the two youths turned round, went home to the old woman and said : " We followed the hunter ; he went into a cave ; we now know the way."

＊　　＊　　＊　　＊　　＊　　＊　　＊　　＊

War came over the King Malna, heathens were they who attacked him. The King spake to the Gurma old woman : " Where is the light-coloured hunter ? " The old woman said : " When thou gavest him thy daughter in marriage, did not thy people bear him company then ? and do they not remember the way to where he lives ? " The King was silent. Thereupon the woman sent the two youths whom she had sent before as spies that they might now carry the King's message to him.

The two men departed. They slept in the same place in the bush and went on next morning. Then they came to Torse's cave. They entered in, but saw neither him nor his wife. They only saw Lumbu, Torse's son. Lumbu asked them : " Whence come ye ? " They said : " Thy father Torse came to our place ; King Malna gave him his daughter to wife. Now heathens are overrunning the kingdom with war. The King bade us come hither to pray Torse to deliver us, as he erstwhile saved us from the Buffalo."

Lumbu said : " It is true that Torse was my father and Wobega my mother. But my father and mother both are dead. My father Torse came to your aid, without knowing Malna. So now I also will help my grandfather. Let us hence ! "

Lumbu went with them to the King's city. Lumbu drove the heathens to flight and slew many of them. Then he went with Malna's men of war to Bialdi. Tindana was a King in his own country. Lumbu went to him with his warriors and stayed by the river near the country of Tindana to rest. Here he remained with his warriors.

Tindana (just at that time) had collected workers from his nobles who were to help him to cultivate his lands. The nobles had given them to him, but said : " Do not suffer any work to be done in the fields on Thursday. For Thursday is a holy day. Neither let the women fetch water from the stream." Tindana gave no heed to the warning but suffered them to work on Thursday as on each other day.

Now there was a son of Tindana's (?), Oashierro by name, who had a daughter (?) of Tindana's, called Meshiobro, for his bride. Meshiobro went to the place where the people were at work in the fields in the bush and saw that her lover was thirsty but had no water. So she took a jar to go down to the stream to draw water. She came to the stream and saw Lumbu seated there.

When she saw him, she was so terror-stricken that she threw down the jar and ran away. Lumbu ran after her and said : " Have no fear ! Do not run away ! " When she came back he asked her : " Why didst thou run away when thou sawest me ? " Meshiobro answered : " My father hath in his fields labourers who are thirsty, I came down to the stream to draw water." He said : " Draw thy water, carry it up into the field and then tell thy father that I, Lumbu, am here by the brook."

Tindana took a jar, drew water and filled the jar. He took it and went with the oldest man to the stream where Lumbu was sitting. Lumbu said : " Thou art Tindana and bring'st me water in this jar ? The jar is not good." Then he took some clay from the stream and gave it to Tindana. He said : " Fashion it into a vessel in the shape of a gourd bottle." Then he took an ear of durra and gave it to Tindana, saying : " Plant it to-day ; it will sprout to-day, grow and be fruitful." Then he took a pumpkin seed, gave it to Tindana and spake : " Plant it ; it will sprout, grow, and even to-day ripen into a gourd bottle." Then said Lumbu : " Let thy daughter grind flour from the fruit which the durra thou hast planted will bear, and fill it into the gourd bottle. Let her fetch water in the bottle jar even now to be fashioned. Let her then bring them both to me."

Tindana departed and did as Lumbu had bidden him. The grain and the pumpkin seed were planted and sprouted and grew and bore fruit. The pot in the shape of a gourd bottle was fashioned, and when the sun was high in the heavens Tindana's daughter went to the stream to draw water. She poured the water on to the flour in the gourd bottle. She mixed it and brought it to Lumbu.

When these things had been done Tindana sent to Lumbu,

saying : " My grandson, come unto me, I will give thee a house."
Lumbu obeyed the call, and Tindana's compound was allotted
to him for an abiding place. Tindana said to his daughter : " A
dog that devours an egg must pay for it ! It was thou who
madest Lumbu come hither. For this reason will I give thee to
him in marriage."

Thus it was that Lumbu received Tindana's daughter to wife.
She bore him a son. The child grew into a boy who went with his
uncle (?) Tindana into the bush to tend the cattle. One day the
lad saw a partridge and killed it with a bowshot. The uncle said :
" Make a fire. We will roast the partridge ! " The boy did so.
Then they roasted it. The uncle gave his nephew only the head
and one leg. The rest he ate himself.

When the boy came home he told his mother : " I shot a
partridge, and my uncle bade me make a fire. We roasted it.
Then he gave me nothing but one leg and its head. He ate the
rest himself." His mother said : " Be silent and say nothing to
thy father."

The boy went again next morning into the bush with his
uncle to tend the cattle. The boy killed a guinea-fowl with a
bowshot. His uncle said : " Light a fire." The boy made a
fire. His uncle roasted the guinea-fowl. Then he ate it ; but he
gave the boy only one leg and the head. When they came home
the boy told his mother : " I shot a guinea-fowl. My uncle bade
me make a fire. He roasted the guinea-fowl. Then he gave me
nothing but one leg and the head. The rest he ate himself." His
mother said : " Be silent and say nothing to thy father."

Next morning the boy again went into the bush with his uncle
to tend the cattle. The boy killed a hare with a bowshot. His
uncle said : " Light a fire." The boy made a fire. Then the uncle
roasted the hare and gave the boy only one leg and the head. When
they came home, the boy did not tell his mother, but his father,
Lumbu. He told him all that had happened.

Lumbu listened to it and went to Tindana. He said : " My
son killed the game, but the meat was taken away from him. If
now in the future thou shalt slay an ox, I give up my share of the
flesh and claim nothing but the tail and the hide." And thus it
came to pass. Every time when Tindana killed an ox, Lumbu

received the hide and the tail. That happened until there were twelve of them.

When Tindana had made this (humiliating) division twelve times, Lumbu one day asked Tindana's son : " When thy father hath slain an ox for the fetish and the young dance, where does he then stay ? " The son of Tindana made answer : " Then my father lies upstairs under the roof." (N.B.—The houses, therefore, must have been two-storied.)

Now when the time was at hand for the next ox to be slaughtered, Lumbu secretly sharpened his knife and hid it in his sleeve. Then he crept stealthily into the upper chamber of the house in which Tindana slept and cut Tindana's throat. Then he went home.

When Tindana's wife went to take her husband hot water that he might wash himself, she found the King dead. She screamed, so that the people ran together. They all cried out : " Who hath killed the King ? " Thereupon Lumbu stepped forth, saying : " I slew him." And he further said : " Whose son do ye call Yornesorberi ? (Bushman). That is not the name of my son. My son is called Nyergele and my name is Nyergele ; that is, I have taken vengeance for the insults which ye have done unto my son."

When Lumbu had slain Tindana, he, Lumbu, was King.

\*      \*      \*      \*      \*      \*      \*      \*

Comparison of the beginning of this legend with Sunjatta's will show them to be very closely related. The Koba antelope's place has been filled by a buffalo. The old woman who gives the fair-skinned hunter information is called Malé. She does not change herself into a buffalo. But here the buffalo also has one horn of gold and one of silver. The tail cut from the buffalo is here also considered a proof of victory—the hunter here also has a maiden for his guerdon, not, it is true, disfigured like Sugulun-kurmang, but without feet. As Sunjatta is exiled, so here the hero also goes away. Heathen tribes invade and threaten the existence of the land. The valiant champion is recalled and misses the direct succession to the throne, just as in the Sunjatta legend the two conquerors of the Koba also not only do not found the kingdom afresh, but the one who does so is the son of the rescued damsel. Thus we find versions of the same legend we were enabled to gather from the mouths of the bards on the Upper Niger, which are not very divergent.

If, now, we examine this legend more closely in respect of the names and ask ourselves whether it may not afford us further points of connection, the answer will be more than satisfactory. The principal thing is that the King's name is Malna, and his country Malé. In the Dagomba district, Malé is the name given to the great Emir of the West's country, or Maliland. And, moreover, the suffix " na " in the Dagomba tongue has the same meaning as the Mossi word " Naba," which is " king." The King of Dagomba is there called Dagomba-na, in Mossi speech Dagomba-naba. The ruler or King of Bingoland is, in Dagomba, Bingo-na ; in Mossi, Bingo-naba. Therefore, Malna is nothing but Malé-naba, *i.e.*, King of Maliland. The local conditions are a satisfactory explanation of the variation in the names of the countries. Here the conquering hero, Torse, cannot hail from Memaland, the home of the Tungara ; he must necessarily derive from Bingo or Gurma, in sympathy with historical events. The other legends of these lands teach us, as a matter of fact, that the now reigning dynasty of Mossi and Dagomba came from Gurma, or Bingo, while Mandingoes coming from Mandeland formerly ruled over the West African-Soudanese kingdoms, which had been settled upon from time immemorial. It is, then, self-evident that Torse of the Dagomba legend could not have come out of Mema, but must needs be traced from Bingo or Gurma.

Now, in these countries, Torse, or Turrsi, is the name given to a distinctly legendary race whose special attribute was a fair skin. " Si " is a plural ending, and, consequently, Turr, or Turre, remains as the name of a race of light complexion. These Turre, however, are also of frequent occurrence in Mande history. In this also they appear as a fair nation who came from the North. In turning over the ample store of legends I was able to collect in the course of years and bring home, I find that the details of the mythical contest with the " laidly worm " are most clearly preserved among the light-coloured nations. Therefore, I turn my attention to the North, and will illustrate the point from those districts where the legend is still current in full vigour and form, and begin with the recital of a bardic song from Massina, the country to the South-west of Timbuktu.

There the Saga runs like this :

2. Traditional history from Massina.—Hambodeju (a Fulbe) was a king's son. When Hambodeju was ten years old his father died and Hambodeju, together with the kingdom, was taken over by his uncle and educated at his court. He used to play with his uncle's children. One day his son, in the course of a wordy quarrel, said to Hambodeju : " What business hast thou to be here at all ? Thy father is dead. The kingdom belongs to my father, thy uncle. Thou hast no right here at all." Hambodeju immediately ran to his mother and asked her : " Whose is the kingdom ? Does it belong to my uncle or to me ? " His mother said : " Thy father was this country's lord. When thy father died, thy uncle usurped the throne. But thy father left a very good horse. Its name is Bonnujuwadi. Thou canst take it whenever thou wilt." Hambodeju said : " It is well." He went away. He went and took the horse Bonnujuwadi out of its stall, called his Mabo (jester and also squire), gave him a horse and gun as well, saying : " Come, we are going to war. If I win the victory I shall wage a campaign against my uncle and see whether I cannot get back my father's kingdom." He rode off with his Mabo.

He arrived with his Mabo at the Sahel. After riding through the Sahel for the space of ten days he came to a small village. He asked : " To whom does this village belong ? " A man said : " To the Burdam (Tuareg)." Hambodeju inquired : " Who is King of this land ? Who has the soldiers ? " The people told him : " King Elle, the King of the Tuareg." He made them show him the way and rode on to the town.

King Elle had one son and one daughter. The son, named Hammadi-Elle, was accustomed to mount his horse in the evening and go for a ride with his Mabo. When Hambodeju was nearing the Elle's abode he met the youth Hammadi-Elle and said : " Good day ! " Hammadi-Elle also said : " Good day ! " Hambodeju asked : " Who art thou ? " The other made reply : " I am Hammadi-Elle, a Burdam, the son of the King of the Burdam. Who art thou ? " Hambodeju said : " My name is Hambodeju, the son of a Fulbe king." Hammadi-Elle said : " What dost thou

here ? " 	Hambodeju said : " I have some things I would speak
about with thy father." 	Hammadi-Elle said : " Hearken, Hambo-
deju, thou hast a good horse, let us ride a race and see which of us
two shall be first in the town." 	Hambodeju said : " It is not
worth while, for I shall be first anyhow! I do not care for a
race." 	Then Hammadi wanted to excite him to race, snatched the
cap off his head and galloped off with it.

Now Hambodeju said to his Mabo : " Give me my sword."
The Mabo gave him the sword and then he galloped after Hammadi-
Elle and caught him up. He lunged with the sword and struck
Hammadi-Elle on the back of the head. The King's son fell dead
to the ground. Hammadi-Elle's Mabo immediately galloped from
there and into the town. He met King Elle and spake : " Thy son
hath this moment died." King Elle asked : " Did death come out
from heaven or earth ? " The Mabo said : " There is no need to
reach so far. A Fulbe, lately come, hath put thy son to death."
All the people had assembled in that place. There were very many,
because next day a great festival of sacrifice was to be solemnized.

After Hambodeju had slain the King's son Hammadi-Elle,
his own Mabo said unto him : " Hambodeju, it was wrong of thee
to kill this King's son when thou wouldst go to his father. It was
not wise. Wilt thou still seek out King Elle ? " Hambodeju said :
" Notwithstanding will I go in quest of King Elle." The Mabo
said : " If thou do this, then art thou a Grintiwal and a Garantáwal."
(The first means an undaunted hero, the second, a generous one.)
Thereupon they rode into the township. A vast concourse of people
was gathered together in a great square. When Hambodeju saw
this, he made his horse rush rearing upon the crowd, brandished his
sword and all the assembled Burdam fled asunder in wild haste.
King Elle sent this message to Hambodeju : " Lodge in the city
this day. I will judge the matter to-morrow in the great
assembly."

Hambodeju took up his quarters in the house of an old woman.
But she knew not that it was he who had killed the son of the King.
He said to the old woman : " I prithee bring some water for us
and our horses." The old woman said : " Alas ! it is not an easy
thing to get some water. There is no water. We have, the truth
to tell, a great pool, but in it lives a mighty beast whose name is

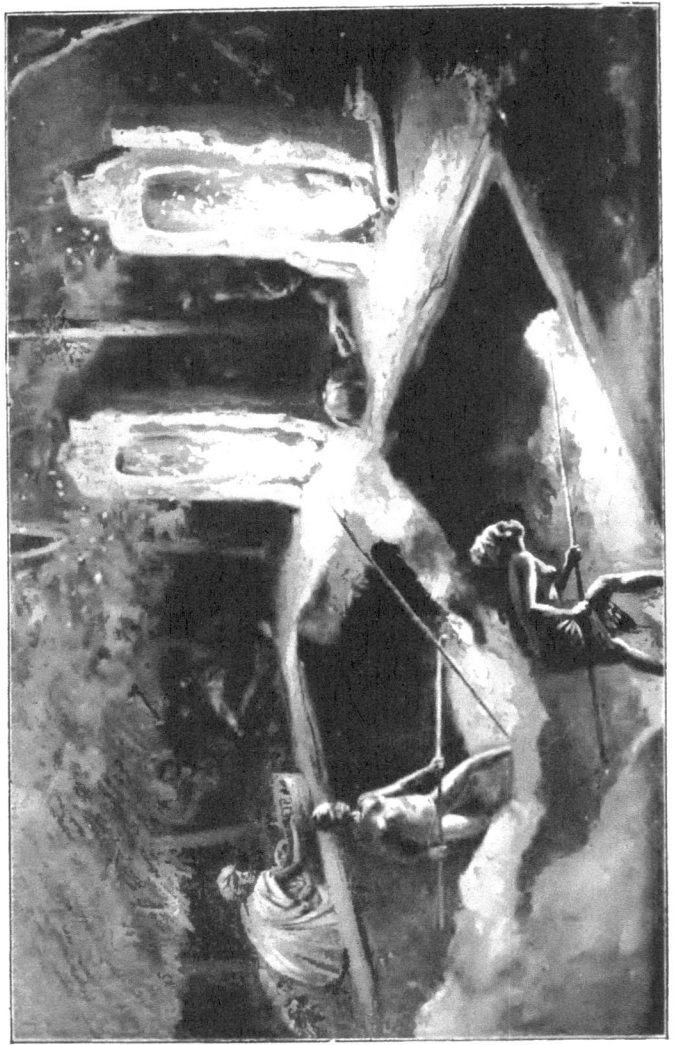

Iron Foundry

Iron foundry in Nupeland.

(By Carl Arriens.)

[Facing p. 164.

Kurua. This animal has three heads and its lair is in the pool. So that we be allowed to take water, the city has in every year to send one of its loveliest virgins into the lake as a sacrificial offering to the Beast. Now to-morrow is the day of the great sacrifice. This is the reason why there are so many people in the town. The girl to be immolated is Fatumata-Elle, sister to Hammadi-Elle, who has to-day been slain. But now, since just to-morrow is the day appointed, Kurua will not suffer anyone to draw water from his pool and none will dare, for the three-headed Kurua is terrible." Hambodeju asked : " Which is the road to the lake of the monstrous Kurua ? " The old woman said : " It runs by here. If thou goest down there, thou wilt soon come to it."

Hambodeju said to his Mabo : " Put the Faram (that is the little bridle with which a horse is led to water and to the ford) on Bonnujuwadi ; give me my sword and lead the horse behind me." They departed. They came to the pool. Hambodeju put his sword ready in his hand for the battle and spake : " Now, my Mabo, do thou lead me Bonnujuwadi into the lake." The Mabo did so. When the horse and the Mabo stepped into the water, Kurua reared its head in astonishment out of the deep. Hambodeju raised his sword on high and drove at it. One severed head fell off. Kurua lifted up the two remaining. Hambodeju struck yet a blow. The two heads fell down. Then Hambodeju called to his Mabo : " Is Kurua quite dead ? " The Mabo said : " Yea, it floats upon the water, dead."

Then he went and cut off the monster's tail, and gave it to Mabo with these words : " Take it with thee." Then placed he by the shore his shoon and the leathern sheath of his glaive across them, to serve as after-proof that it was he who had waged this combat. They took some water with them, went back to their abode, and Hambodeju said to the old woman : " Here is water. Take and drink."

Next morning all the Burdam folk foregathered in the square. They came together in great crowds, for this was the day on which the King's daughter was to be offered up to the Kurua and, after that, all might drink again. So they were all assembled. King Elle said : " We will give judgment on the Fulbe man who slew my son Hammadi-Elle." But the Burdams cried : " Leave that till later. Only first let us drink our fill for once. Only let us sacrifice the virgin to the beast Kurua first, so that we may drink." King Elle said : " That is true. Let us to the pool."

All the people present wended to the pool. There were nigh upon a million. This million of people desired to see the maid delivered to the monstrous Kurua, and then to drink. The girl destined that year to be Kurua's victim was conducted thither. She was Fatumata-Elle, daughter to Elle, King of the Burdams, sister to Hammadi-Elle, the slain. The girl went to the edge of the lake. The monster Kurua made no stir. The maid waited. The monster Kurua neither showed itself nor troubled the water.

The crowd grew impatient and shouted : " Further in ! " Fatumata-Elle went further into the lake and stood still. The monster Kurua was nor seen nor stirred it. None of its three heads was visible. All waited. The mass of people grew impatient, shouting : " Further in ! " Fatumata-Elle went further in. Fatumata-Elle went as far as the middle of the lake. There she stood expectant. The monster Kurua neither stirred nor moved. None of its three heads appeared. All waited. Fatumata-Elle waited. The whole gathering waited. But nothing happened. Then one among the crowd cried : " Kurua has died." All the people shouted : " Kurua is dead." One called out : " Some man ought to go into the lake and see whether Kurua be dead or liveth yet." They all shouted : " Let some one go and see." There was a multitude of more than a million heads gathered together to assist at the spectacle of sacrifice. But among all the million people there was not one to be the first to dare even to approach the edge of the pool of Kurua.

At last one man, armed with a spear, adventured fearfully to the edge of the lake. He thrust the spear several times into the water and then cried : " Kurua is dead ! " Some others now came to the shore and found the shoon and sword-sheath of Hambodeju. They shouted loudly : " Some man or other must have killed Kurua. He hath left his shoes and dagger sheath behind him as a token." The people cried : " Thus must it be." The shoes and knife scabbard were brought to King Elle. He said : " He who hath slain Kurua left these things behind. Now we shall be able to find out who it is." Thereupon all the people rejoicing commenced to drink and carry water away. And Fatumata-Elle came back out of the lake whole and unscathed.

All the folk were assembled in the great square of the city. King Elle spake : " Now conduct hither the Fulbe that we may sentence him." All the million of people was gathered round in a circle. Fatumata-Elle, the rescued, was seated next to the King ; in front of the King were the shoes and the scabbard found on the shore. Hambodeju was summoned.

Hambodeju went through the city streets. Behind him came his Mabo. He carried the Kurua's tail beneath his coat and sang :

> Where others fail through fear
> Hambodeju is fearless;
> Where others flee in flight
> Hambodeju stands firm ;
> When others evil do
> Hambodeju is away.

Hambodeju came to the great square on which the million people were foregathered and went straight across to the open space where King Elle was seated. There lay the shoes and the blade-sheath. All this world saw the blade-sheath, the shoon, and saw, too, the Fulbe who slew Hammadi-Elle, the son of the King.

Hambodeju strode right across the great open space surrounded by the people, went up to the kingly seat, did not turn towards him, but took up one of the two shoes placed there and drew it on his foot. He took up the other of the two shoes and drew it on his other foot. He drew forth his dagger, fitted it into its sheath and stuck it in his belt. Then he thrust his hand behind him, took from Mabo's hand the monster Kurua's tail, laid it at the King's feet and spake : " Here ! " All the people here ranged together saw all these happenings. This was seen by the Elle, this was seen by Fatumata-Elle, sister to slain Hammadi-Elle ; and when she saw it, she said : " My father, give me in marriage to this Fulbe, for never will I be wife to any other man. Kill me before thou give me to any other man to wife."

King Elle regarded his daughter. He regarded Hambodeju and spake : " Take thou my daughter Fatumata as thy bride and, moreover, I will grant every wish of thine within mine power to bestow." Hambodeju said : " I came not hither to get me a wife.

I am Hambodeju, the son of the Fulbe King of Bongo in Konariland. My uncle filched my kingdom from me and I am come to pray thee give me an army wherewith to come into mine own again." King Elle said : " I give thee the hand of my daughter to wed. The army thou needest I willingly give thee." So Hambodeju married King Elle's daughter.

Then Hambodeju sent a messenger to his uncle with this message : " Put on thine harness, for I come into the field against thee. Cause thyself to be made a pair of shoes whose soles are of iron. For I will follow and hunt thee until thy soles of iron shall be worn quite away. I know that not only one woman of the Fulbe hath borne a brave son." Hambodeju set out with his forces in battle array. The two armies met. Both sides fought very valiantly and death-defiantly. At last the victory lay with Hambodeju's side. He beat his uncle's troops to flight and followed in pursuit of the foe as it fled.

When he had galloped a space he saw his uncle sitting by the wayside. He was waiting for his nephew Hambodeju to fight with him. Both seized their spears. They hurled their spears. The spears shivered to pieces. They hurled fresh spears. These, too, shivered to pieces. But then Hambodeju laid hold of his horse's belly-band, drove in upon his uncle with it and with it slew him. Then afterwards he struck off the head of his uncle.

Hambodeju was made King. He took over his uncle's warriors. One half of his domestic slaves he kept, the other half he sent to Elle, his father-in-law. He ruled in his city of Bongo in Konariland all the days of his life.

\*      \*      \*      \*      \*      \*      \*      \*

The bardic songs of the ancient tribes on the border of the Sahara were taken over by the Fulbe. They had no original chivalrous poem and singers of chivalry, and, just as they assumed the poetic art and form of song native to the Sahel district between the Soudan and the Sahara, so they again lost them when they moved into other lands. There is no Mabo, no knightly bard and no poem of chivalry to be found in the East among the Fulbe in Mossiland, the Houssa States or in Adamawo. The race of troubadours and the songs themselves cling almost closer to the soil than those who dwell upon it.

And as it is with the singer, so also is it with the songs. It is immaterial whether we hear such a song from the lips of a Fulbe or a Mandingo. It is an attribute of those who inhabit the fringe of the Western Sahara. And it is here alone that we grasp the meaning of the legend of the dragon who guards the water. Here, where people are so conscious that water is an element essential to life, the dragon who prevents people from going to the wells and pools is easily explained. This leading idea, which would be quite out of place in a land like Dagomba where there is plenty of water, could only have arisen here. But this is not the only point which is clearer in the legends of the North. The idea of the virgin rescued from the dragon is worked out much more definitely in the construction of the Massina tale. This presents a typical variation of the Perseus myth. It is as plain as plain can be. It is clearly perceptible as the basic form from which the Mande and Dagomba legends are derived. And, consequently, it is also widely disseminated in the Northern districts.

There would be no difficulty in appending a whole series of related Sagas, all native to the tract of country between the mouth of the Senegal and the middle Niger near Timbuktu.

Mention has just been made of the identity of intention which exists between these legends and the myth of Perseus and Andromeda. The dragon which Poseidon in his wrath sent into the land of Cepheus, King of Ethiopia, also waits for the sacrifice which the King must bring in the form of the lovely Andromeda, a child of the King's. None other than Ammon, the King-God of North Africa, announces the imperative necessity of virgin immolation. The legend is not, in reality, Greek, but North African, and especially popular in Joppa on the Carthaginian coast. And in this way the extension of this myth, which found its way to the Hellenes from the lands lying to the north of the Sahara and across the lands to the south of it, becomes at once quite intelligible. It is simply a Libyan legend.

This Libyan element, so distinctly preserved in this mixture of Soudanese traditional history, reminds us that the mediæval traveller, Leo Africanus, has a story that the mighty empire of the Songai, stretching far along the banks of the Niger had been founded by a ruling family "*della stirpe di Libya*" (of Libyan descent). Now, in the celebrated Soudanese historian, Abderrahman ben Abdalla's Tarikh es Soudan, the history of the foundation of the Songai kingdom, which happened at the beginning of the seventh century, is enshrined. He gives an account of how two brothers miserably clothed in skins (the dress of the Libyan tribes then) came to Kukija (or Kuka) on the Niger, into Songai-land, where (as opposed to the religion of Mahommed) heathenish Gods were adored. A demon which ruled in the land lived in the form of a fish in the river and from time to time appeared when the water was high. Once, when he came up again, the elder of the two skin-clad youths took up his spear and killed it. Thus he became the founder of the Sa dynasty of the Songai Empire and this is ample warranty for assuming the same descent for the Mande.

A similar dragon-myth, then, respecting the ruling family which Leo Africanus assures us was of Libyan descent, is here also as current as among many other tribes native to the North or North-east which are called fair-skinned. If Islam is concerned to represent these founders of states as immigrants from Mecca, as descendants and reverers of the Prophet, it does precisely what old Christian legend did, namely, appropriate with haste in the East the groundwork of the Tale of Saint George. That the dragon story, therefore, did not come in with Islam, is proved by its dissemination and its absence, historically, in the genuine mythology of Mahommedan Africa. And, furthermore, we find other forms of this dragon-contest legend in the Soudan which, as they spread southwards, are very antique and yet so very primitive in character as to present no difficulty in tracing the original connection of their inner meaning.

I will give just one of this older type of story and select a version current in the Houssa countries, in order to show how the same material is developed on the same lines both in Africa and Europe. A certain likeness between the naughty boy, Dan-Auta, and the early mischievousness of young Siegfried, is quite noticeable, without, however, necessitating the assumption of an analogous philogenetic origin.

3. Legend of the Houssas in Katsena.—A man married a girl.

He went into the bush with his wife and lived far away from men. He tilled his fields and harvested (his crops). The man and woman made everything they needed themselves. After the man had been married to the woman for about half a year, she became big and afterwards bore him a child. The child was a girl and its name was Sara (or Ssara). Afterwards the woman bore yet more children (*nota bene*, it should at once be stated that the tale-tellers do not know what became of them), and, finally, one tenth child. This was a little boy and because he was the youngest they called him Dan-Auta.

Dan-Auta was still quite a little fellow when his father fell sick. He said: " I am going to die." He called Ssara and said to her: " I am going to die. Always keep Dan-Auta by thee. Always watch over Dan-Auta. Take care lest Dan-Auta either scream or weep." Her father said this and died.

Dan-Auta was still quite a little fellow when his mother fell sick. The mother said: " I am going to die," called Ssara, and said to Ssara: " I am going to die! Always keep Dan-Auta by thee. Always watch over Dan-Auta! Take care that Dan-Auta never scream and never weep." This her mother said and died.

Ssara was alone in the bush with Dan-Auta. He was a little boy, crawled about on the ground and also walked a little. But Ssara and Dan-Auta had plenty of food. They had a whole rumbu (granary) full of dauwa (sorghum or durra); they had a whole rumbu full of maiwa (late penisetum); they had a whole granary full of adja (panicum); they had a whole granary full of geero (early penisetum); they had a whole granary full of ground-nuts; they had a whole rumbu full of beans and a whole granary full of maize. Ssara said: " We shall have enough to eat till Dan-Auta is big enough to till his own farm."

Ssara went out and ground durra into flour to cook a meal for herself and Dan-Auta. When she had ground the flour, she brought it into the hut in a calabash in which she cooked and where Dan-Auta was sitting by the hearth. Then Ssara went out again to fetch firewood from the bush. When she had gone, Dan-Auta ran to the calabash in which was the flour and upset it. Then he fetched ashes from the hearth-place and mixed it with the flour which lay on the ground. Ssara came back in a little while. She saw what Dan-Auta had been doing and said: "Kai (thou)! My Dan-Auta! Thou throwest the meal, which we were going to eat together, on the ground? Fie!" Dan-Auta sobbed. (At this part of the story, the narrator always imitates the sound made by a child about to cry.) Ssara quickly said: "O, Dan-Auta, do not cry. Thy baba (father) and thy inna (mother) said thou must not cry! Do not cry! I was only vexed because thou threwest away the grain on which we must live till thou art big enough to till a farm."

Ssara went out. She took another sort of grain out of the granary and ground it to meal. Ssara worked at the grindstones. Dan-Auta took a burning piece of wood from the cooking-place, ran to the rumbu, where the durra was and set light to it. The rumbu was alight. The rumbu was burnt to the ground. Ssara saw it burning and came running. She screamed: "Kai! Dan-Auta! Thou burnest down the whole rumbu! What shall we both live on? I am only a woman (women do not work in the fields in those countries); thou art still so little that it will be long before thou canst manage to work the farm. What shall we live on?" Dan-Auta sobbed. Ssara quickly said: "Dan-Auta, do not cry! Thy father and mother said thou wert not to cry! Do not cry! I was only vexed that thou didst burn down a granary with grain on which we must live till thou art strong enough to manage a farm."

Ssara went out; she prepared the food. She brought the food and ate with Dan-Auta. Then they both lay down and slept. Next morning, while Dan-Auta was still asleep, Ssara arose, took the pot and went to fetch water. When she was gone, Dan-Auta woke up and saw that Ssara had gone. Dan-Auta got up. He went to the fire-place. He blew the fire up. He took a wisp of straw and set light to it. He ran out with the blazing straw wisp and fired all the rumbu in which lay the geero and adja and the beans and the ground-nuts. Ssara saw the fire and ran up. She saw that all the rumbu were burning, that all the grain was burning. Ssara screamed: "Kai! Dan-Auta! Thou burnest up all we have to eat. Now, we have nothing left!"

Dan-Auta sobbed. Ssara quickly said: "My Dan-Auta! Do not cry! Thy father and mother said thou wert not to cry! I was

BRONZE-CHASING WORK III.

1. Pani (oku) (incised).
2. Egun su = bee's foot (incised).
3. Fokuagi (punched).
4. Sanbara (incised).
5. Elaa = snake track (do.).
6. Kambali koko = small leaf (incised).
7. Dunori goga = vaulted ceiling (incised).
8. Elaa (punched).
9. Cluka = bush path (punched).
10. Kambali.
11a. Olue bako = horse belly.
11b. Lenimatugi = lemon pip (punched).
12. Sanbara = net (stamped).
13. Ekuloko = horse foot (do.).
14. Djani bagi = horse trapping (stamped), mistaken.
15. Teme baka = circle (stamped).
16a, b, c. Akali fara = grasshopper teeth (stamped).
17. Eti-bi-danji = cat's-paw (stamped).
18. Kambali (stamped).
19. Pata = horse (do.).
20. Sero = hand (do.).
21. Lenimatugi (punched).
22. Peradi = beetle (stamped).
23. Ful sakuro = broken mouth (stamped).
24. Eti-jakumbara = lizard's head (stamped).
25. Newer fashioned die (Kambali ?).
26. Akali fara = grasshopper teeth (stamped).
27. Newer fashioned stamp (combination of Ecchi hyacchu, dog's knee and Lenimatugi).

[Facing p. 184.

only vexed because we now have nothing more to eat. But never mind : I will look for food for us ! "

Ssara took Dan-Auta on her back and tied him (in the country manner) tight with her dress. Then she went into the bush. Ssara came to a path and went along that path. Ssara went with Dan-Auta into the town and went with him into the quarter where the King lived. The King's first wife took Ssara in. There, with the King's first wife, they lived.

She gave Ssara and Dan-Auta food for many days. Ssara always carried Dan-Auta on her back and never put Dan-Auta on the ground. The other women said to her : " Why dost always carry Dan-Auta on thy back ? Why dost never set him on the ground and let him play like the other women ? " Ssara said : " Let me do after my own way. Dan-Auta's father and mother said Dan-Auta was never to cry. If I keep Dan-Auta on my back, he will not scream. I must be careful that Dan-Auta do not scream."

One day Dan-Auta said : " I want to play with the son of the King ! " Ssara put him down on the ground. Dan-Auta played with the King's son. Ssara took up her pitcher and went down to the water. The King's son took a stick, Dan-Auta also took a stick. They both played with the sticks. The King's son and Dan-Auta beat with the sticks. The King's son and Dan-Auta thrust with the sticks. Dan-Auta poked one of the King's son's eyes out and the King's son fell down.

Ssara came up. She saw that Dan-Auta had poked out the King's son's eye. But none else was by. The King's son screamed. Ssara set down the jar, picked up Dan-Auta and ran out of the house with him, out of the King's quarter, out of the town, into the bush as fast as she could run.

There was nobody in the house but the King's firstborn. He screamed. The King heard his screams and said : " Why screameth my son ? " The King's women ran up ; they saw that one of the King's son's eyes was poked out and screamed. The King heard the screaming of his forty wives and came along. The King saw that his son had had an eye poked out ; he called out in a loud voice : " What is this ? Who hath done this thing ? " The child said : " Ssara came into the house with Dan-Auta. I was playing with Dan-Auta. I took a stick. Dan-Auta took a stick. I beat with the stick. Dan-Auta beat with the stick. I thrust with the stick. Dan-Auta thrust with the stick. He poked out my eye. Ssara came, picked up Dan-Auta and ran off with him." The King said : " Search the town over for Ssara and Dan-Auta. Bring Ssara and Dan-Auta unto me ! "

All the King's Dogari ran through the town. All the King's people ran through the town. Every house was opened. Every house was searched for Ssara and Dan-Auta. Every house-master said : " Ssara and Dan-Auta are not within my compound."

The Dogari and all the King's people searched in all the houses. They did not find Ssara and Dan-Auta. Then they all came back to the King, saying : " We have thoroughly searched all the compounds and houses in the town. Ssara and Dan-Auta are no longer in the town."

The King called the people together ; he summoned all the soldiers and all the horsemen. The King said : " Ssara and Dan-Auta have fled out of the town. Ye must find them. Ye must find them and capture them, even if they be gone into the water. Ye must find them and capture them, even if they be gone into the earth. Ye must find them and capture them, even if they be gone into the air. I, the King, will go with my horsemen and search in the bush." All the King's horsemen went forth from the town into the bush to look for Ssara and Dan-Auta. People went east and searched. But they did not find Dan-Auta and Ssara. People went south and searched, but did not find Ssara and Dan-Auta. People went north and searched. But they did not find Ssara and Dan-Auta. For two days the people searched in all directions. But Ssara and Dan-Auta were not found.

Ssara had been running for two whole days with Dan-Auta on her back. Then they heard the horsemen coming. The King, with his horsemen following, came up with her. There was a very big tree there. Ssara said : " I will climb up this tree and hide myself and Dan-Auta among the leaves of this tree ! " With Dan-Auta on her back, she climbed up the tree and concealed herself among its leaves.

The King and his riders came to the tree. He said : " I have ridden for two days. I am weary ; I desire to rest ; set up my karaga (bedstead made of little reeds) under this tree. I would seat myself upon my karaga." His people set up the karaga under the tree. The King sat down upon it. He sat under the bough on which Ssara and Dan-Auta were sitting.

Dan-Auta looked down upon the King and said : " Ssara ! " Ssara said : " Kai ! Dan-Auta ! Be still ! " Dan-Auta sobbed. Ssara quickly said : " My Dan-Auta, do not cry ! Thy father and thy mother said thou must not cry. Do not cry ! Say what thou wilt." Dan-Auta said : " I want to relieve myself. I will do so on the King's head." Ssara said : " We shall be put to death. But thy father and mother said thou must not cry. Do so, then ! "

The King looked up at the tree. He saw Ssara and Dan-Auta, and shouted : " Bring axes hither ; we will fell the tree forthwith ! " The people ran and brought axes. They began to fell the tree. The tree began to quiver. The people cut deeper into the tree. The tree began to sway. The people cut away half the trunk. The tree began to lean to one side. Ssara said : " Now I shall be caught and put to death."

A great Shurua (falcon, also Shirma) was flying across the bush. It came close to the tree, where Ssara was sitting with Dan-Auta. The tree began to bend down. She called to the bird : " My Shurua ! see ! they will kill Dan-Auta and me if thou dost not take us away." The Shurua heard Ssara and came down. The tree sank sideways, but the Shurua took Ssara on one shoulder and Dan-Auta on the other. The tree fell over. Then the Shurua flew high up into the air with Ssara and Dan-Auta.

It flew with them quite high up in the air across the land. It flew quite high up in the air, always higher and always higher. Dan-Auta looked at the bird ; he saw how the bird twisted his tail (the steering movements are meant) and said : " Ssara ! " Ssara said : " Kai ! Dan-Auta ! What wantest thou now ? " Dan-Auta sobbed. Ssara quickly said : " My Dan-Auta ! Do not cry ! Thy father and mother said thou must not cry ! Do not cry ! Say what thou wilt ! " Dan-Auta said : " I want to take hold of the bird's tail." Ssara said : " If thou dost so, the Shurua will let us drop this minute and then we shall be dashed to the earth. We shall both die. But thy father and thy mother said thou wert not to cry. Do it, then ! " Dan-Auta said : " I do not care whether we die or not." He took hold of the Shurua's tail. The Shurua clapped his wings together. Ssara and Dan-Auta fell down.

Just when Ssara and Dan-Auta were quite near the ground, a great Gugua (whirlwind, waterspout) was tearing across the land. Ssara saw the Gugua and called out : " My Gugua, behold ! we shall be dashed to the earth and die, unless thou catch us up and put us (gently) on the ground." The Gugua came near ; it picked up Ssara and Dan-Auta and put them (gently) on the ground. Ssara and Dan-Auta were in a strange land in the bush.

Ssara walked with Dan-Auta through the bush and came to a path. Ssara and Dan-Auta followed the path which led to a large town. This city was larger than any other city. It was surrounded by a mighty Birni (wall). There was a great iron gate in this wall which was shut every evening when it grew dark. For every evening, when the darkness fell, came a huge Dodo. This Dodo was as large as a donkey, but it was no donkey. This Dodo was as long as a python, but it was no python. This Dodo was as strong as an elephant, but it was no elephant. This Dodo had eyes which shone in the night like the sun at noon. This Dodo had a tail. Every night it crawled to the city. That is why the wall with the iron gate had been built round the city. Ssara and Dan-Auta followed the path until they came unto the great city

They entered the city ; they went through the door. By the wall, near the gate lived a Sohua (*i.e.*, an old woman). Ssara and Dan-Auta went to the Sohua. Ssara spoke to her. Dan-Auta listened. The Sohua said : " I will take thee and thy brother in. But every night a huge Dodo comes before the city and sings with a loud voice. Then everything in the city must be silent. If anyone were to answer it, the Dodo might come into the city and kill us all. Take care that little Dan-Auta does not scream at night and then ye can lodge with me."

Dan-Auta heard all this. Ssara and Dan-Auta lodged at the Sohua's by the wall near the great gate.

Next day Ssara went into the city to get food. While she was away, little Dan-Auta also went out. He took a billet of wood here and a billet there, carried the pieces of wood to Sohua's house and hid them behind the wall. Dan-Auta ran about and gathered a great deal of wood. He stacked the wood up behind the wall. Dan-Auta looked at the wood-stack and said : "That is wood enough!" Then he ran into the city again. Here Dan-Auta took away one Makodi (the round, hard stones with which the millstones are chipped off) here and another Makodi there. He carried the Makodi to the Sohua's house and hid them by the wall. Dan-Auta carried nearly one hundred Makodi to the hiding-place and laid them on top of the wood billets. Then he looked at the heap of Makodi and said : "There are enough Makodi. All I want now are tongs." Dan-Auta ran into the city, went to a forge and took the tongs. He carried the tongs to the Sohua's house and hid them near the wood pile and the Makodi behind the wall. And none knew all that little Dan-Auta had gathered and hidden.

When evening came, Ssara said to him : "Come, now, into the house, my Dan-Auta, for the great big Dodo will soon be here and then he may kill us!" Dan-Auta said : "I want to stay outside to-day." Ssara said : "Come in!" Dan-Auta sobbed. Ssara quickly said : "My Dan-Auta! Do not cry! If thou wantest to stay outside, stay outside!" Ssara and the Sohua went inside and shut the door. Dan-Auta stayed outside.

He sat down before the Sohua's house. She and Ssara and all the other city folk had gone into their houses and shut the doors after them. Little Dan-Auta was the only one in the open. He ran to where he had hidden the wood and the Makodi and set fire to the wood. It made a great fire. The Makodi lay in the fire and grew very hot. When Dan-Auta had been sitting by the fire for a while, Dodo came out of the woods towards the city.

Dan-Auta climbed on to the Birni and saw Dodo coming in the distance with eyes shining like the sun and like a fire. Dan-Auta heard Dodo—for Dodo sang with a strong voice all through the bush :

"Wuajinni agarinana ni Dodo!"

"Who is there in the city like unto me, Dodo!"

When Dan-Auta heard this he sang down from (his place on) the wall into the bush in answer to the Dodo :

"Naijakai agarinana naijakai ni Auta."

" I am like unto thee in this city, I am like unto thee, I, Auta ! "

When Dodo heard this, it came closer to the city. It came quite close to it and sang :

" Wuajinni agarinana ni Dodo ! "

When Dodo sang this, all the trees in the bush quivered and the dry grass began to burn for a great space round about.

And Dan-Auta sang :

" Naijakai agarinana naijakai ni Auta ! "

When Dodo heard this, it climbed on the wall. Dan-Auta climbed down and went to the wood pile where the Makodi were red-hot in the fire. And Dodo sang out across the city from the top of the wall with a mighty voice :

" Wuajinni agarinana ni Dodo ! "

When it sang this, the iron gate shook and all the houses shook. It was as though one hundred smiths smote upon their anvils at the same time, or as if ten thunderstorms broke over one river. All the trees in the city withered in the glare of the fire which shone out of Dodo's eyes ; all the city folk within their houses heard it and felt the heat beating through the walls ; all the people were so terrified that they thought they would die. And not a soul in the houses dared to open his mouth.

And now Dan-Auta seized a red-hot Makodi with the tongs of iron and sang :

" Naijakai agarinana naijakai ni Auta ! "

Dodo climbed down from the Birni. Wherever Dodo trod, the earth chasmed. Wherever Dodo turned its eyes the walls gaped. Dodo opened its jaws and roared :

" Wuajinni——"

But Dan-Auta hurled ten red-hot Makodi into the yawning maw. Dodo gulped them down and hoarsely sang :

" —agarinana——"

Dan-Auta threw ten more glowing Makodi into the yawning maw. Dodo gulped them down and hoarsely sang :

" —ni Dodo ! "

And now Dan-Auta again threw ten red-hot Makodi into the yawning maw. Dodo gulped them down and groaned. Then Dan-Auta hurled all the remaining red-hot Makodi in the throat and sang :

"Naijakai agarinana naijakai ni Auta !"

Dodo died. Dan-Auta looked at Dodo. Then he went into the Sohua's house. She had a kororo (leather bag) in which there was a wuka (little knife). Dan-Auta took the kororo, went out again to where the dead Dodo lay and cut off Dodo's tail (utshia) with the wuka. This he put into the kororo. Then he went inside the house with the bag, lay down beside Ssara and fell asleep.

And now there was no sound at all within the city ; not even the tiny ants were heard ———

Next morning the people came out of the houses and ran to the Serki. The King asked the people : "What was it ?" The people said : "We cannot tell. We were like to die with fear. It was on the side where the gate of iron is." The King said to the Chief of the huntsmen (Serki Mahalba) : "Go thither and see what it was !"

The Serki Mahalba went thither. From afar he saw the Dodo dead and approached it slowly. The Serki Mahalba said : "That is the mighty Dodo. The mighty Dodo hath been slain !" He ran back to the King and said : "A man hath killed the mighty Dodo and cut off its tail !" The King said : "Is the mighty Dodo verily dead ?" The Serki Mahalba said : "The Dodo is dead !"

The King said : "I will ride there myself and see it !" He mounted his horse. The Dogari surrounded him and accompanied him to where the Dodo lay dead. The King said to the Dogari : "See ye whether it be dead indeed." The Dogari went there, slow of foot. They came back running and said : "The mighty Dodo is dead and its tail has been cut off." The King dismounted. He approached the Dodo with measured tread and saw that the Dodo was dead. He gazed upon it and said : "This Dodo which hath threatened our city from the time of our forefathers of the olden times, this Dodo who hath made many die from terror, this mighty Dodo now lies dead within the city. A man slew it ! A man cut off its tail. Let the man who slew it and cut off its tail come unto me. Let him lay the tail before me. Then will I give him one-half of my city and he shall be King after me !" Thus spake the King. Then he mounted his horse and rode back home.

All the people heard what the King had spoken. Then one,

who had a horse, went home, cut off the horse's tail, went to the King, showed the tail, saying : " Behold, I slew the Dodo in the night." And another, who had a cow, cut off his cow's tail, went to the King, saying : " Behold, I slew the Dodo in the night." And another, who had a camel, went and cut off his camel's tail, went to the King and said : " Lo ! I slew the Dodo in the night." And one, who had an ass, went home, he cut off the ass's tail, went to the King, showed him the tail, and said : " Look, I slew the Dodo in the night."

The King said : " Liars are ye all ! Take ye the tails of the horses and cows and camels and asses and carry them home again. Search for the man who the mighty Dodo hath slain ! " There was an old man there, who said : " I do not think it was a man of this city who slew the mighty Dodo. I think it must have been a stranger. I, like many others too, heard his voice in the night. The voice was not that of a man, but the voice of a boy. It must be a stranger boy who dwelleth near the gate of iron, yet who it is I cannot say ! " Then the King said : " Near the gates there lives an old wife with whom at times strangers have their lodging. Inquire ye of the Sohua ! "

The people went and called the Sohua. She called Ssara and went with her to the King. The Sohua said to the King : " This woman Ssara and little Dan-Auta lodge with me ! " The King asked Ssara : " Did little Dan-Auta slay the mighty Dodo ? " Ssara said : " I cannot say. He must himself be questioned." The King said : " Summon little Dan-Auta ! "

The King's people came to Dan-Auta.

They said to Dan-Auta : " Come with us ! The King desires to see thee ! " Dan-Auta arose. He put the leathern wallet on and went with the people to the King. The people said to the King : " This is Dan-Auta ! " The King asked him : " Dan-Auta ! Didst thou slay the mighty Dodo and cut off its tail ? " Dan-Auta opened the leathern wallet. He drew forth the mighty Dodo's tail and gave it to the King. The King said : " Yea, Dan-Auta is the one who slew the Dodo."

The King gave Dan-Auta a hundred women, a hundred camels, a hundred horses, a hundred slaves, a hundred cows, a hundred robes, a hundred sheep and one-half of the city.

Old Nupé chased bronze vessels of the 15th century, about ½th of natural size.

And it is since the time when the Dodo lived that the Houssas build Birnis (ramparts) round their towns.

\*    \*    \*    \*    \*    \*    \*    \*

There are many variants of this charming tale current in the Houssa and Nupé countries. There is no difficulty in proving its dissemination from Mossiland to the furthest East and South. The substance of it is mostly all kinds of mischief done by two children of men on their wanderings, in flight, as it were, and whom the legend eventually often places in the sky where they remain as senders and preparers of storm. And thus we get into touch with the mythological content of the legend.

Yet we gain more available material for our own research for proof of migration, related civilizations and historical connection if we follow the leading idea of the contest with the dragon which also reaches its culmination in the history of Dan-Auta. We saw that the Fight with the Dragon came from Libya as a chronicle of heroic deeds; heard that the Mande in the West attribute these to the founder of the first Islamite Emir Empire; and that versions of it are also current as well in the advanced posts existing in the districts of the most distant South-east. We saw that the Songai on the Niger glorify the founders of their kingdoms and civilizations with it, and are able to ratify the conclusions arrived at by establishing the fact that the Houssas also are familiar with it by their original history of Dan-Auta. For they, like the Songai, say that the founder of the royal family, Bayajidda, a man from the East, came to Dowra, there slew the great Serpent which lived near a well and prevented people from getting water and thus freed the country from a terrible scourge and married the Queen of Dowra. H. R. Palmer also heard the legend in Kano. But what they told me was that Bayajidda was a Persian who, as already mentioned, came from the East.

We have learnt, then, that the Libyan inheritance from the North, from the Sahara, spread over the whole breadth of the Eastern Soudan; that it was incorporated in the West with traditions relating to the origin of the first Mahommedan Emir rule and in the East with the traditional history of the Persian migration from out of the East. In the introductory chapter of this part of the book I gave a sketch of the two streams of culture from the Western Powers which broke upon each other on the Niger-bend and pressed onwards under the banner of Islam in historical times and also of the Eastern Powers which now, for the first time, may be characterized as Persian. Both of these streams came into collision within historical periods. But the Libyan element in particular, which was so observable in the Fight with the Dragon, was the cultural heritage of them both.

We will, then, pay somewhat more attention to the stream from the East, which we now recognize as having flowed from Persia.

Mossi-Shâmâns.
( *Drawn by Fritz Nansen.* )

# CHAPTER XXIII

## A RACE OF EMPERORS AND KINGS

### (HISTORY OF THE MOSSI NATIONS)

The Mossi are the outposts of the stream of civilization from East to West, and as such had to bear the brunt of the advance of Islam from the West, North-west and South-west —The Mossi tradition, which describes the events which occurred between 1289 to 1908 A.D.

WHEN the heathen power on the Upper Niger and the Senegal was broken by the Emir Diarra, as the protagonist of the Mahommedan faith in the year 1235, and the door thus opened to Islam and the Moorish traders, commercial relations between the Sahara and Western Africa were developed with a rapidity which could bear no other construction than its being the revival of similar relations at a very early period indeed. For a vellum MS. records the names of seventy-four rulers before the Fulbe dynasty in Gana, which there occupied the throne in 300 A.D., running through twenty-one generations, and relates that they obtained great quantities of gold from the Southern countries, that is to say, from the Gold Coast hinterlands. In West and Central Africa seventy-four rulers meant on an average a period of one thousand years, so that, assuming this calculation to be correct, it brings us approximately

495

to the time coterminous with the appearance of the Carthaginians on North African sea-borders. But, granting the possibility of its exaggeration, the mere statement of this very ancient trade in gold proves that the road really existed in very olden days and was merely re-opened by the champions of Islam.

The carriers of Mahommedanism on the Libyan and Moorish route along which the stream of gold flowed northwards shortly afterwards, were the Mandingoes. The highway was not opened up by fighting men, but by travelling merchants called Diula. These founded Kong, which was not a military capital, but a centre of commerce. The Diula controlled the gold-countries in the South and while the Mandes led by the Emir Diarra marched down the Niger in the North, conquered the countries with the sword and made it accept the Faith of Islam, the Mande-Diula crept, so to say, on stockinged feet through the auriferous districts, insinuated themselves into Ashanti and pushed on to the Dagombas among whom they must, according to all living tradition, have occupied a very prominent position.

At first the great heathen countries in the centre remained untouched. The Mali ruler only sent his emissaries into these regions from the North, and we still find the remnants of these old families in the Jarsi (a compound of Diarasi ; the families of these Jarsi are the Kone and Fofana). The Jarsi, or Morenga, were time and again pushed aside by the Mossi and attained no power. Force of arms was no more capable of completely subjecting these nations from the direction of the North of the Niger than the Egyptian kingdom was able to maintain a permanent ascendancy over the desert tribes in the East and West.

While, however, the strength of the warlike invasion from the valley of the Niger was unproductive, the trade propaganda of Diuladom continually crept further southwards. Finally, about one hundred and fifty years ago, the Tshokossi advanced under Mande leadership to the north of the German colony of Togoland as far as Sansanemango. This noiseless progress in the South went on without interruption ; the violent invasion from the North was a piecemeal occurrence.

Islamite Mande power thus held the heathen tribes dwelling in the Niger-bend and drawing their resistance from the East in a

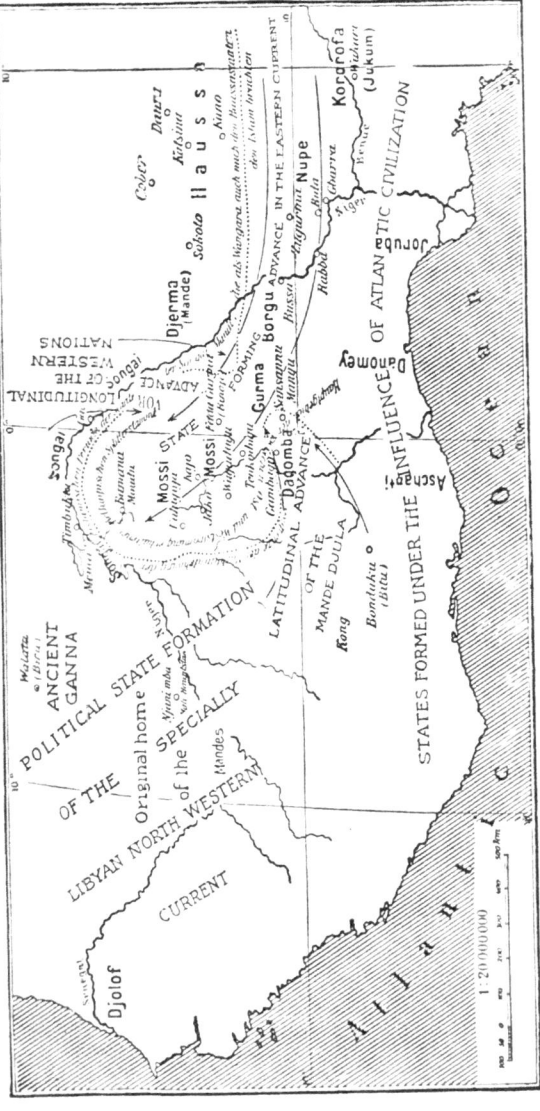

MARCH OF CIVILIZATION IN WEST SOUDAN IN THE MIDDLE AGES.

Translation of the German *within* the dotted lines: Region mainly inhabited by the Ethiopian "disciplive" tribes preserved between streams of migration from the East and the West.

Translation of the German *outside* the dotted lines: Limit of sphere of power exercised by the States formed during the Islamite period by the Songol Mande, who also brought Islam into the Hausa States — to the Watzata.

firm grip.   The sharp pricks inflicted from the Niger and the Diula-Volta countries came closer and closer together like a pair of slowly grasping pincers which seemed to be fairly near each other as early as the beginning of the fourteenth century.   As shown on the map, only the countries of Borgu and Gurma, next to Mossi, still lay between the approaching cutting edges of the forceps, and then the driving power of Islamite Mandedom was spent.   They cut through the Songai in the North, the Dagomba in the South, but the tough resistance offered by the Borgu, Gurma and Mossi nations made their complete conjunction impossible.   And what El Bekri, the Venerable, had already set down in 1068 A.D., namely, that the natives of these middle regions exterminated all those who fell into their hands (*i.e.*, all Mahommedans), was substantiated.

In spite, then, of its prowess in battle and pliability in trade, Islam's assault failed in its attempt to overcome this central block of heathendom.   This fact brings us face to face with a problem in the history of civilization.   The Mahommedan Mandingo power was victorious all along the line, until it had advanced thus far.   Nay, more, not only had this invasion spent its initial force, but one of its consequences was that these citadels of " heathenry," excited by the approaching wave of elements foreign to themselves, rose in revolt and dealt the spirit which threatened them out of the North-west some pretty shrewd blows to the sensible hurt of Islam's trade and political power.   The protrusion of the southern cutting edge of the pincers resulted in the amalgamation of the central powers (see *infra :* the legend of the alliance of the Gambaga and Bingo kingdoms) ; it roused the strength of the people from its slumbers, and, led by Uidi Rogos, whom we may imagine to have been a great hero, the central powers rebelled against the ecclesiastical emporia of commerce in the North, against Timbuktu and Wallata, in the name of the Mossi, and so thoroughly laid waste these beautiful towns in 1329 and 1480 that the natives of Timbuktu to-day, almost five hundred years later, still speak of it with accents of horror. The famous Sonni Ali, like many of his predecessors, undertook a fruitless campaign against Bingu, the oldest metropolis, which is simply named Be in the North and whose ruler's name was Be-naba. In the year 1498 the Emperor of the Songai made vain efforts to agitate a war of conversion against these defensively consolidated civilized nations by proclaiming a "Holy War." The Libyan-Islamite culture of Mandeland had no other resource than withdrawal. It was powerless to complete the hold of its claws. Its strength was exhausted. At that time the countries on the Lower Niger and Benue had been spared. And it was only that last great wave of Mahommedanism of much more recent date, namely, the movement among the Fulbes which succeeded in penetrating the eastern lands of the Niger and Benue and opening the road to the East in the nineteenth century, but failed to conquer this central block of the Mossi-Gurma-Borgu tribes.

Up to the present time the particulars of this protracted period of growth have only been ascertainable from Mahommedan chronicles. But for those who have read and recognized in them the extraordinary power wielded by the Mande-Songai princes and thus learned how these rulers squandered the gold out of Bitu and innumerable human souls from the South on their pilgrimage to Mecca, the fact that this individual block remained impervious to their influence is a continual source of amazement. And even though the fact of the rapid conversion to Islam of Western Mandingoland, the districts, namely, between the Senegal and the Niger, and the remarkable rise of the states thus founded by Mahommedan culture to great power, are evidence of a very considerable predisposition to this special form of civilization and of the fact that these nations must have been already imbued with a fair amount of political sagacity peculiarly their own and acquainted with methods of organization on an extensive scale, yet, for all that, the amount of resistance shown by that central group which was inaccessible to Mahommedan influences also proves their possession of an equal, though possibly not a profounder or more vigorous, independent civilizing impulse.

In this connection the laws of physical geography, that is to say, the dominant factors in universal history, found their indisputable expression. While the assumption of a former civilization imported from Libya will primarily serve with regard to the West, it is still insufficient to explain matters with respect to the East as far as concerns that part south of the Niger-bend and the Houssa countries. Mahommedan civilization penetrated into the West across the chain of kingdoms which must in former times have been firmly established in the Interior parallel to the coast. The wave from the Sahara was, for this reason, able to make headway and advance to the South, especially by confining itself to commercial methods and avoiding the paths of aggressive warfare. And to the same extent as the influence attained by the Libyan civilization which came from the North the Islamite proselytizers and state-founders were victorious, but no more so, in consequence of the law imposed upon them by the natural physical conditions of the country. Yet neither the Libyan influence from the North nor the Islamite conversion which succeeded it affected the centre, that is, the countries south of the Niger-bend or the Houssa states. Here it conflicted with another stream which was crossing the continent from East to West. Here its force was dissipated because its impact was at right angles to this horizontal current. This horizontal movement of the Soudan is represented by the Adamawa, Nupé, Borgu and Mossi civilizations which tended westwards from the East, and the essential purport of what now follows will be to pursue it, trace its true inwardness and discover its historical growth. (*Vide* the introductory chapter of this part.)

\* \* \* \* \* \* \* \*

This vertical impact has been recorded by Mahommedan travellers and university scholars of the Niger-bend in documentary history. The region in the East which was affected by the horizontal movement also possessed some chronicles; but, as far as they are of any literary value, these have not been discovered. The documents and vouchers of the latter stream of tendency are stored in the retentive power of man's memory.

I can call nothing to mind which so strongly caught hold of and stirred me as the manner in which these records of the Mossi Empire were brought to light. Never shall I forget the moments in which its venerable priests squatting on the ground in front of me, drew five, ten, seventeen, or, I forget how many, strokes in the sand, saying: " This king, this Naba, had so-and-so many sons, of whom this one founded this province, that one founded that province ! " and so on. These men were able to count up thirty-six emperors and their surviving sons up to several hundred, who all lived, acted, founded kingdoms and expressed themselves in characteristic fashion within a space of half one thousand years, taken altogether. They were able to do this marvellous thing because their vocation compelled them to repeat the tale of those who had gone before at the yearly kingly ancestral sacrifices and to recite the names of the royal antecedents in their correct sequence.

I was frequently able to check their statements, which resulted in scarcely perceptible variations. The priests of the collateral branches of the main stem supplied an efficient counter-check; but the principal thing was the opportunity thus afforded of identifying a few facts and leading incidents with the statements of Mahommedan scribes, which made the preparation of a historically accurate genealogical tree possible. The best control of all, however, consisted in the discovery that adding up individual rulers' separate reigns backwards produced the same date as that given by the chroniclers.

A great and rounded piece of work, which, generally speaking, may be considered trustworthy, is, therefore, in evidence. It was naturally not quite easy to induce the high priests to speak, because, on the one hand, even in Mossiland, the zealous and pushful Islamite propagandists, supported by the French Government, try to suppress and discredit " heathendom," and because, on the other hand, modern economic conditions tend to decrease the interest taken by the people in their ancient lore. The consequence is that there are not many old people left both able and ready to unload their store of knowledge and I think I may say that it was high time that the work, of which this book is the outcome, should be taken in hand when I travelled these countries.

\*     \*     \*     \*     \*     \*     \*     \*

The destruction of Timbuktu by the Mossi in A.D. 1329 is mentioned in the historical work whose author is Abderahman Ben Abdalla ben Imram ben Amir, the scribe. The traditional statement of the Mossi priests is to the effect that this annihilation was accomplished by Uidi-Rogo, who achieved it in the fortieth of the fifty-four years of his reign, and this proves that the growth of the Mossi Empire began in the year 1289.

In this particular year there were four kingdoms in the Eastern regions of the Niger-bend, viz. :

Firstly : The Songai kingdom, extending from Niameane upstream along the Niger, and bounded on the West by the Mande kingdom ;

Secondly : The Borgu kingdom, situate on the Niger to the South of the Songai ;

Thirdly : The Bingo kingdom (called Gurma by the Northern tribes), which stretched westwards from Borgu as far as present Dagombaland ;

Fourth, and lastly : The Gambaka kingdom, which lay in the northern portion of the English Gold Coast Settlement.

According to tradition, the most powerful of these four was Borgu (or Bussu). Bingo, or Gurma's sphere of influence was mainly confined to the Niger-bend districts, where its army leaders conducted many campaigns. Gambaka, however, was said even then to have had a city in which the Mande-Diula did a great trade. The remainder of the vast country to the South of the Niger-bend was inhabited by a swarm of small tribes, whose conditions of culture were such as we can study to-day in the Dafina, the province of the Bobo folks. There were several little provinces, or independent princedoms, besides these four great realms, which must have had very singular organizations of their own ; and the chief one of these was Namba, a kingdom of limited area, in the neighbourhood of modern Tekondugu.

Now, the Gambaka-naba had a lot of daughters, but no son. In compliance with an ancient custom he had forbidden his eldest daughter, named Niallanga, or Yendanga, to marry. This girl's mission in life was, on the contrary, that of a warrior princess, to be commander-in-chief of Gambaka-naba's soldiers and carry on wars abroad. This princess was, however, not cheerfully willing to renounce the matrimonial idea. One day there was a difference of opinion between the father and his child; so she mounted her stallion in great anger and rode off. The quarrel originated in a proposal to sack the quarters of the Mande merchants, which the Gambaka-naba wished might be spared at whatever cost. The Princess said : " Thou forbidd'st me to marry, O my father ! and allow'st me only the conduct of war ! But now thou wouldst even rob my free-will in the conduct of war, and refuse me permission to exterminate these Mande-Diula whom I loathe. Therefore will I wage war where it listeth me and do what befits me at my own good pleasure ! " So the Princess rode away.

She rode a great way, as far as the land of Namba. There she met a mighty hunter, whose legendary name is either Riale, or Riaele, or Torse, or Tonsa. He was the King of Bingo's son and thus of aboriginal princely Gurma stock. The Princess, similarly to the Kalunda and Bihe Saga, fell in love with the Prince and abode with him. The fruit of their union was the doughty hero, Uidi-Rogo. The founder Tonsa's tomb is unhesitatingly relegated to the locality of Komtoiga.

Uidi-Rogo inherited his mother's hatred of the Mande and Marenga, as the Mossi call the Songai. Directly he had grown up, he gathered a host about him, was made Naba of Namba, and as Namba-naba began his expeditions to all the points of the compass. He thrust the Marenga and the Jarsi aside all over the country ; advanced further and further north in this campaign and in the fortieth year of his reign reached the Niger, crossed it and destroyed the great commercial centre, Timbuktu, that city of ancient renown. The people there tell tales about it to-day. They say that once a great water from the Sahara came tearing across the city of Timbuktu towards the Niger ; that Timbuktu had once stood and flourished beneath the shade of gigantic forests of Borassus palms in days of old. But the mighty Mossi hero had filled the river in. He caused whole forests to be felled with the axe and the river-bed filled with tree-trunks and earth. He razed the city to the ground and made sacrifices upon its ruins to the black standard which had led his van. Timbuktu recovered but slowly from the blow and its palms took long in growing sufficiently tall again to yield the timber from which the great Songai Emperor was afterwards able to build his great fleet of warships.

When this war was over, Uidi-Rogo left behind him two sons, Ravi-naba and Sonima-naba, in the country north of the Niger. They were a race of mighty heroes, who did not, however, at first co-operate with the Mossi tribes, which were spreading over the South. The popular legend is eloquent on the point that they were not only descendants of the warriors' parent stock, but also well versed in the construction of large edifices. They were extraordinarily cruel and violent and used all the instruments at their command to force the natives to build monumental aids to civilization. The natives' liveliest memory is that of the Uamtananga-naba, described as the Terror of the Land and the brutal champion of Mossi-dom. The story goes that he ruled over the land of N'deraogo Djitti and Gurga. Now, as he often went to and fro to Sabunu, because a woman he loved to madness lived there, the unevenness of the road, which ran through a hilly district, one day caused him to summon all the smiths. He commanded them to make him a good road. They carried out his behest, and made a cutting about forty-four yards wide at the top and twenty-two at the bottom, measurements which Captain Noirée has corroborated, and it is said that this cutting can still be seen. He was inconceivably cruel. Once he saw a woman, with a child on her back, busied in grinding corn with a pestle. The Naba commanded her to lay the child in the mortar and bray it. The frightened creature did as she was bidden, but when the babe smiled at her, she flung the uplifted brayer away, leaped at the tyrant's throat, and throttled him. And this was the way he died.

While the sons of the Empire's founder were behaving like this in the North, and when Uidi-Rogo lay dying, he appointed his nephew Djugulana as Great-naba. This prince waged the original wars against the nations in the West. These tribes were called Ninisi. In this campaign Djugulana at first tried bows and arrows. But the contests in archery gave him no advantage. He could not gain the mastery. So he applied to a neighbouring people, the Nionjonsi, saying : " If you change yourselves into a wind and blow down this town or that, I will give you something good to eat." Then the Nionjonsi made themselves into whirlwinds and blew down all the town walls and dwellings of the Ninisi. Or Djugulana would offer the Nionjonsi oxen or cowrie shells, for which they would also render him similar service. At that time many people could be seen squatting about the country, who sat crouching together, and were lean and always wanting to sleep. If they were roused up and asked : " What ails ye ? " they answered : " It is the Kunugunku (sleeping sickness) which the Nionjonsi were commanded to blow into us by Naba Djugulana." Many folks' legs or arms or other parts of the body swelled up. All these things were the work of the Nionjonsi, who turned themselves into a wind at a word from the Naba Djugulana. And this ruler drove the Ninisi Westwards by these methods.

His successor was Naba Ubri, who is so far rightly entitled to be called the founder of the Mossi Empire because he built the capital city of Wagadugu. His predecessor had unsuccessfully waged war against the Gurunsi, the tribes in the South. Ubri continued the struggle with redoubled energy and was engaged in almost unbroken warfare ; sometimes he spent forty days in the bush without a roof to his head. But he gave himself no rest until he had pushed back the Gurunsi over the Volta and planted his flag in Boroma as a frontier. And, in addition, he conquered a few Northern provinces in the course of his extensive campaigning. He got as far as a town in the North which was simply called Tenga (*i.e.*, earth), at first, but afterwards Ubri-Tenga.

On one occasion Ubri had a desire to conquer the city of Kudugu, but saw that he could not achieve this. And then he was attacked by a fear of a bad end to this war and drew off to Nanjali, where he sickened and died. His people carried off his corpse on their heads. They wanted to take him to Tenkodugu for burial, but only reached Tenga with the remains. The people of Tenga said : " Bury, we beseech ye, the Naba in our town." They answered : " Nay, we will bear him back as far as Tenkodugu." But the corpse-bearers, too wearied to go on at once, lay themselves down and slept. While they were asleep the Tenga people quickly dug out the grave, prepared everything properly and stole the body of the Naba. They had finished by midnight and all had been done in absolute secrecy. When the bearers woke up, their Naba Ubri was entombed, but they did not know where. And so there was nothing for it but to go on without him and return to Tenkodugu. The people of Tenkodugu asked them : " Where is the Naba Ubri ? " The corpse-carriers said : " He desired to attack the town of Kudugu, but then retreated to Nanjali, fell ill there and died. We took him on our heads and would have brought him back here. But while we were taking some rest from fatigue in Tengaland, the folk of Tenga stole the remains and laid them to rest in their own town." Since then the place is no longer plain Tenga, but Ubri-Tenga or

Naba-Ubri-Tenga. And the natives of to-day enjoy a singular privilege, namely, that of stealing the King's property unpunished.

Ubri was succeeded by his eldest son, the Naba Sorroba, whose first act was to summon the great ones of the kingdom, namely, the Uidi-naba, the Lachabe-naba, the Gunga-naba, the Tansoba-naba, the Kamsogo-naba and the Ballum-naba to his side. But when they had stayed with him six days, the Emperor said : " I will now kill an ox on the grave of Ubri, my father. Hearken unto what I say to ye : in future an ox shall always be offered at this time to every Mogo-naba (or Emperor) who has died. And every Mogo-naba shall sacrifice an ox to his dead mother. In days to come that shall be law and custom ! " Thus Sorroba inaugurated the Basaga festival. Naba Sorroba also made other general laws. For instance, he established the custom of the three dances, Uarraba, Chigiba and Uando. He was a great organizer who spent his days in Lugusi, to the south-west of the Wagadugu district.

There is nothing much to say of the reigns of the next two Emperors, Nasikiemde and Narimtori, but the Mossi Empire grew considerably under the seventh ruler, Naba Nasibiri. The two provinces of Kajo and Katenga, whose capital is Uahiguja, attained their individual growth under his rule, not, however, without some very singular events and contests with respect to titular possession. It is necessary for the thorough comprehension of the native accounts to know that whenever a Mossi Emperor created a fresh province by transferring the fief of a country to be conquered or settled anew, a certain " medicine " or magic was carried into the new city from the centre of the Empire as a loan.

Now, Nasibiri had one daughter besides his sons and her name was Pawere or Bi-Kajo. There is a traditional story about her of which the correct interpretation is claimed by both the Jatenga and the Kajo people. Although it may be said with tolerable certainty that the events referred to concerned the Jatenga, I obtained the better version from the Kajos and give it here. The story is that there was a certain charm at the court of the Emperor, known as the " Pem-tiga " and this, like all other " State-magic," was in the keeping of the Gunga-naba. This " medicine " was a protection against arrow-wounds and even against arrow-poison. It was only necessary to strew a little powder scraped off the Pem-tiga upon the wound to ensure its healing. Or, also, before going on the warpath, to turn to this " magic " and say : " If I return unscathed from this battle, I will make thee a gift of a white fowl." This having been said, the protection of the Pem-tiga could be fully trusted. Now, Naba Nasibiri had, according to the custom, enfeoffed his sons with districts at the borders of the kingdom where a persistent struggle with the aboriginal inhabitants was always to be expected. The son, who was settled in Kajo, was especially exposed to constantly recurrent campaigns and suffered great losses in this archery contest with the natives who unceasingly menaced his own life as well.

So Kajo-naba's sister, whose memory is still green in history as the girl Pogo-bi-Kajo, determined to furnish her elder brother with a safeguard and to steal the charm Pem-tiga from her sire. She executed her purpose in the dark middle of the night. One evening the Gunga-naba saw the maiden, the Emperor's daughter, enter his house. He could think no evil of her. But next day he reviewed the Imperial sorcery stores and missed the Pem-tiga. He immediately went to the Mogo-naba and inquired : " Didst thou take the Pem-tiga into thine own keeping ? " Naba Nasibiri said : " Nay ; are they no longer in their place ? " The Gunga-naba said : " The Pem-tiga are no longer in my house. I assuredly saw Pogo-bi enter it yesterday at eve, but I know not whether she hath taken anything away." The Mogo-naba at once despatched horsemen with the Gunga-naba to find either the missing thing or the thief. The riders scoured the whole of the district, but found neither one nor the other. Pogo-bi was already too far away. She had fled to her brother in Kajo and given him the Pem-tiga. When she had done this she herself sent a message to her father the Mogo-naba of Waga-dugu, telling him : " It was I stole the Pem-tiga. My father sent my eldest brother to Kajo and there is so much shooting with arrows here that his life is in peril. Therefore, I brought the Pem-tiga to my eldest brother to use. If Naba Nasibiri desires the Pem-tiga again he must fetch them himself ! " Now, while some say that Naba Nasibiri left the matter where it was, others relate a very singular continuation.

Naba Nasibiri said : " Let the Pem-tiga remain where they

now are. But, come what come will, I will win back Pogo-bi, my daughter, who is the cleverest and bravest of all the women of Mossi. I shall follow her until I regain her." Naba Nasibiri set out with a vast army. The Princess gathered her fighting men and riders about her. She fled across the Niger and arrived at the great city of the Marengas. The Emperor pursued her. He conquered the city, took captive his daughter and went back with her. Thereafter Pogo-bi became the woman warrior champion of Naba-dom.

This ending of the Mossi version is of peculiar interest, because in the chronicles of the Songai for A.D. 1480 we find it recorded that the Emperor of the Mossi arrived at the city of Biro in July, obtained a victory over its warriors and left it again in a month. Curiously enough, this history states that he demanded a woman from the inhabitants who was the daughter of a very learned man and that he married her. It says that the Mossi king first conquered the city, took its people and their families captive, but lost his prisoners again in a battle.

The plain proof of our here having an historical event looked at from two sides, is further confirmed by the fact that the Askia was not satisfied with this result. On the contrary, in the year 1498, he moved in arms against this Emperor, who is referred to in the chronicle as Na-Assira, but in the North Mossi tradition as Naba Assiri. The Songai Emperor demanded the acceptance of Islam from the Mossi Emperor. The latter declared that he wished to consult his ancestors, betook himself to the temple set apart for the purpose and had the experience of seeing an aged person rising from the depths. The Mossi prostrated themselves before the shade of the departed, who in the name of his forbears stated that they would never consent to the Mossi becoming Mahommedans and that they ought sooner to fight to the last gasp against the Islamite armies. But as a matter of cold fact the Emperor's armies failed to subdue the Mossi nation.

This ruler, so important in history, was succeeded by Njiginjem, of whom legend has nothing to say except that he bribed the nobles of the kingdom not to make his son his successor according to custom. And this Naba Kundumje played a very significant part indeed ; the real consolidation and organization of the country, its division into large provinces, must be ascribed to him. He waged many wars and was himself a proficient in archery. He put his own sons at the head of the provinces. His principal achievement was the conquest of the North-west and the creation of the province of the Bussuma-naba, who, for his own part, then enfeoffed his younger brother, Mani-naba, with a district. Kundumje, however, was also the first to be compelled to take up arms extensively against his own relatives, the rebellious Mossi chiefs, and more especially the always independent gentlemen of the North, of the province Jatenga, made his life a burden to him. So then he founded the province of Jako, situate midway between Jatenga and the province of Wagadugu. He also called into being the towns Kumkiesse Tenga, then Tanga and Gjellogo and Powa-Ture in the South.

For whenever a new Emperor was placed upon the Mossi throne, the new ruler's eldest full-brother was formally and solemnly invested, so to say, with the robes of the father departed. He was entitled "Kurita," whereas the other full-brothers were called Kurita-damba. But the Kurita was the king of the exiled full-brothers. For immediately following the coronation, the Kurita and Kurita-damba were banished for life from the empire's metropolis. They lead a very peculiar existence. In general, the Kurita is an object of fear to Mogo-naba. Neither his name nor title are mentioned at court. But the king of the exiles and his brothers have possessions in some distant district or other. They pay no sort of taxes and suffer no punishment for their actions, which are closely akin to those of the old robber-barons. They are, for instance, at liberty to drive off the herds of the Mogo-naba, if they can, with impunity and even to steal the tribute from envoys on their way to the King. They are accountable to nobody. Many provinces of the Empire acquired their independence on these lines. The legend says so with respect to Bulsi-naba and we may assume it to have been so with regard to Jatenga-naba. But several of these Kuritas formerly went beyond the Empire and acquired new provinces for Mossi-dom. One of the consequences of this method was, on the one hand, the spread of the Mossi people and, on the other, the slow but sure process of individual detachment from the imperial bond and the disintegration of the actual Empire of the Mossi.

Unusual good fortune attended the military excursions of the

Emperor Kundumje. When he was warlike in mood he commanded the Tapo-Rane, the flag bearer, to bring him the Tapo-Koare, or imperial standard. Its pole was treated with sacrifices and " medicine " and the banner unfurled in the open country. The Mogo-naba took particular notice of the direction in which the prevailing wind blew out the banner's folds. He then set forth with his troops on the road so indicated, firing their ardour with : " Our flag is flying thither. Thither will we march. There we must and shall be victorious ! " And Naba Kundumje actually was crowned with success. He lost a great many of his men in the course of his reign. But he was not a brutal ruler in other ways and condemned but few to death in Wagadugu. He was, moreover, exceedingly open-handed, gave largely of slaves and women to each of his Tansoba (or generals). Nor was he greedy for personal treasures. His palace was at Kiu to the south-south-west of Wagadugu.

The Saga reports that his son Kuda waged many wars and made his sons administrators of the kingdom. His reputation was that of an excellent ruler, of great ability in the employment of various supernatural qualities. He died at Wagadugu after having been held in great honour.

His son Dangoegoma then occupied the throne, and displayed his father's transcendental faculty to a yet greater degree. The mass of legendary matter gathered round this potentate's name even starts with his immaterial birth.

Even in his father's lifetime Dangoegoma was a great and terrible Tansoba (or general). He was frequently absent for a long time from Wagadugu, busily occupied in the reduction of some outlying district. And he was also absent when his father, the Naba Kuda, died, and consequently the high dignitaries placed his younger brother, the Naba Jotembussuma, on the throne. On his unexpected return Dangoegoma found the place that was due to him already occupied. He immediately proceeded to the large paternal house to the west of the royal palace of Wagadugu and settled down in it. The news of his home-coming rapidly spread and next morning the imperial grandees put in an appearance to offer him their loyal salutation. But Naba Dangoegoma flew at them and said : " How come ye to instal my younger brother as

Mogo-naba without awaiting my orders ? " The great chiefs
prostrated themselves humbly and said : " We crave thy pardon,
but thou wert so long away abroad in the wars that we knew not
whether thou still wert alive. Therefore, we entrusted the kingdom
to thy younger brother Jotembussuma." Then Naba Dangoegoma
at once sent his younger brother, Naba Jotembussuma, this message :
" Let my younger brother leave Wagadugu and fly without any
delay, so that I may not set eyes on him." Wrathful he sat in the
midst of the nobles in the great house of his father. He blew with
his nostrils ; flames leaped from the earth and spread all over the
ground. Then he said : " Lead me to the grave of my father ;
I will see the grave of my father and weep." The great chiefs
conducted him thither. When Dangoegoma stood by the grave-
side, bloodgouts dropped from his left eye, tears from his right.
While this was happening Naba Jotembussuma called the nobles to
him and said : " I thank ye for all ye have done to me. But I
received my brother Naba Dangoegoma's message and now will
go hence. I shall leave Wagadugu. If my eldest brother should
die and ye still think me worthy, ye then may recall me." Then
Naba Jotembussuma went thence. When news of this was brought
to Naba Dangoegoma, he spake thus : " I have erred. I thought
my younger brother wished to do me an ill turn. But now I perceive that my younger brother is a right-loving man. When,
therefore, I die, choose ye not one of my sons to succeed me, but
my brother, the Naba Jotembussuma."

Naba Dangoegoma was fortunate in his wars, and proved himself
to be a potent Bumbande (sorcerer). When he attacked a city, he
quickly turned himself into a raging whirlwind and tore across the
enemy's town. He ruined the walls and the houses and afflicted
the people with sickness. One broke a leg, another had a swollen
belly, a third ophthalmia, a fourth the sleeping illness, a fifth lumbago,
and so on. But many accounts agree that he only waged
such cruel warfare before he became Mogo-naba in Wagadugu,
and not afterwards. After that event he was, on the contrary, a
peace-loving and very good ruler. When he felt that his end was
at hand, he summoned both his sons and said : " I once did my
younger brother a wrong in thinking that there was evil in his heart
and that he wished to usurp my throne. Yet it was not so. Now

I ask of you two that ye seek not to succeed me. I wish Naba Jotembussuma to be my successor. Even should Naba Jotembussuma die, I ask of you that neither you nor your descendants strive for the crown ; for I do not desire that there should be any strife between my descendants and his. As you believe, I shall be under the earth with my body. But I shall be present above in the air. Ask ye, therefore, the earth over my grave, should ye be in doubt what is my will, and I shall make it known to ye."

Having uttered these words, Naba Dangoegoma gave up the ghost. A grave was dug for his intended interment. While this was being done, his sisters sat by the corpse. But, when the dead man was to be removed in order to lower him into the tomb, he had vanished. Search after search was made without finding him. He had passed away into air. And it is known that he still floats about there. But he was looked for at that time in vain and since it was not desired that the grave should be filled a fowl and a ram were sacrificed to him and laid in the trench which led to the tomb.

The Naba Jotembussuma was recalled and made king in obedience to the will of his elder brother. He was very gentle and always endeavoured to carry out his elder brother's wishes, who, as he knew, hovered about him and watched all his actions. He reigned in Wagadugu.

Jandefo, who followed him, is said to have ruled in the kingdom's capital for no less than sixty years. He was not very bellicose, even when fresh to his monarchy, and in this respect, too, was different from the rest of the Emperors of the Mossi. He tried to get rid of an opponent by some secret means instead of by methods of warfare. He invited such as were his enemies to come to Wagadugu. Then he buried some " magic'" on the road which must lead them to his palace. When they set foot within the charm's sphere of influence they would die.

Now when he grew old, he fell a prey to all sorts of whimsies. One day, for example, he said to his people : " I have now been the Mogo-naba for a very long while, and during the time ye have given me such a quantity of cowrie shells, stone beads, cloth, and so forth, that I am sufficiently rich and a-weary of these things. Bring ye me, therefore, in future something else in token of your fealty and truth. Bring ye me ashes and cinders of charcoal. Heap them up in a pile in front of my palace." The people did this, and so arose that little mountain of rubbish which is still shown in Wagadugu as the Tampure of Naba Jandefo. It lies west of the town. It is a regular kitchen-midden, common enough towards the South, in the Gurunsi country, like those I frequently came upon afterwards in Djenn and Adamawa on the Benue river.

Natjeng, the King, had a name as a pattern of mildness. He was greatly esteemed and is said to have deserved his celebrity, because he had several foreigners in his service and induced many merchants from abroad to settle in Mossi. Such was his piety, that he doubled the usual number of the sacrifices on the grave. He offered up two oxen for one, two fowls for one, two dogs in place of one goat—and greater sumptuosity is unheard of in Mossiland, where dogs are considered the most precious of all smaller offerings. He ended his career in Dassuri, where he had lived and ruled for a space of ten years.

It is, furthermore, stated that Naba Namego held the sceptre for five years and conducted a long series of fights against the Busangsi and against Bussuma in the course of his reign. His expeditions were specially directed towards the East and he met with his end during one of these. His son Kiba reigned for two years and was succeeded by Naba Kimba, already well advanced in age when he assumed the reins of government. His feeble hands only grasped them for six years.

Naba Sana, also called Naba Djana, or Naba Gana, by the Mande, was promoted to the sovereignty by the aristocracy on Naba Kimba's demise. But a hard and grievous time was in store for the land directly he was installed into office. A drought set in. This fearful condition of things lasted three years, and during these the Mossi Empire had declined in its vigour. The Electors of the kingdom assembled and after prolonged consultation and questioning the priesthood discovered that Naba Sana brought nothing but misfortune upon the land. So they made arrangements for a great immolation and then went to the Mogo-naba to tell him : " Thou bringest the country nothing but evil ! Wilt thou go willingly or shall we slay thee ? " Naba Sana said : " I will go of my own accord." The grandees gave him a few women and slaves and what else was needful for life on the way, and so he bid his country and Wagadugu farewell.

Then the Electors put the crown on the brow of Naba Gobaga, who wore it ten years. He was a scourge to them all, for he sent all the Pewere-Soba (possessors of powerful " magic ") this summons : " Come to my Court," and when they obeyed it, entered into a friendly alliance with them against all the Electors of his provinces. Then, aided by the Pewere-Soba and the practice of their wizardry, he started making a riddance of all the nobility. During his reign there was no distress, but all the ancient dignitaries were put out of the way. It was the custom in those " good old times," when a good ruler died away from home during a military expedition and left a son, for that son to conduct the defunct monarch to Wagadugu, there to be himself invested with the insignia of royalty. Now, when Naba Gobaga departed this life in Ubri-Tenga this custom was neglected; he was buried where he fell and his corpse was not allowed to be carried to the imperial metropolis. For all the notables were his enemies and rejoiced at his death.

Thereupon Naba Sana was recalled to the seat of sovereignty in Wagadugu. He held it again for six years. But scarcely had he occupied it before the rains stopped again; the same misery was repeated, and his death, which was longed for, took place in Wagadugu.

One of the cruellest tyrants of all was said to be Naba Giliga. While eunuchs had formerly been imported from Gambaka, he inaugurated this custom of mutilation at home and began the exportation of eunuchs. When he was gathered to his fathers in Wagadugu, a very beloved and excellent monarch took matters in hand in Ubi, who governed the land for some eight years and died in his capital. Now and again he assembled his great men and slaughtered a hundred head of cattle. He instituted many sacrificial festivals, gave banquets and gifts to his nobles, and was wont to observe : " My father wrought the country great harm. I will try to do otherwise." His son Uatuba filled the shoes of his father and during eight years of rule made many insignificant incursions to the West, and during one of these also died away from his home.

Then the Emperor Uaraga wore the purple for about seven years, and is credited by tradition as one of the worst rulers of Wagadugu. He commenced a course of slaughter and ruin in Saptenga and continued it nearly as far as La. It seems that the whole district to the North had risen in arms. He took the most beautiful girls into his harem and castrated many of the natives. When he came to La, he said : " This neighbourhood pleases me extremely." He built a great city there and made arrangements for a magnificent harem.

He was displeased with a number of his worthies and the headman of the Kombissiri district was particularly obnoxious to him. He had him summoned and decapitated, putting his own second son in his stead. After that a war broke out between him and Nanon-naba. The battle, in which both sides were heavily smitten, lasted a week and Nanon-naba was almost victorious. But at the last the tide turned in the Emperor's favour, the rebel prince's head was struck from his trunk and the Mogo-naba put his own son in his place. After this success he went back to Wagadugu, lived there for one year more and died in that capital.

His successor, Dumburi, whose son was also "as strong as pepper," is the genuine representative of the ancient " heathendom " as contrasted with the ever increasingly aggressive Mahommedan influence. In him the old religion once more blazed up in extraordinary triumphs. His was a peaceful reign of thirty years, in which he tried and knew how to make the country's religious institutions beneficial to his regency. At that particular time the Nionjonsi dwelt in the land, especially in the townships of Boassa, Tengondogo (? Tenkodogu) and Sangadogo, the first two being in the East and the other in the West. The Nionjonsi were a people with a well-established reputation for extensive learning and a mastery of all things connected with matters of religious observances. So he sent envoys to all the places where the old inhabitants still practised their cult to its fullest extent with this message : " It hath come to mine ears that ye command quite special powers, that ye can, for example, create the wind and change yourselves into a leopard, produce pestilences, and that ye understand questioning the oracle of the earth. Come ye all then to Wagadugu and show me what ye can do, so that I also may show you adequate honours." The Nionjonsi, on receipt of the summons, set out and came to Wagadugu. Naba Dumburi said : " Show unto me now whether ye can make wind!" The Nionjonsi had brought with them their little holy axe, the Tobaga, whose handle was smeared with ox-blood and covered with feathers, and its bearer laid it on the wall. He said : "I need a white fowl." It was brought to him. The officiant priest stepped up to the Tobaga, saying : "Here do I offer thee a white fowl. I will gladly sacrifice it to thee. But lo, the Mogo-naba hath called us hither for us to show thy power. Now, let his eyes look upon it!" The man cut the fowl's throat. And at once a strong wind arose.

The Mogo-naba said to the Nionjonsi : "Now inquire ye of the earth oracle and tell me who of those around me is evil and who good." They interpreted the oracle. Then they said : "Such an one is not well-disposed, but such an one wishes thee well." Another interpreter improved on this saying : "It is not such an one, but it is such an one." Naba Dumburi noticed it all very carefully and when he saw there was a bungler among them, motioned him away ; but those among his entourage whom the wise men pointed out to him as being evilly disposed towards him he promptly dismissed and made up his Court of worthier persons. He did not act like his predecessors, who simply beheaded the untrustworthy.

After that Naba-Dumburi said : "I have heard that ye can also make rain. Is this the truth?" The Nionjonsi said : "We will prove it at once. Give us a white fowl." Thereupon a white fowl was given to them. The master of the Tobaga turned to the small holy axe with these words : "We know that thou hast done good only to our fathers and grandfathers before us (here all the names were recited). Naba Dumburi wants it to rain. That is a thing which is good. Show him that thou canst make the rain to come. I will also sacrifice unto thee a white fowl without blemish." When the fowl had been immolated, the rain began to fall. For the space of seven days the Nionjonsi abode with the Naba Dumburi. Then the Mogo-naba made them gifts of maize and clothing and cowrie shells, saying : "Now get ye back home. When I have need of ye, I will summon ye again." The Nionjonsi departed. The Naba Dumburi caused them to come to Wagadugu many times, asked them for advice, gave them presents, and kept constantly in touch with them.

The Emperor grew very old. It annoyed him that strife and dissensions took place among the dealers in the square north-east of the present market-place. He said : " Let the market be held in the square which lies next to my palace." In this way the locality where it is held to this day was settled.

The champion of the party of the Islamite priesthood was Naba Kom I., who reigned for seven years and was a contrast to the genuinely heathen Naba Dumburi whom he succeeded. His mother was a Mahommedan and, therefore, it was natural for him to be frequently guided by Mahommedans as opposed to the policy of the foregoing ruler, who gave the old native hierarchy great power. The following anecdote will illustrate the growth of this influence. In the early days the monarch was tyrannical and had all who crossed his path slaughtered regardless of justification. One day, however, the Mahommedans interfered and said to him : " It is certainly right that evil people should meet with evil fate. But thou shouldst not put to death without having weighed the right and the wrong in a court of justice ! " The Emperor thought this over. He inaugurated the salaam and became a mild, just and greatly beloved governor.

The reign of his successor, the Emperor Naba Saga, lasted six years. He had to spend the greater part of his life in hard fighting with his paternal uncles—struggles which had their beginning long before he was able to make his processional entry into the Imperial Court of Wagadugu. His father, Naba Kom I., sent him, while yet a boy, to the Court of Giba, or Gipo-naba, in the South, who was a near relative, the fifth son, in fact, of Naba Uaraga. The Gipo-naba simply pitched his nephew out as he was coming in. I could never learn why. Young Saga came to Wagadugu a fugitive and remembered the shame so put upon him. One day, without telling his father, he assembled some troops and attacked his uncle. The first time he had to retire with the worst of it ; but for three years he made a yearly trip to his uncle in battle array. His third campaign gave him the upper hand. He conquered the township and razed it. Many of its inhabitants fled to Gurunga. He killed his uncle and returned to the capital.

A year after that his father turned his face to the wall, and he was elected to fill the vacancy. But this was scarcely bruited abroad before all the surviving descendants of the Naba banded themselves together and took the field against Naba Saga. Their contention was that in the line of succession the uncles had priority, and then the sons of their generation. The Kom sons combined against the Uaraga sons to substantiate their brother's and their own claim to the kingly title. This led to a long and embittered struggle. Victory fluctuated. At first the Uaraga sons got the best of it. They got to Wagadugu, deposed Naba Saga and led him in shameful procession, namely, tied on an ass, southwards as far as Sapone. There the poor dethroned Emperor remained for three long years; then at last his brother's arms were crowned with glory and he was able to make his triumphal entry into Wagadugu, where he finished his reign in about three more years without further disturbance.

The next twenty-nine years were the reign of Lulugu, who was so busy in the wars that he passed hardly a month of them in Wagadugu. The wrestling for supremacy with the Bussuma-naba seems to have started this protracted period of bloodshed. The Emperor shattered his army and position. Then he marched forward. The Kumtega tribe, who seem to have also rebelled at first, made their submission without much resistance. Then the ruler marched further still to Garango and destroyed it. Finally the great war began against the Bussangi. When all these peoples had been overthrown, the victorious regent went back to Mani. Here another battle was fought, in which the Emperor was fatally hurt by an arrow. His body was brought to Wagadugu, where it was buried.

His eldest son, Sagadogo, held sway for seventeen years in all, in the first ten of which he enjoyed good, but for the remaining seven very bad health. There is a story of some particular kind of drink which he took every morning. He managed to arrange several intricate family matters with very great skill. His wretched condition at last grew such that he spent the last days of his life in a hut speechless and motionless.

Naba Karfo reigned seven years. Needless to say, he, too, had to deal with his rebellious relations. The Sondere-naba, named Kollogo, concluded amity with Uidi-naba, and both of these tried to get a following amongst the great ones at court, with whose help they hoped to shift Karfo. But the other Electors set their faces against this and informed Moga-naba of the plot. Naba Karfo lost no time in mustering his host and moved eastwards against the allied revolting forces. He beat them and pursued them as far as Bassoko (in the East). This war cost a great number of lives. When the Mogo-naba had gone back to Wagadugu the insurgent and conquered Uidi-naba soon followed him to offer submission and the Mogo-naba accepted this at once.

Now, the course of events following on this is extremely characteristic of negro diplomacy in general and the dependent relation in which the Mogo-naba of Wagadugu stood to the great Chieftains, whether these be called Electors or hereditary ministers. Naba Karfo accepted the homage of the traitor Uidi-naba, but did not dare to dismiss or supersede him. And yet he would have liked to get rid of him, no matter how. He therefore put this question to a few trusted adherents: " I will give a horse, a wife and one hundred thousand cowrie shells to anyone who has the courage to take Uidi-naba's life quickly and decently. Who dares to do it ? " A brave man called Daogo sent in his name. He said : " I will undertake it ! " Naba Karfo asked : " How wilt thou do it ? " Daogo said : " Give me two arrows." Naba Karfo gave him two virulently poisoned arrows and said : " Tell me exactly how thou proposest to settle this business." Daogo said : " I will creep into the courtyard of Uidi-naba at about six in the evening. Then I shall take away all the hay from the horses, and throw it aside where the moon shines upon it. When I have done so I shall hide. At night a horse will neigh because it cannot reach the hay lying near it. Uidi-naba, like a good master of horses, will wake up and come into the courtyard to see what may be the matter. He will see that the hay has been thrown to one side, will take it from the corner in the moonlight and want to throw it to the horses. That will be a good opportunity, for Uidi-naba will be in the moonlight." Naba Karfo said : " It is well. Go ! " The valiant Daogo went and did all in the manner described. When Uidi-naba stepped into the light to pick up the hay and strew it to the horses, Daogo put the arrow to the string and loosed it against Uidi-naba. Then he ran to the Mogo-naba's palace and said to him : " I managed it so ; Uidi-naba is dead." So Naba Karfo gave Daogo a horse, a

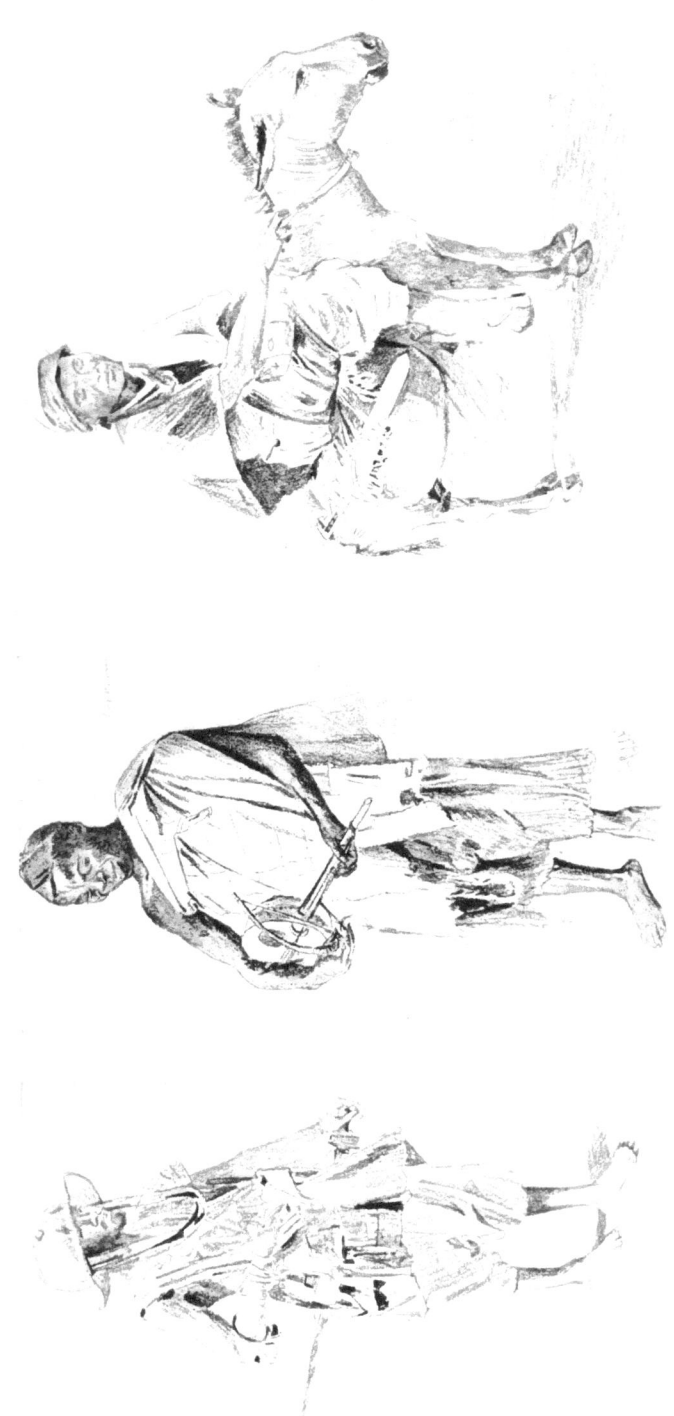

Eisu on their way to the coast lands.

(Drawing by Carl Arriens)

wife and one hundred thousand cowrie shells, and a beautiful garment besides.

The story of the whole matter's conclusion makes it, however, a perfect example of African imperial diplomacy. A few days later Mogo-naba, on thinking things over, came to this conclusion : "This Daogo is a dangerous person." And he gave orders to put him to death. So this was the end of valiant Daogo.

For five years the ruler in Wagadugu was Mogo-naba Bogo, uncle to Karfo, and he left a very bad odour behind him. He is rumoured to have often crept about the city at eve or at night dressed in old and dirty and tattered clothes. And then he eaves-dropped in the compounds listening to all that was said. If he heard anyone say anything bad or disrespectful about himself, the ruler, he had him killed next day by the familiar three blows with a club. The punishment for the slightest offence against his court and family goods during his reign was death ; every theft of a chicken was a capital offence. And report, moreover, declares him a drunkard. He conducted great military raids and plundering expeditions against Garango in the regions of the Bussangi in order to capture slaves, which he then put into circulation like any common dealer in cattle.

His successor, Naba Kutu, sat on the throne for seventeen years. A war against the town of Surruku is the principal incident during this lapse of time. This community's Naba died without leaving a successor and so it sent to Naba Kutu to petition for the despatch of a worthy descendant. The ruler sent them his own son. But the latter behaved so atrociously that after a time the Surrukuans made up their minds to expel him and soon actually carried out their resolve. Then the citizens chose a leader of their own. When Naba Kutu got wind of this there was nothing to do but to marshal an army against the revolting city if he wanted to have his own will respected and his family's authority upheld. The new lord of the city, elected by the inhabitants themselves, was energetic enough to offer resistance to the imperial will and to oppose the Mogo-naba's soldiery. The Emperor was compelled to do all in his power and thus the town met its fate by being destroyed.

Kutu's firstborn, Naba Sanum, ruled for eighteen years and waged war against Bussuma and Bulsi-Bulsena. It was in his time that the first two Europeans came to Wagadugu and the first of them, the German traveller G. A. Krause, got down at Malike; the second, the Frenchman Captain Binger, at Manam. This Emperor procured great droves of slaves in the East, died in Wagadugu and was there buried. He was succeeded by Uoboga, who lived in Wagadugu for eight years, during the time, in fact, which the French penetrators of the period jestingly called the " battles of the standards." Many representatives of the great European Powers then tried various ways of getting colonial expansion. Naba Uoboga also fell a victim of these flag-fights. French colonial history may, perhaps, some day devote a page or two to the closer verification of the details.

Uoboga died in exile. Naba Sigirri was the chief of Wagadugu for ten years, received the French troops now coming into the country as friends and, as described by them, seems to have had no great individual character. Naba Kom II., who ruled in my own time, did not impress me as a gifted person. He died of the smallpox after we had left French territory. The natives were of opinion that he had perished because he had bartered away the Imperial jewels shortly before his death.

And thus that mighty dynasty which once had conquered a gigantic district and offered the greatest opposition to Islam, which came from the West, found its close in comparatively very miserable personalities. The power of the Empire had already been crumbling for a considerable period, because the power of the family was too much divided and disunited in the development of its might.

Songai village on the Middle Niger.
*(Drawn by Fritz Nansen.)*

# CHAPTER XXIV

### THE GIANTS OF THE PAST

## *(Songai Legends)*

The archives of a nation, written and unwritten—The giant founder of the Songai; Nana Miriam, Fono and Fara Maka—The story of the woman Shâmân, Pa Sini Jobu.

THOSE sections of this work are now ended in which we made an attempt to sketch the mode of life of the active and more highly developed Soudanese peoples, and this was followed by a description illustrated with examples based as far as possible on actual observation of the influence exercised on national life by a Libyan-Islamite stream of culture from the North-west coming into contact with an older stream of civilization, Eastern in its origin, encountering a vigorous and determined resistance to any further advance, and finding its expression in the formation of a Mossi Empire which was united in revolt against the further expansion of Islam. Full justice has been done to the Crescent borne on the wave of civilization pressing onward from the North-west in the year 1000 A.D. The immediate object of what is to follow is the indication of the characteristics of the older heathendom, and especially of that marvellous Shâmân religion or doctrine of the higher magical powers and demoniac obsession, which was carried into the Soudan on the bosom of the river of civilization which sprang from the East.

Forwards, then, to the study of the religions of the more highly developed heathen nations!

521

On surveying the noble pagan races of the Soudan I recognize two differing types, namely, the apparently primitive " disruptive " tribes, with their wonderfully lucid system of earthly ancestor worship, and the " State-builders," who particularly cultivate the teaching of magical power, the theories of Angels of Darkness and Light and possession by demons, besides the fragments of other beliefs. This is the religion whose essence and permeation of the Soudan, whose origin and connection will be expounded in the following chapters. I will begin, then, this exposition which will need three chapters in all, by reproducing a few traditions of the nation which dwells on the bend of the Niger, the people whose historical relation to the Mahommedanizing Mandingoes I have already mentioned, namely, the Songai. The Songai chiefs on the edge of the Soudan were the first to yield to the Crescent and produce the first great Emir of the Mali Empire from the western sphere of their power, namely Mema, which is the reason he and his descendants assumed the name Keita or Koita, and this, being interpreted, means man or adherent (=ta) of the Kings of the Songai (=koi).

From the point of view of geographical distribution of civilization it is a vitally important fact that Islam gained its first foothold in the royal family of unmixed Libyan blood in just that part of the Niger valley where the stream proceeding from and returning to the Soudan rolls viâ the Sahara, the habitat of those wandering Libyan nations who were subjected to the current of North-western culture; it is, I say, an important fact that the first and greatest Mahommedan universities (Timbuktu and Jenne) should have been founded just here and that the religious tradition of the older subject races should yet have remained the purest and, of its kind, the grandest amongst all the nations of the Soudan precisely here, in the area most influenced by the schools for teaching Arabian script and men learned in history.

Now, although absolutely natural and in harmony with the laws whose action was also observable elsewhere, this is very peculiar. Leo Africanus tells us that the royal house of the Songai sprang from a Libyan stock. This corresponds with the geographical position of that portion of the Niger valley intersecting the Sahara and inhabited by the Songai, who were the first to be exposed to the inrush of the Libyans migrating through the Sahara and to the Islamite faith which they spread on their course. Therefore the development of Mahommedan literary history " demanded " this state of things as a " condition precedent " of its potential existence.

And, secondly, those forces which I tried to explain at the end of the very first chapter in this book were at work. While the governing classes adopted Islam and the art of writing and thus relaxed their hold upon the Past of tradition, the vast, lower stratum of the people clung all the more firmly to the preservation of their inherited memories. This stratum retained the civilization which, pre-eminently based on the education and growth of national remembrance, preceded the age of the written record. Now, however, since the nation is divided into an upper class, which controls historical literary records, and an extensive lower class, which enjoys a highly developed oral tradition, the simple conclusion arrived at is that the under stratum failed to absorb the written records of events in its mnemonic store in the same way as the upper stratum in the main only wrote down the happenings of the period set down in script. The difference between these two, so to say, " record offices " is so striking as to lead one to believe in an existing law which so operated as to make these two stores of archives of older forms of culture in these countries mutually exclusive. We find scarcely a single thing in the memorial treasure-house of the Songai which is set down to this people's account in their history chronicled according to Islam. Whereas, from the epochs of their heroes and giants the glory of their legendary Gods who were in power before the advent of Islam and the memory of the Shâmâns, in which this people believes to this day, is all the more splendidly preserved.

Here I will give the best specimens from my collection in order to show what was the spirit and philosophy of the pre-Mahommedan Songai religion.

\*　　\*　　\*　　\*　　\*　　\*　　\*　　\*

The Originator of the Race.—The primal ancestor of all the Soroko tribes was Owadia. All the Sorokos from Sansanding to Gao (or Garo), and for a long way down-stream, are descended from him and called Soroko; but the people of Timbuktu and Jenne know them as Sorkai (or Sourkai), and the Bammanas name some of them Bosso. They are not related to the Sommono (of the Bammanas), or, as the South Sorokos call them, the Kommo, or, as the East Sorokos do, the Korongoi. For these are not cf Owadia's blood.

Owadia came from the East. He was so huge that a flood which swept away man and beast only reached to his knee. When he wanted to eat he picked up a Joromo, *i.e.*, a whale (?) (Salé among the Malinke), or a Shobo (hippopotamus), out of the water and held his prey for a bit to the sun to roast it. He was so tall that he could put his booty quite close to the sun. Owadia was very strong and big. He never begged and never lent, but simply took. He ate so much as to create a famine round about him and soon folk had nought to eat. There was a Mahommedan, Sirisi Moola by name, who said to the people : " Wait a while ! " One day Owadia came to Sirisi Moola and said : " Give me a robe ! " Sirisi Moola said : " A robe I cannot give thee, for I have but two, and all the world has only two. But I can lend thee one." Owadia said : " Then lend me such a robe ! " Sirisi Moola did so. Owadia made himself a wrap of it, but it only reached to his navel.

Up to that time Owadia had never lent, but only taken. He was afraid to lend. Now one man after another came. One said : " I lent you some corn, give it me back." Another : " I lent you some rice, give it me back." Then everyone came and wanted to be paid for what he had taken.

Then Owadia fled far away. He came from Mecca to Bammana Moodoo, north-east of Bandjagara, which is on the Niger, above Gavo (or Gao). Then he travelled up the Niger as far as Gura (the same as Gurao at the entrance to Lake Debo), and then up to Sansanding.

Owadia left two sons, one in Gura who begat Fono (or Fuono), and the other in Bammana Moodoo, who begat Fara Maka. Their jurisdiction ended at Kabara (near Timbuktu). All Sorcko are descended from Owadia's posterity.

\* \* \* \* \* \* \* \*

Nana.—Fara Maka was big and strong, but ugly. He had one daughter named Nana Miriam, whom he instructed about everything. He often reclined with her on a sandbank and asked her : " What is it swims here and what swims there ? " Then Nana Miriam would answer : " I think it is that or the other kind of fish." Fara Maka said : " That is not what I want to know. I want to know whether it is male or female." Nana Miriam said : " Father, I do not know." Then Fara Maka would say : " That one is a hard roe, that one is a hard roe, that one is a hard roe, but that one there is a soft roe." In this way Fara Maka taught his daughter everything and his daughter learnt all her father's magic arts.

There was a hippopotamus living then which so devoured all the rice fields that there was great scarcity. It could turn itself into all kinds of shapes and thus elude pursuit. Fara Maka set out to rid the land of the Nile-horse. He took his spears with him. But the hippo had a great many ovens and burning fires on his neck and back. When Fara Maka encountered the beast, he hurled one spear after another at it, but every one of them fell into a fire-pot, melted in it and was swallowed by the hippo. Fara Maka went home after a bootless journey. Now in Gavoland there was a hunter, a Tomma called Kara-digi-Mao-Fosi-Fasi, who owned a pack of marvellous hounds, each one larger than a horse. Their leader was Kunjima Mbana and quite black.

Fara Maka said : " If Kara-digi-Mao-Fosi-Fasi cannot kill this hippopotamus with one hundred and twenty dogs, I do not know what more can be done." He invited the hunter with his one hundred and twenty hounds and prepared a great deal of good, a vast quantity of the best food, so as to make them strong and full of courage. Each single one of the dogs was fastened to a separate chain. The dogs devoured every morsel of the food so prepared. Not a grain of the rice was left for the next day. Next morning Kara-digi-Mao-Fosi-Fasi led the one hundred and twenty dogs to the place where the hippo was. When they got near it, he slipped one dog after another from its leash. One big dog after another leaped at the hippo. The hippo tore one after the other to pieces and swallowed it. He destroyed all the one hundred and twenty dogs and gorged them. Then the hippo walked on and grazed the rice field off. It did not go into the river. Fara Maka then saw that he could do the Nile-horse no hurt.

He went home and lay down in the shade. Nana Miriam lay

by his side and said : " Tell me, father, canst thou, indeed, do nothing to the Nile-horse ? " Fara Maka said : " Even so, I can do it no hurt." Nana Miriam said : " I will go away for a little ; I will look at Gavo." Her father said : " It is well." She got up and went to where the river-horse was.

The hippopotamus said : " Good-day, Nana Miriam." She answered : " Good day ! " and girt her clothes tightly round her loins. The river-horse said : " I know thou art come to kill me. But no one can slay me with weapons. I devoured Fara Maka's spears, I devoured Kara-digi-Mao-Fosi-Fasi's one hundred and twenty dogs. No one can kill me." Nana Miriam said : " I am only a woman, but we will see what happens to-day. We will have patience." The hippopotamus said : " We will see." Nana Miriam said : " Make thyself ready, either thou shalt kill me or I will kill thee this day."

Then the hippo lighted a mighty fire all round itself so that nobody could possibly have gone through it. But Miriam took her charm, murmured some incantations and strewed the powder over the ground. Then all the fire turned to water. But now the river-horse built up a high iron wall about itself so that it was again protected against all human attack. Then Miriam turned herself into a smith, seized bellows, hammer and anvil and very soon smashed up the ring of iron. The Nile-horse was now overcome with a great fear. It wanted to run to the water, so it changed itself into a creek that escaped into the main stream. But Miriam again threw some powder into the water so that the water-course ran dry. Now the hippopotamus had to run on foot and Nana Miriam ran behind it. When it came near the Niger she caused a lofty wall to rise up which ran along the Niger so that the hippo could not break through it to reach the river. Now the frightened animal ran towards Fara Maka. Nana Miriam saw that her father might now capture it and so she leapt swiftly and caught the huge creature by the hind leg. She swung it round in the air and hurled it away. The beast flew so far that one had to march every day for ten years to cover the distance which the beast flung by Nana Miriam in the air flew through.

Fara Maka saw this. He said : " What a splendid daughter is mine ! Nana Miriam, I thank thee ! " Then he summoned all the

Pl. Horse Games.

Horse games before the Galadima's compound in Tshamba.

(Water-colour by Carl Arriens.)

[Facing p. 224]

Kië (Dialli, or Troubadours, singers). He composed a beautiful song and taught the Kië to sing and play it. All the people in the land, all the singers, all the fishermen, all the peasants, all the Soroko sang the song of Nana Miriam.

Then Nana Miriam sent word to all the villages of the Soroko, saying : " Leave all weapons and implements of the chase at your homes, but give good heed to all that happens in the great river and quickly bring every good catch to shore so that it be not lost. For ye shall have such great plenty of meat, such vast store of meat that ye shall not know how ye will be able to dispose of it." Then Nana Miriam asked her father Fara Maka to give her an egg. She broke and, speaking words of power over it, flung it into the Niger. No sooner had she done this than the whole Niger from Gavo to Sansanding was so covered with dead hippopotami that the Sorokos were hard put to it to be quick enough to bring all the meat to land. Wherever there was a Soroko village there was an abundance of dead Nile-horses.

And now all the river-horses but one, which lived very far up country, had been killed, and this particular one was a Nile-mare in foal. Nana Miriam knew this quite well. She went to her father and said : " Give me another egg." Fara Maka asked : " What wouldst thou do with it ? " She made answer : " There is still one river-horse left alive. I wish to kill that one, too, for then are they all destroyed." Her father said : " Forgive me, Nana Miriam, my daughter ! Thou hast done glorious deeds. But if thou kill this last hippopotamus heavy with young, the Soroko will have no river-horse flesh to eat in times to come." Then said Nana Miriam : " How farseeing thou art ! My father ! thou say'st well ! "

She did this Nile-horse no hurt. The Nile-horse heard that Nana Miriam had desired to kill it, but had spared its life because it was with young and the last of the river-horse race at that time. It set out on the road and travelled to Nana Miriam, showed her honour and gratitude, saying : " Nana Miriam, I thank thee ! Thou hast given me my life : Now, I pray thee, let me still keep it." Nana Miriam said : " Go thy ways, thy life is given thee." The pregnant river-horse went away and became the ancestress of all the now living Nile-horses.

And since that time the name of Nana Miriam has been reverenced by all the Soroko. Whenever anyone makes or uses a charm for hunting the hippopotamus he always mutters over it the name of Nana Miriam.

\*   \*   \*   \*   \*   \*   \*   \*

Now for the legend of a mighty Shâmâness (Tungutu) : Pa Sini Jobu. Once upon a time, and very, very long ago, there lived a Bosso woman, whose name was Pa Sini Jobu. There were only four villages then and no others had been built. Pa Sini Jobu is regarded as the ancestress of a Soroko-Bosso tribe which dwells below Jenne ; she attained to extreme old age, and was a mistress of the most marvellous (magic) powers.

Now, when she arrived at the time when women generally get husbands, she sent all her suitors away. She had no desire towards marriage. But there always were many to woo her who would gladly have had her. Wherever she went, there was always a crowd of young people sitting around and talking with her. When the young men came, Pa Sini Jobu always gave them as much fine food as they could eat—rice and mutton. But nobody could leave her house without her permission. If anyone wanted to rise without asking to be allowed to get up he stuck fast to his little sitting-stool, and he was irremovable from the spot without the express consent of the clever Pa Sini Jobu.

Now, one evening a handsome young Bosso also betook himself to the beautiful woman. The pet sheep of the royal household met him and the young man, mistaking the sheep for a jackal, simply shot the magnificent animal dead. Then he went to Pa Sini and passed the night in her house till next morning. Now, this sheep was endowed with a certain degree of sanctity. The fortunes of the royal family were (in some measure) bound up with his life.

The body of the dead ram was found next morning and brought into the King's house. There was great mourning. The King had proclamation made : " Who hath killed the sheep ? " The question " Who hath killed the sheep ? " was asked in every house. But nobody confessed and there was nobody to give evidence as to who had been the slayer of the ram.

Then the King sent tidings through the whole of his realm

saying : " If there be one who can bring back the sheep to life, him will I not only honour highly, but I will make him such rich gifts of gold, slaves, cattle and all other things that he shall not know want for the rest of his days." The King also sent a message to Pa Sini Jobu saying : " Many people go to and fro at your house. Say unto them all that I will recompense him most generously who shall raise up my sheep from death." Pa Sini Jobu said : " I will let them all know, and even offer them the best of all I can give to find out a man who can again bring the sheep to life." Then Pa Sini Jobu called all her friends together and said to them : " I will marry him who can restore this ram to life. I desire no gold, no precious stones, no goods at all from the man to whom I offer myself in marriage."

Then all sorts and conditions of men from the uttermost ends of the earth flocked together ; all who were Tungutu (that is to say, controllers of magical forces ; " sorcerer " is somewhat different. The word " sorcerer " does not convey the thought contained in the word Tungutu). There were some who could stay under water for three days. There were others who could stay buried in the earth for three days. There were people who could change themselves into fire. Each one tried his powers of wizardry. But the sheep was still dead ; he gradually rotted and could not be made living and whole again.

Now, a long way off there lived a man called Yena (or Djena), who heard of the death of the ram, and being a Tungutu, thought he had sufficient power to carry out this difficult task. He took up his staff and came to Pa Sini Jobu. She said to him : " Djena, I have often been told, and I know that quite special powers obey thee. Now, here is a special occasion. This sheep was shot some time ago and is to be called into life again. If thou canst do this thing thou shalt have me to wife."

Djena looked at the carcase. Some jackals had come in the night when it had been shot and torn out a portion of the animal's liver. Besides this it had long been a corpse and was very far gone in corruption. Djena saw that it was a very difficult business. Besides this he wanted to put to the test the magical power of Pa Sini Jobu and so he said to himself : " There is not the least difficulty in calling this animal back into life. But, unluckily enough, some beasts of prey have dragged out a piece of its liver. If, now, thou canst get me those pieces, I can at once bring back this sheep to life."

Pa Sini Jobu said : " If that be all that is needed, it can be done very soon ; nothing whatever can be simpler ! " She called to a slave and said : " Go into the forest near by. There are the ruins of a very ancient city, which was destroyed. There is a very tall Kerebu (baobab) near to them. Next to the baobab there is a deep hole in the ground. Descend into the hole. You will find two jackals there. Tell the jackals to come hither immediately." The slave went into the wood. There, next to the baobab, was the deep cave. He went down into it and found the two jackals all right. He said to them : " Pa Sini Jobu commands that ye at once come to her." Thereupon the jackals set forth and ran to the village where Pa Sini Jobu was as fast as ever they could.

Pa Sini Jobu said : " The King's great sheep was shot dead here one night some time gone. You were passing by and tore out a piece of its liver. Is it not so ? " The two jackals said : " It is true, and since then we have neither dunged nor vomited so that each of us must still have the piece he took out in his belly. Find out then some means to make us purge and thou wilt find the needed parts of the sheep." Pa Sini Jobu said : " Vomit at once ! " The two jackals began to retch and sicked up the lot.

The mess was, however, indistinguishable ; neither was Djena able to reconstruct the liver nor call the ram back to life. He said to Pa Sini Jobu : " Thou hast brought back the parts that were missing by thy skill and use of (magical) powers, so that I cannot marvel at thee enough and I recognize thy superiority to me without more ado, but I am unable to restore the sheep to life."

And therewith Djena returned to his own country.

\*    \*    \*    \*    \*    \*    \*    \*

The King's sheep (King is the same as Sembeng or Kaneka) went on rotting and its stench grew stronger and stronger. The King's wife shed tears all day and all night because it could not be awakened into life again. The King sent once more to Pa Sini Jobu, asking : " Know'st thou of no means at all to revivify my sheep?" Pa Sini Jobu sent word: "It is well. Then I will see to this matter myself. The sheep shall live. But when this has been accomplished, I shall depart from hence. And I shall never marry a Bosso; for the men of my nation are impotent. Therefore I will have nothing more to do with them, but go out from this land."

Thereupon the King caused all the Kië (musicians; the Dialli of the Mandes) to come together to beat their calabashes. The Kië sat around the square. Pa Sini Jobu took her seat on the ground in the midst of them. Because she was a Tungutu, she had such long hair that it reached far, far down her back, and she could sit on her own hair instead of a stool or a mat. This hair was the gift of her (magical) powers. The Kië began to beat time. The Kië played music. They played and sang faster and faster still. Pa Sini Jobu began to get into a frenzy. Her (magic) power was awakened. The Kië played and sang and beat time with ever-increasing quickness. The (magic) power of Pa Sini Jobu grew stronger. Pa Sini Jobu screamed! The Kië beat time. Pa Sini Jobu rose up. She floated aloft. She floated up to the clouds. She changed her arms while up in the clouds into wings, like the great birds have, and then sank slowly down over the ram.

Pa Sini Jobu rested over the ram for the space of six days. During this time she covered the ram with her outstretched wings. On the seventh day she got up. The ram was alive!

\*   \*   \*   \*   \*   \*   \*   \*

Pa Sini Jobu left the town. She wished to have no more dealings with the people (? of her own country). She went upon wanderings and came to a land whose king was not a man; that land's chief ruler was a woman, Na Manj, the Queen. When Pa Sini Jobu was near to the Queen's principal town she sent her a message, saying: "Pa Sini Jobu is coming; come thou to meet her at the gate!"

Na Manj immediately formed up a stately procession, set forth and met the approaching Tungutu. She greeted her in all friendliness and said: "I have heard of thy great (magic) gifts. Do me the pleasure to stay awhile with me so that I may show how greatly

I honour thee." Pa Sini Jobu said: "Thou art very gracious. For a while I will stay with thee."

She made her entry into Na Manj's city. The Queen did all she possibly could to be good to her. All the townspeople came to greet Pa Sini Jobu, to bring her presents and do honour to her.

Na Manj asked her after a few days: "Wilt thou be so friendly as to tell me what thou knowest?" Pa Sini Jobu said: "All that has happened is known unto me. Ask me, therefore, and I will answer thee gladly." Na Manj said: "I have a petition. Here in my neighbourhood there is a kingdom ruled by a King. His people are constantly fighting with my troops, and always, at whatever the hour or place, the King's warriors gain the victory. I no longer know what is to be done or how to do it. My question, then, is, O Pa Sini Jobu, whether thou canst and wilt help us in our need against this King?"

Pa Sini Jobu said: "That seemeth to me no such difficult matter. When thou again marchest forth with thy men in that direction, I will accompany and see what may be done." Pa Sini Jobu continued: "See thou also to it that a black bull, a black ram, a black he-goat, a black tom-cat and a black cock be with us. Whatever happens, I shall need these if I am to go to the wars with and help thee. So make these preparations."

Now, the enemy's King lived on an island in the middle of a great river, so that his residence was surrounded on all sides by water. This vast river was called the Wië. Three Djins lived in the stream (Djins are spirits corresponding to the Houssa Alledjenu). It was these three Djins who helped the King to be conqueror.

Na Manj marched with Pa Sini Jobu and her army to the Wië river. They had taken the black bull, the black ram, a black he-goat, a black tom-cat and a black cock. The Queen pitched her camp opposite the King's island-town. The slaves went to the shores to draw water to carry into the camp.

When the Djins saw the slaves coming, one of them changed himself into a man and sat down on the bank. When a slave came up, the Djin said to him: "There is a Tungutu called Pa Sini Jobu in your company, is there not?" The slave said: "Yea, a woman of that name is with us." The Djin said: "Then go to her and tell her to be so good and come down to the river-bank, where there is one with whom she would certainly like to have speech." The slave said : " This will I do." The slave went back to the camp. He found out Pa Sini Jobu and said to her : " There is somebody by the stream with whom thou wouldst certainly like to speak. This was his message." The Tungutu at once set out and met the Djin. He said : " Thou art Pa Sini Jobu." She said : " That am I." The Djin said : " I sent thee a message, that thou wouldst like to speak with me. I am one of the three Djins who rule the water here, and are bound to defend it against thy friend Na Manj. What does the quarrel between the King and Na Manj concern thee ? Why dost thou wish to enter into a contest with us on account of this matter ? " Pa Sini Jobu said : " Na Manj is my friend, and I think that right is on my side in coming to my friend's assistance in her trouble. What do the Djins concern me, anyhow ? If you obey your King and desire to help him, do so. Then we shall see whose is the greater (magic) strength." The Djin said : " Pa Sini Jobu, thou art very proud, but not well instructed. Thou art a Bosso woman. Why dost thou wish to wage war in this country ? Believe me, thou canst do nothing— nothing at all here. We are this land's Djins. Thou art a strange Tungutu, great and mighty—in other places—but here thy powers avail not. Let it be, Pa Sini Jobu." The woman spake : " Nay, I shall not let it be. I will see what truth there is in thy mouthing." Pa Sini Jobu turned round and went back to the camp.

The Djin went back into the river and called his comrades, all three Djins, together. The Djin, standing on the bank in human shape, said : " I have had a long talk with Pa Sini Jobu. I have dissuaded her from carrying on the war against the King of our island for the sake of Na Manj. But she is too haughty. I could not get anything out of her. What shall we do now ? " The two other Djins said : " What shall we do now ? " The Djins had a slave. The slave of the Djins said : " Will ye permit me to settle this business ? " The three Djins said : " It is well. Do it thou ! "

The slave of the Djins at once set out for the camp of Queen Na Manj. He went to Pa Sini Jobu and said : " Thou art Pa Sini Jobu the mighty." The Tungutu said : " Yea, that am I." The Djin slave said : " I am only a quite insignificant slave of the Djins. But thou canst see the relation in which thou and I stand to each other in this : Thou art one hundred and eighty-three years old and I but seven, and yet I know far more than thou dost. I know thy father, thy kindred, and not less than ten generations of thy forebears. Measure the strength of my years by that, Pa Sini Jobu." Pa Sini Jobu said : "Cease thy chatter." The Djin slave said : "Mock not. Believe me, it will not be good for the troops of Na Manj the Queen to approach too close to the river. Believe that it would be better for thee to keep thy hands out of this business. This river Wië belongs to the Djins and the Djins will not have their rights interfered with by a woman of the Bossos." Pa Sini Jobu said : "Do not chatter, thou small seven-year-old ! But see to it that thou keep out of the way. Thou wilt not matter much either way !" The Djin slave said : "I have done all that I could do ; now it remains for thee to justify thy attitude of pride."

The Djin slave went away and returned to the river Wië.

\*　　\*　　\*　　\*　　\*　　\*　　\*　　\*

The slave of the Djins went to the King, who lived on the island, and said : "Thine enemy, Na Manj, with her troops and with a Tungutu as well, will come and attack within a few days. Then stay thou and thy people all perfectly quiet. Behave as though ye observed it not, but let them go on shooting and storming. Do not stir. What is to be done, I will do." The King said : "So be it ! We will do as thou desirest." The Djin slave went to his lords and said : "I beseech ye, when the battle begins, to stay on one side and not interfere, for I would fain settle this matter out of hand." The three Djins said : "Be it so. We will stand aside and look on."

Seven days afterwards Na Manj and her armed forces and Pa Sini Jobu moved down to the shores of the Wië and set up their tents opposite the King's island. Pa Sini Jobu said : "Now send me the black animals down to the bank." Na Manj said : "It shall so be done." Pa Sini Jobu went down to the bank. She cut the black bull's throat and let the blood which streamed from it trickle into the river ; she cut the black ram's throat and let its blood trickle down into the stream ; she cut the black he-goat's throat and let his blood trickle down into the water ; she cut the male

Pl. Mahommedans at Prayer.

A view of the great prayer on Friday in Bida.

cat's throat and let his blood trickle into the river ; she cut the black cock's throat and let his blood flow down into the water. Then she said to the people : " Now ye may attack them."

Na Manj the Queen's men took up their arms. They began to shoot upon the city of the King. There was no reply from the King's city. The soldiers of Na Manj the Queen shot again and again, until their quivers were empty. But no reply came from the island of the King. Na Manj the Queen said : " Now 'twill be time to cross over the river."

The little Djin slave came out of the water at that very moment. He floated above the water. Then his tongue began to grow out of his mouth. It grew longer and longer, until at last he was able to throw it back over his face to the back of his head. Then this tongue went on growing longer and broader, so that it was spread out like a thick cloud. Suddenly the little Djin slave darted his mighty tongue forward and smote a body of troops in a distant country with it. As far as the tongue could reach every living thing which had been moving about on the plain a little while before was broken and crushed. No life was left upon this tract of land. The little Djin slave lifted his tongue up again and over his head. Again he darted it forward. Another body of troops was broken and crushed under the weight of its blows. Once more he drew back the tremendous form and several times the giant tongue struck Na Manj's nation, and then the Queen and all her warriors were wiped out and of all those people only the one Bosso woman, Pa Sini Jobu, was left alive.

But the small slave of the Djins seized the woman, drew her to him and took her under the surface of the river Wië. He led her to his house under the water. Here the little Djin slave said to Pa Sini Jobu : " This was necessary and inevitable. Thus have I done thee much bitter hurt, but thou thyself wouldst have it so. Yet even now will I show thee a little of the magical power and art of the Djins, and disclose unto thee wherein lies the greatness of thy future. Behold now and mark well what I show and shall teach thee."

Having said this, the little Djin slave took up three pots. He said to Pa Sini Jobu : " Thou seest them all three to be quite empty." Then he took three lids and put one on each of the pots. After a

little while he lifted the lids off again.    Then all three pots were
filled, the first with Dië (blood), the second with Juguduo (leaves),
the third pot with Tungu (sorcerer's charms, the equivalent of the
Kirsi among the Bammana).    Djinnikin asked : " Dost wis where-
fore this is ? "    Pa Sini Jobu said : " Nay, I know it not."

The little Djin slave said : " I will expound.    Mark well and
nothing forget."    Then the little Djin slave told of all the illnesses
and all misfortunes and all life on the earth, and explained exactly
how this or that thing was to be remedied and how this particular
sickness or ill-hap was to be treated.    He explained to her that
all things which could be useful and helpful to earthly existence
in sickness and bad fortune were among the things which these three
pots contained.

The little Djin slave said to Pa Sini Jobu : " Thou didst wrong
as a Bosso woman.    For the Bosso should keep to their fishing and
farming and the business proper to them.    But they should not go
into wars.    The Bosso are not a nation of warriors and should not
bother themselves about warlike activities.    Act on this advice in
the future.    Take these three pots with thee and hie thee back
into thine own country.    Use the contents in the manner I have
taught thee and thou shalt then be held in higher honour than any
other Bosso woman has been before."

Then the little Djin slave gave Pa Sini Jobu the three pots.
She took them and went with them thence.

*       *       *       *       *       *       *       *

These selections may suffice for examples.    Let us now turn
our attention to the " Djins " of the Songai, who are friendly at times,
and at times, unfriendly to men ; we shall find their nearest relations
among the Alledjenu of their neighbours, the Houssas.

Asama, the chief Alledjenu, dancing as a mask before the heathen Houssa in Wukari.
*(Drawn by Carl Arriens.)*

## CHAPTER XXV

### THE DEMONS OF LOVE

### *(Religious Legends of the Houssas)*

Related Songai and Houssa legends—Examples of Alledjenu legends :   Djiberri—Sherandeli—
Gogobirri—Djengere—Kundari—Serki Rafin.

IN the legends peculiar to the Songai the historical element was
seen to have almost entirely disappeared.   And the fact is
still more observable when we give ear to the Houssas, the people
settled in the region lying between those occupied by the Songai
and Bornu tribes.   There are Chronicles of Houssaland just as
much as there are histories of Songai.   Simpler, perhaps, in
character, they may be, but they, as well as the Songai chronicles,
contain some historical substance which, to a certain extent, has
been transferred by the records in writing from the store-houses
of folklore into the field of knowledge owned by the learned priesthood, and, in this way, withdrawn from the archives based on the
memories which the people themselves have preserved.   Therefore
we find that the Houssas, no less than those of their Western
neighbours, offer national legends, but little historical accuracy and

537

a few points of prehistoric connection excepted, are generally bare of all historical interest.

Yet, in turning over the leaves of the Kano records, published by the painstaking industry of Mr. H. R. Palmer, we find that forty-eight kings can be counted who bore the sceptre between 999 and 1892 A.D., and a fascinating introduction as a preface to their recital. In this introduction, and thus at the very commencement of Houssa historical thought, there appears to be a hero, a giant who—again recalling to our minds the Songai legend—fetters and seizes on elephants; a human being endowed with the strength of a giant. And we are still further reminded of the Songai myths on seeing that in the popular Houssa traditions the subverter of the kingdom in pagan times was also a Slayer of Dragons. The original primitive historical connection is obvious. And, moreover, the Kano chronicle gives an account of the ancient heathen cult as practised before the advent of the Founder of Empire, counts up the number of black animals sacrificed by the high priests in the moonlight nights behind a wall in the shade of trees venerable in age—the reader will not forget the immolation of none but black animals referred to at the end of the preceding chapter by Pa Sini Jobu, the woman Shâmân—describes the oracles' wisdom, gives, in a word, an image of the religious observances before 999 A.D. which can be identified throughout with a definite religion in existence to-day. This old Houssa religion is the Bori, a treasure-house of legends which contains a mass of documentary evidence essential to the comprehension of the previous interdependence of the Houssa tribes.

Here we once more have another parallel between the Songai and the Houssa. The Songai traditions are preserved in the religion of the Tungutu, or Shâmâns, and make mention of demonic spirits, the Djins. The Houssa traditions tell of the Alledjenu, certain spiritual beings who can be identified with the Djins. The myths of the Songai describe a mighty giant race and give an account of its beginning. The legendary stories of the Bori people of the Houssa country are chronicles of great cosmogenetical powers and events. But :

The Tungutu faith resisted Islam, which therefore thrust it aside on to the road of decay ; whereas the creed of the Bori adapted itself to Islam in the sects of the Fakirs and Dervishes and so managed to incorporate itself with the faith of Mahommed that it was able to prolong its own life under its wing and its light. And thus both of these variant systems, springing from one religious root, underwent transformations so diametrically opposite as to make their identity almost unrecognizable.

However, their historical growth is clearly and intelligibly reflected in both nations' traditional religion. The Songai segregated themselves in the practice of their religious cult and in this manner attained a more equalized style of their legends and method of life, but anticipated the ruin of both; a state of affairs which need cause no surprise with regard to the Songai, because Islam strode from the Desert and across the plains and they were able to find sanctuary for themselves and their creed on the islands and jungles of the river Niger. But the Houssas were forced to adapt themselves incontinently to the progressive advance of Mahommedanism, because, living in unprotected towns on the level steppes, they could only stem the Islamite wave which tore across the waste by conforming to the new nature of things in their views of religion; the laws which prevail on the surface of the earth primarily compelled them to assist the Mahommedan ideals and subordinate the indulgence of their own cult to the religion of the Prophet Mahommed. In this way they acquired an access of vitality at the expense of a compromise and the loss of a religion encrusted with the mould of the ages.

The legends of the Bori religion form different groups. There are, firstly, the cosmic sun and moon myths, the story of Maikaffo, the lord of the buffaloes, of the primeval lifting up of the sky, then of the building of the Tower of Babel, of the Gods of Volcanoes and Rivers and so forth. As an example of this branch of tradition I quoted Ra-Rana, the Sun-goddess, in the chapter on the Yoruban Thunder-god, Shango. I will here give a typical instance of the first group in the legend of Djiberri, the Mahommedan Gabriel, that is the warrior comet War-lord of the Houssas (Legend No. 1). The second group is historical, and treats of the Alledjenu guild. In this Feri-Uma (Pharaoh), Nuhu (Noah), Namarudu (Nimrod), etc., etc., are all merrily mixed up together and the Saga fearlessly connects the ancestors of the heathen Houssa legends with the prehistoric Worthies of the East. I produce the two legends of Sherandeli and Gogobirri (Nos. 2 and 3) as instances of this type. The third group deals with the actual, terrible demons who dwell in the forest and prairie ; these are the uncanny beings who feel attracted to men out of love for them and afflict them with the fearful signs of possession. The legends of Djengere and Kundari (see Nos. 4 and 5) illustrate this class. We come, lastly, to the lighter forms, the demons who dwell in the water. These predominate in the South. The traditions of Serki Rafin and the legends of the migration of the Alledjenu guided by Ashama may serve as examples (see No. 6, etc.).

These selected specimens sufficiently explain the mode of thought and growth of religion of the Houssas. In the following chapter I shall then give fullest attention to this singular faith and prove that it is sufficiently wonderful to be regarded as an heirloom from the depths of a history which is full of significance.

\*/　　\*　　\*　　\*　　\*　　\*　　\*　　\*

1. Djiberri, the Alledjenu of God (Houssa-Kano). Every Alledjenu and every human has his star in the heavens. When he dies, the ownership of the star passes to some other person. But the star of a very great King is said to fall down at his death.

Owdoo Kaderr(e) (God) has also a star, which is Tarauri-gam-Saki, or also Tarauri Gabas (the Star of the East), namely, the Morning Star.

Djiberri, the God (equals Gabrielu, the archangel Gabriel, who here also becomes an Alledjenu), came to Owdoo Kaderr(e) and spake thus : " Give me that star yonder, Tarauri-me-wutsia-sun (wutsia = tail ; fudu=four). This means the comet which, in this instance, represents the well-known princely standard with six horse-tails. Owdoo Kaderre said : " I cannot give thee Tarauri-me-wutsia-fudu. For that which it demands as an offering of sacrifice (food) is very difficult to get." Alledjenu Djiberri said : " Tell me what it is Tarauri-me-wutsia-fudu eats. I will provide it." Owdoo Kaderre said : " It eats only men. But those alone do not satisfy it. From time to time it must have a King. And that is the great and difficult thing." Djiberri said : " Owdoo Kaderre ! That is a great and difficult thing. But I will show thee that I am the Alledjenu Djiberri. He can achieve it." Owdoo Kaderre said: "It is well! Take thou the star with the four tails. But if thou canst not give Tarauri-me-wutsia-fudu a King to eat it will return to me." Alledjenu said: "I take it. It shall be my flag. I will give it Kings as food." Djiberri carried the comet as his banner, his Tuta. He went forth, stirred up a war, killed a King and gave him to the star for food.

Since then, whenever a comet appears in the heavens there is always a war and the death of a King. That is the reason why in ancient days only human beings were sacrificed to the Alledjenu Djiberri. It was the only sacrifice acceptable to him. More particularly, men were offered up to him on going to and returning from war.

The immolation now to be described is said to be in connection with the Alledjenu Djiberri; but it must be mentioned that the Nupés and Houssas both claim the authorship of this offering and quarrel about their respective claims to its origin.

Formerly, before the Nupés and Houssas went to war, or when a pestilence afflicted a city or country, the following offerings were made in public of old, but secretly now, namely:

|  | Houssa. | Nupé. |
|---|---|---|
| 1. A black male dog | — Bakin-káré | Eki-jiko |
| 2. A black he-goat | — Bakin-bunsuru | Bukunji-jiko |
| 3. A black bull | — Bakin-ẹà | Nanko-jiko |
| 4. A leper man | — Kuturu | Soko-guntshi (*i.e.*, God hath gash-marked him; thus, a holy disease) |
| 5. An albino (male) | — Sabia | Beà-beà |

All these three male beasts and two wretched humans were offered up and butchered in the house of the King, the Lord of the City. The meat was taken from all the five victims and cut into little pieces. Then it was cooked in great cauldrons outside the city walls, stirred up so that the separate parts could no longer be distinguished, the mess of food poured upon an ox-hide (in Houssaland=Klabu) and portioned out among all the town's inhabitants. Everyone had to eat of it. The last sacrifice of this kind is said to have been celebrated at the turn of the years 1908–09, in a suburb of Katsena in fact, and a man who was often possessed by the Alledjenu Djiberri reported to have conducted it.

Now Alledjenu Djiberri was, and still is, worshipped in the Houssa lands in a temple whose most important implements of service are : firstly, a sword which stands erect, called Takobi, and, secondly, a dagger which lies down (I am not quite certain on this point), called Kubé. But the Houssas assert that water trickles down this sword when offerings are made to this their War-God. In the popular imagination, Djiberri is furnished with many weapons, horses and rich armour.

\* \* \* \* \* \* \* \*

2. Sherandeli, the Alledjenu of Kisra, and Nohu (Houssa-Bida).—The Alledjenu Sherandeli (or also Sherandebi) came from the distant East. He dwelt in Gabas before Kisra (the Persian King) came West, and became King in Karishi and in Boussa (on the Niger). At that time the Alledjenu Sherandeli Dan Sherbo lived in a stone. That was in the time when Anabi (prophet) Nuhu was always contending against Kisra. Whenever Anabi Nuhu (Noah) met Kisra in battle at that time he gained the victory. Kisra always and always again lost many peoples and could not fight against Anabi Nuhu without being worsted.

Kisra assembled all his people and spake unto them : " This Anabi Nuhu ever gaineth the battle. He is ever victorious. How can we prevail against him ? What shall we do to counteract this misfortune ? Go ye and seek for something which we can set up in our city so that we may beat Anabi Nuhu in fight." The people said : " We know not what to do. That alone which thou thyself mayst bring will avail."

Kisra the King spake thus : " Even though ye should know of no other thing, let us go to the rock which stands yonder." The people said : " We will even do as thou sayest." The King went thither with all his people. When he had come there, he said : " Here will we build our city. Mayhap that will aid us." Thereupon the city of Kisra was builded round about that stone. Three months afterwards Anabi Nuhu came again and fought against King Kisra. Yet King Kisra and his fighting men were once more vanquished by Anabi Nuhu. Then Kisra, the King, went to the stone

PLATE II. I

The Bori Magadja and Adjingi in Ilorin.

*Photo by Abudu Herreira*

(Facing p. 244)

and spake these words : " O stone ! we have built up our city here. I beseech thee ! I beseech thee ! I beseech thee ! Let it not come to pass that Anabi Nuhu again obtain victory." Now Alledjenu Sherandeli was in that stone. He said : " That is all very well. But if I help ye now, ye will do some evil thing to me afterwards." Kisra said : " Nay, of such kind be we not. How should we do evil unto thee if thou help us now, seeing we are but men ? We are but men, but thou art an Alledjenu. How, then, could we do hurt to thee ? " Sherandeli said : " Then it is well ! But bring me my food." Kisra said : " Tell me the food which will please thee." Sherandeli said : " Give me red cock (djen sakara), red he-goat (djen akuen), red bull (djen sa), red stallion (djen doki), red man (djen mutum), red robe (djen riga) and red cloth (djen sam). These please me." Kisra the King said : " What thou wouldst should be offered thee, that will I give thee. Give us only thine help and thou shalt never be in need."

Kisra the King made sacrifices on the stone : red cock, red he-goat, red bull and red stallion, red man and red robe and red cloth. Kisra poured the victims' blood over the stone. He bound the cloth round the stone. Then he built a house over it. When he had sacrificed, Kisra said : " Now have I given thee all for which thou didst ask ? " The Alledjenu said : " Thou hast done as befitted. Henceforth will we fight together against Anabi Nuhu."

Seven days afterwards some came and cried : " Anabi Nuhu is advancing once more. Anabi Nuhu is once more advancing ! " Sherandeli asked Kisra : " On which day will Anabi Nuhu be here ? " The King said : " He will be here the day after tomorrow." The Alledjenu took up his spear which was as strong and as long as a palm tree. He stuck the spear in the earth in the city's midst. King Kisra made sacrifices of red ˙cock and red goat, red bull and red stallion, red man and red robe and red cloth near the spear.

Sherandeli accepted the offerings and said : " If ever the Anabi should come, carry forth the spear and thrust it into the ground without the city."

Now when Anabi Nuhu was coming, the Alledjenu Sherandeli called all Kisra's men and said : " Take ye your arms. Come with me ! Follow me against Anabi Nuhu ! " All the people assembled ;

all the men took up their weapons. At the eighth hour of the morning (ahansi), Anabi Nuhu arrived with his forces. The Alledjenu said to Kisra's troops : " Come, this day we shall do battle against Anabi Nuhu." The King went out with his army. Twice the men of Anabi Nuhu and Kisra met in the shock of war. Then Anabi Nuhu was conquered. His warriors fled afar off. Afterwards Kisra the King and Sherandeli waged war against many cities. When he went forth with his fighting men, Sherandeli went before him brandishing his spear. Thus, Kisra obtained the victory and thus Kisra became a mighty King. Anabi Nuhu was killed in the wars waged against him because Alledjenu Sherandeli was on King Kisra's side. Only Anabi Nuhu's brother was left alive. (This brother is also called Luma or Ruma.)

Kisra was conqueror in all the wars. He thought no more on Sherandeli the Alledjenu and no longer gave him the food he desired. Kisra remembered not the Alledjenu Sherandeli. For now he departed from Kisra and went to Anabi Nuhu's brother. To him he said : " Come with me. I will go before thee. Fight against Kisra the King. I will help thee ! " Anabi Nuhu's brother said : " So be it ! I come ! " He came ; he contended against King Kisra. That (the war) was in Gabas. And Anabi Nuhu's brother, with Alledjenu Sherandeli, was victorious over Kisra.

King Kisra was driven out of Gabas. He fled to Karishi (in the province Kotangora), fled with all his horsemen to Karishi. Anabi Nuhu's brother pursued him for a long time. Then he turned round and went back to Gabas. Then Anabi Nuhu's brother stayed in Gabas (in the East).

When he had come back to Gabas, he said : " It is true that Alledjenu Sherandeli killed my brother Anabi Nuhu. Yet he hath now given me a great victory over Kisra. Therefore I will never secede from Alledjenu Sherandeli. I will give him all he wishes to have."

Thereafter Anabi Nuhu's brother gave Sherandeli all things the Alledjenu desired and if anyone be seized and thrown down to-day by Alledjenu Sherandeli, one knows that he is a descendant and relation of the brother to Anabi Nuhu.

The popular tale, moreover, states that Alledjenu Sherandeli made the first of all the spears in the world and that the Alledjenu

Sherandeli is older than the Alledjenu Gogobirri. The face and especially the eyes of him into whom Sherandeli has entered, swell, like those of one who has been beaten.

\* \* \* \* \* \* \* \*

3. Gogobirri Bowa, the Alledjenu of ancient Gobir (pagan Houssas ; Wukari). The Gogobirri of the Serki Bowa Dan Goinki was a great King (among the Alledjenus). He was as mighty as Feri-Uma (Pharaoh). He was the first Gogobirri and an Alledjenu who dwelt in the bush. And Bowa Dan Goinki was the first King of Gobirland (Gobir is reckoned as being one of the most ancient kingdoms of the Houssa countries). Now at that time the Serki of Kororofa waged many wars against the Serki of Gobir. The Yukum of Kororofa always gained the day over the Gobirawa. The Serki of Gobir did not know what he could do to prevail against the Serki of Kororofa and the Yukum. One day he went into the bush and prayed to Alledjenu Gogobirri thus : " O Alledjenu Gogobirri ! I beseech thee ! I beseech thee ! I beseech thee ! Help me, aid me against the Yukum ! " Now there stood an old, old, great, great Kuka (baobab).

Gogobirri lived in that old, old Kuka. When the Serki was at his wits' end what more he could do to conquer in the struggle against Kororofa, he went into the bush and once more prayed to the Alledjenu Gogobirri : " Come to mine aid, help me to victory over Kororofa ! " Then he took a great mill-stone which women use, upon his head and went with it to the foot of the Kuka. The King sat down with the mill-stone on his head beneath the Kuka, and sat thus for seven years and nine months, always with the mill-stone (=dutshinika) on his head under the tree.

During this space of seven years and nine months the King's skull was crushed in by the heavy mill-stone. A great hole was made in his head, and he had to wear a turban (=ruoni) afterwards. The King offered up many victims near the tree to the Alledjenu. He immolated one hundred black steers, one hundred black (male) apes, one hundred black (entire) asses, one hundred black (stallion) horses, one hundred black men, one hundred black he-dogs, one hundred black buck goats, one hundred black rams. He made a sacrifice of all these animals close to the trunk of the Kuka tree. The King

only spake these words :- " I offer thee these one hundred bulls."
He said : " I offer thee these one hundred black male apes." He
spake : " I offer thee these one hundred black entire asses " (and so
forth, no longer praying much, but only making sacrifices).

But the King, however, did not require the animals and men
to be brought there ; he did not require the animals and men he
wished to sacrifice to be killed. All he had to say was : " I sacrifice
these one hundred bulls to thee." Then the one hundred black
bulls at once lay dead under the tree. Then the Alledjenu drank
the blood of the animals and men when they had fallen down
dead under the baobab. The spot where the Alledjenu Gogobirri's
Kuka stood was (and still is) not a fertile place, but a rock. Neither
has Alledjenu Gogobirri's Kuka any roots, nor was it growing firmly
on the rock. It just stood there (loosely and unconnected). It
moved about then from place to place, and still does so. But at that
time it went upright. (See *infra* how it was later and to-day is.)

When the King had made the said sacrifices and seven years
and nine months were elapsed, he set eyes on the Alledjenu Gogobirri. (The meaning is that he had inclined his ear unto the King
and made himself manifest.) He had a Mashi (or spear) in his
hand, and said to the King : " Go home ! To-morrow is Friday.
On Friday will I come into the city with this spear. Tell the men
and women that I shall come. Tell the men and women that I
shall call aloud. Tell them not to flee when I come and call aloud.
Tell them that I shall do. them no hurt." The King saw the
Alledjenu. He heard the voice of the Alledjenu, took the stone
from off his head and hurled it to the earth. None have seen the
stone since.

The King went home and said unto the men and women :
" To-morrow cometh our mighty friend, the Alledjenu. Fear not
nor run not away when he cometh and calleth aloud ! " Then
next day the Alledjenu came into the city. The King was in the
market square, where the Alledjenu met him. The Alledjenu held
the spear aloft in the air. He screamed. All the multitude were
afeard. For all the men and women saw only the spear held high
and only heard the Alledjenu's voice. But he himself was visible to
none. The men and women were sore afraid and jumped up to
run away. The Alledjenu said to the King : " Tell the multitude

Zar or Msar dance in Oudurman.

*Drawn for "The News" from a painting by Ethel Packenham.*

not to be afeard, but to seat themselves down." The multitude sat. Now the Alledjenu said to the King : " Henceforth will I abide with thee. Henceforth will I tarry among ye. Therefore shalt thou look neither to the right nor the left ; thou shalt not turn thine head, but thou must only thrust it forward and look in front of thee. If thou shalt remember to do this, thou wilt have power through me to overcome all men and everyone thine enemy." Thenceforth Alledjenu Gogobirri abode in the King's compound.

When now the King was going to war he went to Alledjenu Gogobirri. He grasped the spear and said : " I am about to go forth to war ! Come, aid me ! " Then the Alledjenu led the van of the army. And all followed after him. And now the King could go into any land he would ; he could wage war against whomsoever he would ; he was victorious everywhere under the guidance and with the assistance of the Alledjenu Gogobirri. And thus it came to pass that none dared any longer to make war upon the King of Gobir. All the dwellers in his land were contented and happy.

One day the Adjingi (priest) of the Bori came to the King, saying : " O King ! Thou art the King of all Nations. But we beseech thee to grant us to take thy Alledjenu in our midst, to the end that it abide with us." The King said to the Adjingi : " I cannot part with this Alledjenu nor lend it, for I myself was sore afflicted until I won it." The Adjingi said : " That which thou hast offered up to this Alledjenu is naught but what we be ourselves, namely, thine own possessions. Therefore we pray thee : Lend thy Alledjenu Gogobirri unto us ! " The King spake : " This petition I cannot grant, for that which the Alledjenu devoured before I gained favour in its eyes and since it has dwelt with me, ye cannot afford. Ye would be unable to satisfy the Alledjenu and it would depart from us ! " Then the Adjingi said : " If thou wilt not give us the mighty Alledjenu, grant that the sons of thy Alledjenu play with us." The King said : " Of myself I can say naught as to this. I will hold converse with the Alledjenu myself."

The King went to the Alledjenu Gogobirri and said : " The Adjingi of the Bori came to me. He asked first that thou shouldst go to the people. I told him that the Bori nation cannot give thee enough food. Now the Adjingi begs of me that thy children be allowed to play with the Bori. What thinkest thou ? " The

Alledjenu Gogobirri said : " I cannot myself go with the people. But my little young ones may be with them." The King went back to the Adjingi and said : " The Alledjenu itself cannot come to you. But its little ones can play with ye. I myself can do nothing without the Alledjenu wills it. Henceforth then its children may come to you when ye draw the bow on the Goye (fiddle) (in the rites). The Alledjenu further said to the King : " So be it, then ; my children may dance in the Bori. But each of my children shall, like myself, carry a mashi (spear). Every one who would dance this dance (in my honour) must hold a spear in his grasp." Since that time, whenever Alledjenu Gogobirri enters into a person, he goes to a Kuka with a spear in his hand ; he performs a (pantomimic) dance near the Kuka and eats of the leaves of the baobab tree.

When the King of the Gobirrawa, Bowa Dan Goinki, died, Alledjenu Gogobirri's great Kuka, which had always stood erect up till then and wandered about on the rock, fell down. There now it lies. But it is not dead. It wanders about with all its leaves still on it (thus, with new foliage), upon the stony plain. It does not now move about erect, but since the death of that King moves leaning.

\*    \*    \*    \*    \*    \*    \*    \*

4. Djengere, the Alledjenu King (pagan Houssas ; Ibi).— Djengere is the King of the Alledjenu (this may be misunderstood). Djengere is the King of the Bori nation (that is certainly correct). He comes from a land which lies far, far towards the East.

In this far distant Eastern country, there was a large, large tree with a great hollow in it, which would hold many people. The hollow was as large as all that. But not many people went into it. They were afraid. Only three men ever came. These three men then entered into (or before ?) the hollow tree. And then they spoke into the tree, and in the tree there was the " big thing." The big thing spoke out of the tree, when the three men asked something. The big thing always gave the men an answer to their questions.

(Once) the three men came to the tree and asked the big thing to come out. They said : " We beseech thee ! Come forth and live amongst us." The big thing made no answer. They prayed once more : " We beseech thee ! Come forth and live with us ! " The big thing gave no reply. The three men prayed and prayed. But the big thing answered them not and held its peace.

The three men asked : " What must we do, so that thou shalt come out to us ? " Then the big thing spoke and made answer : " Ye must give me a black bull (baki-n-sa), a black cock (baki-n-kasa), a black buck goat (baki-n-aquea). Give me this. Then I shall be pleased. Then also will I (some day) come forth." The three men threw themselves upon the ground, saying : " We thank thee ! We thank thee ! We thank thee ! " Then they went their ways and brought a black steer, a black cock and a black buck goat. They slaughtered the three animals and returned to their homes. Next day the men came again, bringing a black bull, a black cock and a black buck goat, slaughtered the animals and went back home. The three men came again on the third day and once more sacrificed a black bull, a black cock and a black buck.

The three men sacrificed. Then the big thing came out. They sat about the tree before the hollow. The people's Adjingi spoke again. The big thing came out of the tree's hollow and sat down with them. It spoke with the men, saying : " Ye men, mark ye this : I come out on Friday (Djimoa). Friday and Thursday (Alamiss) are my days. Therefore go ye to your homes again, and return hither on Friday next at seven in the evening (Almuru). When ye then come, I will come forth again and hold converse with ye about this. Call me by name. Call : ' Djengere ! ' Then I shall appear. This do ! " The men threw themselves down, saying : " Nagode ! Nagode ! Nagode ! " Then the Alledjenu went back into the tree again. The men took to the path again and went back into the city.

They waited till the next Friday, then went into the bush again and sat down by the great tree with the great hollow. The men sat down. One of them had brought a Goye (fiddle), another a calabash drum with sticks. The men sat down by the tree ; one played the violin, the other beat the calabash. They called upon Djengere with the music (the names of the Bori Gods are invoked in a rhythm or song, or at all events musically). But they did not see the god (Alledjenu). When Djengere came he kicked one of them. The others neither saw nor felt it. But the Alledjenu threw the kicked one down and entered his head. (The man was possessed then !)

The possessed one saw the God and began to speak. He spoke with the Adjingi, who asked the possessed man what he wanted. The God spoke through the mouth of the possessed and told him what he wanted and what would come to pass (thus prophesying the future). Now Djengere told the Adjingi through the man he had entered into that he was to make everything known to the people. The Adjingi informed all the people. The people brought black oxen, and black cocks, and black billy-goats, and said to the Adjingi : " Sacrifice these animals to Djengere." The Adjingi accepted them and brought the victims to Djengere near the old tree and there sacrificed them.

The family of those thus inspired (literally " thrown down ") by Djengere in the far East (=Gabas) is still known as Jan-Gabas. As it was then, so it is now. When the Alledjenu Djengere (the chief of the Alledjenu) wishes for victims or to prophesy something to the Bori people, if it wants to say that such-and-such a misfortune can be averted, then it announces it through a member of this family (Jan-Gabas) to the particular community's Adjingi, who then explains everything in such a way that it can be " understanded of the people."

One may recognize the inspiration of the Djengere patients by the Alledjenu by their very rapidly swallowing Gauta (white tomatoes) and pouring bucketfuls of Gia (durra-beer) down their throats. Then they also smoke tobacco, and besides this, their testicles are greatly swollen while under inspiration.

\*　　\*　　\*　　\*　　\*　　\*　　\*　　\*

5. **Kundari, the Alledjenu of the Lepers** (pagan Houssas ; Ibi).—The Alledjenu Kundari is the same who in other provinces, *e.g.*, Kontogara, Samfara, Kano, etc., bears the name Kuturu. But this is because the leper is called Kuturu and because the form of possession peculiar to this Alledjenu subjects its victims to the loathsome marks of this disease. Now the Abaqua-Riga gave the

following account of Kundari : Kundari very, very long ago indeed was as sound and vigorous a man as any other. (Kundari, then, was not at first an Alledjenu, but a human being.) He said to people : " I excel all others in strength. I am strong and not afraid. I flee from nothing. From nothing do I run ! " Kundari had a friend, a good friend, named Pati. He heard Kundari speaking so, and said to him : " Thou say'st thou fliest from nothing. Dost thou not run from fire ? " Kundari said : " No, I do not run even from fire. Nor do I run when the fire chases me." Pati said : " I should have to see this before believing it."

Once Kundari went hunting with Pati. They both went so far afield that they were weary. Then they sat down in the shade of a tree. The tree stood among dry grass. The dry plain stretched far, far away, as far as ever one could see. The dry grass at the other end, far behind them, had caught light. Kundari had fallen asleep in the shade of the tree. Pati heard the fire crackling in the distance and woke Kundari up. He said to him : " Kundari, Kundari, wake up ! Kundari ! Kundari ! Get up ! Kundari ! The fire is coming ! " Kundari roused himself and said : " What art thou talking about ? " Pati said : " The fire is coming ! The prairie has been set alight. Now the fire is coming to where we are." Kundari said : " I shall not go away because of the fire ! Run thou away alone." The fire was quite near now. Kundari lay still. Pati took to his heels as fast as he could.

He ran a good way, then climbed to the top of a tree so as to look across at Kundari from there. The summit of the tree was very high, so that Pati could see Kundari. The latter was sitting just as one sits by the fire for warmth (*i.e.*, on one's hocks with one's arms hanging over one's knees, so that both one's feet and hands are turned to the blaze). The fire came closer to Kundari. He did not change his position. The fire was in front of Kundari. He did not shift. The fire went round about Kundari and set light to his clothes. Kundari sat still. The fire set light to his hair. Kundari did not budge. He sat in the middle of the fire. The fire ate away the tips of his fingers and toes ; it burnt Kundari's skin. He did not alter his attitude nor did he die. The fire scorched Kundari in every part of him. He was unable to get up, but he did not change his position. The fire then retreated from Kundari.

Pati came down from the top of the tree and went across the burnt plain to Kundari.

He had not altered his position. Pati came up to him and said : " My Kundari, canst thou come home with me ? " Kundari said : " I cannot get up." Pati saw that Kundari's fingers and toes and skin were burnt and said : " Wait, my Kundari, I will run to the city and fetch some folks. Then they shall carry thee home." Pati ran off to the city, called six men and said : " Take poles with ye and then come ye with me. Kundari is badly burnt by the fire beyond the city. We will lay him on the poles and carry him home." The men came with the poles. Pati ran with the men into the bush where the fire had seized hold of Kundari. Kundari was sitting under the tree. He had not changed his position.

Pati said to him : " My Kundari, art alive ? " Kundari said : " Why not, forsooth ? Only I cannot arise. Nor do I think I can walk." Pati said : " I have brought six men and poles with me. We will carry thee home." The men laid Kundari on the poles. They lifted him up and carried him away. Kundari spoke no word. They carried him into the city. Kundari kept silence. They took him to his house and laid him on his bed.

When they had laid him on his bed, Kundari said : " If the fire kill me (meaning if I die of the burns), I shall return as an Alledjenu. But if then I come as an Alledjenu into anyone's house, all the world shall know it is I who have come. Then nobody will mistake me."

Kundari lay on the bed for the space of three months. He spoke no word during the three months. The people nursed him for three months. Then Kundari died. He never spoke again before he died. Kundari was buried. Eight days afterwards, his grave fell in. There was a hole. The people passed by the grave and saw it had fallen in. The people saw the hole and said : " What this Kundari said is shown to be truth. He is no longer in his grave." All the people said : " Kundari spoke sooth. He is no longer in his grave."

Kundari came again as an Alledjenu eight days after his grave had fallen in. The Alledjenu Kundari entered Pati's house and seized Pati (such a " seizure " or taking possession of a female is in Houssa called Jakama-ta ; if of a male, Jakama-shi ; a woman

thrown down by Alledjenu is called Jabuge-ta ; a man, Jabuge-shi).
Pati, then, was caught hold of by Kundari and at once began to
scream. His wife heard him, ran up, and asked : " What ails
thee, my man ? How is it with thee ? " Pati answered her
not.

The woman asked : " What ails thee ? My husband, what ails
thee ? " The woman asked the man again and again, but Pati
did not reply. He screamed. His wife was frightened and ran
away. She ran to a hunter and said : " Come to our house with
speed. Only come quick and look at Pati. Since this morning
my husband no longer sees me. He covers his eyes and screams."
The hunter said : " I will come with you at once. We will look
at Pati in a moment." The hunter went with her, saw Pati and
spake : " We will sit your man down." The hunter and the
woman wanted to sit Pati down. But they could not. They could
not open Pati's hands. The hands were clenched and pressed together
as hard as stone. Pati's limbs were as stiff as wood. He was as rigid
as a corpse. But tears streamed from his eyes.

The hunter looked at Pati and said : " Now I know all about the
matter. Kundari said : ' I do not run away even from fire ! '
Pati said : ' I must see that first.' Before he died Kundari said :
' If the fire kill me, I shall enter some house as an Alledjenu, and
all the world will know that it is I who am come. None shall
mistake me ! ' But now Pati said to the people : ' I do not
believe that ; Kundari cannot return as an Alledjenu.' Pati
said this because he knows nothing of this kind of people. Folk like
Kundari keep their word if they so wish. Therefore, I say I know
all about this matter."

The woman said : " Abokina ! Tell me what can now be done
to make my husband whole once more ? " The hunter said : " Thy
husband is not sick ! Thou does not understand. I will do all that
is needful." He sent his boy back to his house, saying : " Go
into my house, take the little jar of Magani (medicaments) and
bring it hither." The lad went. The hunter asked Pati's wife :
" Canst thou give me a fowl ? " She said : " Surely I can give
thee a fowl." The hunter said : " Then go and fetch it." The
woman went and brought the chicken. The boy came back from
the hunter's house with the jar of Magani. The hunter said to the

woman : " Now give me some durra ! " The woman brought the durra.

The hunter scattered the grain on the earth and said to the woman : " If now the fowl pick up and eat the millet, it is a sign that it is Kundari who has possessed thy husband. But if the fowl do not pick up the corn, then Kundari is not in thy man." Then he spoke these words into Pati's head : " If thou be Alledjenu, take this fowl." Thereupon the hunter set the fowl on the ground.

When he had set Pati's wife's chicken on the ground it ran at once to the grain and began to peck at it. It very quickly picked up all the grain which the hunter had strewn. He said to the woman : " Did I not at once tell thee that it is Kundari who has got hold of thy husband ? Didst thou see how the fowl picked up all the grains ? "

The hunter now said to the woman : " Bring me now some water ! " She brought water. The hunter took some of the Magani out of the jar and mingled it with the water. He began to wash Pati with the mixture. He washed him above and below. He washed the whole of Pati's body with the Magani water. He bathed all his limbs with the Magani water. He laved every part of Pati's skin.

When he had been thus bathed, Pati began to speak and said : " I have seen Kundari again this day. He is now quite well. His hands, his feet and his skin are now as they were before he was burnt ; Kundari is whole again ! " The hunter said to Pati : " While Kundari was still alive he told thee everything. He told thee he would not flee from the fire. Thou wouldst not believe that. He told thee that if the fire killed him he would come back (to earth) again as Alledjenu. Thou wouldst not believe him." Pati said : " What thou say'st is the truth ! Thou art right. I would not believe Kundari. He hath told me himself this day that it is so. Now it is so. Kundari also told me that he would help me and my wife that we should this year have a child. We shall therefore even have a child this year." The hunter said : " Then you now believe what Kundari says ? " Pati said : " I believe most truly what he says. Kundari also told me to give the child we shall have this year his own name." The hunter said : " Then see thou do so and it will be well for ye and the child."

After that Pati was made whole again. Now, three months after that, Pati's wife was of good hope. Then in due time the child was born. But it was patchy, with black and white spots, like an albino. The child's skin was mottled like a skin burnt with fire. The parents washed it; they washed it with Magani water, but the skin remained piebald. Pati knew not what he should do with the child.

He said : " The hunter helped me. The hunter can surely also help the child." He went to the hunter and said : " The child of which Kundari told me has now been born. But the child is pie-bald, white and black ; the child's skin is spotted like an albino's. It is blemished like a skin burnt with fire. We washed the child with water and Magani. But the spots remain. Now canst not thou give me a Magani to make the child whole and its skin good ? " The hunter said : " None but Kundari can help this child. Give, then, the child Kundari's name even as he himself has told thee." Pati went and gave the child the name of Kundari.

It was a man-child. It grew up and became big. But when it was grown up, the wind (Iska) blew over it every Friday. Then the Alledjenu seized the child. Then the boy could not stretch out its four fingers (i.e., the fingers were convulsedly closed, so that only the thumb was free to move outwardly). That came to pass every Friday. Those who saw it said to Pati : " The thing thou hast brought into the land is not good. It is not at all good ! " Pati said : " What shall I do ? It is my friend Kundari. When my friend comes to me, I cannot prevent him." The people said : " Good, if so be thou canst not loose him, then may the quality (=hali) altogether remain in thy family. We will have naught to do with it."

Therefore Kundari's sickness always breaks out in Pati's, but never in any other family.

\* \* \* \* \* \* \* \*

6. Serki Rafin, the Alledjenu of the Rivers (Houssa-kono).— We now come to a deity which is apparently more widely distributed and enjoys greater consideration and honour among the Bori tribes than any other. This is Serki (king) Rafin (of rivers). In another

place stress will have to be laid on the unusual importance generally attached to the rivers as well as the trees in these mythologies. (See Dodo and Bashama on the Benue river.) Let us now see what the Kano people have to say about the River God. It is a longer traditional tale.

A woman had been married for three years to her husband without having had a child. One day she said to her man : " I will take my water jar, go down to the river and bring up some water." The man said to his wife : " Let be ! Wait ! The sun now stands just midway (*i.e.*, it was noon). Nobody ought to go to fetch water when the sun is in the middle. Nobody does that. Neither do thou so. Wait." The woman said : " What shall I do then ? I have no water for my work. I have used all the water this morning. I want to do my work now. I will not wait till afterwards." The man said : " Do not go ! " The woman said : " Go I will. I must get on with my work." The man said : " Do not go ! " The woman said : " Go I shall. Go I must. I want to finish my work." She took her pitcher and went down to the river. The way to the river was short.

The man waited for the woman. The woman did not come back. The way to the river was quite short. The man waited a very long time—the woman did not return. The sun had already come down to there (about two o'clock)—the woman did not come back. The man said : " I must go and see where my wife is stopping. I told my wife that nobody ought to fetch water at noon. Something has happened. I will go and see where my wife is." The man went down to the river. He came to the river and saw his wife. She was standing in the water up to her hips and could not come out of the water. The woman was held in the water. She was held in the water and was screaming. The woman went on screaming. The man saw how his wife was being held tight in the water and he screamed too. Then he ran away.

The man ran back into the town to his father and said : " Father ! my wife wanted to fetch water to-day at noon from the river. I said to her : ' Let be ! Wait ! Nobody ought to go to fetch water when the sun stands midway ! ' My wife said : ' I shall go ! I want to do my work.' My wife went ; I waited for her. I waited long. I have just been down to look after her. I have seen my wife. She is standing up to her hips in the water and cannot get out of the water. She is standing in the water and keeps on screaming." The man's father said : " I will come down to the river with thee and look at this business."

The man went with his father to the river. The father saw how the woman was standing in the water. The woman was standing in the water up to her hips and could not get loose. She screamed and screamed. The father said : " I will pull thy wife out." He caught hold of her and tried to pull her out. The woman screamed and screamed ; the father pulled ; he pulled hard, but could not get the woman out. The woman was held fast in the water and could not manage to get out. The father said : " What shall I do ? I cannot pull her out." The woman screamed and screamed. The man screamed. The father said : " What am I to do ? " The woman stood in the water. The husband stood on the bank. The father stood on the bank.

Then (after a long time) the woman was able to come out of the water. Nobody held her. Nobody helped her. The woman was able to come out. When she came out of the water she was quite dry. The woman's dress was dry. The woman's hips were dry. The woman was not damp a bit. She went home with the man and his father.

When it grew dark (on the same day) the woman jumped off her bed and screamed. She cried and screamed : " I must go to my spouse by the river ! I must go to my spouse by the river ! " The folk said : " What hath come over you ? Thy husband is not in the river ; thy husband is here in the same house as thou ! " The woman wept and screamed : " I must go to my spouse in the river. I have a husband there in the river who is far better than the one who is here." She wept and screamed and ran out. The woman ran down to the river. She came to the river and wept and said : " Serki Rafin ! I beseech thee ! Serki Rafin ! I beseech thee ! Help me that I may soon have a child. I am already three years married and have no child yet." Serki Rafin said : " Go into thy house. Say to thy husband that I will come to ye if ye will give me what I want. If thy husband will give me that, I will come into your house. Then let thy husband embrace thee again and then shalt thou be of good hope. I will always abide with ye, but ye

must always give me my due." The woman said : " I will immediately run home and tell my man this."

The woman ran home. She went to her husband and said to
him : " My husband ! Serki Rafin will come into our home if
thou wilt give him that which he needs. Then embrace me and
I shall be of good hope." The man said : " It is well, I will gladly
give Serki Rafin that which he needs. But wait. I will first speak
with my father." The man went to his father and said : " Serki
Rafin is ready to come into our house if I give him what he wants.
Then I am to embrace my wife once more and then she will be of
good hope." The father said : " Why should this not be so ? Why
should Serki Rafin not come ? I am rich and can give thee all that
he needs." The man went to his wife and said : " Go and tell Serki
Rafin to come ; tell him I am able to give him all that he wants."

The woman went to the river and said to Serki Rafin : " Come
with me ! My husband will give thee all thou wilt ask for. Come into
our house and live with us ! " Serki Rafin said : " It is well, I will
send my herald with thee. My herald shall speak with thy husband."
The woman went with the herald. Only she and nobody else
could see Serki Rafin and his herald. The herald came into the house
with the woman and said to her husband : " Serki Rafin wants white
cloth, white cowries, white rams and other white animals. But
when thou wouldst make offerings to Serki Rafin thou must always
sacrifice a male and a female white animal (therefore mating pairs)."
The man said : " This will I do ! "

The herald went back to Serki Rafin and said to him : " Thou
wilt receive what thou askest." Serki Rafin came into the house.
Only the woman could see him. The man offered up to Serki
Rafin white cloth, white cowries, white rams and other male and
female white animals. At night the man embraced his wife.
Serki Rafin made a Magani (" medicine ") for the woman. He
made fire in a saucer ; he strewed fine powder on the fire. Smoke
went up. The woman sat herself over the pot from which the
vapour was rising. She threw her garment round herself and round
the pot. All the vapour entered into her mouth and she breathed
it in.

Serki Rafin said : " I will now depart again. Thy wish will
very soon be fulfilled." He went back into the water. A very

few months later the happy event was very near. Serki Rafin came out of the water again (meaning possessed the woman again). She screamed aloud : " Fetch hither a Goye (fiddle). I would dance. Fetch hither a Goye. I would dance."

The people said : " That is bad. Wait till thy child be born. Then thou canst dance again. If thou dancest to-day, a misfortune will happen." The woman screamed : " Fetch me a Goye. I will dance. Fetch me a Goye, I must and shall dance ! " The people fetched a Goye. They played on the Goye and the woman danced to the Goye. It did her no hurt ; she remained sound. She bore a child which was sound. Since that time the Goye is played when a man or a woman is possessed by an Alledjenu.

Some Houssas think that Serki Rafin has a wife in the water who is also an Alledjenu. This Alledjenu is called Magadja Rafin.

Asar or Zar-men (called Bori in the West) taking a meal before the "session."

*(Drawn by Fritz Nansen from photo taken by Edith Frobenius in Omdurman.)*

## CHAPTER XXVI

### THE RELIGION OF POSSESSION, ESPECIALLY AMONG THE HOUSSA TRIBES

African Shâmânism and the basis of Alledjenu religion—Division of the Alledjenu into black and white—Exorcism of undesired possession—Invocation of demons—Prophetic energy —The area occupied by the religion of possession—Nubian forms of this religion—Its origin and antiquity—Its migration.

MY object in this chapter is to discuss the Bori, whose material record is legendary. Some of their legends were given in the previous chapter. The Bori have a religion which is widely spread over the Soudan and very little more than its general meaning and a list of spirits, compiled by Dr. Alexander, have so far been brought to our notice. The Bori's religion prevails from the Nile to the Niger, from the Atlantic Coast regions to the dwellers in the Sahara. The smaller "primitive and disruptive" tribes nowhere believe in it and everywhere it is the dominant, broadly disseminated peoples and, above all, the inhabitants of large non-Mahommedan cities who practise it. It is a most interesting cult, not only because of the extent of its spread, but on account of its relation to its original source.

560

The Bori religion, as stated, spreads from Nubia over Kordofan, Darfur, Wadai, and the Bornu tribes as far as the Houssas, and from the Lake Chad-Niger line to the South right across the Benue river, as far as the Yorubas, and its "runners" may be traced even towards Senegambia. The name of this religion as such varies. The spirits, whose great diversity of office was made evident in the last chapter, are almost everywhere known as Alledjenus, Djins, Jenne, etc. The purest form of this religion is found in the districts lying between the Great Desert, Lake Chad, and the rivers Benue and Niger. It has become largely absorbed in the religion of the Prophet, in consequence of the advance of Islam fostered by the Arabs, as far as regards the East, and is, in fact, here considered to be the "Islam of the blacks," because only the older black races adhere to it, and the more recent tribes pressing forward from the North do not profess it. To the West, however, the Bori has, in part (among the Mande), been fused with the old clan organization of the more ancient stock, and, in part (among the Songai), assumed the position of a pagan religion in violent contrast with Islam, and thus become the religion of those it repelled. This method of its dissemination is a proof that the Bori could not have come into the land at the same time as Islam. Therefore, this religion of possession is an individual form of belief, and this being so, I call it the African variety of "Shâmânism."

Let us be clear about this one thing, namely, that the Soudan is the home of four essentially principal religions, of which the youngest is Islam and the oldest, earthly ancestor worship; the third, the social-cosmogony of the Atlantic races, and, lastly, the fourth, this Shâmânism. Now, the position of the last in relation to the rest is fairly obvious, although it is also perfectly plain that here the different branches of philosophy are everywhere more or less intimately connected and show a tendency to become interwoven. The Houssas have kept the Bori faith freest from adulteration and, as a part of this nation retired across the Benue river into the ancient realm of Kororofa before the invasion of Islam we are enabled to see the clearest manifestations of its oldest form in this section of the Houssa nations. We shall get, then, the best insight into the original significance and import of the Bori among the Benue-Houssa. But neither must we forget that this religion penetrated into Ibi and Wukari (therefore, into old Kororofa), the region of Atlantic social-cosmological belief, and that consequently and as a matter of course this resulted in an amalgamation of the Bori and Atlantis philosophical systems. This fusion is recognizable in the adoption of the number sixteen or eight of the immigrant Bori-Alledjenu, in the transformation of the gloomy black spirits into white ones, but most distinctly in the representation of originally demonic apparitions in masquerades.

The chief introduction of the notion of metamorphic possibility, based on the power of attracting supernatural intelligence or force into the Soudan, is due to Shâmânism. The history of the kingdom of Kororofa, which was given me by the Western Yukum, contains a description of the transforming powers possessed by the King of Kororofa and his royal brother of Bornu, and how they vied with each other in their application. The Songai (on the Niger) and the Tommo (in the Humbori highlands) tell similar traditional tales. Whoever of these peoples stands in relation with demons shares their magical potencies, which play no less a part here than in the legends of the central Asiatic Ural-Altaic tribes, or in the Saga song of Bagda-Gesser-Khan. The Shâmân selected is the favourite designated by the demon's untrammelled choice, and he often has to practise the " call " against his own will. He is moved by the spirit and suffers under the influence of its possession. The genuine Shâmân, so understood, came into Africa with this form of Shâmânism and, therefore, with the Bori.

Animism is the religious basis of the Bori, a philosophy which, through the agency of spirits or demons, endues every object and especially parts of nature such as stones, trees and rivers, with a soul. These spirits are the Alledjenu, of which two kinds are, in fact, assumed, namely, black ones dwelling in the bush, in trees and rocks, and white ones who inhabit the streams. The black ones are honoured with black, the white ones with white, sacrificial offerings. Now, these Alledjenu enter into human beings and thus " possess " them. Sometimes this possession is desired and prayed for from the " daimon " invoked; sometimes, however, it seizes the body of the personality selected of its own accord and from sheer love. In that case the priest can hold converse with the spirit by the mouth of the person possessed. Such conversation, however, requires the use of music, mostly only the guitar, sometimes the Soudanese violin or Goye. It was but seldom I heard of drums being used, and, actually, only outside the Sahara. This fact, *per se*, assures the Bori an individual domain in which it is supreme. Islam, the religion of the Prophet, which (so small was its musical endowment) stopped its ears at the sound of a flute, was content with the rhythmical intonation of a name, whereas Manism and social cosmogony know only the bell and the drum. The Bori alone demands a stringed instrument.

Two priests, one male and one female, are its hierarchs, the former named Adjingi, the latter Magadja. The education and initiation of the Magadja in particular call for definite examination. Adjingi and Magadja are apparently always celibate, but altogether interdependent in the exercise of their priestly office. Neither of them can act without the other. Certain spears or peculiarly formed iron implements are used as insignia of power or as conductors of spiritual energy. The Bassarites explained this to me by saying that the person selected by the spirits as their Shâmân finds on the fields small pieces of iron, called Agomma, which chase him until he picks them up and thereby accepts his election as a priest of this religion. When placed in the hut these pieces of iron then grow into long rods with upper and lateral branches. The Yorubans call them Ille and they are badges of the Ada-ushe. It is these which have been given the intelligible (?) name of " fetish trees " in the literature dealing with Benin.

The Bori's usual appearance in the streets does not convey an impression of a profoundly significant or intellectual company; its procedure reminds one rather more of a skilful conjuring performance than anything else. Martius gives an account in the records of the expedition based on the notes made at Illorin in illustration of this. It runs as follows :

The Bori folk gather for the dance in the afternoon about two hours before sundown. Soon the sounds of fiddles (Goye) and guitars (Molo) strike the ear, accompanied by the calabashes (Koko) either beaten with sticks or, if furnished with grooves, held before the player's chest, who scratches them with his nails in turning them round and so produces a humming sort of sound. Then the Magadja rises to her feet. She wears two girdles of cloth (called

Damara), in which the amulets are sewn, knotted together over her breasts and hips and in her hand she holds a slender rod of bronze. Scarcely lifting her feet from the ground, she steps slowly forwards ; her movements soon get more lively and she follows the *accelerando* music by beating its time on the ground with the soles of her feet. Suddenly she makes a leap and falls on the earth with her legs spread apart, only to get up and repeat this performance. A large mortar is brought along. The Magadja gets on to this and ventures the jump as aforesaid also from this, shaking the firm earth as she falls on it. She does this three or four times, until she falls exhausted into the arms of her attendants, who comfortingly cover her with a cloth while the hitherto breathlessly gazing crowd thanks the dancer and musicians with an ample largesse of cowrie and kola. Then the novices, young girls anxious to penetrate the mysteries of the Bori dance, appear. With lightly balancing steps and waving a cloth in their hands, they dance to the music and then kneel down before the Magadja who, as it were, blessing them, lays her hands on their backs. Another Bori woman is already dancing, a bronze staff resting on her hip, her frenzied eye on the heavens. While all this is going on the Adjingi stands aside unmoved. But now his body is suddenly convulsed, he snatches at the air with cramped-up fingers and stammers words without meaning. The crowd now makes way for him and some women cover him with cloths. The attack is soon over and the Adjingi begins to put on his garments. Chest and body are covered with cloths and several " Damara " are knotted over them. The Adjingi takes his staff in his hand and, thus bedecked, appears in front of the protecting cloths of the women in order to perform the dance and the bold leap from the mortar, and even sometimes from a tree or a house-top, without hurting himself.

Darkness has meanwhile set in and the Adjingi gathers up the last cowries and kola-nuts ; the crowd deserts the square well pleased. I called the Magadja and the Adjingi to me next morning. I wanted them to repeat their performance of the previous day without the gaze of the profane upon them. Neither love nor money could move them ; the Alledjenu was not hovering over them.

Do not let us be led astray by these external mummeries, but let us listen to what the Bori folk told us about their internal ceremonial when we succeeded in gaining their friendship.

The division of all Alledjenu into two kinds is very important. It has been said that there are white spirits and black. The Ibi people definitely state that the white Alledjenu, who always live in the water, are, on account of their colour, called Fari-faru (white-white), while the black ones always inhabit the bush and are called Babaku (black-black), because of their hue.

\*        \*        \*        \*        \*        \*        \*        \*

Girrika Ritual in Wukari.—The following description of the cure of a man attacked and made ill by a Babaku was given me at Ibi :

It may happen to a man who goes out at night to meet a Babaku and fall ill. The Alledjenu can then go on, but the man will lose his wits and be unsound. His family do not know the right treatment to be given him when he comes back. As soon, however, as his illness is found to be connected with an Alledjenu the family goes to the "Gusulfa" or the "old woman" who fills the post of Magadja in the Bori. She takes the sufferer under her charge and summons her partner the Adjingi. Adjingi and Magadja cannot practise separately. The relation between the two is a singular one, but corresponds precisely to that which connects Djengere and Magadja, that is to say, neither can effect anything independently. On every occasion when I had some talk with the Bori folk both of them came, nor would either of them say anything without a previous conference with the other. If one of them could not turn up I had to say what I wanted to the other, who then went away to the absent colleague, had a consultation and only then returned, ready to impart something to me.

Well then, his family has taken our patient to the Gusulfa and she has informed the Adjingi. She asks the family for a red cock ; that means that the fire-medicine is pertinent to the matter in hand. The red cock is sacrificed with the black animals at the initiation of the Magadja. She makes ready for the fire or smoke ceremonial, while the Adjingi goes into the bush to gather all the herbal and other ingredients necessary to the cure.

The Gusulfa takes a jar, some Shuni (blue colour), Masigi (red wood colour), and Alli (white colour made from bones). She then paints the jar with this black (dark-blue stands for black), red and white in rings. The medicine is put into the jar, which is then well wrapped in white cloth and set on one side for three days. This Magani (magic charm) must stay in the jar for three whole days.

After that the decoction suited to the sufferer is prepared. Albassa (onions), Chita (hot peppers), the tree fruit (Kulla), some root-barks of different trees ground to powder and a goodly quantity of Manshanu, i.e., cow butter, are added to the broth. All these things are well mixed and stirred in the medicine-jar and make a strong soup which is well rubbed into the possessed person. A little of it is kept for internal administration.

This inunction is followed by the sacred inhalation, which is called Furare by both Houssa and Nupé. The Magadja puts some fire in an earthenware pot and pours some powdered drugs into it. The patient has to breathe this medicinal vapour and, as it seems, mostly wrapped up in a cloth. After the sick man has thoroughly inhaled his ritual nourishment, he is taken in hand. The remainder of the ointment is mixed with rice and water and he is fed with the mess. Externally and internally he has been made ready by anoint-ment, inspiration and nutrition. But the main thing, namely, the treatment of the sufferer by way of his sense of hearing, is now to come.

" David," a Goye player, a fiddler (and elsewhere, as we shall see, a guitarist), is summoned. It is an interesting point that this individual need not necessarily be a member of the Bori. He may have but the slightest connection with the Bori, but must know their tunes. For when he plays to the sick man he has to recite the names of the various Alledjenu individually, because, according to the real ancient ritual, more honoured now, I think, in the breach than in the observance, every single Alledjenu had his own appro-priate notes, concords, harmonies and melodies. This proceeding then, was a conversation in music, such as is still extant in a flute speech and a drum speech. I do not believe that a guitar and fiddle language is living to-day. But tradition asserts its previous existence. I never could look upon these things as freaks of imagination. There is quite a considerable amount of evidence to show that there was formerly a very singular relation between the guitar and the way it was thrummed. I shall have to discuss this later on in connection with the " hunter's guitar " of the Kanuri and other tribes of the Soudan.

Well, the Goye musician chants the names of the Alledjenu. And when he utters the name of the Alledjenu who has caused the patient's bad case, this Alledjenu returns and " fills the sick one from the crown of his head to the sole of his foot."

· Here there is some confusion in this otherwise lucid account. Before the illness began, the Babaku was said to have attacked the man and passed on after making him ill. Now, in the treatment by fiddle playing, it is stated that the Babaku returns, fills up the sufferer from top to toe and then pursues his way. As the acoustic method of dealing with demonic possession seems to have been the integral part of the ancient ritual I made exhaustive inquiry what the divergence might mean and got a description of the various stages of possession and their symptoms. And I should wish to put down the following as the averaged result of the statements combined :

The man made ill by the Babaku at first screams, falls into a fit, distorts his features and has convulsions. After that he falls into a lethargy. This obviously means that the Babaku throws him down and goes on. When he lies comatose the Babaku is supposed to have gone further. Afterwards, now, when either the violin tones or the guitar thrummings invoke the Babaku's name, the patient again screams, again becomes convulsed, gets very excited, but then relapses into perfect indifference. That seems to be the meaning of the Babaku filling him up from head to heel and then letting go and departing out of him. Probably it is some kind of epileptic condition, and this fits in with the name given to an obvious sufferer from the falling sickness whom I saw in Bida, because there it was called " Bobaku." I had not, however, then gone into the Bori mysteries and knew nothing of a Babaku which, in all probability, is the same as Bobaku.

But to get on with the account of the clinical methods adopted. On the discovery of the originating Alledjenu the Adjingi rubs in the medicine, and then the session continues for seven days and nights in succession with fiddle-squeak and drum-tap.

Three days after that the epileptic is carried into the bush and washed. Then the Babaku departs from the man (or, as the case may be, the woman) he has possessed. Then the general custom is to sacrifice a black buck-goat to the Babaku, cook it and eat it. But no morsel of it may be taken into the village or town. It is an unwritten law that these sinister immolations and all traces of them must be confined to the bush. Not a single pot, not a single piece of crockery used in the arrangement of the ritual is allowed to go back into a human abode. And this buck, too, is the mildest and certainly most usual sacrificial offering made to-day, the part doing duty for the whole. In reality every Babaku demands other and often a great number of offerings of black, either animal or human males, or cloth which is black. But by custom this has been reduced to what we may call the " symbolic " he-goat.

The gloomy Babaku, having accepted his swarthy offering, the priest and assistant members of the community return home with the invalid. Three days after that a white ram is immolated. The black goat was for the Babaku, the white ram is for the Fari-faru. This, too, is slaughtered, cooked and eaten, and this dinner is followed by a great ball and extensive festivities in the course of which the second essential part of the ritual takes place. For now the one or the other of Fari-faru frequently and suddenly inspires these or those feasters, who leap about in mighty bounds, often hurling themselves into the air and coming down flop to the ground on their *gluteus maximus !* It is this part of the ritual which has degenerated and become trivialized into a special bit of fun, and that is why both Professor Mischlich and Dr. Alexander state that this dance is the chief manifestation of the Bori religion. As a matter of fact, this dance is the only thing the Bori show the stranger. But the essential part of the inspiration by the Fari-faru, which the Bori so ardently wish for, is contained in the spirit of prophecy which comes over the dancers. I shall dwell a little more fully on this in describing the ceremonies of the Wukari people. When the festival is over the Bori take the sick person as being now made whole again, back into the bosom of his family. The procession is headed by the Adjingi, the Gusulfa and the Goye musician. The Bori then proudly hand over the convalescent to his kith and kin, saying : " Here have ye once more your child which was ill."

Presents of money are now made to Adjingi and Gusulfa-Magadja. Henceforth the sound man is a member of the Bori community. The whole ceremony is called Girrika. There is said to be a similar ritual performance called Osoodi 'de among the Yorubans, alleged to be a portion of the worship of Shango.

\*     \*     \*     \*     \*     \*     \*     \*

The Origin of the Bori.—Now, what is the source of this singular religion of possession ? I was talking one day with a man in Kordofan about the origin of this peculiar belief not originally inherent in genuine Africans, but certainly only engrafted on their own indigenous creed in historical times. The man questioned said : " These spirits are winds ; they came out of Persia." At first I attached no importance to the statement, yet now, on turning over my records, I find several notes which make it worth some attention. The Houssa, for instance, call their demons Iska, or winds, as well as Alledjenu. The Bori in Bornu maintain that the spirits called Alledjenu, or Djindi, have nothing to do with the demons of their own religion, which are more properly named Kaime, or Kurua, and came in winds. The Moonshees on the Benue inherited several properties of civilization from their neighbours who came from the North. I am not, therefore, surprised to find lewd demons cropping up in their myths, which are explained as being winds or whirlwinds. In the excerpts from Mossi history, reproduced in the Chapter " A Race of Emperors and Kings," the wizard-potentates frequently show their power by conjuring up storms which smite the conquered nations with diseases. Thus on closer examination we on all hands find an ancient form of philosophy completely substantiating the assertion of my Persian friend in Kordofan, which made the demons into winds and spirits of the air.

This offers a pointer to the lands in the East which must be followed in our search for the origin of the Bori and we may pursue this path with less hesitation since we are not primarily forced to leave African ground. For a few tribes in Kordofan also profess the Bori religion as well as the Nubians, but call it Desatir, and say that the demons of possession ride on the whirlwind.

So we have arrived without any compulsion at the East, from which the Bori peoples of Western Africa according to congruent statements received this religion. But the religion of possession prevails to a very large extent on the Nile. W. Ch. Plowden already described it long ago as " Zar," a wide-spread form of religion and civilization in Abyssinia. Enno Littmann recently studied it among the pagan Kumanas. Some of the Fundji call it Bûm, and in Kordofan, too, it is considered very ancient. I found no trace of it among the Shillu and Dinka tribes, nor generally in the Nilotes. From the basis of Abyssinia-Kordofan it had then made a strong northward movement in the last century, and had already gained such a foothold in Upper Egypt in 1875 that the Government saw reason to adopt measures to stay its continued progress. Whereas that famous Egyptologist, E. W. Lane, was not cognizant of its existence in Lower Egypt at all, it is to-day so widely spread under the cognomen " Zar " as to play a great part not only among the lower strata of the populace, but even the better educated class. Paul Kahle published a book about the " Zar " conspiracy, which enables us to gain knowledge of the subtler details of the Egypto-Abyssinian religion of demonic possession. (Magazine : " Islam in 1912.")

A priest and priestess, who are neither blood relations nor married, are also at the head of individual communities who profess the possessional creed in the Nile countries. In Kordofan the priestess is called Amena, in Egypt simply Shesha. She plays the principal part, and, for instance, in Nubia, stirs up the earth with a staff (of wood, but not as in the Soudan, of iron), from whose smell she then ascertains the name of the bringer of pestilence. Here and there the diabolic spirits are divided into black (Desatir tumburra) and white ones (Desatir buri), but in general they are locally grouped. The treatment of those possessed consists in the inauguration of sacrificial and adjuration festivals lasting from one to seven days at stated times and places. I was unable to detect any distinction as to sex or colour in the victims offered up in the East, but I observed that here, too, the result of the adjuration depended on the appropriate clothing of the person possessed and the effect upon him or her of music. In this region, too, every demon has his own tune, which is played on a lyre-shaped stringed instrument in Southern lands, but produced on drums in the North. No agreement can be arrived at with the spirit without his proper melody having been found. But here, too, it is especially the " love " for a person which causes the spirits to fall foul of their victims.

Taking it altogether, Zar and Desatir may be identified with the Bori. Here, then, we can obtain points of view based on phenomenal extension which will help to solve the problem of the origin of the Bori religion. Its general survey is unclouded. The religion of demonic possession in Africa begins in the lands of the East side; follows the Middle Nile through the Soudan to the Niger; undergoes a particularly strong territorial and inward development in the triangle of the Houssa countries and, then, dies away in the West. But I emphasize the point that this religion is not indigenous to the Northern fringe, for it is absent in Tunis and Algeria and lacking also among the older Soudanese " disruptive " tribes. Historically regarded, it is connected with the wavelike movements which broke over the Soudan in the seventeenth century. But it is not our business now to give dates or to look for them. Its growth at various periods of history will claim our attention in the last chapter of all.

However clear the essence of the extension of this religion in Africa may be, yet its inner meaning constitutes a singular phenomenon which most certainly is not of African origin. The suggestion of its indigenous African growth is contradicted by the fact that the neighbouring countries in the East had already brought similar and related philosophies to maturity in ancient times. The stringed instrument is the principal weapon in the armoury of defence against spiritual obsession all the world over. Its birthplace is Asia. Wherever there are drums they are of the tambourine type,  which is peculiarly Asiatic, and not truly African. But who on hearing of the Bori Goye-playing can fail to be reminded of the story of King Saul, who was also possessed by a dark spirit banned by the sweet music of the harp which David played ? Had not Palestine for a long time been a land possessed by "angels," not always the angels of God according to Scripture, but bringing strange diseases in their train. The religion of possession passed over Palestine like a cloud during a period fairly circumscribable in history. Careful researches (cf. Delitzsch) have made it clear that the worship of demons probably only came into, and spread over, Palestine under Persian influence after the Babylonian captivity. It had no doubt reached its zenith of effective power in Jesus Christ's time and disappeared again from Palestine.

Persian influences! There are black and white demons of the Alledjenu kind in Persia. Persia is the neighbour of Ural-altaic Shâmânism, which in primitive days retained still living forms of all kinds of foreign influences, these being, however, in their original nature very closely allied to African Shâmânism. Here we stop short. Our work must not step beyond the region of African wellsprings. The problem we set ourselves will be solved when we have gathered together the threads of the world's history of civilization to a point from which they lead into our own continent from abroad.

The vista opens out. We see a strong stream bearing from the East into a Continent, whose might has long been a thing of the past. We see the path its migration took along that Continent's vertical axis and, after being dissipated in the stream from the East, run out through the sands of the Soudan into the West. We now ask ourselves whether other heirlooms of civilization, whose nature can be determined by history, may not also have been carried along on the waves of this stream? This is the real result of our investigation of the nature and migration of the religion of possession by demons or angels.

Nupé houses with pre-Islamite façade decoration.

*(Drawn by Carl Arriens.)*

# CHAPTER XXVII

### THE DECAY OF A DYNASTY

## (*A Century of Nupé History*)

The wars of succession among the Nupé—Rise of the Fulbe under Mallem Dando—The first plots—Division of the Empire—Etsu, the mighty, expels the Fulbe—Renewed Fulbe dissensions and intrigues—The Houssa General Omar creates order—Extinction of the Edegi dynasty—The Fulbe plot against Omar—Final conquest by the Fulbe—Nupé revolt and slave wars by the Fulbe Kings—Character even among "niggers."

A BRIGHT and varied series of pictures has been passed in review. At first we went from the provincial town to the capital to take part in the modern life of those distant countries of the Soudan ; then we immersed ourselves in the onrush of the waves by which Islam was carried along from the North-west, under Libyan influences, in spite of the opposition to its further progress by the Eastern civilization which was eventually crowned with success. We observed that these Eastern and more ancient forms of culture must have been endowed with features of a highly remarkable character, and I brought the third portion, devoted to the examination of religious legends and cults, to a close by a reference to related phenomena in Western and Central Asia, which stand in no sort of connection with Arabic philosophy and Islam, its nearest neighbours. Taking a bird's-eye view of this motley sequence, we see the Mandingo nation with Emir Diarra, the founder of Empire, as the champion of a recent Mahommedan world-concept in the

Soudan. We see, too, the Mossi nation, with its mighty hero, Uidi Rogo, as the defenders of the right to live of an older form of civilization drawing its nourishment out of the East.

And it is to this civilization and its chronicles that I propose to devote the last part of this book. I wish to describe the triumph of Islam over one of the most wonderful States of the Eastern current, over the Empire of Nupé—the story of a century-long contest, which eventuated in the adoption and re-invigoration of their ancient inheritance of an enlightened policy of culture, a faculty for organization and all sorts of technical excellencies by the victorious Mahommedan dynasty. This dynasty, however, was powerless to do more than effect a pronouncedly Malikitic view and practice of law, such as prevails in the Mahommedan West, and, by strict administration, to strengthen the old institutions in principle, while destroying a good deal; or, in other words, to prove that the intrinsically more active, yet, in principle, much poorer, current of culture from the West did not sweep away that which had been previously alive, but only steeled the sinews of the more ancient and intensive civilization of the East in its struggle for existence.

The study of the growth of religion occupied our attention in the foregoing chapters. We now turn to the political development, the historical record of a people, of a nation, whose roots strike down very deep indeed. The Nupé possess a copious store of written and oral traditions about their past. Now this wealth of material is very much scattered and its fragments are mostly so worn away at the edges that it is not always easy to reconstruct its patterned mosaic correctly. Nay, I did not even find the beautiful vase's pedestal amongst the Nupé themselves, but at two points far beyond this nation's own boundaries, namely, with the Bussa and Nassarawa peoples. The inaugural legend, to be fully set forth in the next chapter, makes the first Nupé King, Ussu Napata, come from the East with King Kisra. His dynasty came to an end in the marriage of the last of this family with a woman of Yoruba. This event was followed by a period of independence from the Southern countries, namely, from Bini, which we may be justified in identifying with Benin, and from Attagara, which means the Atta of the Igarra in Ida. Before that time the South was a dependency of Nupé; it now seceded and compelled the submission of the North in general and the Nupé kingdom in particular. This alternation of government left its echo behind it in the method of official appointment, as I shall easily prove in the following pages.

It was Edegi who, living at the Court in Ida as a hostage, freed Nupéland from its fetters. Innumerable legends cluster round the form of this liberator of his fatherland. He and his descendants were well able to secure both the self-maintenance within, the protection from pressure from without, the continuous development of handicraft and the intensive utilization of agriculture for several centuries. But this Edegi race suffered from a radical evil, namely, doubt as to the line of succession. And this worm at its root brought the dynastic tree to the ground.

The old Lilli in Mokwa started his narrative of the historical growth of Nupéland with these words of almost classical tone: " In olden days (n.b., of the Bini dynasty) there was here (in Nupéland) no paternal authority; the mother and her brothers alone were entitled to a voice as to the children." This means that the line of succession was not through the paternal, but on the male maternal side. Consequently Edegi's two sons, Ebako and Ebagi, were not kings in Gbarra, the chief residential capital in the Edegi period, but were enfeoffed with the Mokwa-Rabé district, while Ramatu, Edegi's sister, appears to have been throned as Queen in Gbarra, and removed her seat to Sugurma when her son was of age and supreme. In the good old Edegi times the succession to the crown proceeded on this basis without a hitch, smoothly and as a matter of course. But after that the patriarchate came closer and closer to Nupéland. Was it the Songai who brought it ? Was it a pre-Islamite social philosophy which introduced the patriarchal ideal, this alluring incitement to fatherly and motherly ambition ? This much is, at all events, certain, namely, that even before the actual foundation of the Nupé kingdom there had been a departure from the matriarchal succession, and, for example, Edsu Masu had already appointed his son Owdoo as Saba, i.e., heir apparent, against the wish of his family and subjects. Nay, more, it would seem as though patriarchal succession had been the more ancient institution in this land and only abolished in favour of the matriarchate by the rulers of the Bini dynasty.

1785–1830.—Be that as it may, the era of misfortune of the last hundred years commenced in this breach of the law of succession and ended in the final suppression of the venerable matriarchate. In 1785 Jimada was the last of the Edsu in Nupé. He reigned till 1799, and mostly in the city of Ragada, near Patigi. His eldest sister was married to one Umoru, a noble of Edegian stock. She bore him a son, named Madjia, who, according to the Edegi law, was the real heir to the throne. But eleven years after he had been King, Jimada did not name Madjia, but his own very youthful son Issa (the Fulbe pronounce it Edrissu), as Saba.

Thereupon Madjia declared war against his uncle. His mother is said to have instigated him and the aristocratic houses who were greatly concerned with maintaining the law supported her action. Tradition represents Edsu Jimada as an incapable person, of whom it was said that even if he had plenty of wives, he had but few children, while Edsu Madjia, his nephew, had but few wives and three hundred (!) children. The confusion thus occasioned explains why a certain Abudu Romanu succeeded in raising an opposing party of considerable power, which was only suppressed by Mallem Dando in 1806.

In 1802 Madjia finally got the better of Edsu Jimada, whom he is said to have killed with his own hand. He was then called to the throne and acknowledged as King by all with the exception, of course, of the adherents of the deceased Jimada. These chose to attach themselves to Issa, Edsu Jimada's infant son, by him officially nominated as Saba, and they took the boy to Adamalelu, where he was kept in concealment lest the King, with a reputation for cruelty, should kill him as well.

This episode would, like many others of old, have passed over without after effects if another quiet and insignificant company had not meanwhile arrived in Nupéland, which set fresh currents flowing. These were the Fulbe. Here, too, they came to the surface as quietly and unobtrusively as elsewhere. I could not ascertain the exact year of their entry, but, according to an MS. preserved in Kabba, Mallem Dando arrived in Nupéland in 1806, and began business by killing Edsu Abudu Romanu, who then had the upper hand, by " magic."

The Fulbe account is this : Two brothers, the sons of the

Fulbe Faté, wandered from Gandu to the South ; they were both
Mallem. One of them, Mallem Allimi, went to Ilorin, quickly in-
gratiated himself with the Yorubas by his magic arts and was made
King. This Mallem Allimi was a sorcerer, a Wulli. The other
and younger, Mallem Dando, or as the Nupé call him for short,
" Manko," settled with his followers in Rabba. But while the
elder rapidly attained the goal of all Fulbe emigrants and became
Chief of Ilorin, Mallem Dando soon came into conflict with Edsu
Madjia. The reason of the quarrel is very obvious. Firstly, it
was reported to Edsu Madjia thus : " One Fulbe Mallem has settled
in Ilorin and the other in Rabba." Then Edsu-Madjia asked this :
" Tell me whether he and his do good." The answer was : " They
do good ! " After some time people again came to Edsu Madjia
and said : " The Fulbe Mallem settled in Ilorin has called the
Yorubans Monafiki (instigators), and now he is Chief of Ilorin."
Then spake Edsu Madjia : " Then take ye horses and weapons and
chase forth the Fulbe who have settled in Nupéland at Rabba."

There is no difficulty about this. The success of the one brother
made the other's swift accomplishment of his own project impossible.
And it is equally easy to understand that Edsu Madjia drove out
the Fulbe from Rabba and that these Nupé-Fulbe retired to the
more successful Ilorin-Fulbe in order to hatch out some new plan
of attack. Edsu Madjia's troops expelled Mallem Dando from
Rabba and pursued him to Ilorin with a view of clearing out this
dangerous neighbouring nest as well. Mallem Allimi gave the
fugitive Rabba-Fulbe a warm welcome. He said to them : " I
am a Wulli (sorcerer), I will shield ye. Not an arrow can reach
you here. But you can catch the Nupés with your open hands if
they do come hither." When Edsu Madjia's Nupé warriors appeared
before Ilorin, Mallem Allimi gathered all the Fulbe about him and
rode out from the gate to meet them. Then these turned tail
and the Ilorin-Fulbe pursued them as far as Eggan on the Niger.
Madjia is said to have awaited the return of his soldiery in Rabba
and, on receiving the news of their defeat, to have gone first in the
direction of Yebba, then to Batsua and then to Laquata, where he
lay for three months.

Now the Ilorin-Fulbe were far too weak to make an assault
upon the might of the Nupé on their own account, and so

took refuge in a trick, in the famous doctrine, *Divide et impera*. When Mallem Dando was in company with the Sheikh Allimi in Ilorin, Allimi asked his younger brother : " Is there none at all in Nupé who hath a claim and desire to be king in Nupé ? " Thereupon Mallem Dando sent envoys to Gbarra and announced : " Allah hath imparted to me that Issa (Edrisu), the son of Edsu Jimada, will be king over Nupéland. This came to the ears of the Nupé in Gbarra and the Elders, who had hidden Edsu Jimada's son in Ademalelu, said to themselves : " Mayhap this affords us an opportunity to instal Edsu Jimada's son. The Fulbe need the permission of a king over Nupéland to return there and to Rabba. Let us apply to them." The Elders sent an ambassador to negotiate with the Ilorin-Fulbe. They said : " Edsu Issa shall be our king. We are willing to help him in this war." They mustered an army, the bulk of which was made up of Eastern Nupeans ; but Yorubans of Ilorin took part in it under Fulbe command. The latter's talent for organization decided the eventual issue. Madjia was worsted by Issa and retired to Mulé in the Sugurma district and, when the Fulbe under Edsu Issa kept on advancing, he was forced to withdraw as far as Augbarra in the Kambarra or Kambali country.

Then Edsu Issa the victorious went back to the East. He sat down in Edda in Trans-Kaduna to the westward of Bida and fortified the town with a wall. Mallem Dando had settled himself again in Rabba after Issa's success and all the other Fulbe, in obedience to the dictates of their policy, took up their abode with the royal court at Edda. Here they incited the King still more against Madjia, because it was their obvious object to stir up the old Nupé dynasty to internal discord and to hound them on to their mutual destruction. Now, one day the Fulbe were talking this matter over in one of their houses. An old slave at the court of Edsu Issa overheard one of them saying : " We shall conquer this Edsu Issa more easily than Edsu Madjia." So he went to his master and informed him what the Fulbe had said. Then Edsu Issa gave orders for the Fulbe's expulsion.

He marshalled a strong armed force and sent it out against Rabba to deal the Fulbe a smashing blow. He succeeded in investing the town. It was strongly fortified and defended itself, but badly provisioned. Edsu Issa hoped to starve it into sur-render. But Mallem Dando stepped in. He sent a messenger northwards to Edsu Madjia at night to tell him : " Come to Rabba and fall upon Edsu Issa's rear. Then thou canst annihilate him." Edsu Madjia came and, almost before he appeared, the whole body of Edsu Issa's men drew off to the fortified town of Edda without loosing a bowstring. But, directly he heard of the alliance between the Fulbe and Edsu Madjia, their leader fled head over heels from Edda to Esa, a place close to Eti and Charati, which is on the now projected railway line. When Edsu Madjia pursued him thither, he again broke up his camp and retired to the East, where he rested in Ekadji, by Kadja, in the province of Agaye.

Madjia at once went back to Rabba and concluded an alliance with the Fulbe. In order to set the seal upon the bond of peace, he gave their most distinguished men three of his own daughters in marriage. Mutafa, a young son of Mallem Dando's, no warrior, but a highly respected and influential priest, got the eldest. Usman Saki, an older son of Dando's, and afterwards first King of Bida, got the second. He gave the third to the Fulbe Majaki, or commander-in-chief, named Mallagao, who was powerful but not related in blood to Mallem Dando. After the splendid nuptial festivities were over, Edsu Madjia again took the field, fell upon Edsu Issa and drove him over the Niger to Toji.

Mallem Dando died about this time, and therefore the Fulbe sent envoys to Gandu, who reported all the events and begged for further instructions and, while Edsu Madjia was close upon Edsu Issa's heels, a decision was come to in Rabba. The envoys to Gandu returned bringing with them a high plenipotentiary from the Emperor of Gandu. Summoned to a conference at Rabba, Edsu Madjia there found a whole army of armoured and fully-equipped cavalry as the escort of Gandu's ambassador. The pomp he displayed is still fresh in the natives' memory. Magnificent garments, such as he had never set eyes on before, were presented to Edsu Madjia to sugar this bitterest possible pill. For the Emperor of Gandu did not recognize his title to kingship as a representative of the ancient Nupean dynastic line. The Gandu ambassador declared that Islam could only acknowledge the son's claim to succeed to the throne, but not the nephew's; therefore, in the Mahommedan view, Edsu Issa was King *de jure* and *de facto* in the ancient Edegi city of Gbarra. However, since he, Edsu Madjia, had allied himself with the Fulbe and given them his daughters in marriage, the Sugurma province would be given him as his kingdom. With regard to the rest of Nupéland round about Rabba, this would be administered by Madjigi, a son of the glorious Mallem Dando, lately deceased, and Madjigi was to set out for Gandu for further instructions.

This decision was as sly as it could be. It kept the two conflicting parties on their legs, properly restricted the spheres of power of them both, and put the reins of government into the Fulbe's grasp. And under the mask of pompous generosity to Edsu Madjia the Fulbe fraternity thus gained its supremacy.

An apocryphal and possibly later tradition records some details of these peace negotiations. While the notables were discussing matters in the presence of Edsu Madjia, under the presidency of the Gandu ambassador, a Fulbe youth is said to have made a humiliating, vulgar gesture to Edsu Madjia's face. A young Nupé standing behind Edsu Madjia, furious at the insult, is reported to have bitten off his finger and hurled it at the face of the Fulbe with these words: " First take this! Later on I will give thee arrow-heads to eat." The Fulbe who was guilty of the gesture of contempt is said to have afterwards been King Usman Saki, and the Nupé youth the terrible Edsu Zado.

All parties were agreeable to this settlement, because for good or ill they were constrained to submit to the will of the Fulbe. Edsu Madjia went back to Sugurma and there in peace spent the rest of his days. He only undertook a few little slave raids against the Kambari. Edsu Issa returned to Gbarra and completed the city fortifications. Madjigi went to Gandu to get his credentials. He came back from there in great state and died three days later.

1830–1846.—Rabba very rapidly grew to be one of the first cities in the whole of Soudan. At that time there were many flourishing towns in Nupéland, chief among which was Gbarra, so renowned for industrial art. An old Nupé told me that Nupé at that time still had one hundred and twenty towns, each of them as large as Bida. Nupé produced more clothing than the Houssa countries. But Rabba took the lead among all the Nupé cities. It was very ancient and had been founded before the Edegi epoch, but not so old as Mokwa, which was described as the mother town. And Rabba was only surrounded with a wall (Ebang) by Edsu Madjia (or Magia) at the beginning of the century before the Fulbe had been banished to Ilorin. The latter, and especially Mallem Dando and his sons, had helped Edsu Madjia in building the fortifications and the palace both by word and deed. In those days Rabba was already so large and its population so wealthy that it had as many as one thousand four hundred horses.

Now, when Usman Saki was made king in Rabba, in 1831, the town was still growing in importance. This ruler must have exercised an unusual amount of influence over his contemporaries, particularly in his youth. Even while his father was living as a simple Mallem in Rabba before being exiled, the young men of the place used to assemble nightly at Usman Saki's, whose little finger had but to be lifted to get their consent. He was not a great warrior, but an orator, a clever demagogue, one who knew how to play on popular feeling, but no more a man of decent character than any one of his brothers or successors. Now, when he became Edsu he began to make use of his power to raise the status of Rabba and it is commonly reported that Usman Saki contributed very greatly to enhance the position of Nupéland in the first sixteen years of his rule. He is said to have frequently done his younger brother Massaba great hurt because he arranged slave raids in Nupé itself. He obviously desired to get this opulent country under his sway by peaceable means and therefore said to his brothers: " If slaves ye must hunt, go to the Bunu, go to the Kukuruku, but leave the Nupé alone ! The Nupé ought to make cloth and so make us rich ! " He sent his brother Massaba to Ladé so that he might make his forays from there on the Bunu and Igbirra.

Usman Saki wanted to get Nupé under his thumb in his own way. He is accused of having tried to poison Edsu Madjia. Once a woman is said to have died instead of the King, and once Massaba, the ruler Usman Saki's own brother, is said to have sent Edsu Zado, Edsu Madjia's son, a warning. And with this Edsu Zado, the most individual, most imposing, and, in its own brutal way, really great personality takes the stage in this drama.

In 1847 Edsu Madjia died a natural death at Sugurma, after two fruitless attempts by Usman Saki to poison him and his sons. Directly he was dead, Massaba sent this message to his brother, Usman Saki : " Edsu Madjia is dead. Take the gold (?) krakras (trumpets) and the silver (?) saddle, and the other~precious things of Edsu Madjia into thy own possession, for they are too good for the Nupé ! " But he sent a different message to Edsu Zado, saying : " My brother has ill-treated mē. He wanted to poison thee and thy father. Let us be friends and allies. My brother Usman Saki will, anyhow, now go up against thee to take away the trumpets of gold, the saddle of silver and the rest of the treasure."

I heard a very 'characteristic anecdote about Zado. Though it may possibly be untrue, it yet sheds an excellent light upon this King's character as old Nupé people still remember it. On his father's death and receipt of Massaba's message, Edsu Zado said to his friends : " I wish to tear Nupéland from the Fulbe's clutches and restore it to the children of Edegi. Ten brave men are worth to me more than a hundred whose hearts are weak. Sound an alarm early to-morrow on one side of the town, saying : ' Usman Saki is coming ! ' Come then to me on the other side and help me to separate the brave from the cowards ! " So it was done. When the news of Usman Saki's approach was bruited on one side of Sugurma, all the faint-hearted raṇ out of the opposite gate. But Zado and his bravoes lay waiting on this side and shot down the fugitives one by one.

Then Usman Saki's forces really came near and Zado took up his little son and a daughter and—took to flight. It was the most horrible flight ever brought to my knowledge. The King and his two little ones, with a few of his faithful ones, fled to the most famous magician in the land. He took refuge at Kanji, or Kanshi, a township near Bussa, on an island in the Niger. He came to this people, famous as sorcerers, and begged them : " Aid me against Usman Saki ! " The Elders said : " How can we old men help thee, the King ? If thou art not stronger than Usman Saki, how should we who be old be so ? But if now we give thee a Chigbe (magical instrument ; Magarri or Ashri in Houssa), will it help thee ? " Edsu Zado said : " That is what I want of ye." The Elders said : " Wilt thou now give us thy eldest son and daughter ? "

Edsu Zado said: "Therefore did I bring them. Take ye them."

All the people of Kanji were gathered together. A great fire was made. Edsu Zado stood by the fire, and over this the people of Kanji butchered the babes of Zado the Edsu. Their father looked on. They stripped the skin from the little boy's back and stretched it over a drum. The father looked on. They stripped the skin from the little girl's back and stretched it over a drum. They burnt the two bodies, mixed the ashes with "medicine," filled them into the drums and plugged down the skins. Zado the Edsu looked on. He saw all that they did. When the drums were ready, the Kanji gave them to him, who took them and said to his followers: "Let all the towns in Nupéland hear the Chigbe I hold in my hands. These drums shall be beaten till Rabba lies in ruins!"

The news of the terrible sacrifice which Zado the King had made on behalf of the Nupé dynasty was borne on the wings of the wind all over the land. From East and West and North and South the people flocked, for such terrific magical things as these must surely bring victory with them. Only the people of Mokwa were loyal to King Usman Saki. They came from Mokwa to Rabba and said to him: "Zado the Edsu approacheth! He hath immolated his own children. All the Nupés are flocking to him." Usman Saki asked of the Mokwans: "Why, then, do ye not also go to Edsu Zado?" They replied: "We cannot desert thee to go over to Zado the Edsu!" The Fulbe afterwards repaid this fealty of the Mokwans most shamefully!

King Usman Saki mustered a great host and sent it to Yebba under Soadjia, in order to break this advanced post of Edsu Zado. The latter sent strong reinforcements there. Soadjia was lured on to the island by a trick, overpowered and put into irons. Then the Nupés beat the panic-stricken and leaderless army and brought Soadjia to Yeni, near by Sugurma. There Zado had concentrated his main strength.

Now this Soadjia was particularly hated by the Nupé because he was the commander of Usman Saki's troops and always sent on expeditions against recalcitrant Nupé. He had always entirely destroyed the towns on these occasions, sold the inhabitants into slavery and thus amassed wealth. Now, when Usman Saki sent a still greater force to Yeni after the capture of his general at Yebba, the Nupés of Zado spent all their fury on Soadjia and struck terror into their opponents by their extraordinary brutality.

A great fire was lighted in the sight of the people of Rabba. First Zado's people showed them the captive Soadjia and shouted : " This is the man ye sent us ! Now ye may have him again ! " They beat upon the two holy drums, danced round the blaze, singing " Here ! this is Soadjia, who always captured and sold folks. He made himself rich by this work. Now let us see how he feels in the fire himself."

Then they hacked off Soadjia's arms and flung them in the flames. They cut off his feet and did likewise. They then cut his body in two down the middle and threw both halves into the fire, so that the whole of him was burnt to ashes. Zado stood by and looked on.

After Soadjia had been sacrificed and consumed in this way, Zado's army took up its arms and hurled itself on the camp of the warriors of Rabba. The terror-stricken armed host was routed and beat a retreat to its capital. Usman Saki raised another. Edsu Zado, to whom came ever more streams of men eager to fight, led his troops from Yeni, between Bokani and Mokwa (closer to the latter), to Kwota. Usman Saki's Maejaki (or Majaki=general), Dagowa by name, was also leading his army there, and there a third battle was then fought, which Zado conducted in person and won. The remainder of Usman's soldiery fled to Rabba. He could not raise a third fighting force. All his persuasive eloquence, all his sending of messages availed him not ; Edsu Zado's name struck fear into every heart. None dared meet him in the open field. All Trans-Kaduna became his and he now ventured upon his final enterprise : he laid siege to Rabba.

The city was rulerless. Usman Saki elected to take leg-bail in time. He first fled to Agaye, and then, circuitously, to Gandu. Here he at first hoped to be furnished with fresh means, but his want of military ability was probably too evident ; and, besides this, the turn taken by events in Nupéland under the guidance of the Fulbes of Nupé was so singular, that Usman Saki had to spend eleven long years in exile at Gandu and was unable to return to Nupé until 1858.

The siege of Rabba holds a peculiar place in the memory of aged Nupés. They liked to talk of it. Zado had encircled the city with a properly constructed ring of fortresses for attack. He posted sentries everywhere, and relieved them regularly; those who attempted to escape from the town were captured and sold. The water supply was cut off. But hunger soon began to pinch the inhabitants. Many died. They began killing each other, shared out the flesh of the dead and devoured it. At last the remaining survivors fled in an inexplicable way. Edsu Zado entered the city and levelled it to the ground. He said : " Now have I satisfied my will. These people can do me no further hurt. Every man can now go home and attend to his own business ! " Then he dismissed the army.

The capture and destruction of Rabba must, as I reckon, have occurred ¯in 1847. Some have given the date as 1846, a difference so slight as to prove the correctness in general of the calculation. The fall of Rabba and the first defeat of the Fulbe dynasty brings the second section of the Fulbe period to a close.

1846–1852.—This moment was the last which afforded an opportunity for the re-creation or restoration of the old Nupé Empire. The Fulbe had been forced across the Niger southwards, and their power was broken. The real Nupé ruler of the Fulbe branch had fled to Gandu ; only his brother Massaba, a first-class plotter, a bloodthirsty fellow, but neither a soldier nor organizer, was left at Ladé, on the south bank of the Niger. He had gathered around him the last of his father's followers and spent his life in catching slaves and selling them for his personal enrichment.

Thus Nupéland proper was free. Edsu Zado ruled in the West, Edsu Yissa, a son of Edsu Yissa, meanwhile defunct, in the East. Some advisers are reported to have advised Edsu Zado to march first to Gbarra and kill Edsu Yissa and then start a war against Massaba. This would undoubtedly have been sound counsel in the interest and direction of the fortunate development of the Nupé State, for Edsu Zado would most certainly have succeeded without great difficulty in getting both of his opponents out of the way by means of his personal ability, the numerical strength of his soldiery and, above all, by the tremendous respect shown him by the entire nation of Nupé. But he was not a Fulbe who was conscious of his aim, but just a plain Nupé man who had done himself well. He disregarded all this advice because he wanted to live in peace.

Edsu Zado's days were not long in the land. He died about 1850 in Borodyi (or Borodgi), which lies between Ebako and Gherkum. As this town is on the road to Gbarra some assert that he had resolved after all to undertake the campaign against Edsu Yissa. Nupéland's miserable fate was sealed with his death. The spirit of discord entered the country from that time forward with giant strides. The poor Nupé people suffered most greatly in the period now at hand. The Fulbe intriguers now manœuvred with marvellous skilfulness and in their able hands the last weak-kneed Nupé Kings were but little better than pawns in the game.

His son, Surugi, became King on Edsu Zado's demise. He must have been a poor enough creature. His father had impressed on him : " Never go with a Fulbe ! " His father's body was scarcely cold when a Fulbe embassy was sent to him. Edsu Surugi received it. He was staying in Yangi, near Rabba, and is believed to have had an idea of rebuilding this city. The Fulbe embassy was the work of that arch-plotter, Massaba. He urged Surugi to adopt the course which Zado ought to have taken, namely, a war against Edsu Yissa. But it would be altogether a different thing whether a Zado or a Surugi waged it. Zado was a warrior of experience, held in honour and a man of broad mind ; Surugi was young, untried, petty and as yet lacking in esteem. Had Zado made up his mind to undertake this war, he would have done so as the closing chapter of large-hearted plans at the prompting of the Nupé nobility. But Surugi began this enterprise incited thereto by the hereditary foe of the Nupé, counselled thereto by the Fulbe, and the seeds of failure were contained in this fact alone. Massaba sent Surugi this message : " I should like to be friends. Keep Nupé for thine own ; then will I take Kaba and the Igbirra lands ; but thou, as my friend, must be sole master in Nupé. Thou must crush Edsu Yissa. He possesses the flag, the ring and the bed of Edegi (the crown jewels, as it were). These things should be in thy hand. Go there and fetch them. When thou hast gained the victory over Edsu Yissa and taken the flag, the ring and the bed of

Edegi, come to me in Ladé. There we will make our alliance."
And Edsu Surugi fell plump into the trap. He sent back word to
Massaba : " I come ! "

He had scarcely put this assurance in his girdle before he summoned all the Fulbe adherents and the exiled Usman Saki's friends
and set out for the South. He made a slave raid in the neighbourhood of Kaba. But Surugi moved up against King Issa, whose
palace was in Gbarra. Massaba kept a watchful eye on the movements of the cousins he had set by the ears. Directly he was sure
of his business he sent the following report to Gandu : " The Nupé
Kings are in conflict again. It is high time to interfere and restore
the Fulbe supremacy." The then Gandu ruler—according to
Nupé statements, Malle-Halelu—first asked Usman Saki whether he
wished to grasp at the chance of going back to Nupé. He said he
would come back when the war was finished and proposed young
Umoru as a capable leader. Umoru declined on the ground that he
had fallen out (?) with Massaba and could not now fight with him
shoulder to shoulder. Thereupon the Emir of Gandu decided that
Situ, the Fulbe King of Ilorin, should settle the Nupé affair. Situ
at once accepted the offer, invaded Nupé with a swarm of cavalry
and soldiery and beat Surugi. Fleeing with his army to Yeni,
Surugi died an apparently natural death in the same year. Meanwhile Situ "arranged" the matter in his own way. He robbed
and plundered on all sides, and this was the beginning of that final
laying waste of the land which others continued.

The Western Nupé proclaimed Masa King when Edsu Surugi
went hence. Edsu Masa also expressed his desire to dwell in Yeni.
The news was sent to Gandu. The Emir ratified Edsu Masa's
election and recalled Situ, especially as that wily old schemer,
Massaba, had sent word to Gandu that Situ was devastating Nupé
to such an extent that it would probably be unable to send any
tribute to Gandu in the following year. This commences a period of
peace for West Nupé from about 1853.

1852-1856.—An unusually able general, a Houssa chieftain named
Omar, had come with the Gandu army led by Situ. His skill had
quickly brought him into fame and when Situ went back to Ilorin
Massaba succeeded in persuading him to remain in his service and
undertake the command of his warriors in Ladé.

This Omar is the second man of truly great endowments in this century whose character shows some very remarkable features. Omar was chivalrous, as by the contract he made with Massaba and by the nature of the difference which parted them proves. He declared his readiness to lead Massaba's troops against the Nupé, stipulated for certain payments, but declared he would have nothing whatever to do with slave-raiding. This statement by the Nupé is extremely interesting. It is obvious that then, too (either already or still ?—which ?), there was a nobler way of thinking in this part of Africa. But there is not even a shadow of excuse for the contrary Fulbe description of this general as a "blood-boltered" tyrant. The appeal made by Omar's knightliness to the Nupé and the hatred evoked by Massaba's cruelty is obvious from the fact that they chose Omar afterwards as their king in place of Massaba, that they followed him faithfully and only deserted him after his last Pyrrhic victory.

So Massaba attached this admirable man to himself, and as soon as he had this excellent general at his disposal he for the first time ventured upon a war against the Nupé. He picked a quarrel on purpose. He sent this order from Ladé to Edsu Yissa at Gbarra : " The kola nuts (the so-called Labodji) growing in Nupéland are in future to be delivered to me." Edsu Yissa sent back this reply : " My father, who was ever a friend to the Fulbe, used to eat these Labodji himself. I, who have ever been thy friend, may, I presume, also eat them." He was unaware at the time that Massaba had engaged General Omar.

So he got frightened when this news was brought to him : " Massaba has sent Omar against thee." Omar was held in great fear. Yissa went to Lobodji and fortified it. But he was unable to hold his own against this terrible commander. The war lasted but five months. Edsu Yissa's resources in Lobodji dried up, his people fled ; he himself was obliged to fly and Edsu Masa opened the gates of Yeni to him. Yissa took shelter under the protecting wing of his cousin's inimical family, and this first episode ends of this particular period.

In the course of this war Massaba is said to have always followed in Omar's footsteps with his army. The Nupé gave him the name of Makundunu (hyæna) because he made haste to carry out his slave raids right and left where Omar had subjugated the country. He must, indeed, have carried on atrociously, because the memory of his barbarities sticks more closely to people's minds than any other occurrences. But apparently the Nupé had lost confidence in their Edegi dynasty. The most natural thing would have been for all the old families to have combined against the foreign invaders and gathered round Edsu Masa, more especially now that Edsu Yissa was also staying in Yeni. But there was no trust to be placed in this direction. On the other hand there must already have been a great deal of respect for Omar's chivalrous method of warfare, for a large deputation of Nupé nobles came, not to Edsu Masa, but to Omar, the foreign general of the Fulbe, who was a Houssa.

The Nupé said to Omar: "We beseech thee to send an ambassador to Gandu. We pray the Emir of Gandu to make thee our Edsu. We shall all perish if Massaba goes on thus destroying our families and laying waste our farms." And Omar said: "Good, I will help ye." He kept his word. He sent back his army and marched it against his own master, the Fulbe Massaba. He sent him word that he, Massaba, had himself broken the contract (?). Henceforth he, Omar, was King of Nupéland. He simultaneously sent a full explanation by an envoy to Gandu. The Emir of Gandu was too shrewd to come to a decision in haste. He would wait and see to which party victory might incline. Massaba was meanwhile pushed back to Mali (or Mari). His uncle, Ilorin's Nupé ruler, then received the fugitive.

But another piece of news reached Ilorin after the message sent by Omar. Madjigi, the first king of Rabba, who had died there three days after his investiture, had left two children, a son, Moru or Umoru, and a daughter, Abiba, who remained single. Umoru had been exiled to Rabba with Usman Saki, but Abiba had stayed in Nupé. Now, as soon as ever Omar had driven out Massaba, whom the whole of Mallem Dando's kindred seemed to dislike quite as much as he did, Abiba despatched a messenger to her brother to this effect: "The Houssa, Omar, hath driven our uncle Massaba away. There is no longer a Fulbe in Nupéland. Come!" This dispatch very clearly shows the solidarity of Fulbe sentiment, of which there is evidence no less clear in the history of the

Senegal-Niger districts than in the Niger-Benue countries. " There is no longer a Fulbe in the land " is always a challenge to throw out a grapnel which may fish up a meal for the maw of a Fulbe. Umoru immediately set out, arrived at Mali and Mari and gathered the wives, children and slaves of Massaba together, sent these possessions to his uncle at Ilorin and then went to meet Omar with the troops he had brought with him from Gandu.

It proved particularly difficult to obtain definite information about the relation which primarily existed between Omar and Umoru, and how this was transformed and developed. The statements of the Nupé and Fulbe were very contradictory. Yet I think myself justified in drawing one conclusion, namely, that Omar was not very highly delighted at the prince's arrival, nor, indeed, had he reason to be.

Although Umoru may not perhaps have been sent over as the official plenipotentiary of the Gandu Emir and as a family substitute for the momentarily impossible Massaba, yet the recommendations and the large cavalcade which the Emir had given him were in themselves a hint for Omar, whose pith, even if not contained in the actual words, was this : " Thou art no doubt a most valiant general, but, if the kingship is in question, we Fulbe will be quite ready to find somebody among ourselves to fill that office." And Omar took the hint. He said to Umoru : " If I am made Serki or Edsu (king) here, thou shalt be my Yerima or Saba ! " And the Fulbe Umoru's alleged answer was : " I do not believe that to be thy wish." This traditional speech and my own reflection seem to convince me that the general and the prince could not have been on the best of terms at the start. Besides which, Umoru, the terrible Emir Umoru of later days, was already then the complete compeer of the rest of his worthy family at the game of intrigue. He sent this message secretly and behind Omar's back to Edsu Yissa, who had taken refuge with Edsu Masa : " If thou desirest to be King over Nupéland, deliver up Edsu Masa to us ; advance against us ! Send thy envoy to Omar ! "

After the war with Edsu Yissa, Omar had first lain in Ishegi (or Etshegi), near Sagbe and Kutigi, then gone into camp at Tatungbasu (near Dabba), and stayed there for a year. Umoru came to the General at this place ; this was the scene of the conference above-mentioned; it was from here Umoru sent Yissa his treacherous summons; Yissa's answer from Yeni was forwarded hither. His message to Omar was: " My father was a friend to the Fulbe. Edsu Masa's father, Zado, was second to none in his hatred of the Fulbe. I myself will be your friend, and, because I think that thou wilt be as well disposed to me as to my father, I inform thee, Omar, that Edsu Masa is planning a campaign against thee and wishes to become King of all Nupé. Therefore, come ! "

And Omar fell into Umoru's trap just as easily as foolish Edsu Yissa. He moved out with Umoru and his army and swiftly arrived at Etzegi(ng), said to be about two miles distant from Yeni. The Nupé now asked Edsu Masa to advance against the enemy. Things would not apparently have been in a bad way at first, but Masa had too little of his father's military blood in his veins. He stayed with his choicest soldiery in well-fortified Yeni, sent out small bodies of troops now and again to harass the camp at Etzegi and in this way postponed a decisive engagement for six months. But then a great piece of treachery settled the fall of the Edegi dynasty for once and for all.

One day Edsu Yissa left Yeni town, in which Masa had generously sheltered him, and showed Omar the way through the lines. Omar gathered his force to strike a terrific blow; the Nupés were beaten and fled in disorder to Kpatatshi, near Lieba. Edsu Masa escaped quite alone on horseback from Yeni and reached Sugurma in safety. Here a Houssa happened to see and recognize the unarmed King and cut off his head in the market-place. He took the head to Omar. This was the end of the last King of the Edegi dynasty.

The power of the Nupé was broken beyond hope of repair. Their old aristocracy fled across the Niger to the Bornu Borgana. They took the road viâ Bussa. But they did not elect a King from the Edegi stock on that side of the river, but Baba, the son of Shaibu. The choice fell upon him because Baba's mother was a Borgana and the Nupé thus hoped to establish a good footing with their present entertainers. And this is how it came to pass that the last King of the Nupés fled to whence, twelve centuries earlier, the founder of the Empire had come. What a marvellous turn of Destiny's wheel !

Yissa, the faithless, was despised by his friend and his foe; he

always followed in Omar's train, and in Bida he died in con-
tumely.

1856–1859.—Omar proceeded to Mofange, and from there to
Modshupa into Kambarriland. He subdued these provinces,
turned about, and marched to Satagi; then to Mule, and afterwards
to Egbe(ng), or Egbei Sugurma. The inconsistency of this episode
struck me as singular when first brought to my notice. While Omar
was popularly reputed to have been an amazingly sympathetic
personality in the previous period, many stories current about
him after the expulsion of the Nupé Kings make him out a most
horrible monster, a perfect bloodhound. The fact that the Nupés
subsequently fell away from him is a proof that his later reputation
was based on very peculiar circumstances.

The actual course of events was told me by a Fulbe who was
proud of the craftiness of his race and whom I had succeeded in making
talkative. Just as Massaba had done before, so now Umoru followed the tracks of the soldierly King. And precisely as the dear
uncle had formerly laid the country waste wherever he went,
so likewise did the charming nephew. Umoru, probably the
cruellest of all the Fulbe princes of Nupé, was not satisfied with
plundering the natives and taking them into slavery; he tied people
together and flung them into fires; he gouged out the eyes of old
folks; cut off their genitals; poured melted lead into the mouths
of the chieftains. Once he impaled a woman, who was the ruler
of a town according to its custom, on an iron stake and said: " Now
wilt thou be mother to a son made of iron." But he committed all
these horrors " at Omar's command." He went to work with
the most subtle cunning. Once, " at Omar's command," he openly
took prisoner a personage of rank and had him tied to a stake in the
heat of the sun. Then he slipped out to him at night, cut his thongs
and let him escape; but bound him to secrecy not to let it be
known that he, Umoru, had unbound him out of good-feeling and in
disobedience to Omar. And in these ways he managed to under-
mine Omar's good name. To the Nupé leaders he said: " Until
you helped him to drive out the Nupé kings, Omar was gentle.
But now he would devastate the land. He compels me to plunder
and catch slaves. I have to hand everything over to him. Omar
is already rich, but he will annihilate you all."

Umoru laid his plans with consummate care. An increasing number of Nupé chiefs attended the nightly assemblies he had instituted. The conspiracy had also been kept secret so well that its fruit was fully ripe when Omar began to rattle his scabbard. He heard in Egbei of Umoru's forays, summoned him and reproached him with them. But the prince now discarded all semblance of humility and showered abuse upon Omar. He said: "He, Omar, had nothing to do in the matter; could never be King, because his father had been only a huckster; even though the pedlar's son had been made a general, he would not be permitted to dictate to him, Umoru, the son of a Fulbe, the first Fulbe King of the Nupés."

The general called his men to the colour; he would expel Umoru with all his Fulbe and Gandu tribe as he had before banished Massaba. And then he discovered that his followers had left him in the lurch. All Nupé went over to Umoru. Omar was betrayed. Umoru banished his late commander-in-chief.

A very graphic account of Omar's flight was given me by an old woman. He had been forced to retreat in the last battle he had ventured to give to Daba and at night told his remaining adherents to restrain themselves and not to fight. He advised them to retire as Umoru advanced until he came back with the fresh force which he was now going to recruit. Then the general fled, accompanied only by his wife and his son Alliadji, to his birthplace in Kamuku-land. There he enlisted recruits. It seems that after the Fulbe-Houssa wars and the progress towards Adamowa made by these Founders of States, a sort of inferior mercenary infantry had come into being, a kind of hireling militia. These mercenary bodies ran hither and thither between those from whom they could expect most booty.

Now Omar's name was even then famous in Houssaland. His appeal not only brought together a considerable armed force, but acted as a magnet on others when he returned to Nupéland. On his arrival, Umoru himself was lying at Edjigi, but his army was encamped at Tatung. Omar hurled himself at the latter, threw it back upon Daba, renewed the attack and forced it towards Sakbe. Here Umoru joined his troops, but many Nupés and former adherents of Omar had, however, meanwhile pondered the situation and come to the conclusion that there was something mysterious in this warm-heartedness of Umoru's towards the Nupé which required explaining. Already here in Sakbe many deserted to Omar.

Here, then, a real pitched battle was fought. Both sides are said to have behaved with determined valour and suffered great losses. Though the victory was with Omar, it was decidedly Pyrrhic. It was plain that his hirelings could, indeed, repel the massed attack of Umoru's Nupés once, but not twice. For the mercenary's profit and advantage lay in the precipitate flight of the enemy. Then he could loot and make slaves and sack. But Omar was unable to put the Nupés and Fulbes to flight. He pushed them aside a good way, but then Umoru retreated across the Kaduna to Bida in seemingly very good order. When the general saw this he is said to have grieved very sorely. When he returned to his camp, all the men and women greeted him with the shout of welcome: " Saki! Saki! Saki! " as the victor. But Omar dismounted, went to his wife and said: " Pack up thy goods. Go back to thy mother. I shall not win twice with such soldiers as these." If this little story is true, it sheds a very bright light on the singular character of this " negro." If, however, it be an invention, it still fits in well with his picture in general as formed in the popular mind.

Umoru saw the position exactly like Omar. He pitched his fortified camp in the neighbourhood of Bida, while Omar himself invested the town and began his entrenchments. Umoru's camp was on the hill now occupied by the English Residency. Umoru fortified this. Omar attacked it and Umoru sallied forth with his forces. He abandoned the fortified position to the enemy and went into Bida which he strengthened still further. The situations were reversed. And, moreover, Umoru spent the five months of his enemy's besiegement to the greatest advantage. He sent envoys to every one of his own kith and kin with these tidings: " Come now. Victory will soon be ours. There is no King of Nupé. But do not fail to bring hither Edsu Baba. Then thou thyself canst be Emir of Nupé." To Massaba, however, the message he sent was this: " We will sink our old differences. The Emirship of Nupé is a matter which concerns every Fulbe. Therefore, thy brother,

Usman Saki, must now be made Emir. The victory will be won very soon. Come therefore ! ''

Now, Umoru, the astute, must probably have quite well known that he could not rely upon his uncle's actual arrival, but that he would; on the contrary, watch like a vulture from afar for the real decease of the lion. And so it happened. Yet Umoru had fully attained what he aimed at. The vultures hopped a bit nearer with a few flaps of their wings when the death-rattle was borne on the breeze. This did not scare Omar, but it frightened the Nupé.

Usman Saki set out from Kabi near Gandu, where he had been living in exile for the last eleven years. An officer of the Emir of Gandu escorted him. He sent a message to Edsu Baba who had also heard of the Fulbe concentration and placed the whole of his forces at his disposal. And Usman Saki sent these troops, composed of the surviving adherents of the Madjia family, in the direction of Bida. He followed them personally at a pretty safe distance and put in an appearance on the field of arbitrament at the very last instant. Massaba's action was similar. The Ilorin Fulbe furnished him with a few bodies of men ; he sent them to Umoru in Bida, and, like a cautious person, tarried himself in the township of Eddhu on the Niger.

When Umoru saw his own side thus reinforced with soldiery, but more especially by the rumoured approach of a greater number of Fulbe leaders, he determined to strike one last blow. He called all the Nupé chieftains together and said to them : " If I am beaten again, ye will have the heel of this Omar and his footpads on your neck. Then will you have to be ashamed of such a ruler. If ye desert me, I may perhaps be vanquished, but then the other Fulbe and Edsu Baba will be here and extinguish ye.''

The armies engaged.—Omar was encamped on the Chekte, Umoru on the Landru stream. Umoru's Nupé attacked Omar's lanzknechts. Omar was worsted and retired to the Bako brook. The rout was general. When Omar was trying to swim his horse across the Chatchaké river in flood, both horse and rider were carried away by the waves ; two of Umoru's soldiers fished out his corpse and bore it to the conquering prince. He had it decapitated and exposed the head on the walls of Bida. The only truly noble phenomenon in this history of a hundred years perished and vanished like a rat which is drowned and hung up on a nail.

But Nupéland at last had its tyrant.  That was in 1857.

\*     \*     \*     \*     \*     \*     \*     \*

If I have devoted more space than usual to this one portion of Soudanese history in this particular book, the reason was not only to present a detailed picture of the struggles between the champions of the Eastern and Western currents of culture in order to follow the thread of our theme ; it was not only to mark the pre-eminent toughness of Eastern national resistance, but to avail myself of the opportunity also afforded to show that there are in the history of these countries and their inhabitants characters and personalities which appear and act as epoch-making individualities.  We here see, just as we in Europe see, significant and insignificant men—men with character and men with none; we see passions, nobility and meanness in operation here, among these races no less than in our own ; we recognize the enormous difference between two " negro " races—the Fulbe and the Nupé—who are as distinct as any two European nations ever are.

We will now, however, bid a truce to historical illustration and turn to the political growth of the States under the influence of the stream from the East.

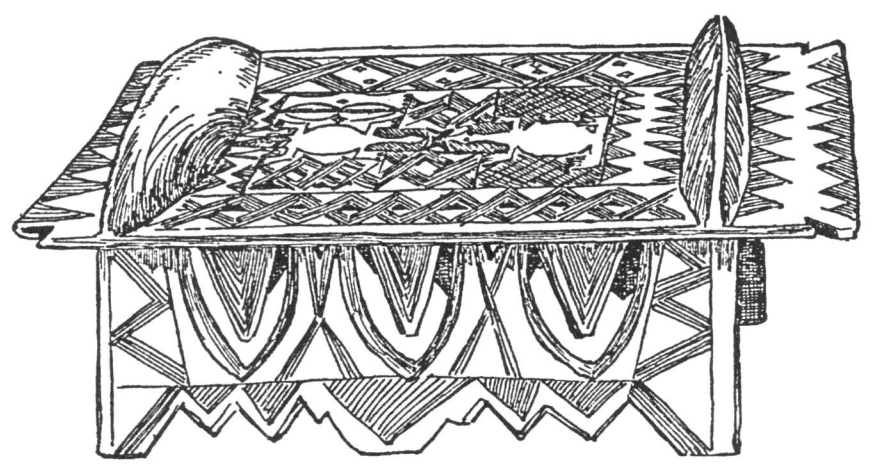

Carved chieftain's seat, about 3ft. 4in. wide. An ancient royal Nupé throne is said
to have been of this kind.
*(Drawn by Carl Arriens.)*

# CHAPTER XXVIII

### THE AFRICAN IMPERIAL PALATINATE

*The official organization of the Mossi Empire—Officialdom in the Nupé Empire—Two kinds of office-holders—Badges of Imperial Power—The Court Jester—The problem of the Court hierarchy—Distribution of the " ladder " arrangement of office—Origin of the principal offices of state.*

SEVERAL distinctive features of the mode of life and of the historical growth of some of the African nations have been brought to the reader's ken in turning over the brilliantly coloured pages in this Soudanese picture-book. We observed the resistance offered to the spirit of Islam advancing from the North-west by the strong stream of Soudanese powers whose current was setting Westwards from the East. We saw that the might of Islam failed to influence the direction in which this current tended. We recognized that a religion of Oriental origin did not succumb to Mahommedan pressure, but adapted itself to it. We shall now see that the forces of Islam could not act otherwise than combine with the sturdy nature of the East-western Soudanese, although they had overcome the old dynasties and the ancient paganism. We shall learn that this type of old Empire continues to exist even when Islam concealed it beneath a veil of its own chosen colour.

I presented two pictures of the historic effectiveness of the more ancient forms of Soudanese vigour in the previous chapters, the reaction, namely, of Mossidom against the Crescent of Mahommed and the Edegi dynasty's destruction by the Islamite Fulbe. The ruling Mossi of to-day are Mahommedans in name and the Nupé of to-day give the impression externally of being a purely Mahommedan kingdom. The mosques in Wagadugu and Bida appear to be the centres of modern spiritual life. Yet for all that the religion of the Prophet failed to alter the political constitution of either of these two nations in spite of a struggle which lasted for a thousand years. The interior construction of these ancient realms is the source of our interest. Our attention will now be arrested by the organization of the powers of government and the life of the Court. The study of the material thus offered will show us the quarter from, and the means by, which the strength of the Soudanese Empire was most recently revived. It will show us the strength of the forces which created the organized, constructive backbone and connective relation of Soudanese policy, that is to say, of the Soudan in its higher development as generally understood. And here, right at the commencement of the two concluding chapters, I indulge the hope of success in an attempt to systematize these forms of government in their historical growth and relation to definite periods. We propose, therefore, to examine the political constitutions of the Mossi and the Nupé, which can be determined by their comparison with a considerable number of similar State-forms, having regard to the question whence the energy was derived which enabled them to withstand the onslaughts of Islam. A thousand years have elapsed since the first mercantile settlement of proselytizing Mahommedans was founded on the fringe of the Soudan. A thousand years have been spent by Islam in the propagation of its religion, yet after this great lapse of time we still see the same form of Empire, the same political organization in existence which must have given the Soudan its power and glory in earlier days. I am inclined to think that the task of acquiring what knowledge we can of the source of this strength is such that its importance cannot well be over-estimated.

\*      \*      \*      \*      \*      \*      \*      \*

Cavalryman in padded armour.

(After a native sketch by Capt. Termnd.)

Let us then try to realize this life as it unrolled itself at the Imperial Court of Wagadugu.

Every morning, after sunrise, long trains of superior dignitaries still appear at the Mogo-naba's palace and offer their obeisance to the ruler by prostrating themselves on the ground, touching the earth with their foreheads and beating it with their fists with upturned thumbs. There are four men at the head of this numerous cortège of higher officials who have always played a part in this Empire's most ancient story. These four are the Tanso-naba, the Uidi-naba, the Lachale-naba and the Gunga-naba. We shall see subsequently that the bearers of these high titles are not only very greatly honoured, but that the power they wielded enabled them under given conditions to dethrone the Emperor.

Each of them has his special duties. The Tanso-naba is the supreme military commander-in-chief. But not that alone. On the decease of a Mogo-naba, the Tanso-naba conducts the business of government in his place until the Emperor's successor is proclaimed. The Imperial Master of the Horse, the Uidi-naba, is perhaps of still greater importance. It was he who formerly in a certain measure ruled the kingdom outside the precincts of the royal palace and his colleagues always held him in fear. It is the Lachale-naba's business to receive the orders of the day every morning as far as the discipline of the palace, the revenue from the provinces and the disposition of work, etc., are concerned. The Gunga-naba's business is to negotiate with the petty provincial chieftains. He summons the rebellious or the disobedient or calls them to order. If and when such negotiation breaks down, he carries the representation of the supreme power a step further by marching at the head of the expedition entrusted with the restoration of quiet. He hews off the hands of the kickers against the pricks and conducts the mutilated offenders before the Emperor for the final pronouncement of justice.

The second official grade begins at the Kammsaga-naba, the Chief of the Eunuchs, whose office is, naturally, not hereditary like the rest. He is always the first to appear at the Court and is responsible for its proper upkeep and what happens there. A whole series of subordinate officials executes his orders as the conductor of public works. The Nemm-naba is the kitchen superintendent. But it must not be assumed that either of these officers, or those now to be named, actually perform their duties in person. They make their own appointments and may in a way be called the Inspectors of the Imperial Palace and especially of the quarters of the harem. Every morning the Poi-naba inquires of the Emperor's first wife as to what may have happened about possible quarrels among the women, possible illnesses which might be traceable to sorcery and other fascinating mysteries. On special days the women are then heard seriatim and the cause of their happiness or the reverse accounted for. Next to him in rank is the Bendere-naba—the Imperial drum-major, who may also be named the Imperial " flatterer-in-chief." He turns up every morning and at all solemnities, chants all the names of the imperial genealogy in a nasal monotone, recites all the great ancestral deeds and benefits by the gracious presentation at intervals of gifts, such as a valuable robe or some rich jewel—provided always that he can flatter sufficiently. The office of Ballum-naba is very important. He arranges the sacrifices over the imperial sacred possessions which he partly stores in some particular corner, but mostly in all the corners of the extremely commodious Royal Compound. His special obligation consists in periodically making the right kind of offerings, the Tjimse, to the spirits of the ruling family's ancestors. The Samande-naba tells the young people of the same age as the ruler the proper boyish games. He is the preceptor of all the sons of the nobility of the highest rank. When the Emperor's contemporaries are thought deserving enough, the ruler gives them each a woman. They remain his friends and under the guidance of the Samande-naba are generally members of his Majesty's entourage.

The Dapoë-naba is the imperial executioner, and, in addition, the master of the slaves and domestics ; the Uidi-danga-naba is the chief of the grooms ; the Kamboë-naba is master of the inferior drummers.

The third rank of the superior class starts with the Gan-naba, who gets his name from the shield (or Gongo). He introduces the guests, but also looks after the guests of honour and, with true African diplomacy, does not always advance their special interests. The Djukugo-naba accompanies the monarch on his yearly pilgrimage to the graves of his forebears and wipes the sweat from his

forehead on the journey with a whisk.    Below him is the chief
warder of the Imperial tombs, who disposes of a whole staff of servants,
each one of whom watches over one of the Imperial ancestral resting-
places.    Then there are the lord of the market-places, the guardians
of the royal quiver, a naba of the beans, a master of the Bogore trees,
a guardian of the propriety of the kingly seat, an upper slaughter-
master, an inspector of the purity of the imperial drinking water,
the officer charged with looking after the heaps of kitchen offal,
the superintendent of the kingly stud, a manager of the poultry yards
and the judicial administrator of the law with respect to cattle
stealing, together with the chief protector of the She-butter trees,
who is ably seconded by the custodian of the baobabs.    Then, below
these in rank, are the saddle-layer, the chief inspector of the imperial granaries, the same of the imperial police spies, the chief
inspector of the matting and inner walls of the palace apartments,
the head of the fisheries, the hierophant of porridge offerings, the
principal huntsman, the chief herdsman and the principal of the
basket-makers.    Then there are the chief of the imperial jest-makers
and jugglers, the royal roofers, the bailiffs of the royal farms, the
imperial purveyor of game, the superintendent of the seasonal
sacrifices, the guild-master of the bronze-founders, the guild-master
of the ironsmiths, and, lastly, a Naba whose task it is to keep the
district south of Wagadugu free from wild animals.

To this third class of officials are attached those subordinated
in rank ; for example, an upper door guardian, an upper way-guide,
and a player on the Lunga drum, as well as a calabash beater, who
are all under the orders of the Bendere-naba.    Then there come the
drummers who play the secondary tempo in the concerts, the blowers
of the Antelope horns, and so on and so forth.

＊　　　＊　　　＊　　　＊　　　＊　　　＊　　　＊　　　＊

And then there is yet a second imperial officialdom, a second
imperial Court State of the same stamp.

Judging from the account of its history as furnished by very old
people, the Nupé kingdom before its domination by the Fulbe was
an unadulterated despotism.    It may well be that the sentiments
and institutions based on long-existing family ties in times of insur-
rection, in peasant revolts and tribal feuds, continued to thrive in

this country unassisted. It may well be that in that bygone period the Nupés were farther removed than they to-day are from being a uniform nation; this is all, in fact, indeterminate but not intrinsically improbable, but it is absolutely certain that the entire population was kept together by a far stronger and more significant feeling of unity due to the uninterrupted rule of the Edegi dynasty for centuries before the interference of the Fulbe with its internal constitution. It was able to look backwards through a vista of many centuries to the mythical heroes of the past, who sired a long line of regents of the same blood and the same ruling family, and this gave birth to an indubitable feeling of solidarity and traditional loyalty which, although it may now be a thing of the past, found its expression in violence and brutality. The units of a people and the adherents of a single royal house, whose scions burgeoned for more than a thousand years without rotting or decay, were naturally greatly inclined to gird a little now and again at despotic power. But, as a general proposition, the nation was content under the sway of this dynasty and, as a matter of course, increasingly so the longer it endured. An Emperor, an imposing figure in the perfection of its power, was at the head of the Nupé realm. As far as the state machinery was controlled and directed by this one individual, this particular despotism was not obviously different from the others in neighbouring countries; but it was especially suitable for Fulbe exploitation. The latter found its entire organization so eminently practical as to be unable to do more than leave it precisely where it stood after its " heathendom " had been overcome. The dynasty changed; the constitution remained. Nay, even the imperial features do not seem to have changed very much in their character; for Nupé blood also runs in the veins of the Fulbe Kings who rule over Nupé to-day! The façade of the structure, then, got a new coat of paint, but otherwise the building underwent no alteration at all.

And it was a tremendous array of both hereditary and elective officials who assisted the Edsu, the Emperor, in the government of this by no means extensive, but extremely populous country. I think we may definitely take it for granted that not a single one of the many high titular office-holders afterwards to be enumerated was allowed to have any will of his own or to act on his own initiative, but that, on the contrary, the despot ruled absolutely as an autocrat without permitting anyone whatever to interfere with, or alter, his own arrangement of affairs.   This is the great difference between the governmental administrations of the Nupé and Mossi nations. And it is easy enough to understand.   The Mossi kings continually enfeoffed their sons with provinces and made them comparatively independent ;  whereas the Edegi rulers renounced this important function on behalf of their descendants.   The consequence, as we shall see, was that one Edegi followed the . other in ordered succession, and this obviated the necessity for splitting up the Empire into separate autonomies controlled by the members of the ruling family invested with regal authority.

Nupé officialdom was formerly classified with amazing precision ; firstly, by birth and, secondly, by rank.   By birth there were the Djitsu (from Edji, son, and su, ruler) and the Edji-Saraki (from Edji, son, and Saraki, or lofty patrician).   The term Saraki, a patrician appellation, may be brought into relation with the Houssa word for King, viz., Serki.   There is an inherent connection between the Djitsu as the nobility and the Edji-Saraki as the patricians.   In former times these two principal classes were the dominant factors in the State, and the sweets of office, consequently, fell to their share.   But no one member of each division could get an appointment which belonged as of right to the other and each of the main divisions was again divided into an upper and a lower grade.   The members of the upper group, be it Djitsu or Edji-Saraki, were called Enako ;  those of the lower Enagi (or Enaki).   The part played by the Enaki of the Sarakidsu of the patricians in the Emperor's service was so subordinate that they were not even mentioned in the list of court office-holders ;  whereas many of the Sarakidsu class occupied such exalted positions that every chief had to kotow to them.   In order to realize their mutual relation, I will at once recount the titles of the Court officials :

Firstly :   The Djitsu class, the Djitsu-Enako group :  Saba, Botun, Makun, Nokodji, Luqua, Rani, Chetcheko, Netsu, Nadjenu, Benu (or Bennu), Gara, Chekwa, Nepherma, Neïdja, Naquena, N'kotshi, Zoeda and Nbandoma.—These make up the group of the highest Imperial dignitaries.   They rank above and below each other in the above-named order.   Their advancement in office was anciently best expressed in the succession to the throne. On the Emperor's death, the Saba became Edsu, the Botun took the Saba's place as the next throne-occupant; the newly-elected Emperor then appointed another Botun, who, theoretically, was the Makun immediately below him, so that the whole lot moved up one step and each inferior took the place of his immediate superior. But in actual practice the rotation was probably often interrupted. The Saba and Botun alone were considered irremovable posts of honour. Once these were both installed, they could not afterwards be interchanged. The position of the others on the other hand, was, however, largely dependent on imperial favour. The above terms are titles and not names. The employment of these functionaries consisted in their investment by the monarch with deputed authority as municipal chieftains or provincial governors to look after his interests. For, theoretically, the Edsu alone was the fountain of all power over the persons and property in the land, and he only delegated his omnipotence to the authorities as catalogued who collected the imposts and tributes on the ruler's behalf and account. The Edu, or fixed tribute, was the real expression of vassalage. The division of the tribute was approximately this: Of each sum of one hundred shillings, the Emperor himself took forty, the Enako twenty, the lesser officials thirty-five between them and the collector-messenger five as Tutshi, or herald's fee. In earlier days all the cost of administration seems to have been defrayed on this scale. If, for example, the Edsu made an Enako a gift of twenty shillings, the latter had to give his Enaki one-eighth, so that he himself retained only seventeen and six. These noblemen are not, be it said, held in such high esteem as one would imagine. For later on we shall see that it was not they, but the Sarakidsu who had the traditional office of crowning the King, and every Djitsu, the Edsu, Saba, and Botun alone excepted, had to dismount and kotow on meeting a Saraki. Furthermore, all these worthies did not, as a rule, live in the provinces they controlled, but in the capital where each of them had a palace of his own, which covered much ground.

Secondly: The Djitsu class, the Djitsu-Enegi group.—This consists of some twenty exalted persons, each of whom has his individual title. All of these are also descendants of the blood-

royal and appointed both to military commands and smaller provincial towns under the headship of an Enako, who, in his turn,
has to hand over to them a corresponding percentage of his own
personal revenue. And, moreover, each one of them takes pre-
cedence over the one next below him in degree.

Thirdly : The Sarakidsu class, the Enako group in civil
administration.—At this group's head is the Ndeji, followed
by the Neffene, Mansoqua, Chapako, Tsada, Makama, Bana,
Ndasa, Cheteko. These, it is true, are "only" Saraki, but
yet the highest office-holders of the State. The Ndeji is he
who crowns the new Edsu ; the first four are the Emperor's
permanent advisers. Theirs is the duty of telling him of his mis-
takes and warning him, should he become too cruel or arbitrary in his
government ; they are the highest in office and supreme. The
five gentlemen below them in the scale are employed as confidential
ambassadors. The extremely lofty position held by the Saraki is
all the more amazing, because this class has no other privilege than
that granted it from time to time by the Emperor in excess of the
rights which are pertinent to the princes. The Saraki are not
allowed to change their places of residence without the imperial
sanction or the permission of his administrative authority. Some
of them are enormously wealthy. There are Saraki who have
slaves and women by the hundred, as well as positions of great
honour at Court, and yet they are no less subservient than the
Djitsu. For the benefit of those who are interested in linguistic
research, I now state that the term Djitsu corresponds to Houssan
Dan-Serki and Yoruban Oma-ba, and Edji-Saraki of the Houssas
is equivalent to Yoruban Omo-lagba. This group may broadly be
said to be the highest of all in administrative officialdom.

Fourthly : The Sarakidsu class ; the Enako group, or the actual
Palace management.—The Sarakidsu of the upper class came to
be called also Esa-Chusi, as the first in rank of the great palace
servants, and also the "Emperor's purses," or "King's counsel in
privy affairs," and the usual employment of some of these personages
justifies the appellation. Their presidents are : firstly, Gabissoidi,
the chief herald, who introduced and looked after strangers ;
secondly, the Natoaki, who arranged the meat and the drink of the
Court, and latterly had to see to the harem ; thirdly, the Sonaji,

the chief equerry, who was also responsible for the imperial bed of state, or throne, as the case might be ; fourthly, the Soajatsu, whose business was to attend to all the other possessions and the domestic upkeep of the Court ; he had, for instance, to provide for a regular and constant supply of kola-nuts. These were the four principal offices in the remotest periods, and were filled with chieftains taken prisoners of war ; that is to say, with slaves of the most superior kind. The positions were honorific, as the titles conferred implied an obligation to see that the duties were properly performed. I am not clear as to whether the positions were formerly hereditary or not. During the previous century their dignity diminished increasingly to the advantage of the Dansitsu, or eunuchs, who now, with similar or identical titles in chief, superseded the old-established " four sovereigns." The four great State offices, then, were in ancient times filled by great men of exalted degree, and are to-day occupied by four less esteemed eunuchs with similar names. Besides these four, the following also played a considerable part in the life of the Court, viz. : the Masentelli, who controlled the private treasury and movable property of the Emperor ; the Santalitsu, specially charged with the care of the horses ; the Wambei, or inspector of slaves ; the Chigilla, or leader of the Kuti priests and keeper of such sacred imperial objects as might be stored in the palace of the sovereign.

Fifthly : Sarakidsu class ; the Enagi group, or Ministry of War. —This is the group which controls the state disposition of the armed forces. The Soa-sudsu is equivalent to the Houssa Majaki. He thus is Field-Marshal-in-Chief, and as such bears the title Majaki under the Fulbe régime to-day. The others were employed according to their ability mostly as leaders of small bodies of troops, or as commissariat quartermasters, but most frequently as conductors of forays and slave raids, tasks calling more for the exercise of cunning than any great knowledge of tactics or strategy. Speaking in general, this group was principally supplemented by elements drawn from abroad, partly because of its high rate of mortality, partly because it most easily and most frequently instigated rebellions, partly because military efficiency is not so much an inherited quality as administrative capacity, and, lastly, because a genius for war often developed spontaneously from the ranks of the privates.

Sixthly : Sarakidsu class ; Enagi group and the Dansitsu in particular.—These eunuchs are : 1. The Nda-toaki ; 2. The Soma-ji ; 3. The Gabi-ssoedi ; 4. The Somfara-ko ; and their respective functions are : first, to act as the King's " spokesman " ; second, to be the King's messenger ; third, to receive all petitioners, officers and officials and to report to the Throne, with the sole privilege of entering the imperial bedchamber ; and, fourth, to instruct the monarch on all questions regarding presents to be made to other princes. This latter office is the same as that of the Houssan Chiroma. All four of these are, as stated, eunuchs from childhood. They were the nearest and most intimate associates of the Crown during the first period of the Fulbe supremacy, and stood higher in favour than all the other official personnel. It is they who dispossessed the ancient holders of the loftiest positions in the State under the rule of the Edegi dynasty.

Besides these male members of the staff, a number of women are also State servants, but space prevents their detailed description here.

\* \* \* \* \* \* \* \*

And now for the Emperor of Nupé in person.

I have already mentioned that the Edsu of old was a genuine despot and brooked no word from any but his Ndeji or his Wauwatsu, or Court fool. His autocracy and just claim to it were fully recognized. The Nupé historical record and tradition show no unnatural deaths from poison, such as happen to the Emperors of the Mossi and the potentates of Yoruba. If many an unsuccessful attempt to this end is set down in the chronicled pages of the last hundred years, it may probably be rightly traced to the influence of the Fulbe. And the high position of the Sarakidsu, and especially of the Ndeji, is all the more striking in this severely despotic and aristocratic régime. There cannot be the least doubt but that the Djitsu and the Sarakidsu were a coalition formed by the corporate officials of two different periods. I will, without delay, call attention to this great distinction, which will be discussed more fully later on. The Djitsu were as precisely subordinated to each other as we found was the case in the Yoruban official world. But the Sarakidsu were not, on the other hand, invested with office in the same way on such an inflexible system ; nor were they so absolutely graded in rank, and the positions they occupied varied but slightly in importance. The chief parallel to the Sarakidsu is to be found in the provinces of the North and among the Houssas in particular.

This bi-partition, one line of which tends more to the southward, or to Yoruba, and the other more to the northward and the Houssas, is all the more significant, since the actual insignia of Empire, the institutions, were, as will be shown, borrowed from the Sarakidsu. As far as the people in general can remember these things and the source of their origin, the following peculiarities as noted down do not derive from the related civilization of the South, but the North :

The Emitsu, the royal castle palace, was always a spacious quarter filled with large courts and edifices and surrounded with massive walls for defence. The Sigifa was reached through one or more entrance halls (called Katamba) and was the ruler's actual abode. He received official visits in the Katamba where all State business was transacted and the Sigifa was sacred to the monarch's private life. The ceremonial and dignity of the Imperial paraphernalia is markedly interesting. When the Emperor gave audience, his custom was to do so half sitting, half reclining on a high sort of bamboo couch (Gado). A mattress was then spread beneath him. The Gado (or Gada) was richly ornamented with metal plates, supported on bronze legs and was, so to say, the symbol of royal dignity, the throne of the Nupé King. When the Edsu had passed away, and his successor was to be installed, this was done by the Njedi's inviting the appointed heir to take his seat on the Gado.

It was not customary in ancient days for the Edsu to speak in person when he was transacting State affairs in the presence of his assembled nobles. He then leaned with one arm on the officer called Soa(n)susu, either on him or against him. By some pressure which he thus put upon this dignitary, he caused him to speak in his name. The Soasusu then knew what the King wished him to say and uttered it. Three essential badges were worn by the olden Nupé Edsu and were also the insignia of his office :

1. He wore a fillet of yellow metal with crossed metal bands on his brow. This metal frame was stuffed with silk, and its name in Nupé was Malfasing.

Cavalryman with shirt and caped chain-mail in Chamba.

*Photo by Les Frères girod.*

(Facing p. 316)

2. He held a stone sphere decorated with yellow metal about eight and a half inches in diameter in his right hand. This sphere with metal ornament is the Rogo. The heir-apparent to the throne, the Saba, carried one similar. This seemed somewhat smaller and the Saba carried it in his left hand.

3. A staff, named Tsukunsu, which the Emperor had to carry in his left hand. There were a larger and a smaller one, both of which had a metal tip of some kind of figure, of which I was unable to get any clear description or explanation.

I think myself justified in saying that these imperial treasures may be called the crown, the orb and the sceptre. They were all three credited with being of great antiquity. They had been carried by Nupé Emperors long before Edegi's time, when they still resided in Gbarra and elsewhere. Edegi is said to have received them, after landing, at the hands of the old families on his progress Westwards through the country. Old people declare that these three Crown jewels, as well as the old Imperial throne, were still in existence at the time of the Fulbe wars, but then hidden in one of the old Imperial graves when Massaba desired to get possession of the treasure. So long as the Fulbe, or any other nation, failed to discover them, the Nupé kingdom could not be conquered. For this reason alone the old inhabitants of Nupé speak of them with the greatest reserve. If it were known where they were, it would not be advisable to make the fact public. I was one day careless enough to mention these Crown jewels by name in the hearing of a Nupé from Sugurma, who was on his way through the town, in Lokoja. He rose up in great anger and asserted that those who had mentioned these matters must have been evilly disposed and deserved to be killed. Then he went away. I could not persuade him to return.

There was, it seems, also the Ifingoa, a gold ring, as part of these insignia, but this fell into the hands of the Fulbe. The Saba wore a silver one of the same kind on his left arm.

This account of the Imperial State would be incomplete without mention being made of the Wauwa-tsu.

The Emperor's court was formerly remarkable for the office of royal jester. In Nupé his title was Wauwa-tsu, in Houssa, Wauwa-serki, and Asiri-oba in Yoruba. Wauwa signifies " crazy."

But he was as sane as sane could be.    Not only so, but the assumption
was that he was very clever indeed ; but he alone was allowed to
play the maddest possible pranks.    The Fulbe prince Maliki  was
the last to keep a Court fool of the old pattern in the ancient royal
Nupé way.    And  this  is  why the memory of the  singularities
and  behaviour  of  such  an  individual  is  still  very vivid  among
the people.

A Wauwa-tsu was, as a rule, somewhat deformed, either dwarfed,
a  cripple,  big-headed  or  in  some  way  misshapen.    His  clothes
were caricatures of the imperial robes.    He lashed the follies of the
great ones of the kingdom, as well as those of the Ruler himself, with
the whip of his wit.    If the Edsu's kola-nuts which the  monarch
dispensed to his Court were not good, he would bring fruit of some
kind  which  was  rotten, spread it out before the King and his Court
and say : " Here are my kola-nuts.    Not very good, perhaps, but at
any rate better than those you get from the Edsu ! "    Should the
King come carelessly dressed into the audience hall, the jester would
appear with a crown of leaves on his head and dressed in bundles
of leaves instead of a robe.    Then he would say : " Look, Edsu !
isn't my crown splendid ?    Aren't my clothes lovely ?    They cost
me less than your own, but at least they are clean ! "

Once upon a time (only the story has been remembered, but not
the actors in it), an Emperor had an exceeding cruel and brutal
Saba (heir-apparent), who  murdered and  tortured people out of
" sheer cussedness."    None ventured to  tell the Emperor of the
Saba's misconduct.    One day there was a great assembly of all the
nobility, at which the Emperor and his Saba were present.    The
Imperial Jester turned up with a wallet which was full.    The Emperor
asked  him :  " What  hast  thou  in  that ? "    The  fool :   " O,
little brother, deserving of pity !  I have medicines in it."    The
Emperor asked him : " Why am I deserving of pity ?    Whom is
the  medicine  for ? "    The  Court  fool :    " O,  pitiable  little
brother !  hast thou not long known that thou art blind ? "    The
Emperor : " What now, blind ! "    The fool : " Yea, little brother,
but soon thou 'lt be well again.  Just drink of this !  Just eat of that ! "
The Emperor ate and drank and, then, the jester pulled out three
little  mice  from  the  pouch, saying : " Now, little brother, thou
art no more to be pitied !  Now thou canst see !  Now thou look'st

upon three little maidens of Bassa whom our dear Saba roasts on a little spit every Friday. Thou art surprised. Thou dost not believe it ? Did I not tell thee that thou wert blind and to be pitied before thou hadst taken my medicine. Now, thou canst see it. Art thou not glad ? I, too, rejoice. The Bassa girls also are glad. Now, our dear Saba takes the three Bassa girls, slits up their bellies. Thou seest it, now, dost thou not ? Thou couldst not see it before ; am I right ? But thou wert blind ! Our kind-hearted Saba slits up their bellies and gloats on the pretty things that come tumbling out. Then he throws them away. Now he catches three other Bassa. O, small brother mine ! before thou wouldst have thought that I took mice out of my wallet. Now that thy sight is restored thee, thou know'st that our so gentle Saba takes three Bassa boys after the three Bassa girls. Thou seest, dost thou not, that I have three Bassa youths in my hand ? Now, dear little brother, I will just see whether thou canst now see more clearly. I will now do nothing more. Tell me only what it is thou canst see." The Emperor said : " I see that our good Saba does the same to the young men of Bassa as he did to the girls ! " The Court fool said : " My dear, dear little brother, how glad am I ! How glad our Saba is ! And all the Bassa are likewise glad." From that moment forward the Saba desisted from his Neronic cruelties.

Another little legend, though not quite so authentic, shows the amount of power such a Court-fool could wield. One of the former Emperors was very avaricious and miserly. He always tried to be out of the way at the hour when it was customary for the nobles to be presented with their morning meal which was theirs as of right. He therefore always came out of his bedroom very late into the Katamba where the Court had long been assembled. One day, when he was as late as usual, the Wauwa-tsu went out right across the courtyard, opened the King's bedroom door and shouted : " My brother Edsu ! thou needst not trouble to come forth to-day ! I will attend to things ! " Then he came back. He took his seat upon the royal chair and said : " I am going to inaugurate a new thing to-day. Ye all know that I am a poor Edsu. Ye, however, are the rich Saraki and the rich Enako and the rich Enaki. Until now I have always given ye very little and bad food. , From now forth it will be best for each of you not only to bring sufficient for his own meal, but also as much more as will fill my one hundred pewter dishes " (wonderfully cast large dishes holding several pounds of meat and rice, which were formerly filled and handed round in the morning). "And then I will have it distributed among my people. Thus shall it be for the future." But the fool knew, as popular memory knows, that from that day the Emperor's parsimony came to an end.

These Court fools, then, were as peculiar an institution as could very well be found. They were unassailable. If a noble, teased or angered to it, hurt the feelings of the Wauwa-tsu, the little monstrosity could kill the Enako with impunity. But just in the same way, as we know from past European history, public opinion, which otherwise never durst venture into the presence of the powerful despot, found its expression under the mask of impudent audacity or foolhardy licence.

    *    *    *    *    *    *    *    *

We will herewith put an end to this descriptive catalogue. An account of the main characteristics of Central Soudanese court-life, as illustrated by the examples from Mossi and Nupéland, has now been given, although one-line of development or the other may here and there show greater historical accuracy in its more significant forms. Generally speaking, the picture repeats itself eastwards of Mossiland in such unmistakably similar colour and form that it is well worth our while to survey the method of its distribution before looking for the original model on which the copies are based.

I have already alluded to the circumstance that the co-existence of Djitsu and Sarakidsu at one and the same Court points to the confluence of two political currents. As a matter of fact, the Djitsu, or " ladder " form, belongs to those nations who were in some way related to the peoples deriving from Yoruba-Benin, with some indications of being the source of their original civilization. I discovered this " ascending scale " form on the Benue River among the Yukum, in the Cameroons among the Bauma, among certain organized communities of the Loango coast, and quite in the South at the furthest advanced post of the area subject to

Atlantic culture. In the Nupé kingdom, then, the existence of the Djitsu is documentary evidence of a connected relation between the dynasties of Bini and Yoruba lands, which is exactly in harmony with their geographical position and the fluctuations in their state of independence or dependence, as recorded in their histories.

The Sarakidsu institution is, on the other hand, a proof of connection with the current setting eastwards. This system of officialism based on hereditary loyalty is peculiar to all those nations whose state-constitution also shows other symptoms of their subjection to the influences of the current flowing from the West. Going eastwards, we find it prevailing with all the Mossi, the Dagomba (and effective from here to Ashanti), Gurma, Borgu and the Houssa. It was rooted with its four principal State offices amongst all the tribes of the Lake Chad basin, the Kanuri, the Bagirmi, the Kanembu, etc. It existed in Wadai. The four provinces of Darfur were still governed by the four arch-officers of State. To the South its ramifications extend to states of primitive institution. I was able to trace it as far as Djur, Boum and distinct Loango types, which have assimilated other characteristics of the Eastward tendency.

This arch-vassalage cannot possibly have come in with Islam from the West. It was foreign to Islam, never native to the Mandingoes, who crushed out even its semblance among the South-western Songai. Neither did it come from the North. Tsemsen itself adopted it, but did not spread it. Travellers from the North were at once struck by its singularity. It died out in Fessan and Gerhardt Rohlfs, a traveller whose practical experience of all North African countries is assuredly second to none, writes about it as follows: "This organization of State appointments is now to be found in the negro kingdoms of Central Africa only (by which, in this connection, the South is meant); and its previous existence in Fessan, where the whole system of Court life in general formerly showed negro characteristics, is a clear proof that in earlier times 'negrodom' extended much farther North." Thus, in this experienced observer's opinion, the system of an official hierarchy was so essentially united with the nature of the Soudanese State-builders as to make even him draw the conclusion that it must necessarily be a " 'negro' institution."

We know that this is not so. The Nasarrawas say : When Ussu Nupeta after having come with Kisra out of the East laid the foundations of the Nupé Empire among the Gwari and reigning for twenty-one years, died, four people were buried with him who had accompanied him as his ministers from the East. These were the Saraki who served him with meat, the Saraki who gave him to drink, the Saraki who ordered his household and the Saraki who looked after his stables. And their sons did the same offices for the successor to Ussu Nupeta.

Prolonging this chain of thought in conformity with the sequence of events and tracing the source Eastwards of the current setting in from the East, we come to Nubia. Nupeta came into Nubia in 641 A.D. Let us verify our references. In so doing we find that at that time there was in Nubia a fully organized Palatinate, an official hierarchy as fully developed and preserved as anywhere else in the districts affected by the influences emanating from Byzantium.

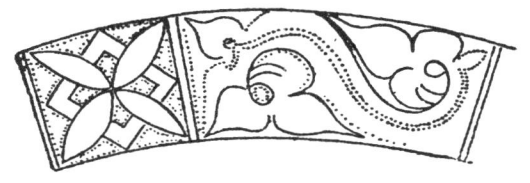

Ornament on middle and rim of Nupé cast pewter dishes.
*( Drawn by Carl Arriens.)*

# CHAPTER XXIX

## BYZANTIUM

What Islam and we ourselves saw in the Soudan—The Kisra legend—Which is Napata-land ?—The significance of Nubia in universal history—Historical basis of the Kisra-Napata migration and its traces in the tradition of such migration—Christianity in the Soudan —Byzantine-Christian customs in Central Africa—Fusion of Byzantine-Persian art-indus-tries in Central Africa with Atlantic elements.

" THE Soudan is a unique, vast, flat and monotonous country ; it is always the same till one gets towards Mecca, where its character begins to change ! " This was how a pilgrim described the land between the Senegal and the Nile, through which he had wandered. He was a Mahommedan pilgrim who had looked at everything with the eyes of a Moslem.

But we ourselves had also made the same journey from the Senegal to the Nile. We, however, as we at once gave him quite distinctly to understand, were not making a pilgrimage to Mecca, and it was perhaps because we modern infidels were travelling this endless ancient pilgrim-way from the Senegal to the Nile that this land did not seem monotonous at all, not flat, but very hilly. We have now nearly, very nearly, finished our journey. And now we will rest for a moment to look upon the waves of the glorious ancient Nile glittering in the sunshine. It is not considered the right thing in African eyes for a traveller to enter a town in dust-stained gar-ments hastily and without careful preparation. For we left the Senegal as prudent and serious folk, and would also enter the land of the Ethiops on the Nile in all deliberation and earnestness of mind.

615

I found the following paragraph in a learned article in a newspaper of the year 1891, and placed it in the forefront of the larger work as an historical memorial, namely : " From everything explorers and ethnographers have told us about this Continent, the history of its population's civilization has its origin in the invasion of Islam (instead of Mahommedanization !). Before the Arabians had brought this religion and its higher culture to the natives there was neither an organized body politic (!), nor a real religion (!), nor a developed industry (!)."—No political organization, no real religion, and no industrial development !

And what was it, then, *we* found ?

We came down to the Soudan from the far distant North-west and pilgrimmed through the Soudan, led by the Islamite legend— came, so to say, with the idea of Islam—and the first thing we saw was that Islam had travelled the ancient road, wrapped up the holy story of its advent and message in heathen old-Libyan legendary vesture and that this was the only way in which it could be kept alive in the popular mind. We saw Islam coming stealthily along the ancient highways. We then observed that its progress was stayed by a Pagan people, by a great wave of ancient culture, which rose up against the zeal of Islam and quenched its flames for a long period ; and that the latter only burst out again from the glowing ashes several centuries later, when it conquered the resistance of the East ; and that Islam had so accustomed itself to the political garb of the Eastern kingdoms that it adopted them and still continues to wear them.

We watched the breaking surf of these hostile waves, and there see again the features of the spirits which once—ah, how long before Mahommed's birth—danced like foam upon their crest. We recognize those haunting forms which David's harp had once to exorcise as his fingers swept its strings. We cast a glance over the quality of the princely retinues. We marked the measured tread with which the Byzantine pallatium advanced from Nubia against Islam in the Lake Chad basin as early as 641 A.D., that is to say, when the Arabian migration ranging along on the edge of the Mediterranean was unconcerned as yet about the far South and the Soudan. And we also saw that Islam was everywhere ready to assume the legacy bequeathed to it by the Byzantium of older date as a

Antique bowl with the cross called Satra or Stana.
(Collection of D. J. A. F. E., 1912.)

[Face my p. 326.

pleasant thing and an institution worthy of respect down to present times.

Victory lay with the Malikite supremacy of the Western stream, after a most strenuous struggle and it was only attained by the recognition of the older strength of culture inherent in the Soudanese East. It is true that the bearers of an Eastern civilization paid a heavy price, and it especially lost all its ancient historical associations with its fountain-head, assailed as it was on two sides, so that to-day the erstwhile homes of culture on the Nile are surrounded by dreary wastes. But that culture on the Upper Nile must have been mighty indeed in its majesty, strong in its construction and powerful in its educational vigour. Only this can explain the fact that it was able to supply Western nations with the necessary energy to withstand the advance of Libyan Islamism for so long a period. And it must have been a magnificent, ancient, well-scoured and comprehensive bed along which the stream from the East poured its waters, so that, despite the influence of the thirsty, parching African sun, it was still able to bring sufficient beneficial civilization to the West to plenish fully all the wells of the Soudan for a thousand years, notwithstanding all the evaporation it suffered during its extended course.

\* \* \* \* \* \* \* \*

The essential legends of olden days, fragments of which can probably still be found in all, but more especially in the Pagan towns, between the Benue and Niger rivers, may be summarized as follows : At the time before Mahommed had conquered Mecca, Kisra, the King of the Persians (called Parsi, Parsena, or Bagdadshi), waged war against Anabinuhu (that would be Noah). Anabinuhu (some say it was not he, but the King of the Ruma ; the Ruma are the Hellenic Romans, or Græco-Romans) had occupied Egypt (Masr). At first Kisra was the conqueror. But then Anabinuhu, who was an ally of the King of the Ruma, was the victor. Then Kisra fled up the Nile and came into the land of the King of Napata, or Nupeta. Kisra said to the King : " I cannot return into my own country, because there the King of the Ruma would put me to death ; grant me permission to stay in thine own country. I have many people with Lifidi (wadded armour) and Sulke (mail tunics) to fight for thee, if so be thou wilt let me remain." Napata the King said : " I will first hold talk with my Alledjenu ; my Alledjenu is the Alledjenu Issa." King Napata spake with the Alledjenu, who told him : " Let Kisra depart westwards and subdue all the land, and do thou follow him. Thy father-will keep guard over this country. But thou thyself shalt be a great King in the West."

King Napata called Kisra and said : " Go thou in front and conquer all the nations to the West. My Alledjenu said that I was to follow thee." Kisra said : " Thus will I do." Kisra set out with an array of his own Lafidi and Sulke and a host of Napata's men. He came to Borgu after a long journeying (Borgu on the Niger is meant). Napata followed him at first as far as Gober. There he took unto himself a wife. She bore him a son, from whom all the Goberawa are descended.

Kisra sent many warriors to the West. He subjected the whole of Borgu. He put Kings over them everywhere, and, according to Albrecht Martius' researches in 1912, these were : in Boa (three days' march to the west of Nikki), King Birjerima (Jerima in Houssa equals Crown Prince) ; in Kika (four days west of Nikki), King Bruka ; in Lessa (two days from Kissiden), King Wagana ; in Wu-enu (three days west of Nikki), King Kora (this Wu-enu is not identical with the one to be named later on) ; King Djaru, in Dari ; in Borish (five days from Nikki), King Sakka ; in Teme (four days west of Nikki), King Schemé ; in Madeguru (four days from Teme), King Kora (?). Kisra made Jiro the first King of Nikki and at the same time his brother and afterwards his successor, Sheru Shikia, ruled in Wu-ene, three hours distant from Nikki.

The legend designates three regions as the sphere of Kisra's power : Umaisha, or Amar, on the Benue (which means the country round about the townships and not only the townships themselves) ; then Borgu, with the Kontangora provinces and Gurma ; and thirdly and lastly, Ambara, which means the country of the Yorubans.

The reports here are certainly very divergent. Some members of the final Kisra commission I called together from many different parts at Lokoja maintained that Mesi, Kisra's overlord, who was identical with Napata, had conquered the Yorubans. It is however at all events certain that Yorubaland was ruled at that period by a new dynasty, which came into the country by way of Borgu. I afterwards got statements in confirmation of the fact in Yoruba itself and shall subsequently also refer to these.

Kisra only lived in the district of Paiko in Gwariland for ten years and a half. He then founded the city of Karishi, which lies three days' march to the north of Kontangora in Dakarekareland. After residing there for four and a half years he went over to Bussa. He resided alternately in Karishi and Bussa. His brother represented him wherever he himself could not be. After ruling for a further sixteen and a half years he died, and was buried in Bussa twenty-eight years after the Hedjira, or 650 A.D., according to our time-reckoning. Another legend states that Mahommed, after following the two great Kings, Kisra and Napata, had waged a war shortly before or after Kisra's death against Kisra's nation. Mahommed's warriors were again beaten and then for a long time ventured no attacks upon Kisra, Napata and their successors.

As already stated, Napata, or Nupeta, remained for a longer period at first at Gober, from whence he often returned to the East, and there on the Nile administered justice. But after Kisra's Maijaki (general) had conquered all the land as far as the Benue he retired to Gbarra and there, in the nineteenth year after the Hedjira, or 641 A.D., founded the Nupé kingdom, which he went on ruling for twenty-one more years. Upon his death he was succeeded by his son. Thirty-four descendants of Nupeta in all reigned over Nupé and Yoruba paid them tribute during the whole of the time. After that the Yorubans again got the upper hand. When Nupeta died, there were buried with him the Saraki who gave him his drink, the Saraki who served him with meat, the Saraki who managed his household and the Saraki who looked after his horses.

Kisra's descendants sent yearly tribute to the East to the river Feriuna (*i.e.*, Pharaoh's river, the Nile). They founded several large cities and kingdoms and spread the name of Napata in the land. All the townships which to-day bear the name of Napata were founded by him. They brought many craftsmen from the East, who built great houses and decked them out bravely. Everything they did they caused to be written down on hides of animals, but not on paper. The leathern manuscripts were preserved for a long time and then buried with Edsu Zado to prevent their falling into the hands of the Fulbe. As long as the descendants of Napata lived according to the laws made by their fathers before them the Islamites could not prevail against them. They only lost their power when they ceased to pay tribute to the East. This is the pith of the Kisra tradition, as pieced together from various sources and generally accepted wherever it is prevalent. Napata's son is as good as forgotten. But many, very many people can tell one of Kisra and there is an enormous amount of legendary material about him preserved in the Bori communities, a few examples of which were given in the chapters dealing with the Bori. Let us now try to realize these legends' purport.

     *      *      *      *      *      *      *      *

The land from which Kisra came with Napata is in general called " in the East " or " by Pharaoh's river." The Arabian story-tellers now and again also call it Misr or Masr, and, therefore, Egypt ; but we may say that this is to be regarded as a modern confusion of ideas, and the more so as the Kisra legend expressly says that the Persian king at first fled up the Nile and so had arrived at Napata's kingdom before he began moving to the West. Napata can, however, be nothing else than the ancient kingdom of Nubia. If, now, we want to understand and determine the full worth of the Kisra legend and whether this tradition deals with the traces of actually experienced historical events or with recent interpolations which came in with Mahommedanism (for the Kisra legends also play a part in Islam), we must necessarily turn to ancient Nubia and get a clear notion of its constitution and its previous significance in history.

     *      *      *      *      *      *      *      *

Nubia is the ancient classical land of Ethiopia. In olden days its inhabitants were considered to be the most pious and the oldest of all mankind. This view and statement must have been handed down from the Egyptians to the authors of antiquity who were their

Saddles with crosses on the pommel, from Basset and Gober.
*(Drawn and coloured by Capt. and M.)*

[To face p. 332.]

neighbours as settlers in the lower portions of the Nile and must in the course of history have frequently had quite considerable commerce with them. The Egyptians obtained their supplies of black slaves, ivory, timber, gold, and so forth, from Nubia. The trade must have been an extremely old and, for many centuries, an extremely intensive one. The zenith of its commercial intercourse was reached when an Ethiopian dynasty ascended the Egyptian throne out of Ethiopian Nubia about 840 B.C.

In many quarters it is still assumed that this Ethiopian kingdom, which the ancients called Napata or Meroë, in accordance with the site of its metropolis, was indebted to the " primitive " Egyptians for its most important elements of culture. For reasons to be fully set forth in the (third volume of the) scientific edition, I, from the standpoint of ethnology, must unhesitatingly reject this supposition. I would only in passing now point out the extremely important fact that the Nubians possessed an individual and independent religion in the earliest known times, the cult of which impressed the Egyptians, who gave accounts of it to the authors of old, with its unquestionably self-existent and primeval establishment on the soil and that in obedience to the call of this religion the King was doomed to death by the priesthood and did not end his life as Nature decrees. But we shall recognize this as a sure sign of a quite distinct form of ancient civilization and religion, which we may assert could only exist as a primeval, but never as a divergent type, or as a secondary typical variant such as the Egyptian, if, indeed, there be any connection whatever between them.

That the age of this primitive religion is, however, beyond calculation is proved by an absolutely appalling sentiment of conservatism, explicable only by its continuous practice in the course of thousands of years and its permanent driving force among the inheritors of this particular form of civilization down to this very day with regard to its regular observance. These particular customs are now, when the conditions precedent for the continuing vitality of such an ancient form of culture and this primitive form of faith have long since disappeared from the rest of the world's surface, to be regarded only as petrifactions or, as it were, ossifications. At the very outset, then, of our investigations of the Nubians and their neighbours we are met by an essential singularity, namely, their strict adherence to simpler religious laws and a severely ritual religion. Devotion to religious thought is a very old heritage of these nations, the distinctive features of which can easily be followed down the lapse of tens and hundreds of centuries. Their primeval, pre-Egyptian religious observance was proverbial among the ancients.

When Nubia was conquered by Egypt the former took up the ideas of the Egyptian priesthood with a sincerity and loyalty which made this people renew the struggle for the possession of the temples of Isis time after time long after that priesthood had become Christianized. When polytheism had had its day, the Nubians adopted Christianity and we see them in the most intimate relations with Byzantium as early as 547 A.D. But the connection was not made viâ Alexandria and Egypt, but on the direct waterway and across the Red Sea. Islam stormed forward and oppressed the Nile countries with all the weight of a migration of nations. But Nubia had already satisfied the craving for a newer faith by getting into touch with Byzantium and consequently declined either to allow the approach of Mahommedanism or its hospitable reception with truly astonishing vigour and strength of determination. It did so successfully for almost one thousand years. When the Islamites began to oppress the Christians in Egypt, the Nubians sent their threatening cry: " Stay your hands and look to yourselves ! " ringing down the Nile with both energy and effect. And the Islamite government of Egypt was not only unable to dominate this Nubian Christianity in the course of the centuries, but spared the Christians in Egypt from fear of the Christians in Nubia. When, however, these tenaciously faithful Nubians at last, in consequence of a deficiency in imported civilization, lost ground and finally adopted Islam, they displayed the same amazing devotion to a religious ideal. When the Mahdi was sovereign in Omdurman, these tribes were his most submissive adherents, the most phantastic defenders of the religion of the Prophet and the Khalif. Their loyalty was unshakable. The tyranny of the Khalifati and the cheerfulness of willing sacrifice shown by its adherents in its service would have been impossible in any other modern country but this, where the tradition of love of, and surrender to, religious ideals are part and parcel of the very air and become incorporated in the flesh and blood of all the nations that inhabit these lands.

The force, then, which has thus held sway here for centuries is pre-eminently powerful. It is a primeval force which endows every growth introduced from outside with sheerly infinite vitality, so that to this hour the single seeds of that form of civilization are traceable in their posterity in their turn. The inhabitants of the Upper Nile solemnize the ancient festivals of the Egyptian cult to this day. In the past century (and possibly in the present) the King-Priests are doomed to death according to Pagan custom in the Nuba hills and the advanced posts of the heirs of this pre-Egyptian Imperial religion in the South. The young branch of the Axumitic kingdom has preserved the Byzantine-Christian form in the neighbouring country of Abyssinia. It is a power possessing not alone the faculty of propagating itself within its own boundaries but of transmitting itself into other countries, right across to West Africa. It is the source of the current from the East with which we became so well acquainted in the course of one part of our work.

This is the Nubia and Napata, in the extended sense of the word, from which Kisra and his overlord, Nupeta or Napata, are said to have come, and most assuredly came. If now we compare dates historically ascertained with those assigned to them by tradition, we establish the actual fact that the Kisra legend can be completely and without the least violence brought into accord with the events chronicled in history, because :

The Persians, who at that time were ruled by Kosrav II. (*i.e.*, Kisra), the Sassanid, occupied and garrisoned Egypt in the year 619 A.D. Their reception in the land of the Pharaohs was not hostile. But, notwithstanding this, the energetic Græco-Roman Emperor Heraklius, seated on the Byzantine throne, regained the upper hand and in 629 A.D. the Persians had again to evacuate Egypt. Now there is, however, a certain tribe in Kordofan, a country adjacent to Nubia and to the south of Egypt, which calls itself Bagada and affirms its descent from Bagadi, who, as they say, came with his wife bearing a child upon her shoulder out of Persia into Egypt. And in this way we can trace the remains of Persian races in the immediate vicinity of Nubia, and thus there is an increasing probability that not all the Persians migrated back again to Asia, but rather that many of them settled in Africa and went Southwards towards the sources of the Nile.

With this clue to guide us on our way to the West similar fragments meet us on every side.

I pass over the inexact statements of the Forans and get on to firmer ground once more in Kanem. Here the legendary tale is this, viz. : that the Bagdad people came with Issa (Jesus) to Kanem and prepared the land, so that when Mahommed's Mellems came down from the North and West there were already many in it who could write. They at first wrote in the manner of the Bagdad folk, and only afterwards learnt Arabic. Here then we once more meet the Persians as representatives of Christianity.

Going another step forward, the Houssa countries offer us ample material. Our own great Heinrich Barth proved that the assumption of the learned Sultan Bello to the effect that the original place of settlement of the Houssas, the famous city of Gober, had really been founded by the Copts, still prevailed in the land and that in his own (Bello's) time it was governed by families belonging to the race of the Batsherawa. The name of this family on the Niger was given to me personally as Bagtshadi, which is undoubtedly related to Bagdatshi ; for, according to Barth, Gober's contemporaneous sister town (Dowra) claims the fame of having had a proselytizer of its own named Ali-el-Baghadi. This dynasty is named " Parsawa " in the legends of the Bori. The Dowra legend, known also to the first editor of the Kano chronicle, H. R. Palmer, makes the founder of the Houssa States come from Bagdad and states that he was the first to introduce horses. But in the Moslem record of Kano, Bagodda, the son of Bowo and grandson of Bayajidda, is given as the founder in 999 A.D. of the Houssa city of Kano which subsequently became so powerful. But before its second foundation by the Persian dynasty this town was still of so little importance that the earliest Arabian books of travel do not even mention it. All they tell us is that it had been founded by the Persians prior to the introduction of Islam ; and Bayajidda is, moreover, referred to as a non-Islamite Bagdadshi. Kano was far more recent than Gober and Dowra, the two most ancient towns in the Houssa states, two cities both older than the ancient capital of Nupé, of even greater antiquity than Gbarra ! As now the birth

Ifa tray with " Mesi-period " string and dove decoration, from a grave near Offa.

*(Collection of Pa. G. I. A. E. F., 1912.)*

(Faces p. 624.)

of Gbarra is attributable to the Kisra-Napata dynasty about the year 641 A.D. or to the very early days of the Perso-Nubian migration and conquest, the date assignable for the second foundation of Kano, stated as being 999 A.D., can quite easily be brought into harmonious connection with that given in the record of a Persian dynasty which, according to that record, had already been reigning for a considerable period over the Houssa countries.

Now, extracting the quintessence of all these statements from the Islamite era, which are mostly preserved in writing, we arrive at the conclusion that the pre-eminent civilization of the Houssalands was established by a dynasty, the original basis of which was taken to be Persian (Parsowa=Bagdadshi), a dynasty, however, which observed the Christian religion. And this accounts for the fact that in Bello's time the Gober nation were held to be Copts. The descendants of this dynasty planned the construction of the important cities of Houssaland and when Islam continued to seep into it more and more in the fifteenth century were called Bagdadshi in accordance with the practice adopted by the Arabian chroniclers of that period.

Now the meaning of this is that the older written documents prove in the main the same things as the oral traditions of the Koarra countries (for so I call the districts situate between Illo and Lokoja on the Niger) and of the Niger-Benue corner. For I have already stated above that, according also to the Kisra legend, Napata left behind him a son in Gober. This shows us that both in the legendary and MS. records the Napata nation and the Kisra nation are consolidated in the term Bagdadshi. The deduction, then, is that the Perso-Nubian invasion of the seventeenth century, which came in with the current from the East, was a Christian invasion. A fact which the Mahommedan writings take particular care not to mention. It goes without saying that Kisra, *i.e.*, Kosrav, the Persian king, did not initiate the civilizing movement in person, but that the term Kisra may be regarded as some form of generalization, such as "Lord of the Persians." And it is, moreover, an historical fact that the Persians had already established a very intense association with the Copts, *i.e.*, with Christian communities, which must have greatly facilitated their subsequent transition to Christianized Nubia.

Hence the Kisra traditions most brilliantly stand the test of comparison with more ancient written and historical material. They prove that this strong current of influence, the power of establishing Empire and the institution of state primacies came from Nubia, from ancient Napata. Individual events further teach us that this union of Central Soudan with Nubia never entirely ceased and, also, that the consciousness of the actuality of such an old-time bond has since its inception never been quite dead ; for the fact that the older designation of Kisrawa, Kisratshi, Nupatshi, or Nupetshi, subsequently replaced the term Bagdadshi almost along the whole line, hardens our opinion that more recent Islamite immigrants and scribes knew it to have been so, and, consequently, translated it in the manner with which they were most familiar. And besides, this is the only way in which we can explain the retention of the dates of the foundation of these kingdoms in the popular memory, whereby they were so clearly preserved in the Islamite method of reckoning time. If Islam in general makes no mention of Christianity, it does so on the same principle which it has applied to the whole of the Soudan. The governing law of Islam is to represent Islam, Islamite life and Islamite culture as the only things worthy to be called human and to label everything older than itself as " pagan," or to eliminate it as thoroughly and quickly as possible from the national memory. This political recipe imported by the Fulbe from Mandingoeland also induced them everywhere to commit to the flames all the old MSS. and chronicles they could find. They put this principle in force in all quarters, as the French explorers in the West also discovered. And if they failed to accomplish their purposes of destruction in the Houssa and Koarra countries, this is no more than additional evidence of the exuberant vitality of the civilization wafted on the stream which flowed from the East, a culture whose related connections could never be expunged from human consciousness. The decisive influence which Islam was able to exercise upon these traditions and the feeling of historical association and origin consisted in nothing but the substitution of the Islamite conception of history and the method of recording it for those which existed previously.

What, however, fills us with profound astonishment is the

perception we have gained of the marvellous power of expansive culture which enabled these ancient Nubians to become the directors of the stream of civilization flowing from the East through the central Soudan as far as the Upper Niger, enabling them to transmit a policy and a religion of Byzantine origin to these far-off lands, and to acclimatize these so thoroughly as to form a bulwark against the invasion of Islam setting in from the North-west. And, therefore, in precisely the same manner as Nubia and Nubian Christianity on the Upper Nile held up the advance of Islam from the Egyptian side, Kisra and the Nupé-Persian Christian culture combined were strong enough to offer a resistance to the progress of Islam on the Lower Niger, in the Houssa countries and in the Niger-bend for the space of about one thousand years. And so we see in the Mossi in the Niger-bend that nation who were the bearers of the civilizing State-creating forces, whose birthplace was Byzantium and Nubia. For it was this force which drove them to political consolidation, although they themselves apparently remained Pagans in religion.

\* \* \* \* \* \* \* \*

But even Islam was powerless to deny the older predominance of Christianity in the Soudan and the contiguous Sahara entirely. The Goberawa do not stand alone as being Christian in origin. Even Ibn-Khaldun states that all the South-eastern Saharan nations had been Christian, with the exception of the pagan Senhadja who inhabited the North-western Sahara and were not as yet, therefore, animated by the spirit of a younger religion and thus best predestined to carry Mahommedanism on the north-west current into Mandeland and the Soudan. We find it stated in the French version of the Tarikh-es-Sudan that Abu-Abdallah-Ez-Zohri, according to the Paris MS., No. 1,873 (folio 5, right, line 13), the dwellers in the Soudan, whose capital was Ghana, were Christians up to the year 469 of the Hedjira, that is to say, up to 1076–77 by the Christian computation of time, and only then adopted Islam. Here, then, is documentary proof of my own contention! And the road pursued by Christendom is pointed out by the great traveller Ibn-Batutah in the passage where he speaks of the downward current of the Niger, which, continuing the traditional view of the ancients, he assumed flowed into the Nile. He says : If one travelled up-Nile, one came to Kowkow (Gao), then to Mooli (the present Mowli), who inhabited the independent region furthest away from the central seat of the Mali kingdom ; from there to Yufi (=Nufi or Nupé), one of the most important realms of the Soudan, but in which no Arabian dared set foot, because he would be put to death there. Thence the river flowed into the land of the Nubians who professed Christianity. And so the Arabian account of the Koarra districts also directly connects with Christian Nubia and we can be quite independent of the learned Leo Africanus' testimony, which states that in his own time the countries situate between Bornu and Nubia were still Christian. In the passage describing the eastward deflection of the river Niger and the statements he gathered from the Songai, Heinrich Barth amply confirms the strength of the bond of union between the Niger nations with the olden Eastern lands, which were to the effect that this was the locality where the primeval highway of the Pharaohs entered Nigeria from the Nile. But the independence of the Songai kings from the Far East was maintained for a lengthened period. According to the MS. in the Paris National Library it can be traced back to a Christian-Nubian relation and with all the more justification, because the time alleged for the foundation of the Gad dynasty of the Songai Empire (beginning of the seventeenth century) coincides absolutely with the date assigned by the Nupé and Borgu tradition (namely, about 640). The growing power of the Western stream, reinforced by the influence of Islam and Mandeland, here destroyed Christendom and forced it back from Songai to Borgu.

I shall prove in a moment that Christian ethics were still for a considerable period effective in the lower courses of the Nile ; and evidence of the fact is contained in written documentary history. The Benin Emperor's ambassador to the Court of Portugal in 1486 stated that the ruler of Benin was vassal to a mighty Lord in the East, who invested every successor to the throne with a staff, a helmet, and a cross of bronze as the insignia of his office. This King's title was Ogane. The report says that he never showed himself, but lived in strictest seclusion. The custom of Kisra's successors in Karishi and in the Borgu States is alleged to have been identical. Now the Yorubans derive their Mesi dynasty from Borgu and their story is this :

There were two Shango once, an older one from Yoruba, the Shango Takpa, and a more recent one from Borgu, the Mesi-Shango. This Mesi, they affirm, had come into Yorubaland as the leader of the Alledjenu, and had been the first of all the Mesi (the now obsolete name for " King "). He had appointed all the remaining Mesi as his viceroys. At first Mesi-Shango had been superior to Shango-Takpa for a long time. Then, however, his Mesi had been expelled by the conquering Shango Takpa. Shango Mesi, the founder of the younger Yoruba kingdom, was represented by a rider on a horse. And it had also been this Mesi-Shango who had required his nation to be good and not to thieve.

If now we have first seen that the Christian State-forming forces coming from the East were known to incoming Islam and Arabian science in the North-west, the last mentioned sources tell us that ambassadors from Benin, in the year 1486, got precisely the same information in the South respecting the still prevalent tradition about the Mesi dynasty. The Arabian reports and the Kisra legends tell us how effectively Christianity operated on the southern fringe of the Sahara in Central Soudan and towards the North-west. The Borgu and Yoruba-Benin accounts bring to our knowledge the influence exerted in still more recent times by this Borgu Christianity on the West Coast countries. Thus we also obtain an important point of attachment for the fixture of dates. According to the statements of the Benin envoy, this enfeoffment was still practised in the year 1486. Therefore, the Borgu dynasty's supremacy must at that time still have been in effective operation. The bronze cross, of which the plenipotentiary speaks, still, however, hangs on the neck of the representative of the Kisra dynasty in Karishi to-day.

The Yoruba tradition ends with the words that it was also the Shango from Borgu who had asked that his nation should do good and no longer steal or lie.

This final sentence, which at first seemed to be particularly questionable and to have a strong smell of the missionary kitchen, must, in spite of such a suspicion, yet be looked upon as an essential and genuine part of the Mesi legend.   For I find an almost identical phrase in a Shango legend which I noted down in the West a year earlier.   It runs thus :

He (the God-King) first commanded obedience to the truth and the hatred of lies.   And he forbade people to poison each other. Thirdly, he forbade the Yorubans to steal from one another and set his face against one citizen going into another's house and taking anything away which did not belong to him.   If any should break one of these three commandments, the God-King Shango would kill them.   It is clear that this version also includes the same basic idea.

Here the ethical demand finds a definite, formulated expression which evades correlation with any one religion of antiquity and has been preserved in these peculiar Koarra countries alone.   In these similar precepts of morality are widely distributed and firmly established in precisely the same connection.   Thus, for example, as old Gurma people told me in 1908—when the kingdom's founder, Djaba, came down on earth, he said : " My people shall not be Usuano. Nor shall they be Djon-djone, *i.e.*, thieves."   And he also said : " At the present hour the peoples are few.   But there shall be a great number of them.   Ye shall wage war against other nations, but amongst yourselves ye shall always be at peace."   The Kisra legend attributes quite the same injunctions to the founder of the Borgu kingdom in the passage describing his residential stay in Karishi.   It states : " Kisra was wont to live in a space set apart, where he was hidden from every man's sight.   When the people came to worship him, they heard his voice from behind a wall.   The voice spake these words : ' Lie not, steal not, be ye not stirrers up of strife, and keep ye peace among one another.'   Whenever the people came to Kisra in Karishi, a herald stepped forth and showed them the Cross which Kisra wore round his neck and which the chieftains of Karishi wear on their breasts to-day as a token of their authority."   And, to sum up, the legend of the inauguration of the Nupé Empire embodies this leading principle, which is short and to the point : " Nupeta demanded that which was good and forbade the evil."

It follows that the guiding idea in the traditions of all the nations of the Koarralands is identical and uniform to a **degree** that almost compels the assumption of their interconnection, which, again, thoroughly confirms the purport of the Kisra legends. And thus the Byzantine seed sown in Nubia on the soil of Africa blossomed and bore fruit on the Niger.

\* \* \* \* \* \* \* \*

Now that we are in a position to follow up the line taken by the Nubian Christian influences as far as their extension into the Koarra districts of the Niger and the important upheavals they there exercised, we can arrive at an idea of the origin of those remarkable customs and peculiar handicrafts which strike us so greatly as being the expression of a more recent and more highly developed form of civilization in these countries and foreign bodies introduced into the African nature.

In making Nubia, and its original sources, and especially the reference to this kingdom's Court officialdom, my points of departure, I am guided by the clue afforded by our method of investigation. It is only in more recent times that Nubia, I mean the Christian Nubia of the Byzantine period, has become a subject of more than common interest to Europeans. The leather MSS., difficult as they are to decipher, which shed a brilliant light on the condition of things at that time prevailing here in the valleys of the Upper Nile were only recently discovered. Professor Karl Schmidt, the discoverer of some of these handwritings, was so good as to bring the literature on the subject to my notice and to supplement it with the result of his own interpretation.

The upshot of it all is that Nubia was not won for Christendom by way of Egypt, but, on the contrary, was missionarized from Byzantium direct. And this is in harmony with the fact that the constitution of the Nubian Imperial Court corresponds in the general as well as in the particular with that of the Imperial Court at Byzantium. The kingdom of Nubia was divided into four provinces, viz. : Nobadia (or Nobatia), Balagulia (or Balakulia), Pacharas and Kurti (or Gurti) which was both a city and a province. The King of Nubia had a Palladium, a Palatinate, as had also the Emperor of Byzantium. This arrangement came to us in Germany what time Otto the Great married the Emperor of Byzantium's daughter.

It came into Central Africa when Nubia extended its sway to the further West in the period above outlined. In one of his descriptions of Court life in Adamowa, on the Benue, Siegfried Passarge says: " Therefore the ceremonial institutions at a Soudanese Royal court are exactly similar to those of the courts of Germany in the Middle Ages," etc. This for us is no longer matter for surprise. We, who have followed the thread of development from Byzantium through Africa in the stream of civilization which flowed from the East, can clearly see that a similar state of things originating in the same source and in the same ages, did of necessity exist and persist here in Africa no less than in Europe, where the same Lord High-Stewards and the same cupbearers performed the same offices at the Round Table of a King Uther or Arthur as at the Imperial Byzantine Court.

It is not, however, the institution of officers at Court alone which we can understand by this method of determining the extent of their growth and distribution. The ancient investiture of the King of Nubia with crown, sceptre and orb has been already described; I have also described the consideration shown to the Court-jester in the Southern portion of this Continent as the exponent voice of the people's demand for the administration of justice.

But that which is most essentially significant for me is the fact that we can still find living proofs of the ancient existence of Christianity in these countries in a heritage of the strangest kind. The dynasty, which came from Napata to Nupé, is to-day called Issa-tshi, i.e., Issa-people in the vernacular. This name was resumed by Edegi. Now, " Issa " is also the appellation given to Jesus the Christ by the Arabians. It might accordingly be assumed that Jesus Christ had already been adored as " Issa " in ancient Nubia, or that the name of Issa must have taken the place of an older designation in a still older epoch with a completely conscious retention of the person therewith identified in consequence of constant intercourse with Arabians, who were always increasingly gaining the upper hand, and the spread of the dominant Arabic language. Moreover, the word " Issa " is met with in an extraordinarily large number of essentially significant compound terms. One legend, for instance, has been preserved, which brings one custom into relation with a particular event which tradition asserts was renewed at Edegi's return from the South and the restoration of the Issa-tshi family.

Issa had a maternal uncle (it must be remembered that after the establishment of the Bini dynasty the matriarchate was in the ascendant), whose name was Ma-Issa. He was living in Gbarra when Edegi came back out of Atagara. When Edegi came to Gbarra, he said to Ma-Issa : " Why is there no King here ? How cometh it that here each acteth after his own desire and obeyeth no Lord ? This nation no longer respecteth any person. But now it shall once more learn to know a chieftain. It is a stiff-necked people. Therefore will I gather together all their sins and I will slay a man. Then they will see that I am a man of might." Ma-Issa said to Edegi : " If thou must needs kill one, kill me !" Next morning, when all the people came to pay obeisance to Edegi, Ma-Issa stayed away. Edegi said : " Why hath my mother's brother stayed away to-day and refraineth he from doing honour unto me ? Ye see that ye have grown disobedient and have no more respect. Go ye hence and capture Ma-Issa." Ma-Issa was captured and brought unto Edegi. Ma-Issa said : " I perceive that it is needful that thou kill a man so that thou mayst create respect for authority. Then do thou kill me. But if now thou wilt be King of all Nupéland and then become a very great King, then do thou remember me, and if, invoking my name, any should petition thee and say unto thee : ' In the name of Issa !' then do thou spare him !" Edegi granted Ma-Issa's request. Ma-Issa was killed. All the people cried : " He who will kill even his own mother's brother will spare none other." They obeyed him and henceforth took off their caps before Edegi, threw themselves upon the earth when they met him and strewed sand upon their heads. Thus they honoured him. Edegi was the Lord of the Land. But he did according to the words of Ma-Issa and spared whoso prayed for mercy " in Issa's name " and swore that he was innocent.

I, however, am inclined to think that we shall be able to find further proof of the once so powerful Byzantine influence, in some other remarkable customs. In the Nupé and Houssa countries there are a number of localities which are called Nassarawa in Houssaland, but Sa-ji or Issa-ji in Nupéland. According to tradition, the localities referred to obtained these names in quite definite and always identical circumstances. Down to this very hour the name of Sa-ji or Nassarawa would be given to a town in this part of the Soudan under the following circumstances. The people of town B make a sudden attack on the people of town A, surprise and over-whelm A and take all its inhabitants prisoners without the loss of a single life on either side. The victor in this case, according to a custom alleged to be immemorial, says in the Nupé tongue : " Soko tshe mio ! " or in Houssa speech : " Allah ja tamakeni," *i.e.*, " God bless thee." Then in compliance with ancient usage the successful winner of the *coup-de-main* must leave all the old folks in A. But he then takes all the young people out of it and settles them in a new site C, generally situate between A and B, and this receives the name of Nassarawa or Issa-ji. The inhabitants of C are now considered to be a sort of sacred and inviolable slaves, slaves of God, so to say, and the B folks may not in any way injure them. More than that, the C folk are exempt from the payment of tribute.

It is perfectly obvious, then, that the term Nassarawa can be brought into relation with the Arabic for Christians, namely, " Nassara," and the corresponding name " Issa-tshi " with the word used for Jesus the Christ, which is Issa. The use of the same term for Christ and Christians, used by the people without the least consciousness of its importance, is all the more remarkable from the fact that they had no inkling whatever of the significance attaching to their statements. They are themselves no longer con-scious that Nassara in this connection stands for Nazarene and Issa for Jesus. The custom itself has been obsolete for about a century and has certainly lost its meaning for a very considerable period. Kueho of recent years and, at an earlier period, probably also Dangadi, a town situated between Bida and Jauri on the Manjara River, is said to be the last Issa-tshi town which was founded in this sense ; its inhabitants have been Issa-ji or Issa-tshi since Edsu Madjia's days, and, as such, also enjoyed the vigorous defence and protection of Edsu Zado as a people holy and set apart.

I wish to keep as far as I possibly can from matters linguistic, but I think I must here make one observation which may perhaps be of great importance. In ancient times a distinctly recognizable cross was a part of the decoration of the saddle pommel of the

Mesi Art. Pl. II.

Ifa tray with string ornament, from a holy tomb near Ọ̀yọ́.
(Collection of the G. A. F. E. 1912.)

[Facing p. 634

princes of Gober, Asben, Bussa, etc. The present day Bussa people call this cross " Somo." But from the North its name was given to me as " Starra " and in Nupéland its designation was " Sarra," the " t " being almost elided in pronunciation. If Heinrich Barth brings the word Mesi from these countries into relation with the Messiah, and Anjellus with angel, I think there is justification for seeking some kind of connection for this word " Starra " with the Greek term for cross, namely, " Stauros."

There can be no possible doubt but that the Cross played a predominant part in these regions as a symbol of holiness. Since I have just referred to Edegi and his correlation to the echoes of Christendom, it must here be mentioned that the daggers of the Nupé, which are in all points identical with the Tuareg hilts (except that the latter are still more indicative, because of their superimposed hammered cross-tips, than the Nupé daggers, which are cast in one piece), are popularly called " Ede-sarra." Obviously this compound term is formed of the words Ede, or Edegi, and Sarra, or cross. The cross as such, with three limbs or points, moreover, occupied a very prominent position indeed. The hereditary transmission of this cross-hilted poniard can be traced, particularly on the Upper Benue, down to later times.

A cross was erected on the thwart of the vessel on which the Emperor occasionally travelled on the Benue river or crossed any other stream. There was a cross fixed on the partition-wall which separated the royal sleeping chamber from the surrounding apartments and ancient tradition asserts that the Emperor used to kneel before it at morn and eve. In days gone by, sacrifices used to be made before this cross on Sundays or Thursdays (these two days were easily interchangeable among the Soudanese tribes in a fashion inexplicable to me). And, above all, there was a holy cereal food, which was also called " Issa," appropriate to these offerings at definite seasons of the year.

Now, Martius was, however, informed by the Bussa folk, the descendants of the Kisra family from Persia, of an extremely singular festival. He obtained the following description of this so-called Gani holy day.

Kisra's royal kinsmen and descendants have their seats on estates of varying extent, granted them by the grace of their King, all over the country round about Nikki (to the west of Bussa). The custom of exchanging children, little boys of from five to six years of age and little girls of four, amongst each other for the education which befits their rank, obtains in the families of the blood royal. The five-year-old boy is then taken to the court of a relation where he has to look after his tutor's horse in the capacity of a groom and is trained in the use of arms as well as in horsemanship, but need do no work on the farm. This course of instruction lasts from five to six years, but it sometimes happens that a strict teacher will keep the lad entrusted to his care for longer. The " boarding school time " of the girls occupies only four years. When the preceptor thinks his esquire's education sufficiently advanced not to reflect disgrace upon him, he gives him a horse and goes with him and his family to the next Gani festival at Nikki, where the groom's family also assembles.

This Gani Feast (which corresponds to our Easter), so-called from Gani, the month of the vernal equinox, is the annual christening ceremony of the princes and princesses of the royal (Kisra) family whose education has been finished. When all the participating families and their god-children have foregathered in Nikki, the King appears before his palace portals one morning and takes his seat upon mats and skins. The Kakaki, or trumpet blowers, take up position behind him and a little in front of him on either side a drummer with a Balabakaru drum (the Houssa Tambari). The Nokogich, the chief of the women, also flanked by two drummers, stands on the King's left. The Royal Barber accompanies her and behind her come the flock of princesses who are to be baptized. Seven little temples stand in two rows in the square fronting the kingly compound and in front of each of these a row of uniformed bodyguards, the so-called Kiliku, is drawn up. Right across the square the male god-children and their fathers sit mounted on their steeds.

Immediately the King appears, the first of the princes to be christened gallops forward, dismounts at half the distance from the throne, and touches the ground with his forehead in salutation. His mouth covered with his hand, the King sits in silence, but the Kiliku answer for him thus : " The King gives thee greeting ! " The prince repeats this act twice or thrice until he kneels at the

Carved planks and beams from Yoruban temples

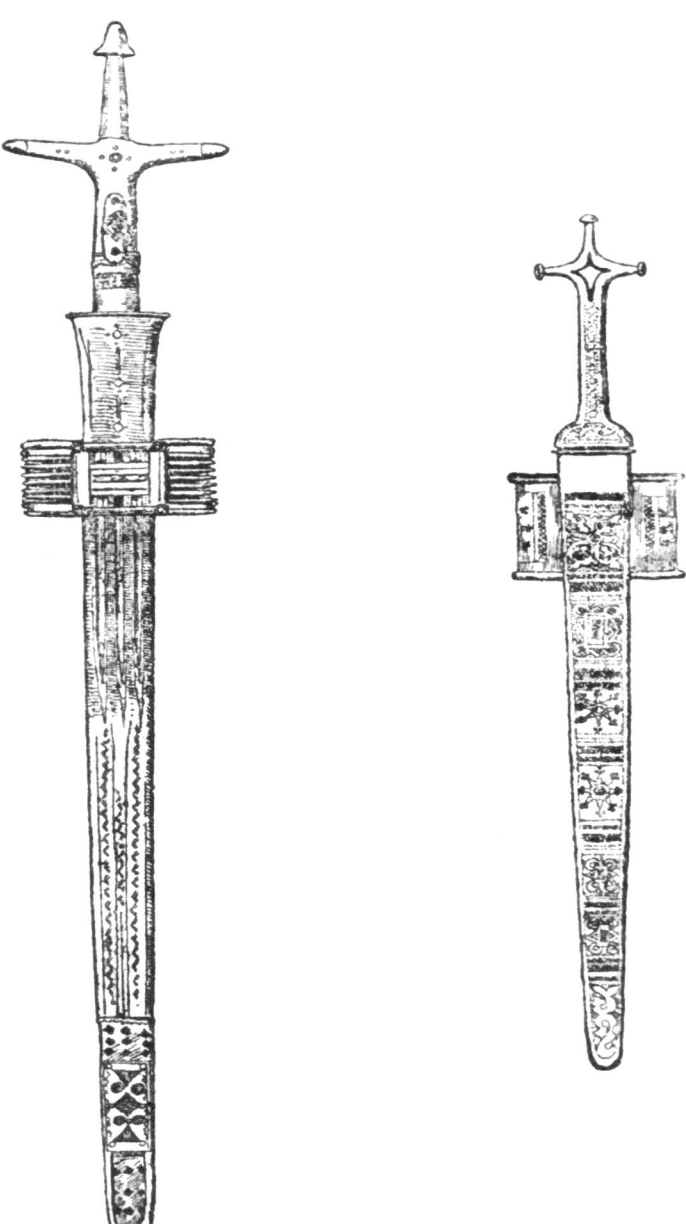

Tuareg and Nupé daggers with old Christian cross hilts. Scabbard and handle of the small right-hand Nupé dagger are cast in yellow metal.

*(Drawn by Carl Arriens.)*

King's feet and the drums begin to beat. Then he turns to the Nokogich, who pours a little water on the head of the figure kneeling in front of her from an antique silver ewer and tells the Court barber to shave his head. Then the Nokogich gives the hitherto unnamed prince an ancient name of the race of Kisra, which is forthwith proclaimed with a loud voice by a herald standing at the King's side to all those present. Then the baptized returns to the King, and on his knees receives from the royal hands a new tobé, a horseman's cloak, a sword and a fully caparisoned horse.

The prince at once assumes the garments while the (bodyguard) Kiliku form a circle round him. The Nokogich receives the old robes and horse of the prince, a portion of which presents she gives to the barber. The latter often gets cowries given him by the parents of the god-children.

When all the princes have been thus received into baptism, it is the turn of the girls, whose hair is also shaved off and who, kneeling down before the King, are presented with a dress by him after the Nokogich has named them. After that all go home. The men return in the same afternoon to the same square where the King receives them in audience. They step forward singly, again kneel down before the ruler, who greets them, distributes gifts, enfeoffs the god-children and expresses his good wishes for the coming year. The entire holiday company makes a pilgrimage next day to Ina, which lies three days' march to the west of Nikki, in order to sacrifice a white bull at the shrine of Tobé.

The following story is told of this sanctuary, situate in a hut (called Bundiru), with only one little window or entrance hole in it : Once when Kisra and his nation were waging war in Gabas (the East), they were one day pursuing the enemy. Then they suddenly came to a great water which parted asunder and allowed the foe in his flight to get across it. But when Kisra and his army attempted to follow, the waves closed in over them and many were drowned. Now, when Kisra was ruler in Bussa, one of his people—Jessarunu—with his brother, Shinajenako, whom Kisra had first left as viceroy on the line of march to the East, also came to Bussa. Kisra gave Jessarunu a great iron as long as a man's arm, like an iron hammer (flail), and commanded a temple to be built in Ina, in memory of those who had been overwhelmed by the waters and had

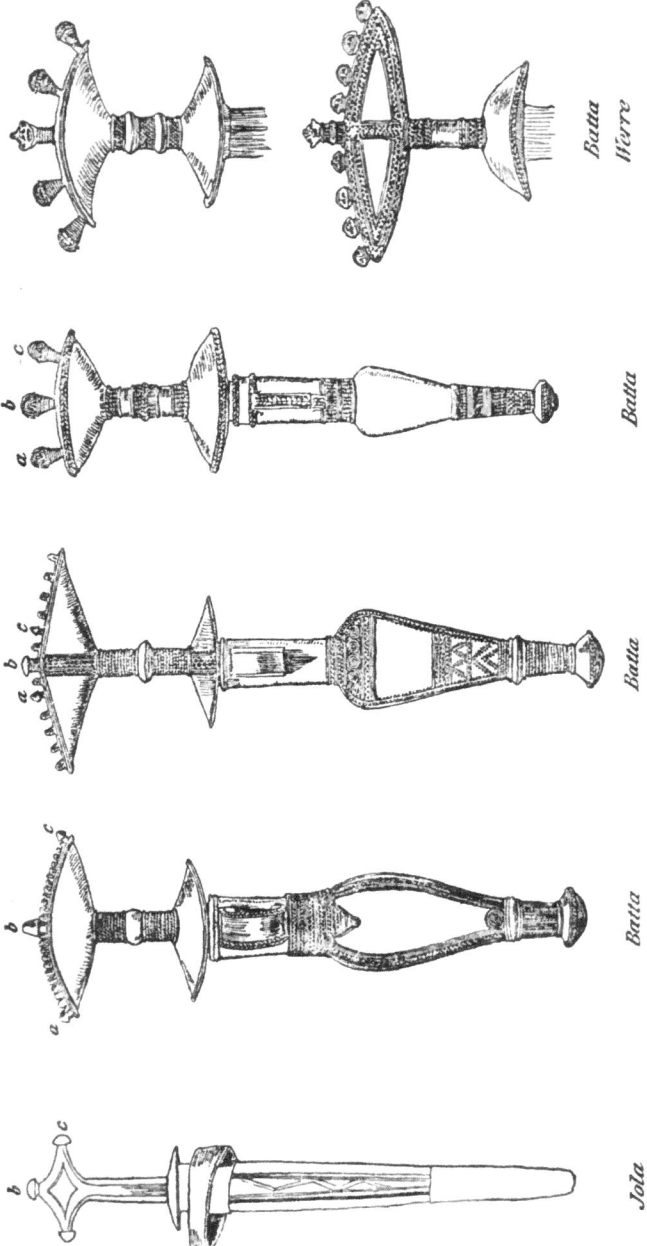

Daggers with bronze scabbards and handles, ¼ natural size, from Benue. The Yola dagger has preserved the original form of the cross-shaped pommel a, b, c. The one depicted in the centre also has the three a, b, c knobs different in shape from the remaining ten, which are curled.

*(Drawn by Carl Arriens.)*

perished. Thereupon Shinajenako fashioned the shrine of Tobé, *i.e.*, a male seated figure of clay, ornamented with poultry feathers, in whose inside the iron hammer is hidden.

\* \* \* \* \* \* \* \*

The preservation of the story of the parted waters and the army which was swallowed up when they closed again, this memory of a primeval myth, is exceeding strange in connection with this Christian baptismal festival at Easter time. We are involuntarily reminded of Jewish traditions, and I must here mention a suggestive remark which I heard only once (from the Mallem of the Maliki quarter in Bida) in this connection, namely, that the Massaga were descended from Anabi Nuhu (or Noah) and had come into the land with Kisra. I repeat it for the sake of the sequence of thought and hasten to add that the Massaga themselves disputed their descent from Anabi Nuhu, and, consequently, their Jewish origin. I refer to this solely because Paul Staudinger and others constantly refer to the great achievements in handicrafts and art-industry of the Jews in Africa and because I cannot call to mind ever having heard in the Soudan of the industrial accomplishments of the Jews with the exception of this one hint.

We may, however, state this one thing with some certainty, namely, that a considerable impetus was given to industrial art at the period of the Perso-Nubian immigration. Legend itself says : The posterity of Kisra and Napata caused many artisans to come from the East, who built great houses and beautifully decorated them. A great deal of the flourishing art-industry of to-day in the Koarra and Houssa countries might be traceable to this influence. Nay, more, direct proof of the fact in some departments can be given.

First of all, in weaving. A Nikkiman, who was a member of my Borgu expedition in 1909 to Bassari, said that at certain festivals the holiday clothing in ancient days consisted only of leather and skins, but that Kisra's followers had introduced cotton and the loom. The first part of this must be unreservedly accepted as being correct. Leather garments are in use at the present day as the dress appropriate for pagan solemnities from the Sahara to the Mossi and Bussa. But these are Libyan in origin ; for the Libyans were from times immemorial renowned for their able and, in part, very artistically decorated leather work and garments. But the loom, spoken of by my Nikkiman, can only have been the male pedal loom, for whose history in Africa I have so far failed to get any firm starting point. Stuhlmann very recently insisted that its use in Africa cannot possibly be very remote. He quite rightly says: " The cultivation of cotton seems to have spread only gradually over Persia and Arabia from India." (Excursion into Aures.) This assumption of the famous geographical authority on the distribution of vegetation confirms the correctness of my Nikkiman's assertion, because the pedal loom and cotton must, judging by their distribution, have come into Africa simultaneously. But now male labour is an absolute necessity in the use of the pedal loom. Everywhere in the region of the African distribution of the Perso-Nubian pedal loom the men spin, weave, embroider and tailor, except where the picture is obscured by older Libyan and Atlantic events. And thus we can understand what we are told, namely, that before the destruction of the ancient city of Jauri, in the northern Koarra states, a family had formerly practised the art of manufacturing cloth from cotton, " the thread of which stood upright like the prayer-carpets of the North." This kind of work was only done by the men of a family.

This cannot have been anything but those handsomely patterned plush-stuffs which have been brought to light in Egypt and Nubia at the excavation of Christian places of burial or churchyards. Although, now, this plush-weaving family has died out, we were still able to send similar textile material from Ilorin in Yorubaland over to Europe, the production of which Albrecht Martius was able to study *in situ*. Here, in Yoruba, in the region of the Libyan Atlantic hand-loom, its use naturally passed over into the hands of the women. But the decorative patterns are identical with those of the Koptic-Nubian plushes. They belong to the ribboned border style.

Now, this style predominates in Yoruban decorative ornament. The reader will find a quantity of Yoruba carving in the following plates of very fine execution, and one antique Ifa tray on which this ornament is combined with doves, the favourite bird of the Christian artificer. According, however, to a man from Mesiland's statement, this ribbon ornament is in direct connection with that King Mesi, whom we found succeeding the Borgu-Kisra dynasty. This Yoruban version coincides exactly with the essence of the matter and the distribution in general of this particular style. It is seen on all Nupé and Houssa clothes, whose extraordinary decoration make such a complete impression of being the misunderstood application of ornament to Byzantine and Persian dress. This style prevails in the embellishment of old palatial edifices in Nupé; it appears on the saddle-cloths from Borgu; it beautifies the calabashes of the Lake Chad nations; here and there it appears in its greatest perfection in bronze-chasing and on the great cast pewter vessels. It is the same style of ornament which was brought into North-western Europe from Western Asia about the beginning of the Christian era, and there effected a change in the decoration with animal forms; it is the one which triumphed in the ribbon form of Longobardian decorative art, which went down the Mediterranean, which inspired the Kopts, and thus, in this relation, taken altogether, becomes intelligible to us in Central and Western Africa as an importation of Perso-Byzantine origin.

This ribbon ornament also appears here and there in the work of the Nupé bronze-chasers. But in this instance it is used in combination or mixture with other patterns, which are completely isolated here in Central Africa as, in fact, is bronze-chasing in general. The special habitat of workers in this metal is Bida; there are, however, also a few in Kano and Katsena, and some in the other Houssa towns at the times when these were flourishing as well. But these bronze workers were in every instance Nupés, and were everywhere called people from Nupéland. It is only in the Far West, in Salaga and Dagomba, that there are chasers of bronze as to whose relation with Nupé I am insufficiently acquainted. The style of the Gonja district bronzeware diverges a little from the purely Nupean. But tradition says that the metal workers of Gonja at one time came from the East in common with the Nupés.

The spirals and double spirals, waves, tendrils, berries and sparse grape-bunches, blooms, more or less luxuriant acanthus leaves, and the egg and tongue pattern are the staple of this form of industrial art. Its application always reverts on principle to the employment of the double spiral, so that patterns directly akin to those of Mykene appear in the more ancient and simple specimens, which may naturally in the most favourable case be regarded as a form of atavism. These patterns have throughout assumed a secondary mannerism in guild and general use, as can be seen from the vernacular names given them, such as cat's-paw, lemon-pip, leopard-spots, snail-shell, mouse-belly, grasshopper-tooth, etc.

The articles themselves are food-dishes, water-cans, boxes for sulphuret of lead (for colouring the eyelids), kola-cups, inkstands, spoons, and so forth. The older the specimens the finer are the patterns in execution, and they get worse, more careless, and more degenerate the more recent they are. The best that I saw dated from the fifteenth century. The decoration is no longer to-day worked out from, and upon, the cast complete, but simply soldered together from tin imported from the coast.

I availed myself of every opportunity to get into communication with the best experts in Oriental industrial-art, such as Sarre, Zittmann, Wulff, etc., about these singular and beautiful objects and asked them for their opinion. Summarizing the information given me by these specialists, the conclusion I draw is that this entire style most certainly originated in the East but took on an absolutely African character. Some of the form and ornamentation recalls the Persian, some of it the Byzantine and some of it the Koptic style. It is impossible to obtain an absolutely decisive judgment on the point. A good deal of it is certainly reminiscent of Islamite art-industry and this drew its inspiration from the same source as our Nubia-Persian invasion of the Soudan. It is beyond all possible question that, according to tradition, this branch of craftsmanship was already being practised in Gbarra in the pre-Islamite era and I therefore think myself justified in definitely assuming its introduction to have occurred during the rule of the Kisra dynasty. The metal workers in bronze themselves say that they received their art and craft from the river Benue (but not from Islam), and the simple reason for this is that the nations on that river most indubitably understood the making of bronze in ancient times and many, many centuries prior to the Kisra-Napata invasion. Therefore the Perso-Nubian craftsmen made use of an industry which they already found in full growth on their arrival. The smelting and casting of bronze were known in the land when the art-craftsmen were summoned into it out of the East. They only added the art of chasing to the art already existing. The material had been gained in the country before they entered it.

The process of development which the glass-bead industry underwent can be similarly explained.

As I have already explained in the first part, the ancient Atlanteans of Yorubaland were thoroughly versed in glass smelting and the use of glass. The glazed earthenware we found is conclusive proof of the fact. The black brown glass of Ebolokun and that made by the Nupé Massaga are in all respects identical. It follows that the manufacture of glass was known in these lands as well. On the other hand, its prevailing forms in both districts are entirely different. Amongst the Nupés, bracelets of glass are the principal output; a symptom of close relationship with the peoples of the Sahara. For these glass rings are an imitation of the stone armlets which the Tuaregs have used from of old. If the beads vary occasionally in the North and South both in their ancient and modern forms, this is in consequence of a constantly fluctuating change in the fashion, a source of alarm also to the merchants importing these goods from abroad. Thus here, too, there is an exchange between the South and the West and East, each of which gained an impetus at a different time and in a different direction. It is quite certain that in the Koarra lands the Perso-Nubian civilization penetrated into the sphere of influence of Atlantic culture, overstepped its boundaries and imbued the latter with renewed vigour. We previously (in Vol. I., page 340, in the chapter on Atlantis) distinguished two periods in the history of Atlantic civilization corresponding with traditional and recorded statements and all actually ascertained facts, a period, namely, of efflorescence in the era of antiquity and a period of mediæval renaissance. The latter must necessarily have had its rise at the time when the reinvigorated Nubian-Persian culture, of which Byzantium was the source and origin, reached and revitalized the region subject to the power of Atlantic culture. And now, since this Kisra era showed its strength especially in the construction of political States, we can easily understand that it was precisely this mediæval renaissance in the provinces affected by Atlantic civilization which was this time influenced from the interior instead of from the coast and should have been able to bear heavily upon the expansion of the sphere of this particular civilization's political influence to such an extent that the legends still told stories about the expansion of the Benin Empire at the arrival of the earliest European merchant-traders, which would have given rise to a political union between the Ivory Coast and Congoland.

I shall later give a volume to show the extent of the sphere of influence of this amalgamation with the culture of the Middle Ages and the manner in which it was expressed in tradition, industrial art and decorative work, as well as in the political institutions of the nations of the Soudan.

In this place, however, we must be satisfied to place it on record. The appearance in the Soudan of a few legacies of civilization is now easy of comprehension. Padded armour and shirts of mail, definite sword-forms and portions of saddles, tobacco pipes, etc., are not difficult to understand when seen in their relation to this immigrant form of culture. The explanation of some of its indications, especially those associated with architecture, are not equally facile, and there is just as little illumination on this point to be gained from the ground-plan of a mosque with regard to the line of development taken in the erection of buildings as in that of a palace compound. I could only demonstrate the influences exercised respectively by Mahommedanism and Nubianism in the course of a lengthy dissertation based on the help which our copious material would afford us.

\*     \*     \*     \*     \*     \*     \*     \*

Elaborations of this kind are not, however, by far of so much importance as answering other preliminary questions. The problem with which we started in the first part of our labours was the determination of the extent of the attribution of civilizing influences in the Greater Soudan to Islam and its transmission by others on the fringe of its actual sphere of influence. The significant result of our investigation was that Islam only gained strength in, and gave strength to, the North-western political States of the

Libyan nations and that the broader Soudan from the Niger-bend to its far Eastern boundaries received a higher form of post-Christian culture through the Perso-Nubian immigration. We also ascertained that the first success of Islam had been built upon a previously stable Libyan influence. The Pagan Senhadja had prepared the soil which Islam cultivated. The expression I would use to describe this condition of things in this : Islam found a cultural predisposition ready to its hand, a readiness for its own acceptation which was due to Libyan ideas.

Now this brings us face to face with the other question in contrast to this, namely, whether the Nubian-Persian civilization, which had so vigorously and successfully pushed its way forward in the current from the East, was really the first which followed this course, or whether it did not rather encounter a tendency in its own favour of such strength as to render its striking success easy to understand as an edifice which was reared on previously existing and more ancient foundations. To furnish the answer I must anticipate some portions of what is to follow, and say that we are now in a position without any difficulty at all, to point out a sequence of symptoms of an older form of culture and pre-existent political conformations finding their strongest expression towards the West, and such as existed in Perso-Nubian form on the Eastern Nile, but were instinct with vitality as far as the Upper Niger.

· I alluded at the beginning of this chapter to an essential peculiarity of these more ancient realms in the passage referring to the first fascination exercised upon us by the name " Nubia." I drew attention to the proverbial piety of the ancient Ethiopians monumentally manifest in this country, a people who devoted their Kings to a sacrificial death in obedience to a primeval ritua cult.

The Shilluk, Djur, Kredj, and Shari tribes, many nations in Northern Cameroon and Nigeria, observed this prehistoric custom or—as will be more fully explained directly—still observe it to-day. We can trace it right into the Bend of the Niger, and if the four arch-princes of the Mossi formerly met every few years at regular intervals and took counsel together regarding the Emperor's conduct and his eventual death, or if the Guild-masters of the Mande smiths—that is to say, the nobles of the old Pagan

The founder of empire or holy horseman in Yoruban sculpture of more recent date.
(Collection of the G. I. A. F. E., 1912.)

and aboriginally settled races—acquired the right of deciding the life and death of their kings at the great nocturnal ceremonial smelting festival, these things are, in fact, none other than the echoes of that ancient phenomenon and custom, whose birthplace in Africa was the Nile, which amazed the authors of classical antiquity—for us they are the evidence of the prehistoric migration of nations in the westward stream of civilization—and the monuments of a period and form of culture which I designate as Ethiopian, inasmuch as it was indigenous to Africa and spread over that Continent which immediately concerns us. According to all the provable traces which have so far been available, this Ethiopian civilization must necessarily have followed a similar course in the Soudan from the Nile to the Niger to that pursued by the Perso-Nubian. Their starting-point and goal were fairly identical. It is, however, possible that the main stream of Ethiopian influence trended rather more in a southerly direction than the Perso-Nubian. These prehistoric Ethiopians had created the cultural predispositon which facilitated, the adoption and success of the Perso-Nubian invasion. The expansion of Ethiopian civilization, therefore, implied as much for the Byzantine-Nubian-Christian form of culture as the Libyan implied for that contained in the Arabic-Mauresque-Mahommedan.

Eternal are the ways, and the only things that change are the individuals and nations that wander along them. Consideration of the splendour and greatness of these essential features of the history of civilization must inspire us with admiration and wonder. Eternal are the ways, and no less eternal the laws to which mankind is subject when it proceeds along the track laid down by the course which civilization has pursued. I have shown the inhabitants of Nubia immersed in the life religious from prehistoric times until the present day. The realms of Ethiopia were aboriginally ecclesiastical kingdoms. The Kisra-Napata dynasties took their way Westwards as Priests and Kings combined. In ancient days humanity was never able to free itself from the holy law of Nature which controlled the road whereon the dark-skinned nations travelled.

If now we propound the final problem, whether, namely, the human races of the North never had knowledge of this furthest province of venerable and ancient Byzantium at the period of its greatest power and glory, we must make this particular train of thought our starting-point. Can it possibly be the fact that this mighty triumphal procession of Byzantine-Nubian culture, which influenced the remotest portions of Africa and called into life renewed greatness and gave it fresh impetus, could have remained unknown to the North ? It is scarcely thinkable ! Is it not rather credible that some indication of the glory of Central Africa should have been preserved in the historical documents of the races of the North ? I, for one, believe in their existence.

For I think that if my old friend from Bokani still remembered the tradition of the payment of tribute to Byzantium, the neighbouring countries must also be credited with a memory of such occurrences. Neither is it a difficult matter to prove that the more ancient Christian era possessed some knowledge of the significance of the pomp of Christian royalty in the heart of Africa in precisely the same manner that classical antiquity was familiar with the piety of primeval Ethiopia. That splendid hero, Parsifal, as depicted by old Wolfram of Eschenbach, of late quickened my pulse as I read him again. Then the figure of the black and white King Feirefi, whose blood was mixed, stirred me, and once more I came upon the passage in which the Christian son of the King of the Moors, whose sceptre was extended over the land in the far, far East, was called Prester John. " The Kings who came after him all bore this name." When the ambassador of the old Emperor of Benin came to Portugal, he said that his lord received the insignia of power in the symbol of a cross at the hands of a sovereign called Ogane. There was even in those early days a suspicion that this name was a corrupted form of that pertaining to the Priest-King John. The knowledge of a great Central African Christian Church Empire was very deeply implanted in the nations of that age. How great in those days was the part which the rich " treasurer from the land of the Moors " played in legendary lore ! And the belated historical record of the New Testament even led the three holy kings, the wise men from the East, to the Virgin Mary, the Mother of God.

Now, however, we have again arrived at the borders of the Dark Continent. We can once again hint at the thread which

connected the world outside with its centre, and we place the clue
in the hands of the specialists. For we personally are only
explorers of Africa insufficiently qualified to understand all
that the history of civilization has established and verified on the
further shores of those oceans which lap the shores of the Continent
of Darkness.

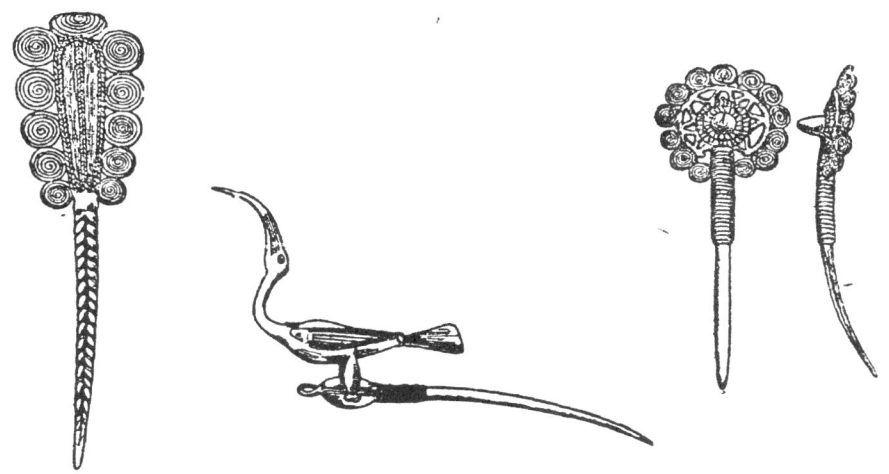

Bronze ornaments of ancient Ethiopian craftsmanship: Muntshi hair-pins.
*(Drawn by Carl Arriens.)*

## CHAPTER XXX

### THE JOURNEY INTO THE COUNTRY OF PROBLEMS

To Porta Atlantica—Two spirits and two regions—Coast gossip—The savage Muntshi of the forest—Savages of superior grade—Djenn—Up the Benue—German Cameroon disease—The Fulbe robber-knights—Hostile reception—On ways untrodden—Amiable " savages "—Meeting of the " nations "—Hill folk—The blameless Ethiopians—Rainy-season and dry-season roads—Down the Tarraba in boats—Lokoja—Round Africa to Kordofan—Meeting with our own people—Down the Nile to Egypt—" Let there be light "—and there was light in the earliest greying of the dawn.

FAREWELL ! The shrill blasts of the Kakatshi, the trumpets of the Emir of Bida, rend the air. Horsemen tear through the streets bearing messages to that place and this. Long trains of porters have already passed through the city gates. Nupé nobles and high-born Fulbe princes have assembled with their retinues to unite in one long procession and give us escort out of this city, the heir of departed Byzantium. Fare ye well, O industrious artists in glass ! Bear us in memory, O tireless polishers of gems ! Ply still your hammers, O deft-fingered chasers of bronzeware ! Good-bye to all this glorious beauty ! Thanks once more to thee, my charming host ! Bida, my lad, take up the bugle and blow a blast to bid thy namesake town a brave good-bye !

And then this lovely city of Nupéland, this ample treasure-house of Byzantine-Persian-Nubian splendour lies behind us—and as early as April 18th, 1911. Let us now journey into the hills to the primitive people, the disruptive tribes, the unsophisticated simple ones. But we will first set out faces Nigerwards, and the river whereon I first set eyes (in 1906) at Bamako, that bore me on its stream upward to Timbuktu in 1907, and which I crossed at the end of 1910 at Jebba when I left Yorubaland, now carries us to Lokoja.

To Lokoja ! To Porta Atlantica ! It was in a measure a step to the rear, a pace or two towards the Coast, which we took in gliding down the Niger to its point of confluence with the Benue. There were, however, many reasons compelling us to this course. Partly because we had to re-equip at Lokoja, where lay our base of supplies ; partly because the water-way up the Benue was more convenient for bringing us to the Northern Cameroons ; but partly, also, because I wanted once to meet the Spirit of the Coast and confer with it before again withdrawing into the Interior and the remoter regions of the heart of the Continent. For Lokoja lies on the Porta Atlantica, at that point on the Niger and the Benue where the stream from the Sahara and the Soudan of the West mingles its waters with those which flow from the Central Soudan. This is the spot up to which great ships can come, the place which gives access to the zones of the Coast for those who come from inland, while for those who come from the sea-shores it is the route to the Interior. Here the Spirits of two distinct regions meet and grasp hands.

And how vast the difference between these two, the Spirit of the Coast and the Spirit of the Up-country districts ! They come into contact everywhere but never will harmonize. They are in disagreement and feud in Western Africa wherever they may come into conflict there.

The West-Coast Spirit is effeminate and ever foreign to the soil. Although it may be European in its nature *ab origine*, it is no longer European in its essence, yet its vitality none the less depends on the close connection which the marine traffic maintains. The Spirit of the Coast sighs with languor if a fortnight slips around without news from its European home. The Spirit of the Coast has its being in an ideal of the love of order and in a constant craving to imitate European methods and is equally active amongst Europeans and Africans. The Spirit of the Coast loves ease of life, sits in the lap of luxury, but fears the sun. The Spirit of the Coast cleaves ever to the written record and the nearness to the sea. Closeness to the ocean is, as it were, its fetter, which robs it of the great African freedom of action and energy for work. But the Spirit of the Coast is cunning and preoccupied with schemes for making profit and money ; it ever hatches new causes of complaint that ever has its birth in laxity of effort, but never in the storm and stress of the struggle for existence. The Spirit of the Coast is industrious, but always tosses groaning on a bed oppressed with fever, whereof it lives in two-fold terror, because the air it breathes is rife with germs that breed disease. The atmosphere which the Spirit of the Coast absorbs is venomous. Poisonous, too, its speech. Alas ! of all the evils to which the white stranger in Western Africa is exposed, I know of naught more difficult or necessary to acquire than the victory over the noxious exhalation of the Coastal mind, neither white nor black in colour, neither European nor African in temperament, but a bastard and a mongrel, in whom the vices of two races and two Continents are intermingled. It is difficult to overcome. But those who have made this Spirit subservient to their ends have been for aye the greatest colonizers of the West of Africa.

The Inland Spirit of the Steppes of Africa sweeps swiftly and fitfully across the plains. It is a Spirit endowed with strength ; in love with space because it can freely move and range across it. The Inland Spirit is like a gigantic bird of passage with a mighty breast and widespread pinions ; and on its heels are spurs with which it kills ; and in its head are eyes wherewith it scans the region over which it soars. The Inland Spirit is one of power, of action and of will. The Inland Spirit is full of vigour and of might, not cunning like the Spirit of the Coast, not intent upon acquiring lucre and well-being, nor for ever thinking of an end in view. For what it delights in is activity for action's sake. The struggle for life in sheer joy of battle ; the joy of movement ; these inspire it with happiness and vital energy. It cares not whether death awaits it on the other side of the movement or the thing achieved.

Our camp on Stirling Hill above Lokoja, overlooking the confluence of the Benue and Niger.
(Drawn by Carl Arriens.)

Stirling Hill about the middle of last century.
(From an English steel engraving.)

The Inland Spirit is a heroic, divinely splendid, strenuously operative spirit, always unconsciously wandering on the edge of its own grave and that of its deeds. Almost everything of greatness and power accomplished in Inner Africa was perfected under this Spirit's banner. Neither is it less great in quantity than fine in quality. We are, however, ignorant of most of it, because none but master minds can bridle the exuberance of this Spirit and guide its stubborn strength into channels of well-directed usefulness and consciousness of purpose.

Where these two Spirits meet, they are in conflict. Each of the colonies in Western Africa knows the consequences of this feud in its historical development, as well as in the organization of to-day. There are two different zones where the working of one of these two Spirits is clearly visible in the life of every West Coast colony, be it German Cameroon or German Togo, French Guinea, or the English Gold Coast. All the Coast lands breathe an atmosphere distinct from the Interior's, and, in consequence, are differently administered. The guiding principles of both are mostly in the violent opposition conditioned by their geographical configuration. And the chasm yawns the wider always, especially as the Coast Government demands taxes and an increasing ratio of civilization from the up-country regions, but is involuntarily compelled to expend all the revenue at its disposal principally in the consolidation of the elements of culture on the Coast. These opposed interests will remain irreconcilable until the establishment of direct communications through great high roads combining the Coast with the Interior and conflict will only be subdued and compromise effected when intellectual control of administrative and economic undertakings has its headquarters in the Interior.

This distinction in the leading ideas is most sharply defined in Nigeria, which is divided into a Northern and Southern Colony. Nowhere can the contrast between the two regions be better observed than precisely in North and South Nigeria, because in many respects diametrically opposite methods of government are there in force. The Christianized black and his aspirations prevail more or less in Southern Nigeria. The white race, as such, is dominant in the Northern province and insists upon the subordination of the weaker aboriginal system.

Now, as we were coming from North Nigeria, the poisonous breath of the Coast could not but come out towards us. This venomous blast's prosaic title is "Coast scandal." The enormities brought to one's ears on the West Coast of Africa transcend all credibility. Even the old charts designed by the seafarers of Africa depict marvellous animals and wonderful men which do not exist in reality, but are the creations of the coast-dwellers' prolific imagination. We full well know now that these fabulous beings are not actually living, but the Coast's fertile fantasy breeds them and indulges itself in inventing descriptions of the up-country Europeans' manner of life. And since the mind is so greatly oppressed with the weight of the terrible climate, it generates noxious stories as well. Everyone who can read is aware of the stories told in the Press of the day and even in the Imperial Parliament, of the horrible things done by the Europeans who live in the Interior. Yet I have personally, nevertheless, experienced the fact that the up-country European is larger-hearted and morally superior, simply because he possesses greater mobility of mind and vigour in action.

Now we had just had some little difference of opinion with a Government official in Southern Nigeria and it was only quite natural and entirely a matter of course that West-Coast gossip had to be interested in us, because certain English newspapers had further embellished and exaggerated the matter in question. I had already heard all sorts of things in Bida. The Spirit of the Coast had been particularly busy with my own personal character and not only through officials, but young traders as well. The tale went round that I always carried a pistol and threatened to shoot every native (there was not even a single pistol in the whole of the Expedition's equipment!). Rumour would have it that I was a German officer dismissed from the army in disgrace (I had never even been inside a uniform!). It was reported that I had been expelled from the German Colony of Togo by its Governor (while all possible honours had been conferred on me by Count Zech). I was accused of ignorance of any other than the German language, of having only attended an elementary school at home and of never having seen the inside of a university. The character given to my poor colleagues was partly that of persons who had been recalled, partly of such as had incurred the Emperor's extra-special disfavour. It was noised abroad that there had at first been seven of us in South Nigeria, but that I had sent six of us home because of dissensions. It was said that the Governor of Northern Nigeria, who had just at that time renewed his pressing invitations, had turned us out of the colony, etc. Coast scandal had taken us to its bosom and only a general and exceptionally significant good feeling restrains me from particularizing the hatchers-in-chief of these fairy-tales by name.

All these wild flights of fancy had predetermined the intention to receive us very badly in Lokoja and to make the place as uncomfortable for us as possible.

And, as a matter of fact, only a very small house had been prepared for our largely increased expedition. The accommodation for my staff of interpreters, swollen by now to about forty, had to be distributed all over the town! Naturally, nothing more than a visit shortly after our arrival to the Cantonment magistrate and the C.O. of the regiment stationed there was necessary in order to establish a better understanding by a little conversation, obtain permission to build our camp on Stirling Hill and then to pave the way for very amicable relations. It was precisely here, here in Lokoja, whence the most odious and repulsive stories had been wafted to us overland from the Coast as to the prevailing "Coast gossip," that we were afterwards able to conclude the sincerest friendships and I shall never forget the delightful hours we were permitted to enjoy at the hospitable regimental mess, hours which we were enabled to return to our English guests at Stirling Hill. When we set our faces inland in June these charming Englishmen escorted us on board ship and, on bidding us Godspeed, once more deplored the miserable and sordid results of that scandalmongering which was the curse of the Coast.

The dreamy sentiments inspired by African river navigation soon enveloped us. We had involuntarily to recall all we had gone through during the last few months and the last few weeks. We came back from up-country and touched the Coast district at Lokoja. We there encountered its evil atmosphere and got the better of it. We parted from all as friends. Yet in spite of it, I had to put a question to myself on the Benue, and must repeat it here in my European home, namely, this : Is there any real necessity for the constant recurrence of these petty differences, these tongue-waggings ? I ask myself, is it digni- fied that Europeans should so far lower themselves as to adapt their mental attitude and speech to the meannesses peculiar to this country ? Is it quite impossible for the European to govern and complete his task here, without falling a victim to this ancient pestilence which rages along the coasts of Africa ? Can we not find means to counteract it ? Is it quite beyond us to learn to practise the power to do and to will and to recognize cheerfully the achievements of others here to the same degree as this is done in the Interior ? Is constant battling with these miseries an absolute necessity ?

\* \* \* \* \* \* \* \*

The Spirit of the Coast invents fables and relates miracles. It creates phantasms which never existed. It exaggerates the difficulties of the traveller desiring to go inland ; it exaggerates the glory and power of the interior cities and principalities ; it caricatures the simple inhabitants of the provinces and depreciates them. But it was these less sophisticated countrymen whom we longed to reach as we went down the stream of the Benue river. Our objective was the investigation of the " savage " nations who had not been drawn within the magic circle of the superior and younger civilization of the Oriental builders of political States. We wished to look up the " wild " races who dwelt in the unlopped forests, in the everlasting, aspiring, impenetrable forests, and the smaller " disruptive " tribes who mostly live in the hills and inhabit both sides of the Benue valley. Our intention was first to visit the forest Muntshi on English territory, and afterwards the hill tribes, the disruptive tribes, in North Cameroon ; for the Colonial Secretary had obtained for us a not inconsiderable grant in aid of the funds necessary for the purpose of obtaining information about them.

Former expeditions had made us sufficiently acquainted with both these species of the human race. My first opportunity of studying the " wood-men " was in the Congo-basin, and before being initiated in the higher diplomatic arts as practised in Africa I had been forced to go through a fight, but afterwards concluded a treaty with them on the Sankurru and Kassai rivers. I was familiar with the hill and "disruptive" tribes in the great Nigerbend, the Volta valley in North Togo. I had at first seen them from afar through the spectacles of Islam, and with the eyes of more highly developed races, as quite primitive and comparatively miserable creatures, quite devoid of civilization; but afterwards, at close quarters, I had come to know and esteem them as uncommonly industrious, active human beings of ability, with strong faculties of ethical perception. And I was now anxious to get the chance of prosecuting my earlier study, test the result of what I had already learned and once more put to the touch all those problems which force themselves upon the ethnologist in view of the strange forms of civilization he meets with there, and of which some explanation is desirable.

We travelled slowly up the Benue as far as Ibi and were most cordially received by Captain Ruxton and his wife as well as by Dr. Pollard. The new equipment was soon got together; the practised leaders and interpreters quickly arranged the baggage, and very shortly after our arrival we were in a position to put our best leg forward towards the Interior. Our first goal was Wukari, in which the capital of the kingdom of Kororofa of ancient renown is to-day to be seen. This realm is peopled by the so-called Yukum, or Djukum. They are a nation extraordinarily like Yorubans in dress, in legendary lore and general characteristics. They have the same system of oracular divination, the identical style of divine worship, though somewhat degenerate and transformed under the influence of the nations which surround them. The old metropolis of Kororofa of which the most ancient records make mention is situate at a great distance from Wukari. It is a city in ruins, a mighty area of fragments, which the natives most carefully and fearfully avoid. For not only can the old chroniclers relate marvels about this place, but the legendary tales of the aborigines also agree that Kororofa was flourishing even before Bornu and the Houssa States had begun their mighty career of progress. Kororofa prospered and grew in importance, because it possessed within its boundaries a great treasure which gained the ancient kingdom numerous friends at every period of time. Ancient Kororofa was a country of smelting ores. The sulphuret of lead with which the Houssa women painted their eyelids was an article of export from this land. Pewter, which competed strongly with that from Bautshi, came from Kororofa and this was cast into artistic cups and dishes in the Northern States. Gold and silver came from Kororofa. But above and beyond all other wares from Kororofa came the bronzes with a reputation which is maintained in popular estimation as well as exemplified in many antique examples. The art of casting metal was a special attribute of ancient Kororofa.

Such was Kororofa's fame that the King of Bornu went South and made a treaty of friendship with the great King of Benue after waging a successful war against the Houssa States. The powerful ruler of Kororofa then, together with his ally, the Bornu King, constructed roads through marshes and forests, the last remains of which can still be seen in long stretches of rising ground, for the highway consists of a high-piled dam or causeway. There is a book about the history of Kororofa which begins with fantastic tales about the magic power an erstwhile King possessed and how he overcame the King of Bornu by means of his sorcerer's might. This wizardry was, however, insufficient to protect the Kororofan King completely; the ancient nation's sphere of interest extended Northwards more and more. Silver was carried down from the Atlas mountains; bronzes came from the West and the peoples only continued to contend against each other for the possession of the sulphuret of lead mines. The gold mines were forgotten and only the most aged inhabitants have any knowledge of their whereabouts.

Kororofa decayed. This city, once so mighty, was destroyed and its King took refuge in his flight in present-day Wukari, whose original founders were the pagan Houssas, the exploiters of the mines. The Yukums continued to degenerate. They went down the swift road of decadence to which all nations, tribes and individuals are doomed in this region of the tropics unless they receive a strong influx from other lands. At present the Yukum are a miserable lot, a folk inordinately addicted to petty matters of devotional exercises, and all sorts of occult practices. They are devoid of all resilience and, without the ancient documentary records and oral traditions, none would suspect that these people had ever played a prominent part in the history of these districts.

We took up our quarters in Wukari at a place which was all the more endeared to us because the compound included the lodging where our great compatriot, Robert Flegel, had once lived and endured great suffering. The poor fellow had been sorely smitten with sickness and had passed many bitter hours in solitude. But the natives still bear a kindly memory of the first white man who had penetrated this region. The Yukum must, beyond question, be regarded as an anciently civilized, but now degenerate people. But to-day they are of no account whatever. The neighbouring races, therefore, who are generally called " Muntshi," appear all the more important to those who visit these countries. Speak but the word " Muntshi " on the Middle Benue and the bystanders will at once assume their most serious expressions. Then heads are uplifted and then the intensest interest is awakened all round. For the Muntshi are the most feared of all the peoples living in these parts. They are the most dangerous man-eating cannibals and the most terrible thieves. They are decried as immoral, cruel, unbridled in violence and malicious. Mark well, this is the verdict in the language of those who come up the river Benue from the Coast. The bad name of the Muntshi was created by those who came from the South-east. The Yukum told me themselves that this reputation is recent. The Muntshi were certainly a nation that was formerly held in fear, but at no time was their character said to be so base and abominable as to-day, at a time when the opinion held by the Fulbe and the Europeans turns the scale.

Much that is horrible will surely be heard of the Muntshi when the history of the first colonization of these countries comes to be written. They conquered both the shore districts of the Benue ; they discharged clouds of arrows at every boat that laid its course down or up stream ; heavily poisoned arrows fatal to those whom they wounded. It is true that they were not openly hostile to the first-comers from Europe, but then they burnt down the factories and looted them. The chronicles of these lands will therefore without doubt relate that the Muntshi are really and truly a particularly barbarous, predatory, quarrelsome and uncivilized people.

But is it not incumbent upon me to give this the lie here and to put an end to this method of history ? Am I not compelled to enter my veto if, in the eyes of " general opinion," a particular

people is vile, only because the Europeans failed to understand it ?
The " savagery " of the Muntshi in olden days consisted only in their
claim to be allowed to save their souls in the way they considered
most suitable to themselves. They wanted to live as they liked
and their life was always strenuous, passionate, free and full ; an
existence in which love and war, the heartiest friendships and the
fiercest of feuds worked together in definite proportions. But then
at the beginning of the last century, when the Fulbes stormed
over the land and the Empire of Nupé was finally conquered ; when
Mallem Dando's dynasty ascended the throne in Bida ; when, besides
this, they could no longer carry out sufficiently profitable slave raids
and forays in their own provinces, they went further afield to the
mining districts of the Benue and came into contact with the
Muntshi. The " evil " Muntshi were pagans and were universally
held to be cannibals. Barbarians of this sort were a welcome find
for the rapacity of the Islamite, and the Fulbe prince hurled himself at these " miserable heathens," grasping in his fist the standard
of high morality which he boastfully waved in the beams of the sun.

The Nupean Fulbes had waged successful wars all over the land
in the North, the South, the West, and in the Interior. But when
they encountered the Muntshi, their progress was stayed. The
" miserable heathen " poured forth thousands upon thousands
of venomous arrows from their ambush at the edge of the forest
upon the advancing Fulbe leaders and overwhelmed them.

The Fulbes made three campaigns through the district and then
the " miserable Muntshi " had got rid of this foe once and for all.
Now, however, their warlike soul had sprung to life and now they,
who had themselves not been left in peace, began to harass other
people. Their hordes swept over the country far and wide.

This was the time when the Muntshi gained their evil reputation. I pass over the tales of the later times told me by the
" wicked Muntshi," but I am afraid that there is a good deal of
truth in them. The Europeans who push forward for commercial
profits into these regions are not always remarkable for ability and
tact. And the principle enunciated in the Duke of Mecklenburg's
presence by my esteemed friend, Captain Ruxton, must cause
surprise. For what he said was this : " He would gladly grant
English prospectors and all classes of traders permission to enter

The expedition marching through North Cameroon in the autumn, 1914

To face p. 384

Muntshi territory, but withhold it from missionaries and exploring travellers." Neither the English prospectors nor the young merchants are (not, at least, in the opinion of the Muntshi, who are, after all, entitled to be heard) always overburdened with education and too keen a sense of justice.

But at last we came to the land of the Muntshi from the land of the Yukum. The road ran through forests with open spaces into a district of extensive plantations and afforestation areas ; we found women and boys busily engaged at this work on every side. We rode uninterruptedly for a couple of hours between Donga and Satalu through plantations which belonged to one small village of no more than five hundred souls. We enter it.

Just as we expected ! What a contrast to the towns and settlements in the Benue valley in Nupéland and in the province of Yoruba ! No fence, no road. A broad square around which are built the mighty conical roofs. Men and women in the open with nothing but a loin-cloth : and then only when they are married. And it seems that marriage takes place among the Muntshi somewhat late in life ! What an absence of bashfulness among the women who at once come up to offer us food and drink, lay a hand upon our shoulder and burst into the heartiest peals of laughter at a joke and gladly hand us their babies to play with. What beaming smiles from the men and boys whose sharp-filed teeth glisten in the sun ! What hospitality !

And then—what is that peculiar-looking ornament shining on that beautiful woman's neck ? Does it not look like an antique bronze necklace ? What a curious, bird-shaped hairpin it is which she is putting into her neighbour's head-dress ? What extraordinary bronze spirals decorate the foreheads of the men ? How beautifully forged the spear-heads and the iron rings and chains ! Just look at that beautifully shaped bronze tobacco-pipe ! There is no doubt but that we are among a people whose art and industrial develop-ment stands high indeed.

Evening falls. The white-skinned stranger has expressed a wish to be allowed to see one of the mystic dances. The stranger gained the goodwill of the people during the course of the day without difficulty. A huge wooden signal-drum is pushed into the middle of the square, little field-drums as well as flutes and a kakatshi trumpet taken as a war trophy from the Fulbes, are brought along too. The moon goes up. The folk have forgathered in their hundreds and hundreds from the surrounding villages, laughing and chatting; the women talk to the white man and are by no means shy. The first taps of the drums resound; the flutes join in and develop a charming air to which some men and women dance a measure. All the hundreds assembled begin to move their shoulders and hips in imitation of the dance leader's movements. The time gets quicker. The steps get quicker and stronger. More flutes join in until the whole of the vast, old, primeval forest re-echoes with the tunes and the glad shouts of the joyfully excited throngs of human beings who madly whirl about in circles.

A gift of a few beads increases the joy of the proceedings. Separate dancers perform here and there. The melodies are changed. The musical sense tries busily to obtain fresh combinations and variations of rhythm. The shrieks of the women grow sharper and sharper; the shouts of the men become louder and wilder. A passionate excitement I have never before in all my experience witnessed seizes the crowd. We enjoy the sight till far into the night. Then we have to ask for a little less noise, for some of our people are very ill and need consideration. One word is sufficient and the multitude disperses in the distance.

I lie me down on my camp-bedstead under an open veranda and am just dozing off when notes of music are wafted across the village which sound quite unfamiliar. The voices are strange. The women are singing duets. Two high sopranos sang a charming and tender air in a delicate, trained tremolo. This was not the song of a barbarian race; this had nothing in common with the passionate abandon which we had just heard outside. It sounded like a love song, and, as we afterwards heard, was a greeting in song offered by two friends of a girl who had been married that day. When I woke up next morning at five and the réveillé was blown, I only found a few old and very young people left in the village. The entire adult population was already at work in the fields and only returned late in the evening.

What an extraordinary mixture it all was. This unrestrained excitement and this industrious labour; this busy occupation, this artistry; these ancient ornaments on the neck and in the head-dress; this cunning craftsmanship of the smiths; this graceful flute-playing and the enchanting song of the maidens. Can these "savages" really be said to be "savages?" Are these vigorous people, with their exuberant feeling for art, their astounding power of work and uninterrupted interest in progress and their strong impulse for the extension of knowledge, not to be considered as being on a much higher plane than the lazy, languorous, corrupted Yukum? May not these folk become much more important units for the furtherance of the efforts we Europeans are making to socialize and colonize on African soil; than the used-up and now merely historically interesting powers of many "more highly developed" races?

\*     \*     \*     \*     \*     \*     \*     \*

We visited the Muntshi, who live in the forests, from our base at Ibi; then the Chamba tribes, who are the advanced posts of the farthest West and whose main body is at home in the districts of German Cameroon. Once I was hurriedly called back from the Wukari to Ibi. Duke Adolf Frederick of Mecklenburg had brought his travels in the countries of Lake Chad to an end and was voyaging on the Benue to the coast on his way to Europe. The reunion which was celebrated on board the Herzog-Expedition steamer and charming Mrs. Ruxton's drawing-room was most delightful. His Grace told me much about his successful work in the Musgu regions and especially described the state of affairs in Northern Cameroon to me. I learnt that the North-eastern boundaries of the French and German Cameroons had been thoroughly investigated ethnologically, so that the supplementary examination of South and West was an essential task which it was considered desirable should be undertaken by me.

Then the entire expedition moved over to Ibi. Here now began the times of heavy sickness. The first symptoms of serious inflammation of the lungs appeared among my people. I personally had my first bout of black-water fever; then I went down under a violent dysentery. Dr. Pollard nursed me with the most unselfish devotion, so that, comparatively hale and hearty, I was able to get aboard the steamer of the firm of Pagenstecher, who always placed their resources at our disposal in the most hospitable way and to whom we owe a great debt of gratitude. Our way lay at first over Djenne, a town in which I was able to make my first observations on the peculiar worship of skulls and ancestors, as well as my first notes and studies of Ethiopian architecture in Central Soudan. The people were externally, perhaps, still more primitive than the Muntshi, but the signs of civilization they showed all the more interesting on that account. We got on shore at Garua.

We were now in the German colony, where Captain Schwarz and Dr. Range cordially welcomed us. We lived in the Pagenstecher warehouses and this firm satisfied all our necessities in the friendliest fashion, making all the preparations for our route. The Government stud-farm furnished us with excellent mounts and through the good offices of the Resident the Fulbe authorities supplied us with no less excellent interpreters. Then we set forth.

We were now at the height of the rainy season, and at the beginning of the time which overwhelmed us with all sorts of trouble. From now onwards, until our adventurous return to Lokoja, the expedition suffered an unbroken series of diseases. No sooner was I passably convalescent than Arriens succumbed to a very bad attack of malaria which often rendered him unconscious for hours at a time. It was precisely then that I learned really to admire this man's character. He always battled against the fact of his illness and would never admit it existed. The worse his condition, the more was his energy and it is a remarkable thing that his impulse to work, which at any time called forth the admiration of us all, now grew greater than ever. It took him months to get over the worst of his illness and he returned to the coast a mere skeleton covered with skin. We treated him with a new preparation of albumen, called Riba, and to this I attribute his ultimate recovery from his utterly deplorable condition. Martius was let off with comparatively less fever and so was enabled to nurse his senior comrade-in-travel with greater devotion. But our people were in no better state than ourselves. Dysentery spread. And when we arrived at the hills, inflammation of the lungs attacked a great number of them. I had thirty-eight cases altogether on my hands for treatment in Chamba, on the middle Faro river.

It was not to be wondered at that the column's health deteriorated steadily in the further course of the march. The valleys we went

Crossing a "break" in the rainy season, 1911, in North Cameroon.

*To face p. 390.*

through were like sponges. The smallest brooks, which are water-less in the dry season, had swollen into rivers many yards wide and deep and all the lower-lying land was one vast marsh under water. I cannot even now understand how it was we managed to make this journey through the valley of the Faro with the horses. They were sometimes so carried down-stream by the force of the current that we gave up all hopes of being able to save them. The natives themselves said that no such inundation had been known within the memory of living men.

Our first destination was Chamba, an urban Fulbe settlement, situate at no great distance from the foot-hills of the Atlantica mountain range. I wanted to stay here for a few weeks in order to study the organization of the petty tribes dwelling round about on the hill-tops and valleys of the district.

We arrived at Faro with the van of the column rather late in the afternoon of August 28th. Although messengers had notified the Galadima of Chamba several days in advance of our arrival, we were surprised not to find a single canoe on our side of the stream which by now had grown into a mighty river. I therefore had first of all to send to a neighbouring hamlet to hunt up a vessel of some kind or other, so that the Fulbe ruler might be informed that not a moment was to be lost in sending across boats of sufficient size to effect our passage over. The worthy Galadima, however, did not hurry himself in the least, although he must have heard the bugle signals for quite a while, nor did he come himself to superintend the work of his people, but sent an old imbecile of a slave, who did not know what to do when he got to the banks. The horses were got across with exceeding difficulty and I galloped up the acclivity to the town. Arrived at the Residency camp, I sent a message to the Galadima, begging him to put in an appearance. But his high mightiness failed to come out and said he was just about to engage in his devotions. Then I went myself. I found the old gentleman not at his prayers, but at his food. The highly-placed Fulbe was so innocent as to forget even to greet me. I had never met with such a piece of gross impertinence of recent years. So I started the conference at once by asking him what could possibly be the reason that he was behaving more indecently than any naked " savage." My interpreters gave due weight to what I wanted conveyed and I very plainly told his worship that as I, of course, had permission from the Residency to occupy the official compounds, I should personally refuse to allow him to occupy them or hold any communication with me unless he promptly paid me a visit of apology and offered some explanation of his extraordinary conduct. And, in addition, I told him that I should know what to do. I gave orders in his hearing to a soldier at the same time to march to the next-dwelling competitor of this worthy Galadima and request him to get in touch with me as I did not care to have anything to do with the present headman of Chamba. The good Galadima got a sad shock when he heard that I was going to summon his Fulbe colleague directly to Chamba. He was quite a good fellow at bottom, but recently indulged in some impudent conduct to a German customs officer with impunity, and his comb wanted cutting a bit. And he had, moreover, quite special reason for not liking our presence just then. He viewed with alarm the possibility that his hitherto illegitimate exercise of power might suffer restriction.

In order to make what follows intelligible I must enter into a somewhat detailed description of the condition of things in those parts of Northern Cameroon, called Adamowa. The final result of a war, which the Fulbes had everywhere waged for some decades, was the conquest of these countries and the forcing back of their Pagan inhabitants to the hills. When the European powers occupied the territory, they discovered that its rule was parcelled out among a number of Fulbe princes who were oppressing the people in their own peculiar way. At first the German Resident officials could not do otherwise than recognize these princely authorities and come to an agreement with them respecting the levying of taxation. The Fulbe chieftains, for their part, afterwards squeezed still more forced labour, cattle and cash out of these hill-folk as far as they could lay hands upon them. They had become men of great substance as the years rolled on and had gathered together thousands upon thousands of slaves within their chief camp. The slave trade, as such, had become impracticable and therefore a new use had to be found for the employment of the captive human material. The slaves were compelled to keep the vast tracts of country which their Fulbe lords had acquired in cultivation for them. I place it on record here that this Fulbe agricultural method of tillage by slave-labour formerly produced, and now still produces, but very meagre results and quite the reverse of those attained by the " disruptive " tribes who were driven into the hill country and which can aptly be said to be models of what farming should be. The labour of enslaved beings who are thus fortuitously associated will only become profitable in Africa when the owners understand how to use it. But the Fulbes are thoroughly ignorant of all that pertains to the cultivation of land and its economy.

While, now, the Fulbes have their fields tilled by slave-labour in the valley districts which they subjugated, they continue every now and again to go with more or less pomp and circumstance into the hills and forcibly levy contributions from the wretched " disruptive " tribes, and use these for the payment of taxes. This method of collection goes on to-day with varying leniency and without bloodshed, because the terror-stricken and expatriated tribes regard the Fulbes as the deputies of the ruling white Government. Now even before my arrival in the German Cameroons, that is, since I had been in Donga and sent an embassy from there into the Dakka and Chamba hill districts, I had caused the report to be spread that I was authorized by the German Government to set free these innocuous hill-denizens from their tyrants and to get into direct relations with the " disruptive " tribes. This news would be naturally liable to be strengthened after I had sent envoys from Garua to the Fulbe rulers of the various districts, asking that delegates of the principal tribes might be sent into Chamba for a conference with me. The very busy and polite intercourse by letter in Arabic which my secretary carried on with the natives had most successful results. And the princes of Marua, of Rëi-Buba and of 'Ngaurdere fell in with my wishes with particular readiness. But the petty chief of Chamba, to whom I was nearest with my column, began to get frightened that I might block his pathway to his milch-giving kine in the Atlantica mountains. He, consequently, was evilly disposed towards me from the start and tried to fob me off in the same way as he had succeeded in doing with the German customs officer. Now, however, as the good Fulbes are not entirely in mutual agreement, the simple sending of a message to the nearest Fulbe chieftain living in the South must have caused a fear in the heart of the Galadima lest a competitor might be raised up in his own town, who, as the white man's friend, would in his own good time skim the cream off the milk which might be left over.

And so this excellent Galadima turned quite amiable during the same night. He took post himself on the bank till towards dawn and directed the difficult passage which, fortunately, a starlit sky made easier, so that Martius and myself could throw ourselves upon our beds at four a.m. with the pleasing sensation of having happily overcome a very perilous and somewhat critical situation.

I at once set about the necessary work next day. I sent a few interpreters into the hills to inform the nearest so-called Komaï tribes that I wished to conclude a treaty of friendship with them. I laid some especial stress upon my not coming in company with the Fulbe, so as not to scare them. We would have a little friendly palaver together about their ancient habits and customs, and they could tell me of their grievances if they happened to have any. I sent my most capable people and left no stone unturned for the next few days to ensure the success of the negotiations. I need scarcely say that I did not begin by overwhelming the people with presents, but that our chief concern was to make it perfectly clear to them that what we, as Europeans, desired was to shield them from injustice and oppression and to be their true and very good friends. I bade them deal directly with my own folks and hear what these had to tell them about the way we had accomplished our labours in other countries. Then they would know that we had no evil intentions and were at all events in a position to be better friends to them than these Fulbes who had been their worst possible neighbours for a very long time. The negotiations were difficult and protracted. The people were greatly alarmed. But, when they heard how I had put the esteemed Galadima in his place, they showed much greater confidence. The first of them came and were received in a friendly way. Then they told me that they once had inhabited the whole of the extensive Faro valley and had there had their fertile fields. I went outside with them and they showed me the places where the ridges of their ancient agricultural holdings were still visible under the grasses. I promised them to do all that in me lay to see that they should return from these

Dwelling of the Konia in Xdera, overlooking the East plain.

inhospitable hill districts, where agriculture could only be pursued in narrow dales of stony soil and reoccupy their former holdings, without reverting to the " Fulbe system." We became friends and the very people who a few years ago had aimed their arrows at the Europeans because they feared that the troubles inflicted on them by Fulbes would be yet further augmented, these very people invited us to come up upon the heights. The Komaï and Namdji, the Bokko and the Chamba, the Durru and the Dakka, or whatever else their names may be, came in gradually after each other and all proved to be splendid fellows with whom it was possible to get on the most cordial footing of amity—people whom we shall in a moment describe and who can lay claim to our respect in every possible way.

And the worthy Galadima's bad temper also improved. He saw that it was no good kicking against the pricks and that the wisest course was to adapt himself to the new trend of things. He began to try and regain our goodwill with handsome presents of cattle and after we had let him see that we knew our way about quite well and he had put the Government quarters in his charge into very badly-needed repair from top to bottom, our relations with him also became less strained.

But how terrible was the misery of which I got a glimpse in those days ! What happy times must those have been when the industrious smaller tribes inhabited the valleys and the spacious levels smiled with standing crops ! Would it not be a very fine and noble task to free the land gradually from the misery of these galling Fulbe chains ? Was it not apparent from our earliest experiences how intolerable the sufferings of the country under this scourge still are ? Would not the substitution of the free activities of the industrious and able agricultural " disruptive " tribes in the place of the enforced and miserable slave-tillage be an object well worth striving for ? Would it not of a certainty pay to despatch a few practical young officers into this district who would relieve the Resident, already overburdened with arduous work, of this additional labour ?—the labour of again so organizing this country on a basis of liberty and economic prosperity as to give it the important and honoured position in the colony which is its due ?

\*       \*       \*       \*       \*       \*       \*       \*

The heavens smiled upon us most benignantly on the day we climbed up the Komaï-Atlantica hill range. The morning had been dull and grey, and rich in unpleasant experiences. My old non-commissioned officer, Bida, had fallen a victim to lung trouble for the second time on this trip; several of the boys had again got dysentery; I myself had an attack of malarial fever. But when the sun broke through, brightening the surface of the flooded Faro valley with its warming beams and painting the lofty heights in brilliant hues; when the horses neighed merrily and the procession took the road, we all felt bright and cheerful. For we were going towards a pleasant experience, namely, the peaceful conquest of a little nation, the friendly compulsion of a people with lovable souls. It was most certainly a curious cavalcade which wound its way at first through the valley plain and then along the hill-side. Neither a rifle nor a machine-gun, neither a cutlass nor a sword, neither a spear nor a bow was to be seen. The hill-dwellers who had come down as our guides were also entirely unarmed. We had to get off our horses and send them back when we arrived at the precipitous parts of the ascent which was both rocky and steep. We climbed up to a little waterfall, formed by the 'Nderabrook, cleared it more or less gracefully by leaping it and before long reached the " magnificent " village where the Fulbe had told us there was nothing offered one to eat but arrow-heads !! The aspect of the first Komaï hamlet we entered was wonderful. Immense blocks of granite here and there concealed the huts, which were squeezed in between the clefts and fissures. The tiny compounds were shaded by very few trees and if the dwellings were already difficult to see on account of the rocky surroundings the corn which was growing in every available spot forbade the least peep at the life of the community. The peculiar attributes of these hill and field folk were already most plainly apparent. Not a particle of ground was untilled, not a crack in the ground unsown. Not so much as a single square yard of space is allowed to lie fallow.

But, now, did not these natives fly in alarm from the strangers whose colour was white ?

By no means at all ! Even the women stayed where they were. They stood on the flat boulders and taller blocks which are as a rule used as threshing floors, as drying or play grounds and were only distinguished from the everyday appearance of things by the freshness of the bunches of leaves with which they covered their nakedness. There was no fear, no terror written on their faces, nothing but amazement. The dear inhabitants of Atlantica were friendly to us from the very first day and only begged one favour of us, namely, not to ask them for corn for our people, because they had none for themselves. The granaries were, in fact, everywhere very far from full, and the reason was not only that last year's grain was almost entirely consumed and this year's not yet harvested, but that the Fulbe had commandeered a great quantity of it in view of the approaching Mahommedan festivities. I, of course, assured these good folk that their wishes would be complied with and took care that the necessary quantity of ready-cooked porridge cakes and condiments for our people were daily brought from Chamba. There was only one untoward incident during the whole of our stay. A young Fulbe scion who called upon us one day without being asked had immediately tried to extort some food from the natives. I had this gentleman soundly flogged in the eyes of several Komaï, a proceeding in which I felt all the more justified as it could only increase the confidence to be reposed in the European.

The dwellings where we lived were miserably small. The idea of building any sort of Government offices or Residence was entirely out of the question here, as rock-boulders were piled like Pelion upon Ossa and any construction could only have been erected by the destruction of some of the native plantations—which would not, naturally, do. So thus we were very wretchedly lodged in the small, pitiable chamberlets, in which for want of more ample space the aborigines also have their homes.

But then a world was disclosed to me which had an infinitely magic charm in this tiny little room of mine. In climbing about these hills we very soon visited and made the acquaintance of many other hamlets. We attained a considerable elevation and overlooked with delight the magnificent stretch of the Adamowa plain, cast our eyes across it to the towering heights to the East and the 'Ngaundere mountains in the South-east and accustomed our eyes to distant vision and the enjoyment of grand and noble natural scenery. While we were luxuriating like this, blessing after blessing was our portion.   No sooner had the other hill-folk heard (and they did so very soon) that the white new-comers were sincerely wishful to set up relations with those who made their homes upon the hills, than members of the most of the oddest and quaintest little peoples made pilgrimages to us from all the distant high-lands round about.   At last there was a complete collection of assembled nationalities.   And when my good friend the Ardo of Reï-Buba sent me Mundang and Lakka, Sarra and Falli across the intervening marshland; when an embassy from the old Batta prince arrived as well and the footing with the Dakka and the Chamba grew more intimate, the villages hanging on the slopes of the Atlantica mountains swarmed with people speaking different tongues who could hardly understand each other, but were all ex-tremely glad to enjoy a freedom of movement which had not been theirs for many years.   And my estimation of these peculiar tribes increased from day to day, for one after another of them poured his lore and faith into my greedy ears.   And in this way they all unrolled before me a world which seemed to me far more splendid, larger and nobler than the view which was spread before our gaze in the level Faro plains beneath our feet.

I propose now to say a word or two about these beings.   But in so doing I shall have to hark back further than in any other portion of this book.   At present I will only speak about the little peoples who dwell on the South of the Soudan between the Nile and the Senegal.   They are the tribes known in the Nile districts as Nuba, and further off as the Wadaï and Fertit races;   in the Chari basin as the heathen Bagrimma (specially the Sarra and Lakka);   in the Northern Cameroons as the pagan Adamawo tribes;   in Central Nigeria as the Bautshi;   in Northern Togo as the Tamberma ;   on the Gold Coast and in French Soudan as the Gurunsi, Bobo, Lobi, etc.   They form a chain of nations whose distinguishing common characteristic is literally their extreme variability, strange as this may sound.   They are little communities, rarely consisting of more than some eighty individuals, existing in a few localities only.   Their main marks of distinc-tion are their mental exclusiveness, that each of them dwells in its own private and hidden corner, its own particular hill or dale, and only come into contact with the general population at a few

Kwala women crushing the corn for the evening porridge in the Atlantika mountains.

(To face p. 402.)

market towns. Looking from the valley, the eye will often see three or four hills, and it is said that on each of them a totally different speech is in vogue. These small " disruptive " tribes have several hundred idiomatic expressions at their command. I am unable to say to what extent these languages have a common basis of construction, but the great number of vocabularies which we and our friendly collaborators have collected in the course of years, prove that lexicographically at least they are quite different.

The first and most observable characteristic of these tribes is the isolation of their small settlements and the isolation of their vernacular tongues. I now set down the second one as being their infinite devotion and disposition to useful labour. Such an assiduous industry in land-cultivation, coupled with such a complete absence of industrial occupation, cannot be paralleled in any other section of Africa's numerous varieties of population. And a further feature is that they show the same progressive scale in their social organization and the same gradations, namely, a definite systematic arrangement based on four or five different periods of life which harmonizes with the stages of development in their philosophic and religious systems.

And now we come to those points which are probably the most interesting in these strange little people from our own point of view : I cannot do otherwise than say that these human creatures are the chastest and most ethically disposed of all the national groups in this world which have become known to me. And this is no less so among the tribes on the Nile than in the Senegal-Soudan Province ; no less so among those in Adamowa than in the district of North Togo, or among those of the North Gold Coast than those in Nigeria. I have nowhere whatever found human beings living their family life so naturally (however incomprehensible in many respects this may be to ourselves) ; nowhere have I met a people who maintain their moral cleanliness so strictly and so entirely as a matter of course as these little tribes. All of them are convinced in the core of their souls of the existence of a single Supreme Being or God, whose single Will is the sole guiding principle of this world ! And the fact that they regard their dead with the tenderest piety and reverence is in complete accord with both these views. They are beyond all question the inheritors of those ancient religions which prevailed at the time when the Egyptian power was at its height in Nubia, and their forebears were called the "blameless Ethiopians" by the writers of classical antiquity. Therefore I think that I may have a right to include these little tribes which agree so absolutely in their characteristics in the term "Ethiopian."

I say that these peoples are more imbued with a sentiment of real religion than any I know. And I must call attention to what I intend this to convey, and in what the difference consists, so as to make it clear. The reader will involuntarily imagine that I looked upon these people from the standpoint of our own ethical, Christian, lofty, profound religion which loves this world. But I see them in their proper place in the process of development of mankind. They have no moral sense in the meaning we attach to the word. They most assuredly know nothing of the subtleties of the Sermon on the Mount. They are singular and bizarre, entirely old-fashioned, and, in many respects, now decidedly beyond our comprehension. But the reason why they are the most religious is because they have the power to devote themselves unreservedly and unshakenly, without hesitation, confusion and unsteadfastness, to a firm faith in the eternal laws of natural forces and family life and the rightness of their convictions. I never saw the smallest sign of any magic amulet on a single one of them! I never saw a single charm upon their persons. I never observed the least attempt at making sorcery a substantial help in bolstering up lack of belief and imaginative power. All the nations which incessantly have recourse to amulets and charms of any kind whatever possess neither ancient faith nor strength of spiritual vision and, with regard to religion, stand on a lower plane than my Ethiopians who care for none of these things.

Never have I come across people who so truly held in honour their begetters. And yet they are the most terrible barbarians with regard to the remains which we see in the bodies of our beloved ones. For it is in our view horrible and repulsive to observe that they are able to cut off the heads of their dead parents or tear them from the corpses. It is so brutal and so cruel, that the mere thought of it revolts us. And yet religious feeling prompts these people to such an act as this. For they need these skulls. They need them, they cannot dispense with their possession; they are their most cherished family treasure. The poor defunct cannot return, but is for ever separated from his family which can never be increased and multiplied unless the skull be set up in the home itself or in the family receptacle for funereal urns and there receive its offering at the proper seasons. This is why they use these skulls; this is why they must needs obtain them, even if they can only do so by the perpetration of a barbarous custom. Then they enshrine it in their homes and before they themselves enjoy a morsel, they pray the deceased member to come back into the bosom of the family and sacrifice a portion of every grain of corn and a drop of every liquid draught to it. Then, too, when a girl of the clan gives her hand in marriage to a young man, either her father or her mother takes the newly-wedded to the skull; they offer it some food and drink and fervently pray the dead to come back now and give his own family his power again. And the youthful wife takes of the grain which was laid in offering on the skull and consumes it. When, then, a child is granted to the young people, they hail it as their forebear come again to life.

This philosophy is deeply rooted in the belief of this species of the human race. It is as impregnable and firm as a house built on a rock. I think this is a proof of profound piety, and I always found the same deeply religious feeling whenever I followed these lines of inquiry. These customs seem brutal and barbaric to us, but the deepest conviction is the source of them all. Is it not a most unhappy thing that these people, who are such industrious workers in the field and so greatly steadfast in the strength of their belief, should be victimized by so pitiable and unproductive a people as the Fulbe?

And I ask myself: How vast and mighty must that wave have been which, incomputable ages ago, swept along on its crest these singular nations over the Nile and across the entire Soudan right away to West Africa? Never did I observe greater homogeneity than precisely in these "disruptive" tribes among different nations of identical origin. Nowhere did I come across a greater decadence of speech, greater and more incisive separation, and yet more convincing correspondence of character than in these Ethiopians. And if still further evidence should be thought necessary to prove the profundity of these peoples' religious life and habit of mind, I will say in addition that they still practise the prehistoric custom of the Ethiopians referred to by Pliny and Diodorus the Sicilian : they doom their Kings to their death within a few years of their reign and do so because otherwise the earth would no longer yield the fruits upon which they depend in due season. The custom is dreadful and cruel. Yet how tremendous that civilization must have been which once found its expression in such mighty immemorial customs ! Ought it not to be within the bounds of possibility to come upon some traces of the period and general connection of an ancient Ethiopian culture ?

\* \* \* \* \* \* \* \*

Then I went down into the valley again with Martius. Arriens stayed behind in the most lofty 'Ndera village, because I thought that the air of the hills would be far better for him, weak as he then was, than the moisture-laden, swampy valley. When we got back to Chamba we found the state of things had greatly changed. The Galadima had at last seen the folly of his conduct and took a lot of trouble with his headmen to make our stay as pleasant as he could. After finding how simply and easily we had established our connection with the hill-dwellers independently of his assistance, he had, after all, come to the conclusion that his best course was to accept the situation cheerfully.

The life we at first led in Chamba was delightful and still more ecstatic afterwards in Kontsha, which was further South. Our threads had been spun in all directions. At that time I had some people in British Bornu and some in the French Chari district. A few careful observers investigated Bayaland. Others of my expedition stayed in the courts at Reï-Buba, 'Ngaundera, Marua and Yola. Small detachments were in Bautshi and the Kano region. Others again wandered through Kontangora towards French Southern Soudan and I sent the main body off under Bida's leadership. Bida, always subject to pulmonary attacks, seemed unable to stand the mountain air. So he went down the Benue on the German relief transport and then travelled slowly from Lokoja to the Northern Yorubas in order to organize a journey

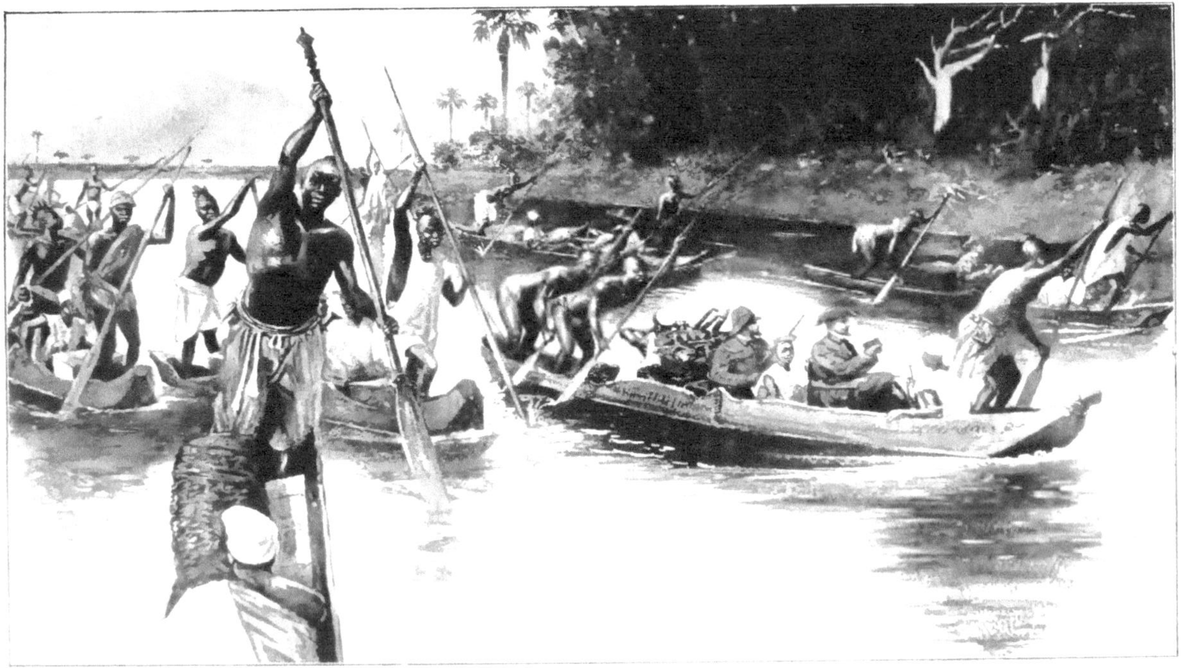

with special objects for research which I wished Martius to undertake at some subsequent period.

After despatching all the requisite correspondence with the native princes and making the necessary agreements with the different envoys, I sent for Arriens to come down from his sanatorium. The Galadima gave us a gorgeous feast and then we went along the Faro valley down to Kontsha. We were obliged once more to plod through marsh and morass, to lift our sick across rivers raging like torrents between huge boulders and to get our horses across dangerous places without loss or injury. They were troublous days.

We spent the next few weeks in Kontsha. The life in our camp grew ever more varied. Captain von Stephani sent us still more representations of different tribes from Banjo ; we spun fresh threads across into English territory. The rainy season was over and the sun had dried up the valleys. We set out upon the return journey through the rocky mountains to the Upper Tarabba. A new district which was as dry and arid as the other had been damp and swampy and almost devoid of population. A region where Nature was all stone stared us in the face. Our night camps in this wilderness were the cause of renewed sicknesses produced by the heavy fogs which settled down upon us ; yet we arrived at the English frontiers, near Beli, fortunately without the loss of a single life.

The day on which we crossed the border was beautifully fine. The English customs-officers had erected triumphal arches in the most delightful way to give us welcome and made all possible preparations for our friendly reception in this wild and inhospitable region. Our means of transport were the only things which were deficient. I sent back the majority of our German carriers from here and only a few dozen Houssas remained in our service. It was difficult to raise porters in the country itself and Captain Ruxton's relief company, which he sent from Ibi, could only arrive in a few days. Therefore we had to stow the greater portion of our luggage and the collections in boats. As these were remarkable for being so miserably small and as I had, moreover, no very great confidence in my leaders who were much more accustomed to marching on the firm-set earth than floating on the water in these regions, I made up my mind to trust the greatest portion of the baggage to the boats, but to conduct the transport myself. And so Arriens, Martius and myself squeezed ourselves into these frail vessels, and, accompanied by the hearty send-off of the British and German frontier officials, we went down the beautiful river. Although my followers had to suffer a great deal from the heat of the sun in the daytime, the coolness of the night air and heavy mists neither made our camps on the sandbanks any too pleasant nor improved the condition of the whites any more than that of the blacks. We were, however, compensated by the beauty of Nature, the aspect of which, as seen from boats, is very different from its appearance to the European on a steamer's deck. On our arrival at Ibi we were able to charter some steel-built boats. Captain Ruxton and Dr. Pollard again most good-naturedly made arrangements to ensure our comfortable departure and we were able to set out on our return to Lokoja a few days after our marching column turned up.

The firm of Messrs. Pagenstecher again received us very hospitably. The British officers and Mr. Maxwell Lyte had prepared a most cordial welcome for us. Our former camp on Stirling Hill, which we found was in truly excellent condition, saluted us. The thirteen large buildings we had erected were, with one exception, in first-class preservation, and for this the camp superintendents received their due meed of praise. Bida with his retinue came to meet us. He had an adventurous stretch of road behind him and brought with him much useful information which proved available for the route which Martius was to take.

The Expedition's state of health was wretched. Poor Arriens, who was very weak indeed, was the greatest sufferer of all, so that I cannot sufficiently wonder at the persistence with which he did his necessary work in spite of all. Martius also fell a victim to the West African demon and I myself recorded my fifth attack of black-water fever on this journey. Our servants from the Coast drew their breath with difficulty and tossed about with fevered groans in their apartments. But we were not the only sufferers, for things were not much better in the English camp. It was an evil time!

But, of course, the needed work had to be got through, come what might, and I here again noted that really strong constitutions get over such periods as these best, if they do not give up their active occupations altogether. Martius' task was the hardest to perform, for he took charge of packing the collection. But here the English Government again came to our assistance with the greatest friendliness and helped us over all the smaller difficulties and, when we were once more passably well in health, we were able to enjoy another splendid evening in the officers' mess. A communication to the effect that an English official of high rank had contributed a substantial sum in aid of the Expedition's funds, which was subscribed in the name of the "Darwin-Tyler Exhibition" in token of appreciation of the importance of our accomplished work, was a source of great joy to me in those days and this addition to our resources was earmarked for the further prosecution of historical research. It was given in that spirit of hearty goodwill which the British Government maintained from first to last throughout all our relations.

I placed the conduct of the expedition Westwards in the hands of Martius towards the end of December and he led the column back to Yebba and the Northern Yoruba districts, while I took ship in company with Arriens. My artist now sailed back to home and convalescence with the greatest speed. I myself, having spent a few days in Las Palmas, took my passage to Marseilles in a French steamship, then again left Europe from Genoa and, together with my wife and brother, the painter Hermann Frobenius, travelled to the Red Sea. I had the great pleasure of making acquaintance with Mr. Wingate, the Sirdar, the famous Slatin Pasha, and that most charming personality, Father Ohrwalder, in Khartoum. First of all, we went to Kordofan, and pitched our camp for purposes of study in El-Obeid. After that we moved to Omdurman, where we were able to devote several weeks to serious work. Here we had the good luck to meet our fellow-countrymen in Dr. Türstig and his wife, who had chosen this out-of-the-way place as a residence from love of science. The hours we spent in their society here were so full of charm and instruction as to make the time of our stay one of the pleasantest I had enjoyed in African camps, in spite of the sandstorms and intense heat. Here, also, I was delighted at being able to shake hands with my Houssa and Nupé friends, who had left the Nupé country not quite a twelvemonth ago in order to meet us here as they had promised.

They had made excellent and most effective notes upon the road to supplement what we ourselves had been able to find out both on this and the further side of Wadai and Darfour.

When I afterwards came back through Egypt to Europe in May of the same year, on a voyage, the results of which filled up a serious gap in the extent of my knowledge and philosophy; when the temples, the tombs, and the art-treasures of mighty, ancient Egypt, in their imposing massiveness and artistic value, had made upon me the greatest impression of which I was capable; when such good friends as Professor Schweinfurth and Carl Herold had inducted me in the magic circle of a world of fairyland, it was borne in upon me that a definite stage had been reached in the course of the studies we were pursuing. So I resolved upon the publication of this book.

\*　　\*　　\*　　\*　　\*　　\*　　\*　　\*

Turning back the pages of history of the last twenty-one years, I think of the then generally current opinion with regard to African people and African civilization. I go back to the article quoted on page 1 of this book, and at this moment I call up before me all that we have achieved and what the alteration of the opinion held twenty years ago and the views held to-day, may mean. There can be no doubt but that the whole presentation of the picture has been changed. What we see now is not a mere sterile and stagnating conglomeration of humanity. We no longer see a Continent which lay beyond the reach of interest in the history of the world, in a state of deplorable apathy, asleep to progress and dreaming its day away. What we see is that the African and his civilization are an important factor in transmitting forms of culture. The quickening pulse of universal history in Europe and in Asia, which beat in human life for thousands of years, had its echo in the hearts of African humanity. Whoever put a finger on the Coastlands of this block of African earth sent a thrill into its very heart. We have seen the ancient Ethiopians who were so pronouncedly religious and the people who carried on a primeval form of profoundly significant civilization. We have surveyed the road along which the influences from Ethiopia first travelled to the East and along which those from Byzantium, Persia,

Down Stream.   Pl.  II.

Night camp on the Expedition on the sand banks of the Juba

[To face p. 414]

and Nubia, in combination, followed afterwards. The North-west was shown as the sphere most subject to the influx of Libyan civilization, and Islam was carried into Africa on this wave of action. We learned to recognize the fact that the older power and the older feelings were of higher ethical value than the influences exercised by the much-belauded younger Islamism. We set our eyes upon the monuments of an ancient colonizing civilization on the Atlantic coast of Africa which were brought to light again, and we observed some forms of life worthy of comparison with the so much admired and astounding standards set up by classical antiquity. The picture is entirely different to-day. We have been enabled to present some entirely new facts.

We must not, however, allow ourselves to forget that we are still only in the infancy of our knowledge. We have, so far, only found fresh lines of influence and development and, in forming a judgment of these, may at first be guilty of errors here and there. But what I personally consider to be the principal result of the knowledge we have now acquired consists in the indubitable fact that Africa may be regarded as a land always deeply susceptible to cultural movements and a store-room of riches in which reverberate the tones of all possible periods. Yet I am not prepared to say that what we have so far discovered represents an average standard of all the influences to which this Continent has been submitted. To either over- or under-estimate one subject or the other lies in the very nature of things. Works such as the present book cannot possibly do justice to all sides at once. It would be too much to ask for such a superhuman feat. But it will, none the less, be my particular task to do my modest utmost to assist in any further efforts to obtain fresh information in the future when called upon, and to uphold the constant conviction that the main body of this interesting subject has still to be collected. I must, however, still put one question, in spite of it all ; in spite of conscious achievements ; in spite of our own conviction that our knowledge is still imperfect and un-organized, namely : Is it not marvellous that such great and far-reaching elements of civilization, transmitted by such eminent forces here among this despised Africanderdom, should have been so long effectively preserved ? Is the fact itself not a proof of the receptivity and adaptability of the races which inhabit this Continent ? Would it really prove to be such a difficult thing to raise these busy and industrious creatures to the position of very valuable co-operators in the civilization of the whole of the world ? And again : Does not the fact of the brilliant conservation, excellent preservation and almost imperceptible transformation of their more ancient inherited factors of culture constitute a proof that these nations themselves, although incapable of effecting much without extraneous assistance, are giants in strength with regard to transmitting an already existing and well-developed, socially, politically and religiously organized, civilization ? Does this not supply the evidence of the greatness of the mistake committed in the policy of inciting the people to exercise their own intellectual activity with our own modern factors in civilization productively on the Coast, where its results are only grotesque and most undesirable symptoms ? Ought it not, indeed, to be possible to make something better and more valuable out of these people than mere imitative simians by educating them ?

To carry the light of knowledge to these nations has proved a task beyond our Northern civilizing powers for hundreds, nay, even thousands of years. It was very, very, very dark indeed in Africa. But then the Interior was reached. We searched its heart, whose beating Islam had not stilled and the vast Continent said : " Let there be light ! " We, now, may say : " And there was light ! " and, in so doing, praise not ourselves, but those who lived before us in this Continent. This book may be closed with the words : " The light was ! " The sun which sheds its rays upon our acquired knowledge and our intuitional perception is not the sun in its noontide blaze. It is only the light of the earliest dawn, whose glow is reflected on the high top of some few peaks and promontories of its past development. So far it is but little we have seen of the general outlines, but still we are able to say :

" And the light was ! "

THE END

*Printed at The Chapel River Press, Kingston, Surrey.*

# ImTheStory.com

Personalized Classic Books in many genre's

Unique gift for kids, partners, friends, colleagues

Customize:

- Character Names

- Upload your own front/back cover images (optional)

- Inscribe a personal message/dedication on the
  inside page (optional)

Customize many titles Including
- Alice in Wonderland
- Romeo and Juliet
- The Wizard of Oz
- A Christmas Carol
- Dracula
- Dr. Jekyll & Mr. Hyde
- And more...

# BRICK BY BRICK

## *THE BIBLICAL STORY OF CHRISTMAS*

Photography by Pippy McGuire

This book is dedicated to my family and all brick lovers.
May you always find joy in the word of God.

ISBN-10: 1979187681

ISBN-13: 978-1979187688

# TABLE OF CONTENTS

# MEET THE EXTENDED FAMILY OF JESUS

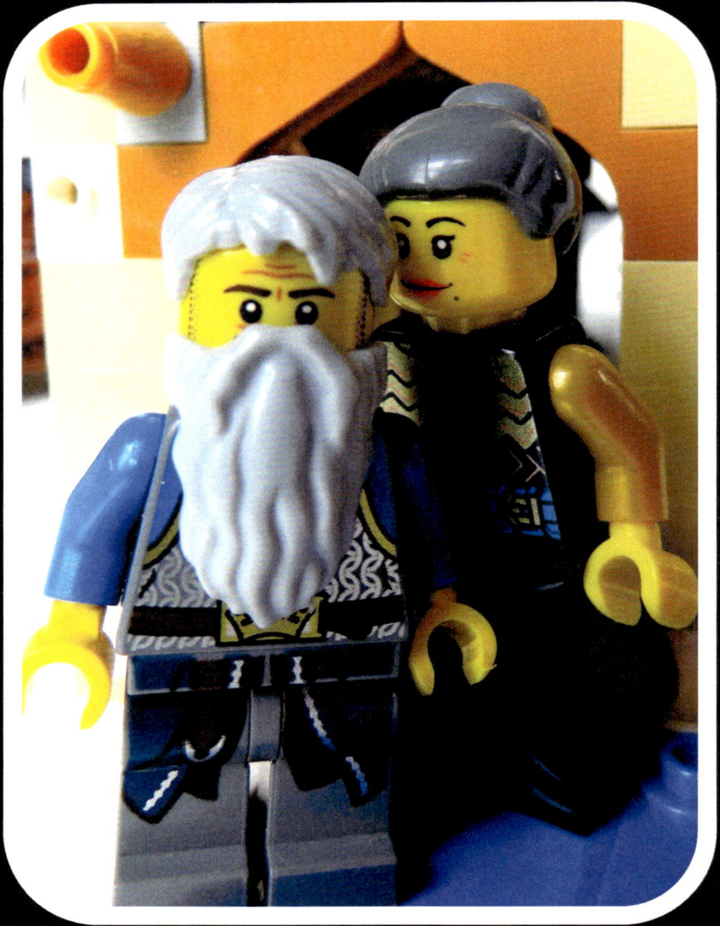

## Day 1

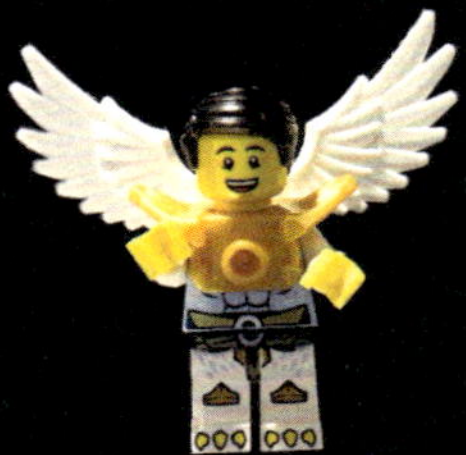

**BRICK BUILD:** ITS YOUR TURN TO CREATE! GET OUT YOUR OWN BRICKS AND BUILD ELIZABETH AND ZECHARIAH. NOW MAKE THE TEMPLE FOR ZECHARIAH TO WORK IN.

Luke 1:5-10

In the reign of Herod, king of Judea, there was a priest named Zechariah, who belonged to the division called after Abijah. His wife, whose name was Elizabeth, was also a descendant of Aaron. They were both right-eous people, who lived blameless lives, guiding their steps by all the command-

ments and ordinances of the Lord. But they had no child, Elizabeth being barren; and both of them were advanced in years.

One day, when Zechariah was officiating as priest be-fore God, during the turn of his division, it fell to him by lot, in accordance with the practice among the priests, to go into the Temple of the Lord and burn incense; and, as it was the Hour of Incense, the people were all praying outside.

# AN AMAZING GREETING FOR ZECHARIAH

**Day 2**

**BRICK BUILD:** BUILD THE ANGEL GABRIEL AND PUT HIM IN THE TEMPLE TO SURPRISE ZECHARIAH. IF YOU DONT HAVE ANY BRICK WINGS GET CREATIVE AND USE SOME PAPER OR TISSUE TO MAKE HIM SOME.

And an angel of the Lord appeared to him [Zechariah], standing on the right of the altar of incense. Zechariah was startled at the sight and was awe-struck. The angel said to him: "Do not be afraid, Zechariah; your prayer has been heard, and your wife Elizabeth will bear you a son, whom you will call by the name John. He will be to you a joy and a delight; and many will rejoice over his birth. For he will be great in the sight of the Lord; he will not drink any wine or strong drink, and he will be filled with the Holy Spirit from the very hour of his birth, and will reconcile many of the Israelites to the Lord their God. He will go before Him in the spirit and with the power of Elijah, to reconcile fathers to their children and the disobedient to the wisdom of the righteous, and so make ready for the Lord a people prepared for Him."

# ZECHARIAH QUESTIONS THE ANGEL

**Day 3**

BRICK BUILD: FIND A NOTEPAD FOR ZECHARIAH TO WRITE ON BECAUSE HE WON'T BE TALKING FOR A WHILE. BUILD THE PEOPLE WHO ARE WAITING FOR HIM TO COME OUT OF THE INNER COURTS OF THE TEMPLE.

Luke 1:18-25

"How can I be sure of this?" Zechariah asked the angel. "For I am an old man and my wife is advanced in years."

The angel answered "I am Gabriel, who stands in the presence of God, and I have been sent to speak to you and to

bring you this good news. Now you will be silent and unable to speak until the day when this takes place, because you did not believe what I said, though my words will be fulfilled in due course."

Meanwhile the people were watching for Zechariah, wondering at his remaining so long in the Temple. When he came out, he was unable to speak to them, and they perceived that he had seen a vision there. But Zechariah kept making signs to them, and remained dumb. And, as soon as his term of service was finished, he returned home. After this his wife, Elizabeth, became pregnant and lived in seclusion for five months. "The Lord has done this for me," she said, "He has shown me kindness and taken away the public disgrace of childlessness under which I have been living."

# THE BIRTH OF JESUS FORETOLD

**Day 4**

BRICK BUILD: WHAT A SURPRISE GABRIEL IS BACK! BUILD YOUR OWN SCENE WITH MARY AND BRING YOUR ANGEL GABRIEL TO GREET HER!

Six months later the angel Gabriel was sent from God to Nazareth, to a maiden [named Mary] He greeted her, saying: "You have been shown great favor - the Lord is with you."

Mary was was wondering to herself what such a greeting could mean, when the angel spoke again:

"Do not be afraid, Mary, you have found favor with God. You will conceive and give birth to a son, and you will give Him the name Jesus. The child will be great and will be called 'Son of the Most High,' and the Lord God will give Him the throne of His ancestor David, and He will reign over the descendants of Jacob for ever; And to His kingdom there will be no end."

Mary Asked: "How can this be? "For I have no husband."

Gabriel Answered: "The Holy Spirit will descend on you, and the power of the Most High will overshadow you; and therefore the child will be called 'Holy,' and 'Son of God.' And Elizabeth, your cousin who was barren, is herself also expecting a son in her old age for no promise from God will fail to be fulfilled."

Mary exclaimed "I am the servant of the Lord, let it be with me as you have said." Then the angel left her.

# MARY VISITS ELIZABETH AND ZECHARIAH

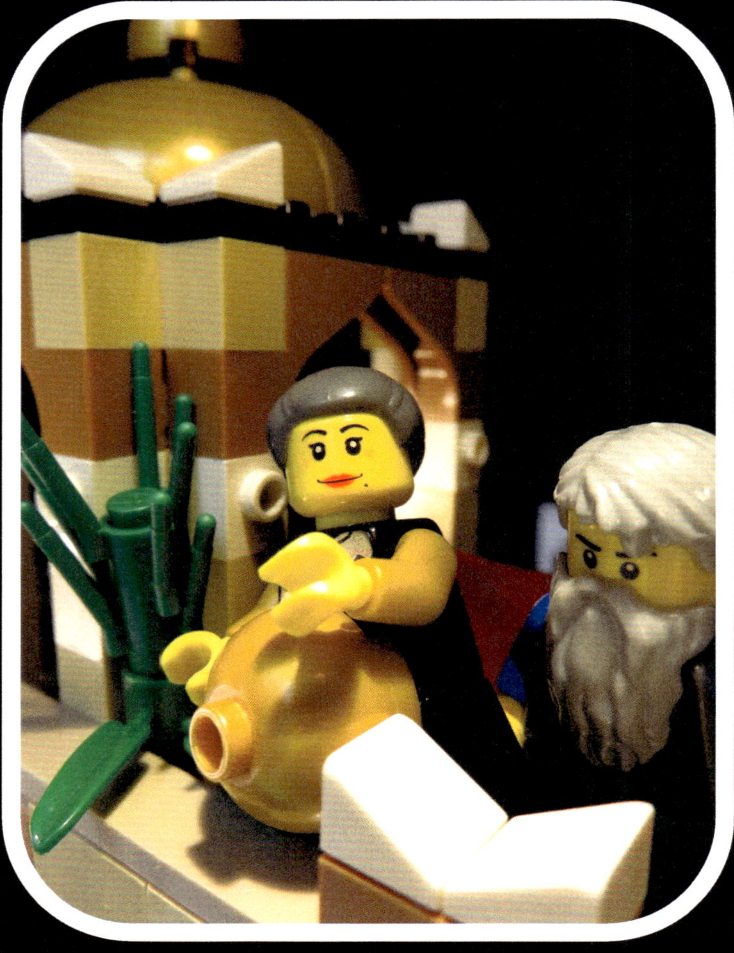

## Day 5

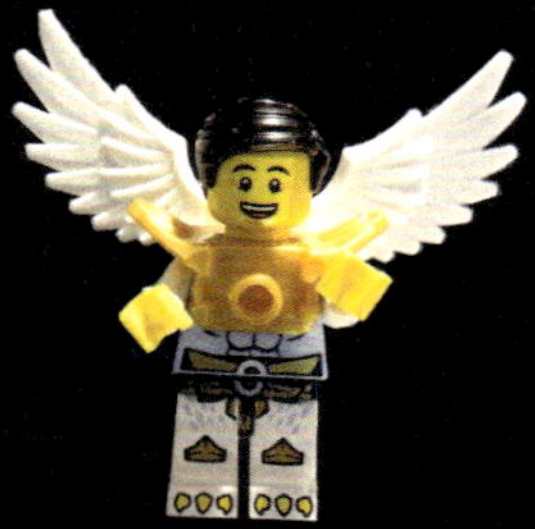

**BRICK BUILD:** MARY IS GOING TO VISIT HER RELATIVES! BUILD HER A SUITCASE TO GO ON A TRIP.

Luke 1:39-45

Soon after this Mary set out, and quickly made her way into the hill-country, to a town in Judah; and there she went into Zechariah's house and greeted Elizabeth. When Elizabeth heard Mary's greeting, the child moved within her, and Elizabeth herself was filled with the Holy Spirit, and cried aloud: "Blessed are you among women, and blessed is your unborn child! But how do I have this honor, that the mother of my Lord should come to me? For, as soon as your greeting reached my ears, the child moved within me with delight! Happy indeed is she who believed that the promise which she received from the Lord would be fulfilled."

# MARYS RESPONSE

**Day 6**

BRICK BUILD: CREATE THE SCENE WHERE MARY AND ELIZABETH MEET. BE CREATIVE AND BUILD THE HOUSE WHERE MARY STAYED WITH HER RELATIVES!

## Luke 1:46-58

And Mary said: "My soul exalts the Lord, and my spirit delights in God my Savior, for He has looked with favor on his humble servant girl. From now on all generations will call me blessed! For the Almighty has done great things for me, and holy is His name. He has mercy on those who revere Him in every generation. Mighty are the deeds of His arm; He has scattered the self-satisfied proud, He has cast down the mighty from their thrones, and He uplifts the humble, He has filled the hungry with good things, and the rich He has sent away empty. He has stretched out His hand to His servant Israel, ever mindful of His mercy, as He promised to our ancestors for Abraham and his descendants for ever."

When Elizabeth's time came, she gave birth to a son; and her neighbors and relatives, hearing of the great goodness of the Lord to her, came to share her joy. Mary stayed with Elizabeth about three months, and then returned to her home.

15

# ELIZABETH AND ZECHARIAH NAME THEIR BABY

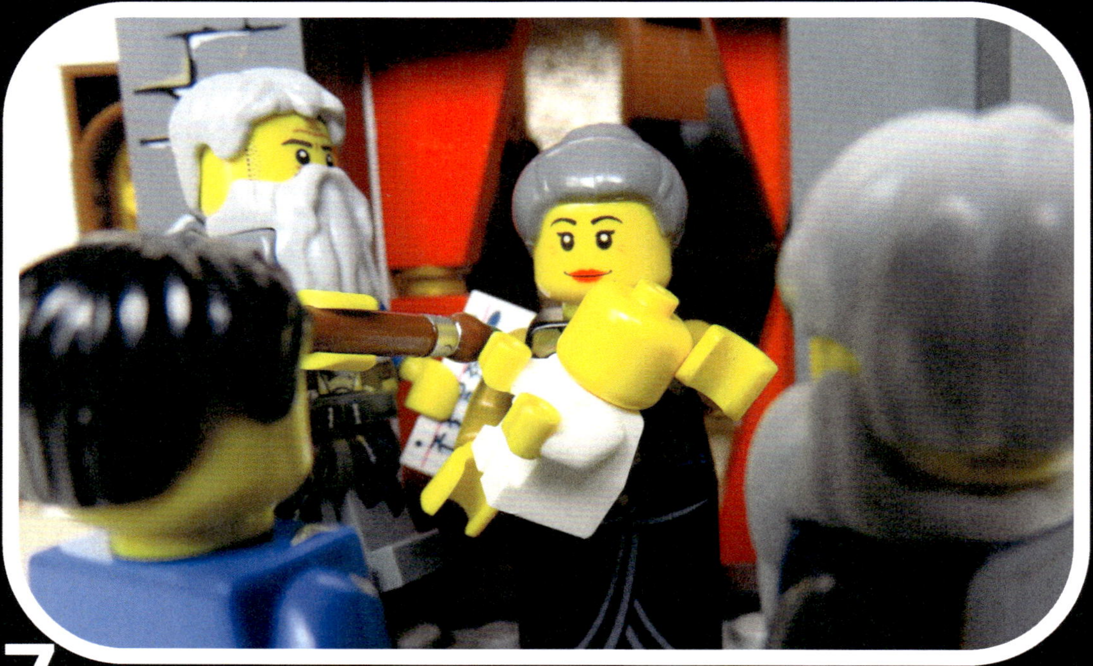

## Day 7

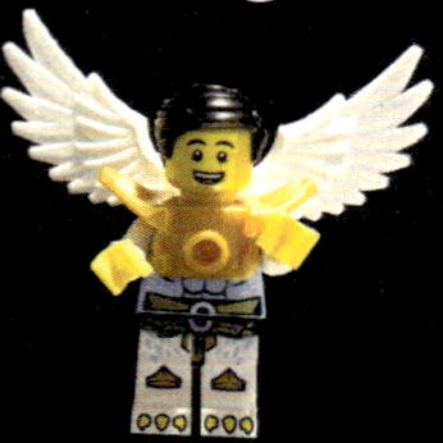

**BRICK BUILD:** CREATE THE SCENE! BUILD ALL THE FRIENDS NEIGHBORS AND RELETIVES THAT COME OVER FOR BABY JOHNS DEDICATION PARTY!

Luke 1:59-66

A week later they [Zechariah, Elizabeth, their neighbors and relatives] met to circumcise the child, and were about to call him 'Zechariah' after his father, when his mother spoke up: "No, he is to be called John."

"You have no relation of that name!" they exclaimed; and they made signs to the child's father, to find out what he wished the child to be called. Asking for a writing-tablet, he wrote the words — 'His name is John.' Everyone was surprised; and immediately Zechariah recovered his voice and the use of his tongue, and began to bless God. All their neighbors were awe-struck at this; and throughout the hill-country of Judea the whole story was much talked about; and all who heard it kept it in mind, asking one another — "What can this child be destined to become?"

# JOSEPHS DREAM

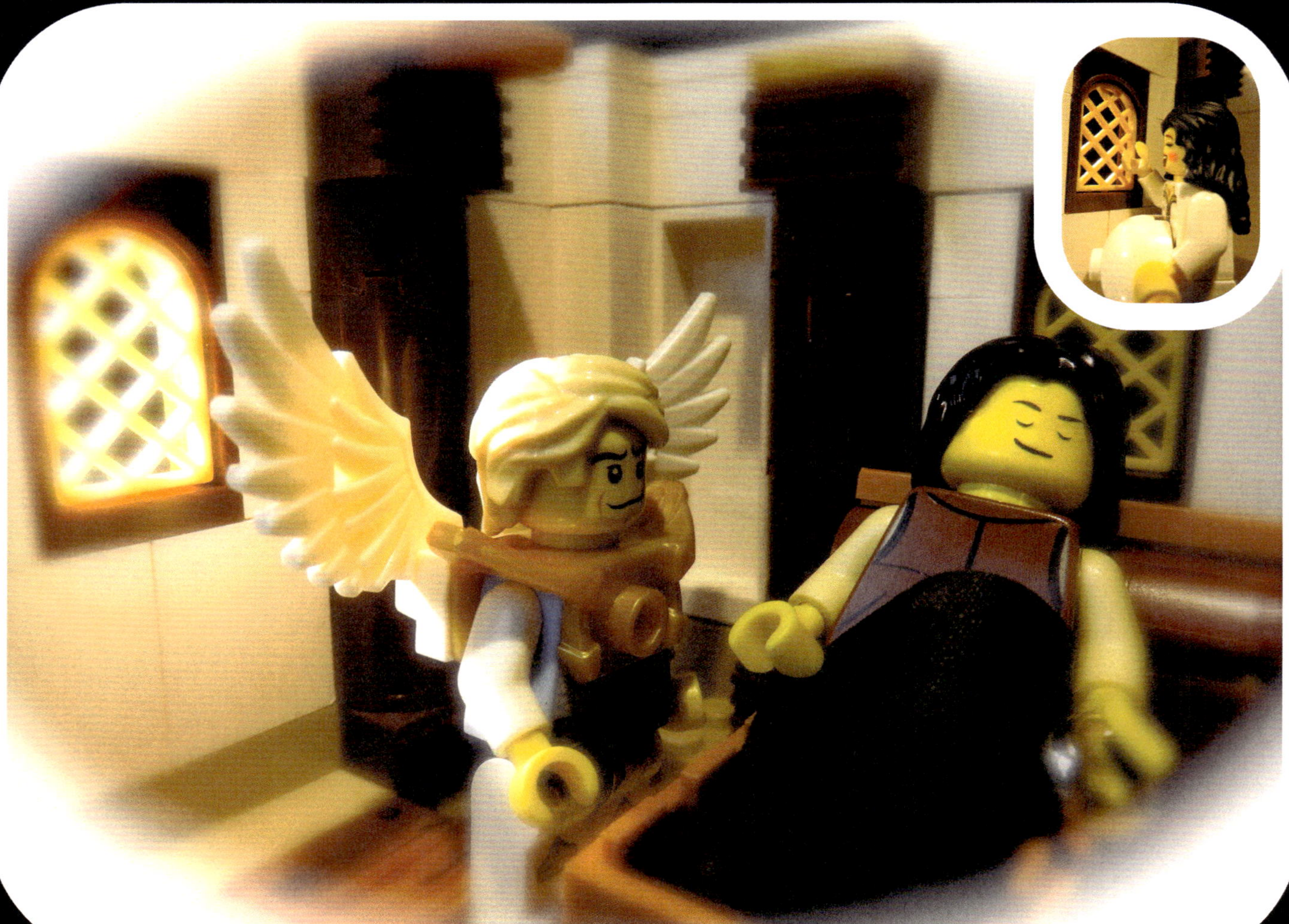

## Day 8

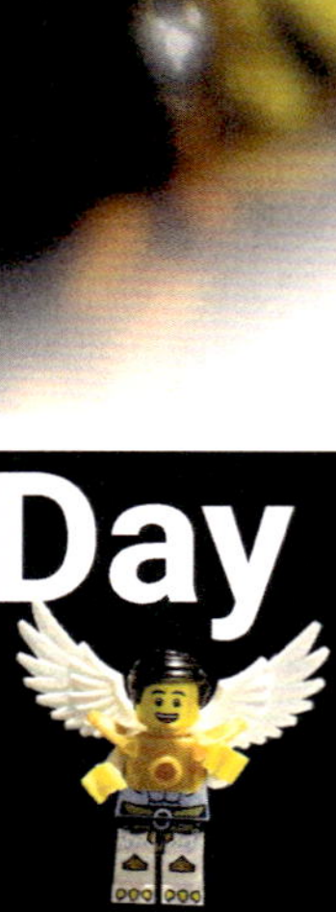

**BRICK BUILD:** JOSEPH IS GOING TO BED! BUILD HIM A BED AND LAY HIM DOWN TO SLEEP! LEAVE ROOM FOR THE ANGEL TO APPEAR TO HIM!

This is how Jesus Christ was born: His mother Mary was engaged to Joseph, but, before the marriage took place, she found herself to be pregnant by the power of the Holy Spirit. Her fiancee, Joseph, was a just man and, since he did not want to disgrace her publicly, he resolved to put an end to their engagement privately. He had been thinking this over, when an angel of the Lord appeared to him in a dream.

The angel said to him "Joseph, son of David, do not be afraid to take Mary for your wife, for her child has been conceived by the power of the Holy Spirit. She will give birth to a son; name Him Jesus, for He will save His people from their sins."

All this happened in fulfillment of these words of the Lord by the prophets, where He says — 'The virgin will conceive and will give birth to a son, and they will give Him the name Immanuel' — a word which means 'God is with us.' When Joseph woke up, he did as the angel of the Lord had directed him. He made Mary his wife.

# A DECREE FROM CAESAR AUGUSTUS

## Day 9

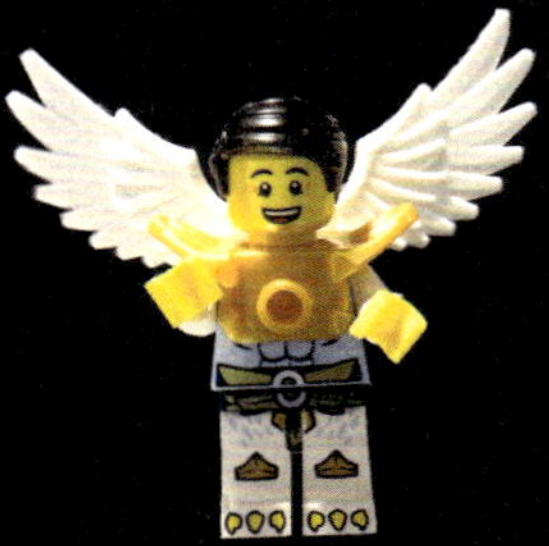

**BRICK BUILD:** THE SOLDIERS ARE OUT IN FORCE! BUILD SOME SOLDIERS TO DELIVER THE MESSAGE THAT EVERYONE MUST GO TO THEIR FAMILY'S HOME TOWN TO PAY TAXES.

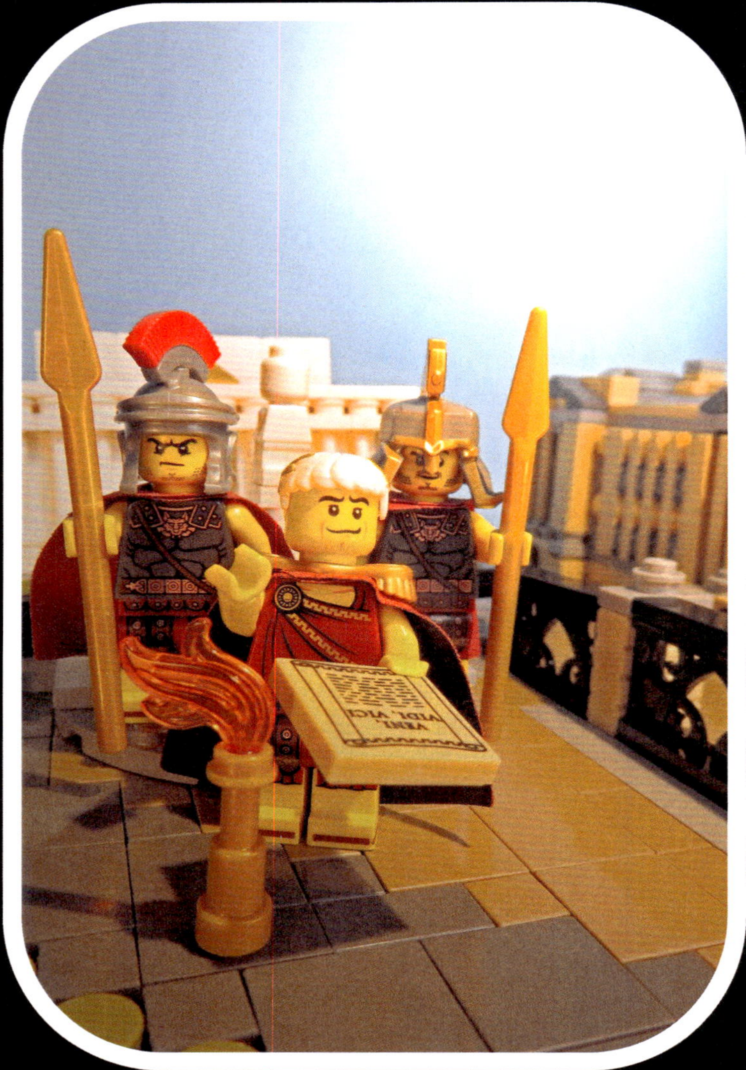

## Luke 2:1-5

About that time an edict was issued by the Emperor Augustus that a census should be taken of the whole Empire. (This was the first census taken while Quirinius was Governor of Syria). And everyone went to his own town to be registered [to be taxed]. Among others Joseph went up from the town of Nazareth in Galilee to Bethlehem, the town of David, in Judea (because he belonged to the family and house of David) to be registered with Mary, his engaged wife, who was about to become a mother.

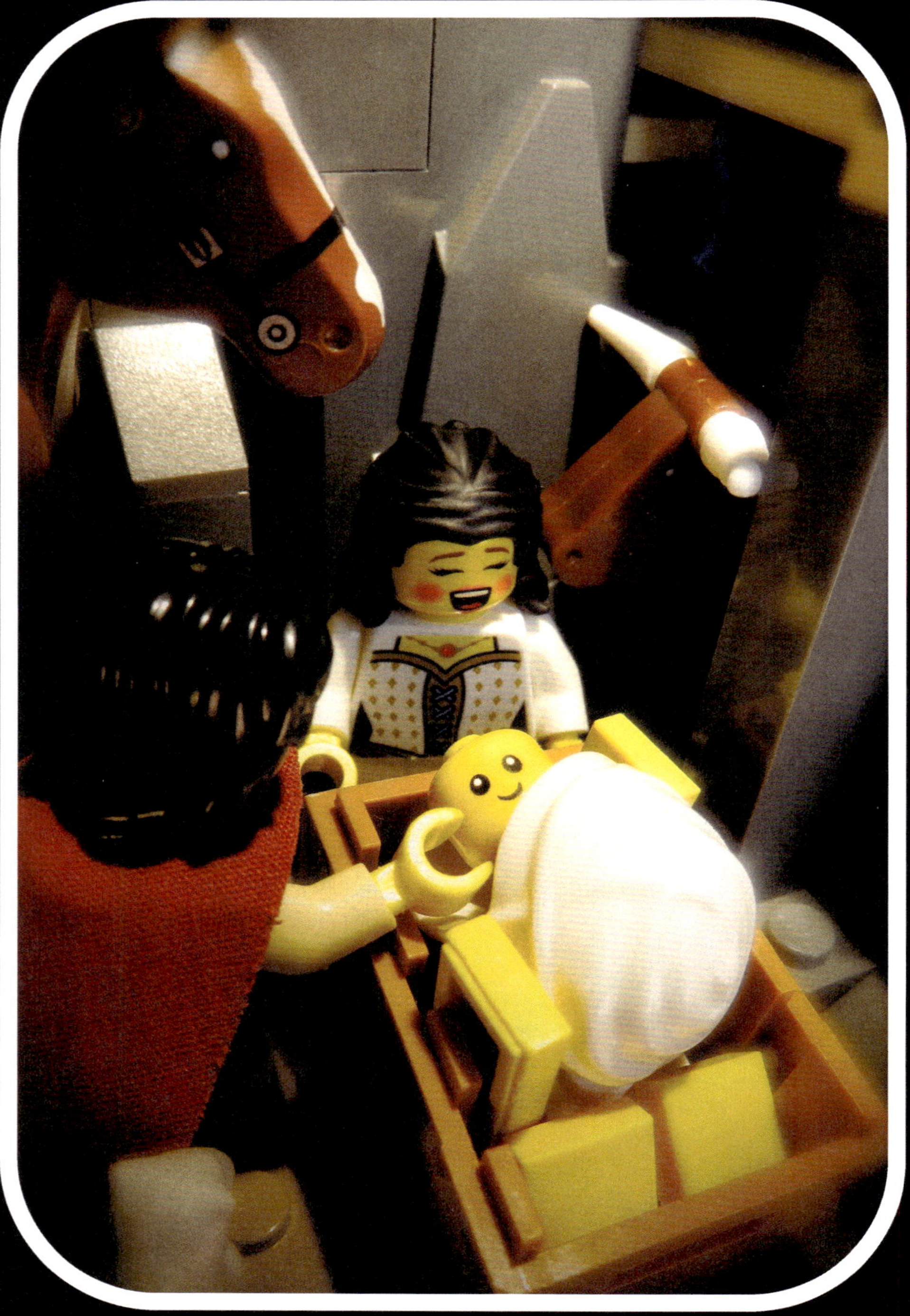

# JESUS IS BORN

## Day 10

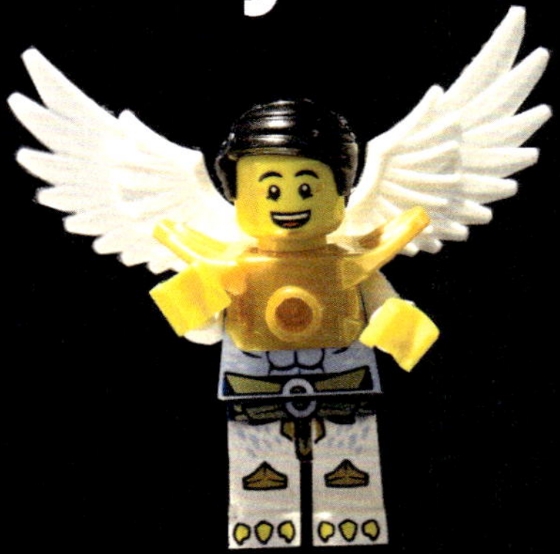

**BRICK BUILD:** THERE IS NO ROOM AT THE INN! BUILD A PLACE FOR THE ANIMALS AND A MANGER FOR MARY TO PUT BABY JESUS IN. DON'T FORGET TO BUILD BABY JESUS!

Luke 2:6-7

While they were there [In Bethlehem] her time came, and she [Mary] gave birth to her first child, a son. And because there was no room for them in the inn, she swathed him around [in swaddling clothes] and laid him in a manger.

Matthew 1:25

. . and to this son he [Joseph] gave the name Jesus.

# SHEPHERDS IN THE FIELD

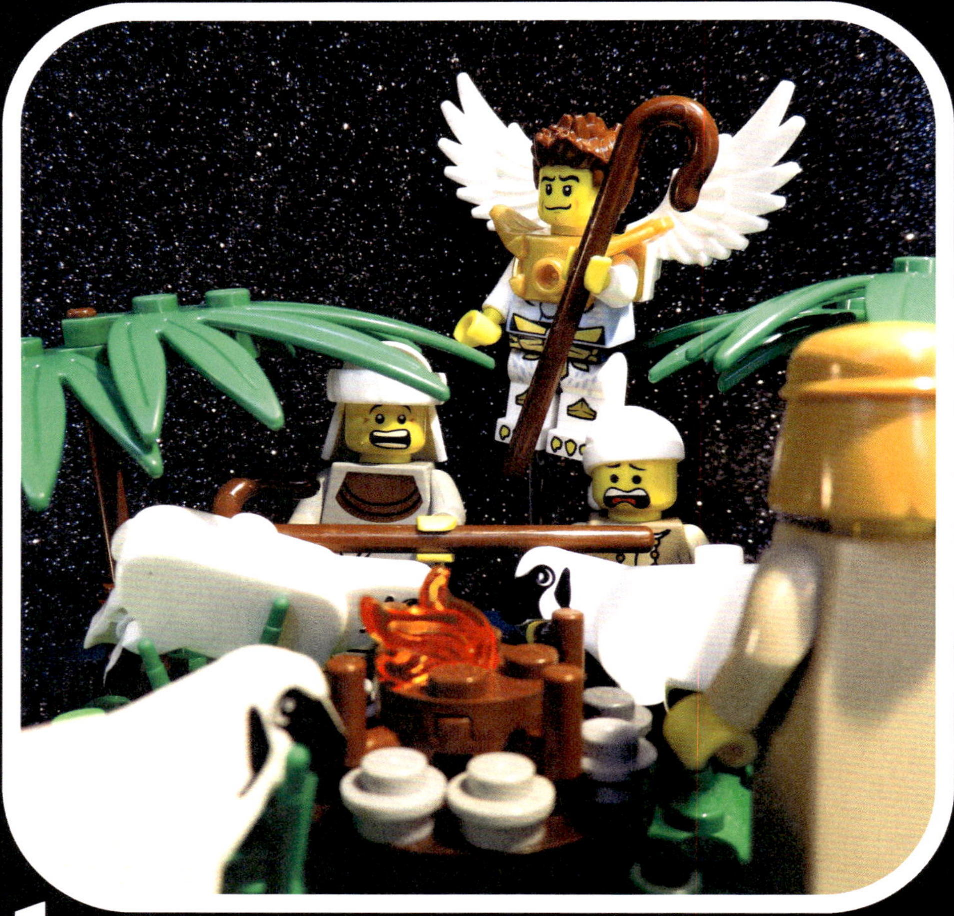

## Day 11

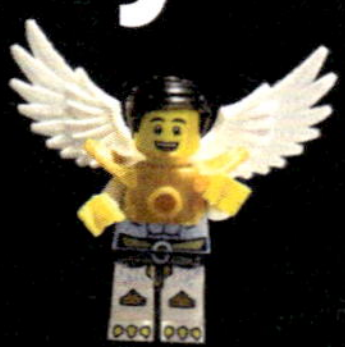

BRICK BUILD: THE ANGEL REALLY SURPRISED THOSE SHEPHERDS! BUILD A FIELD WITH SHEEP AND SHEPHERDS.

Luke 2:8-12

In that same country-side were shepherds out in the open fields, watching their flocks that night, when an angel of the Lord suddenly stood by them, and the glory of the Lord shone around them; and they were seized with fear.

The Angel said "Have no fear, for I bring you good news of great joy in store for all the nations. This day there has been born to you, in the town of David, a Savior, who is Christ the Lord. And this will be the sign for you. You will find the infant swathed, and lying in a manger."

# A MULTITUDE OF HEAVENLY HOSTS

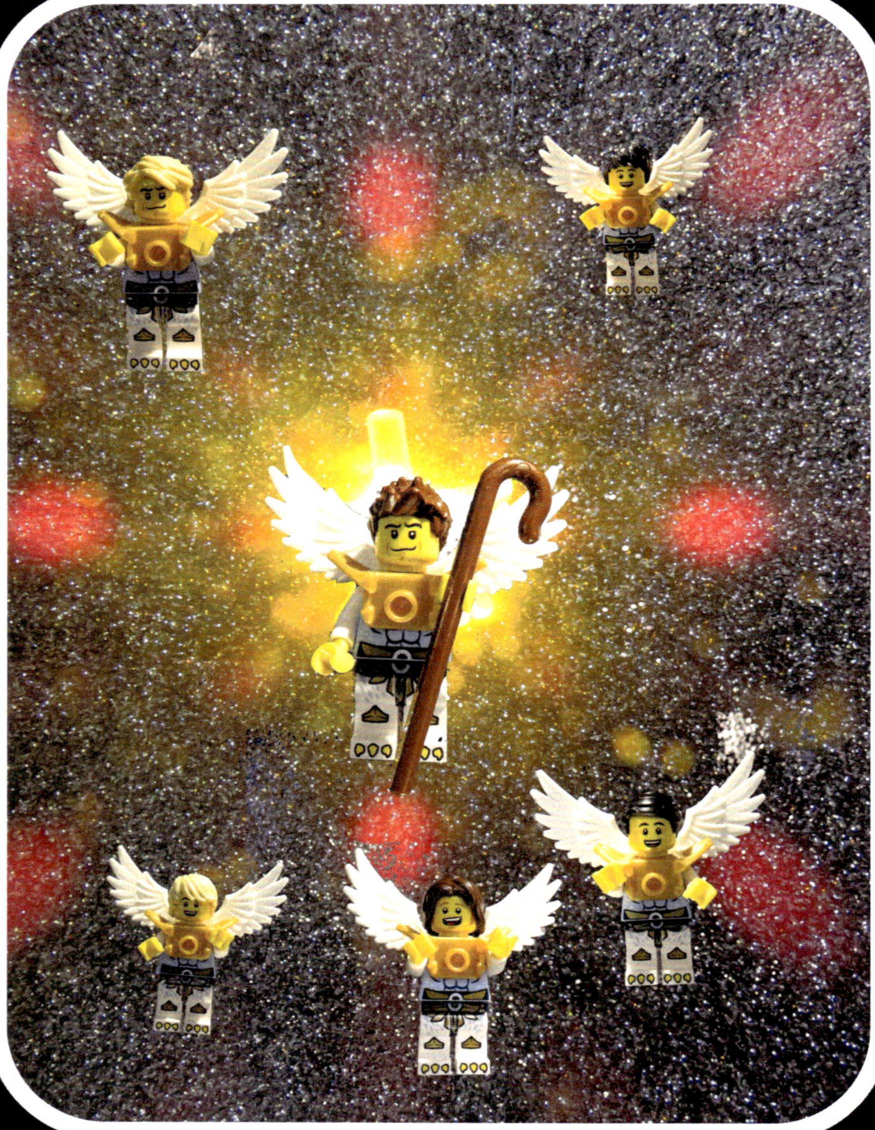

## Day 12

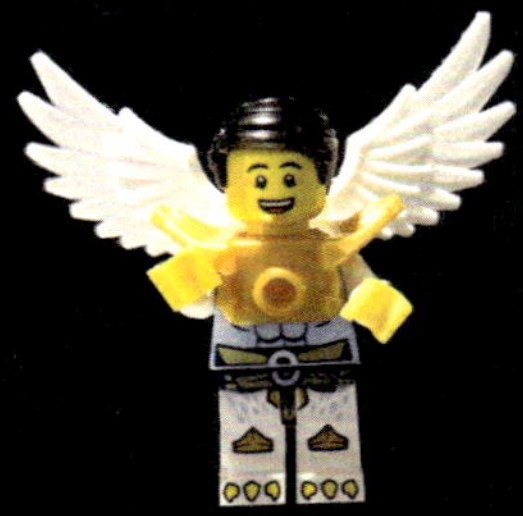

BRICK BUILD: TIME TO GET OUT ALL OF YOUR SPARE FIGURES AND GIVE THEM WINGS! USE PAPER OR TISSUE IF YOU DON'T HAVE ANY BRICK ONES. HELP THE ANGELS ANNOUNCE THE BIRTH OF CHRIST.

Luke 2:13-15

Then suddenly there appeared with the angel a multitude of the heavenly Hosts, praising God, and singing —

"Glory to God on high, and on earth peace among those in whom He finds pleasure."

Now, when the angels had left them and gone back to heaven, the shepherds said to one another: "Let us go at once to Bethlehem, and see this thing that has happened, of which the Lord has told us."

# THE SHEPHERDS FIND JESUS

## Day 13

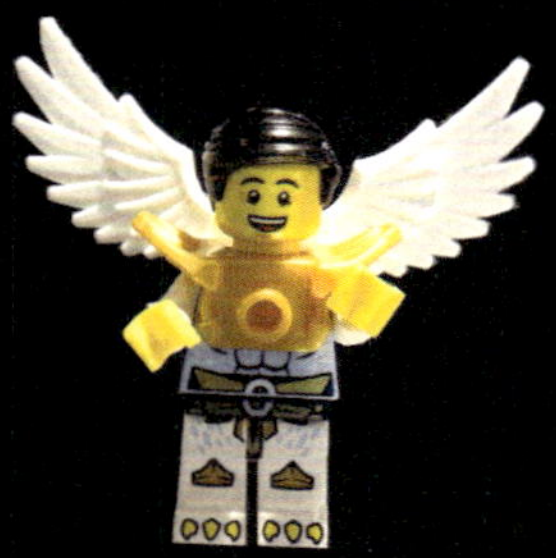

BRICK BUILD: BRING THE SHEPHERDS YOU BUILT FROM THE FIELD TO THE MANGER TO MEET BABY JESUS!

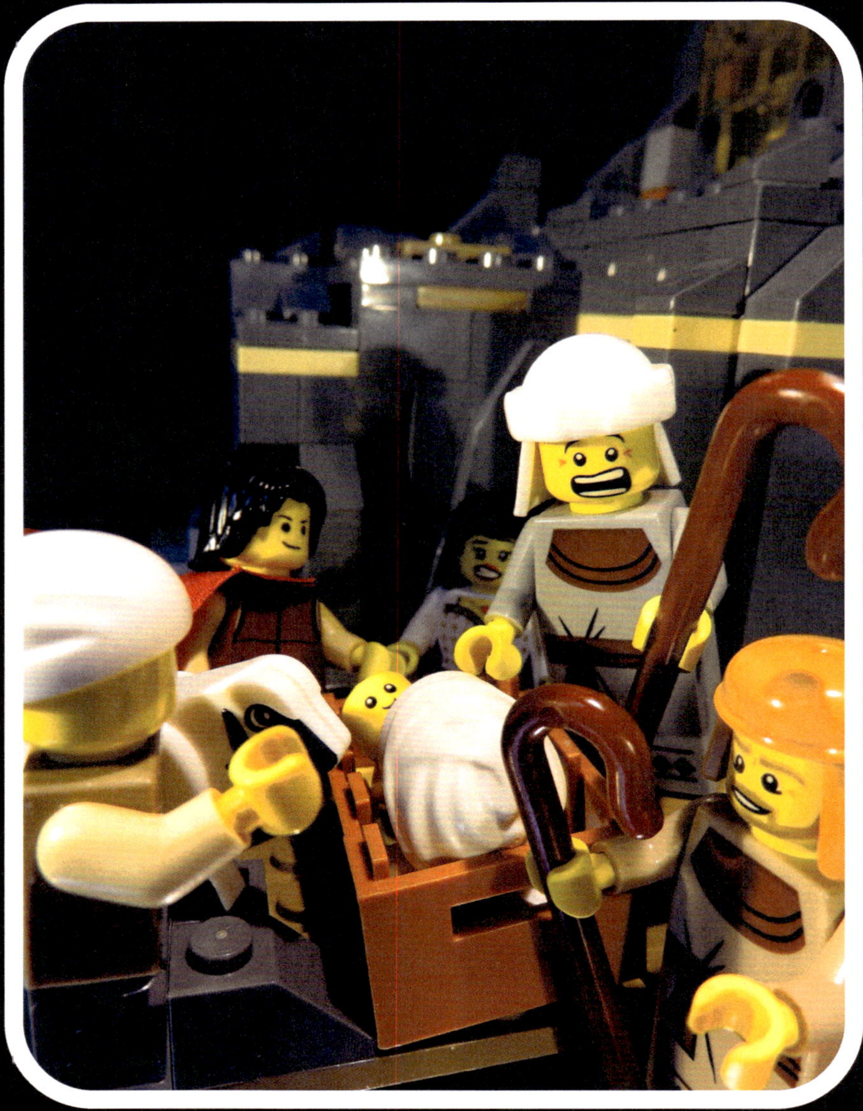

## Luke 2:16-20

So they [The Shepherds] went quickly, and found Mary and Joseph, and the infant lying in a manger; and, when they saw it, they told of all that had been said to them about this child. All who heard the shepherds were astonished at their story the shepherds went back, giving glory and praise to God for all that they had heard and seen, as it had been told them.

Mary treasured up all that they said, and thought about it often in her thoughts.

# JESUS PRESENTED IN THE TEMPLE

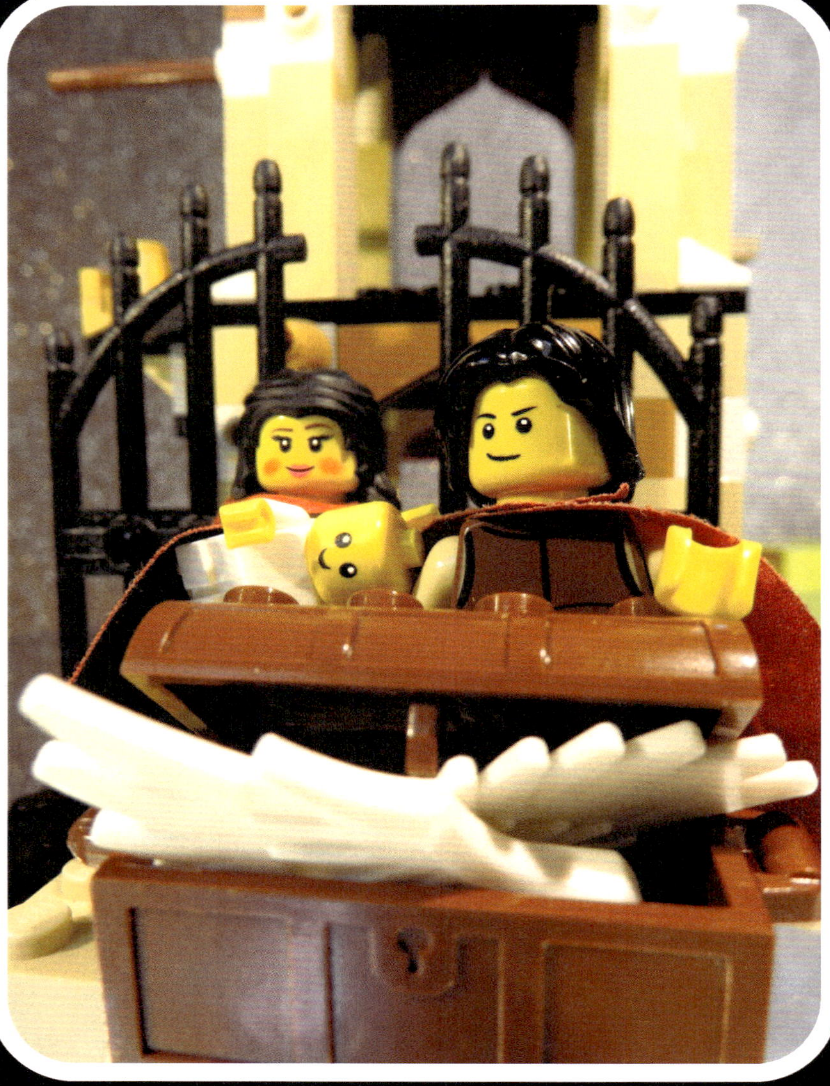

## Day 14

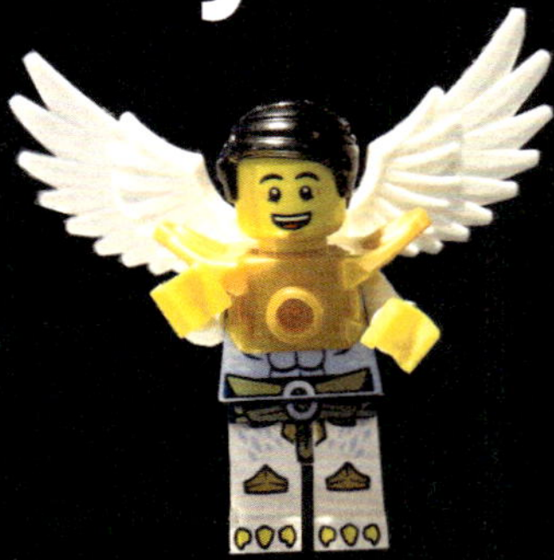

**BRICK BUILD: JESUS IS GOING TO BE DEDICATED TO THE LORD! BRING MARY, JOSEPH, AND JESUS TO THE TEMPLE FOR HIS DEDICATION.**

## Luke 2:21-24

Eight days after the birth of the child, when it was time to circumcise Him, He received the name Jesus — the name given Him by the angel before His conception.

When the period of purification of mother and child, required by the Law of Moses, came to an end, His parents took the child up to Jerusalem to present Him to the Lord, in compliance with the Law of the Lord that 'every first-born male will be dedicated to the Lord,' and also to offer the sacrifice required by the Law of the Lord — 'a pair of turtle-doves or two young pigeons.'

# SIMEON

**15**

BRICK BUILD: SIMEON HAS WAITED HIS WHOLE LIFE TO MEET JESUS! BUILD SIMEON AND LET HIM HOLD BABY JESUS.

There was at that time in Jerusalem a man named Simeon, a righteous and devout man, who lived in constant expectation of the consolation of Israel, and under the guidance of the Holy Spirit. It had been revealed to him by the Holy Spirit that he should not die until he had seen the Lord's Christ. Moved by the Spirit, Simeon came into the temple courts, and, when the parents brought in the child Jesus, to do for Him what was customary under the Law, Simeon himself took the child in his arms, and blessed God, and said: "Now, Lord, you will let your servant go, according to your word, in peace, for my eyes have seen the salvation which you have prepared in the sight of all nations a light to bring light to the Gentiles, and to be the glory of your people Israel."

While the child's father and mother were wondering at what was said about Him, Simeon gave them his blessing, and said to Mary, the child's mother: "This child is appointed to be the cause of the fall and rise of many in Israel, and to be a sign much spoken against -Yes, the sword will pierce your own heart and so the thoughts in many minds will be disclosed."

# ANNA

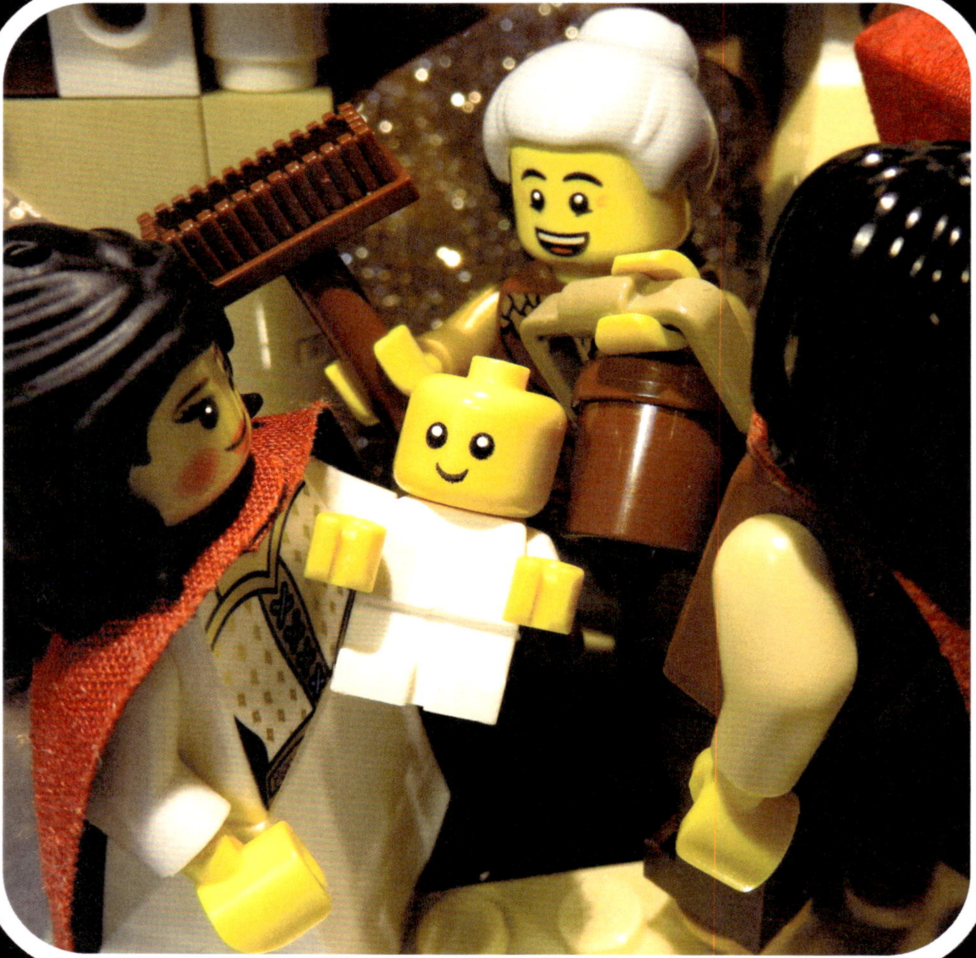

**Day 16**

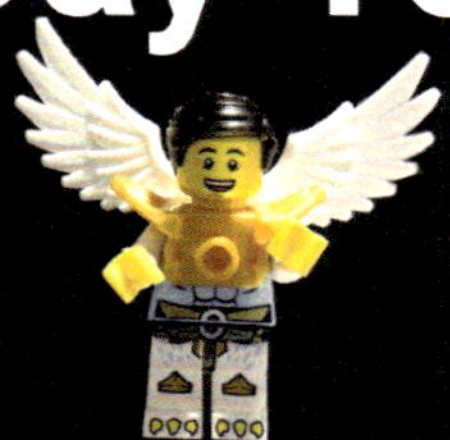

BRICK BUILD: ANNA IS EXCITED TO MEET BABY JESUS. BUILD ANNA AND HELP HER TELL EVERYONE ABOUT BABY JESUS!

There was also a prophetess named Anna, a daughter of Phanuel and of the tribe of Asher. She was far advanced in years, having lived with her husband for seven years after marriage, and then a widow, until she had reached the age of eighty-four. She never left the temple courts, but, fasting and praying, worshiped God night and day. At that moment she came up, and began publicly to thank God and to speak about the child to all who were looking for the deliverance of Jerusalem.

# WISE MEN FROM THE EAST

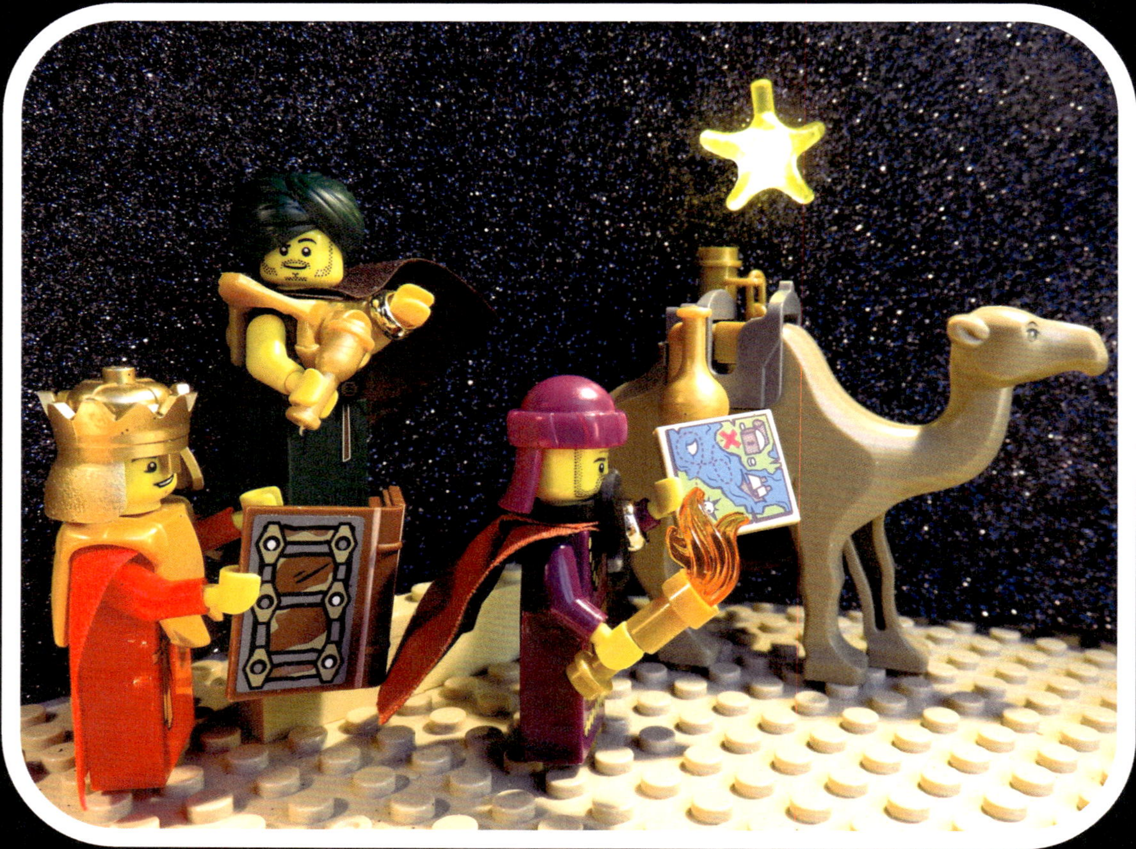

## Day 17

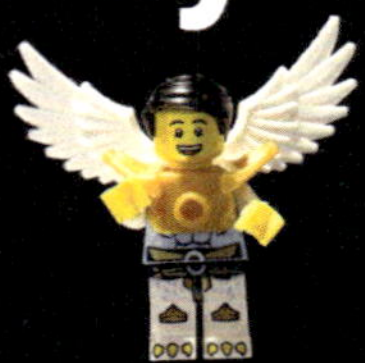

BRICK BUILD: THE NEWS OF JESUS BIRTH IS OUT. THESE WISE MEN HAVE TRAVELED A LONG WAY TO FIND HIM. BUILD SOME WISEMEN AND SEND THEM ON THEIR JOURNEY TO BETHLEHEM. DON'T FORGET TO BUILD A STAR FOR THEM TO FOLLOW!

Matthew 2:1-2

After the birth of Jesus at Bethlehem in Judea, in the reign of King Herod, some astrologers [wise men] from the East arrived in Jerusalem, asking: "Where is the newborn king of the Jews? For we saw His star in the east, and have come to worship Him."

# HEROD CALLS THE CHIEF PRIESTS AND TEACHERS OF THE LAW

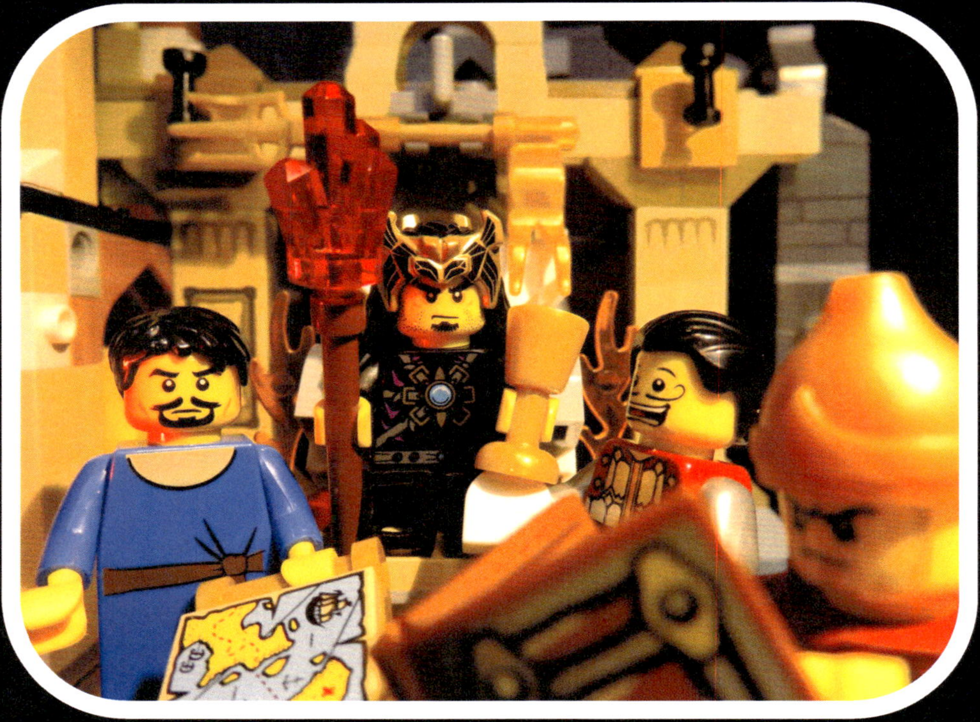

## Day 18

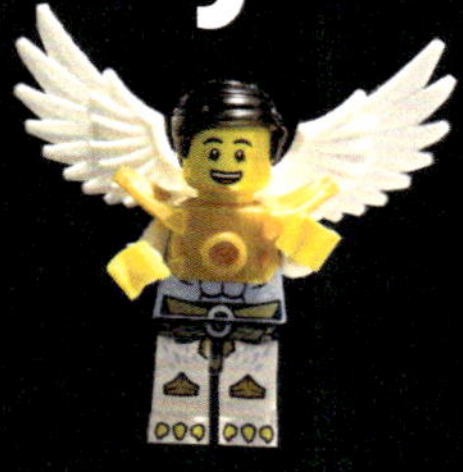

**BRICK BUILD:** KING HEROD HEARD THAT PEOPLE WERE LOOKING FOR A "NEW BORN KING." BUILD KING HEROD AND HIS PALACE.

Matthew 2:3-6

When King Herod heard of this, he was much troubled, and so too was all Jerusalem. He called together all the chief priests and teachers of the Law in the nation, and questioned them as to where the Christ was to be born.

"At Bethlehem in Judea," was their answer, "for it is said by the prophets ——

'And you, Bethlehem in Judah's land, are in no way least among the chief cities of Judah, for out of you will come a ruler — who will shepherd my people Israel.'"

# HEROD MEETS WITH THE WISE MEN

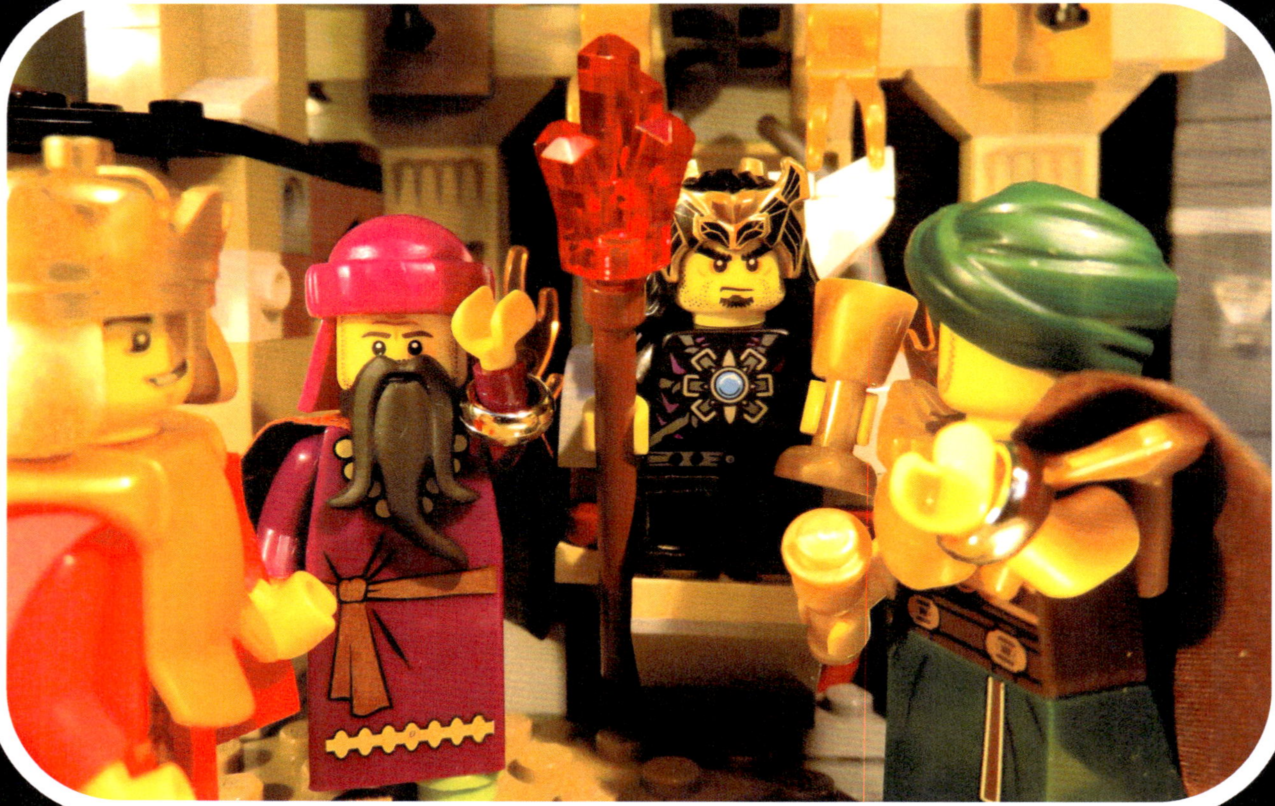

## Day 19

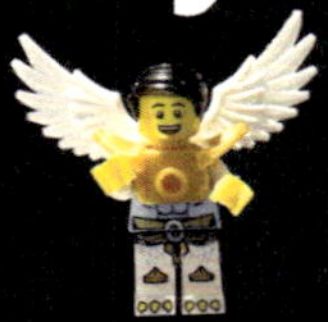

**BRICK BUILD:** KING HEROD WANTS TO KNOW MORE ABOUT THIS "NEW BORN KING." BRING THE WISE MEN YOU MADE TO MEET WITH HEROD AT HIS PALACE.

Matthew 2:7-9

Then Herod secretly sent for the astrologers [wise men]. He found out from them the time of the appearance of the star. Sending them to Bethlehem he said: "Go and make a careful search for the child. When you have found Him, bring word back to me, so that I, too, can go and worship Him." The astrologers [wise men] heard what the king had to say, and then continued their journey. The star which they had seen in the east led them on, until it reached and stood over the place where the child was.

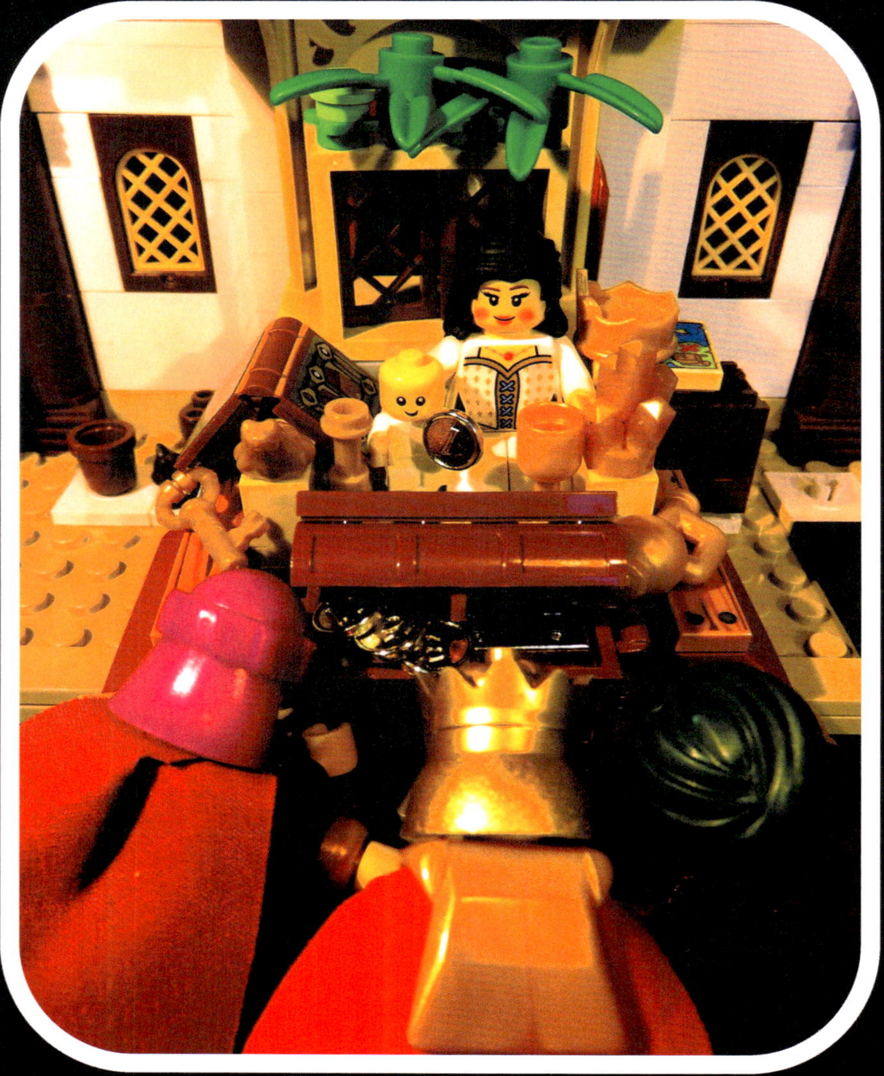

# THE WISE MEN MEET JESUS

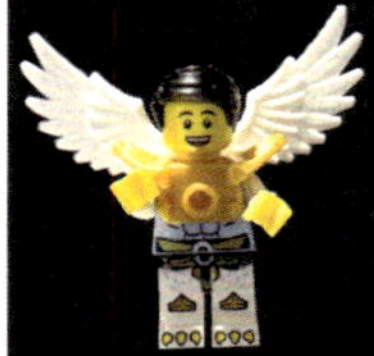

## Day 20

**BRICK BUILD:** HOW EXCITING THAT THE WISE MEN HAVE FOUND JESUS! BUILD THE HOUSE JESUS IS NOW LIVING IN AND BRING THE WISE MEN TO MEET HIM. DON'T FORGET TO BUILD THEIR GIFTS OF GOLD AND SPICES TO GIVE TO JESUS.

When the child's parents had done everything required by the law of the Lord, they returned to Galilee to their own town of Nazareth.

Matthew 2:11-12

At the sight of the star they [the wise men] were filled with joy. Entering the house [where Jesus and his family were], they saw the child with His mother, Mary, and fell at His feet and worshiped Him. Then they opened their treasure chests, and offered to

the child presents of gold, and spices of frankincense, and myrrh. Afterward, having been warned in a dream not to go back to Herod, they returned to their own country by another road.

# THE ESCAPE TO EGYPT

## Day 21

**BRICK BUILD:** URGENT! IT'S TIME TO MOVE! BUILD A SCENE OF EGYPT AND HELP JOSEPH, MARY AND JESUS MOVE THERE AS THE ANGEL INSTRUCTED.

## Matthew 2:13-15

After they [the wise men] had left, an angel of the Lord appeared to Joseph in a dream, and said: "Get up, take the child and his mother, and seek refuge in Egypt; and stay there until I tell you to return, for Herod is about to search for the child, to put him to death." Joseph woke up, and taking the child and his mother by night, went into Egypt, and there he stayed until Herod's death; in fulfillment of these words of the Lord by the prophets, where He says — 'Out of Egypt I called My Son.'

# HEROD WAS ANGRY

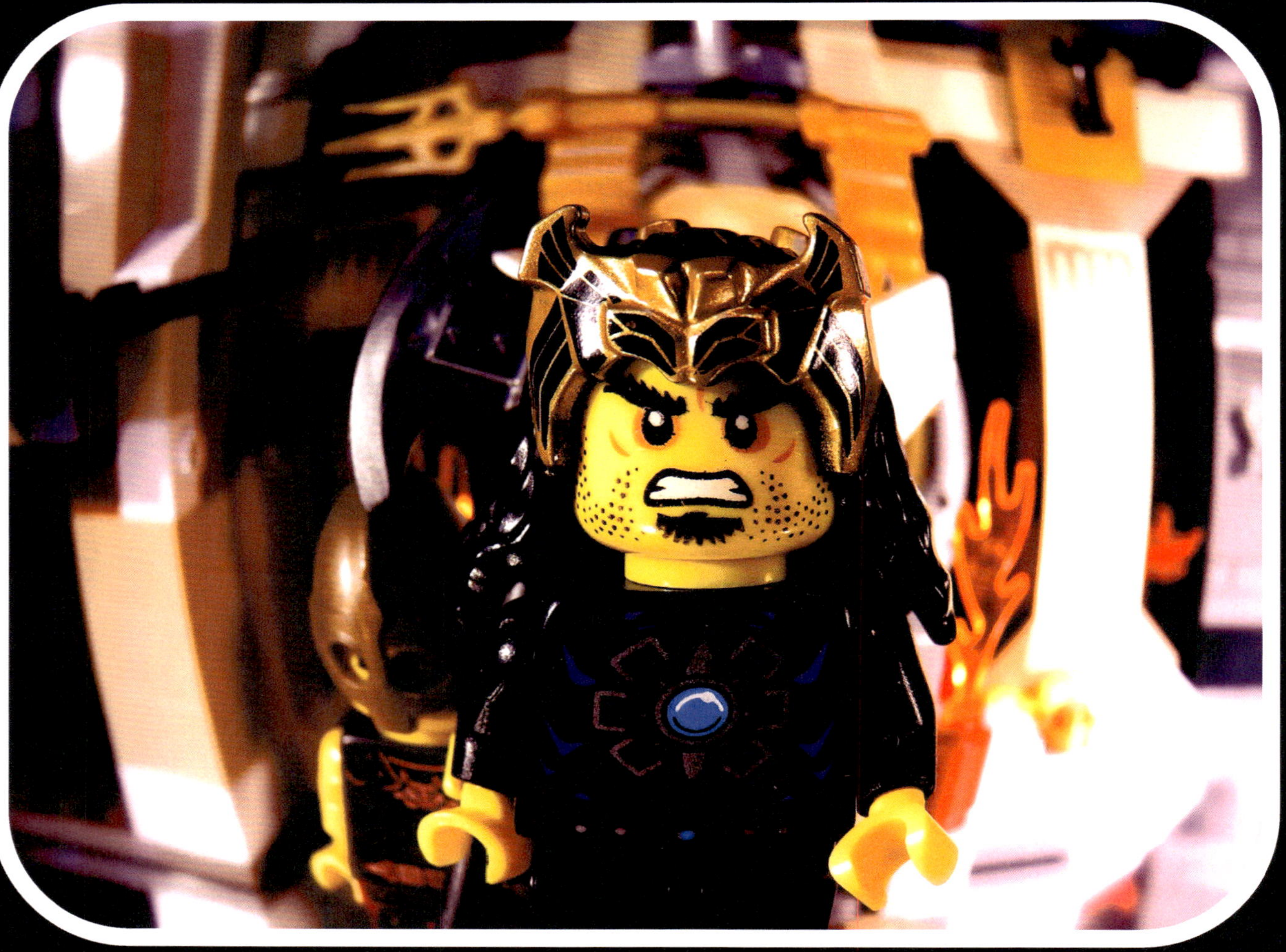

# Day 22

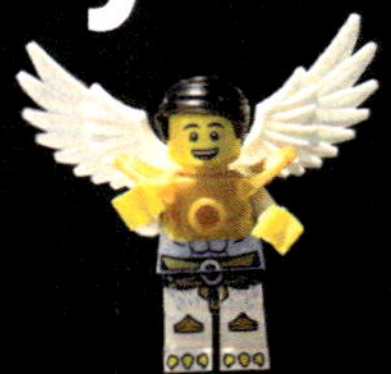

**BRICK BUILD:** ANGRY KING HEROD HAS SENT HIS SOLDIERS TO FIND JESUS. BUILD SOME SOLDIERS AND SEND THEM AROUND BETHLEHEM TO LOOK FOR "THE NEW BORN KING." THEY WON'T FIND JESUS OF COURSE BECAUSE GOD HAS ALREADY SENT HIM TO SAFETY IN EGYPT!

Matthew 2:16-18

When Herod found out that the astrologers [wise men] were not coming back, he flew into a rage. He sent out an order to put to death all the boys in Bethlehem and the whole of that region, who were two years old or under, guided by the time which he had learned from the astrologers [wise men]. Then were fulfilled these words spoken by the prophet Jeremiah, where he says — 'A voice was heard in Ramah, weeping and mourning loudly; Rachel, weeping for her children, refusing all comfort for they were dead.'

# RETURN TO NAZARETH

## Day 23

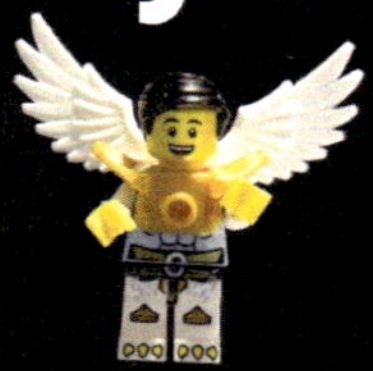

**BRICK BUILD:** IT'S TIME TO MOVE AGAIN! BUILD A HOUSE IN NAZARETH FOR JESUS TO GROW UP IN. NOW MOVE JESUS AND HIS FAMILY OUT OF EGYPT AND INTO HIS NEW HOUSE!

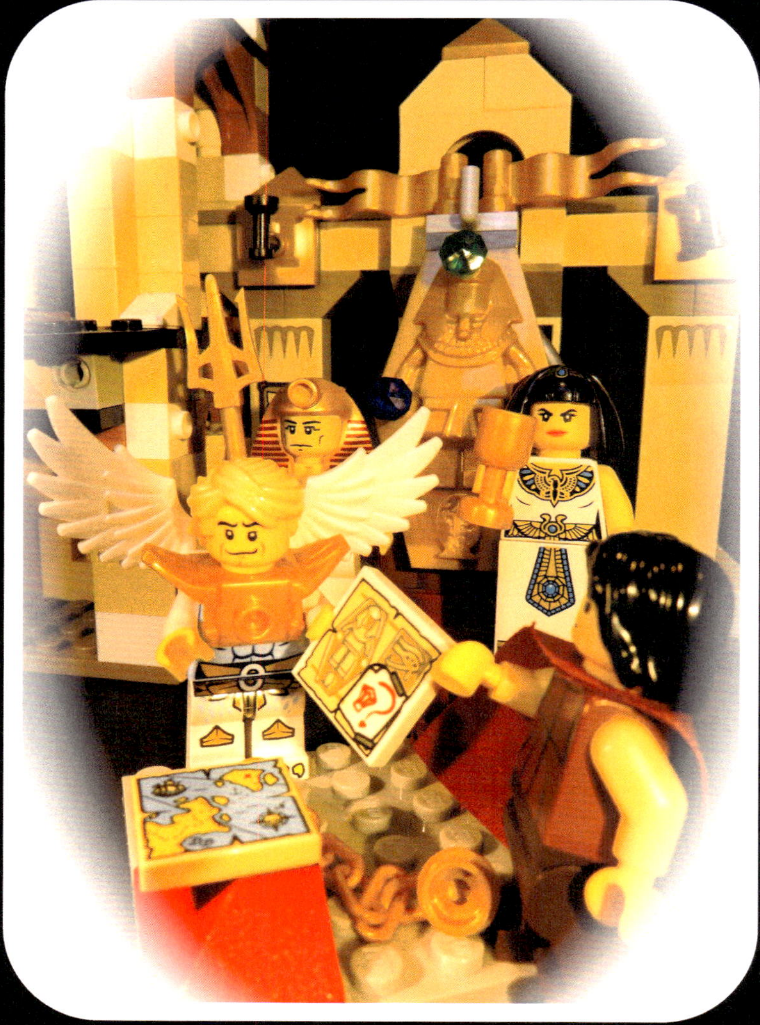

# Matthew 2:19-23

But, on the death of King Herod, an angel of the Lord appeared in a dream to Joseph in Egypt, and said: "Get up, take the child and his mother, and go into the Land of Israel, for those who sought to take the child's life are dead." He woke up, and taking the child and his mother, went into the land of Israel. Hearing that Archelaus had succeeded his father Herod as king of Judea, he was afraid to go back there; and having been warned in a dream, he went into the part of the country called Galilee. There he settled in the town of Nazareth, in fulfillment of these words by the prophets — 'He [Jesus] will be called a Nazarene.'

# PRAYER TO UNDERSTAND CHRIST'S LOVE

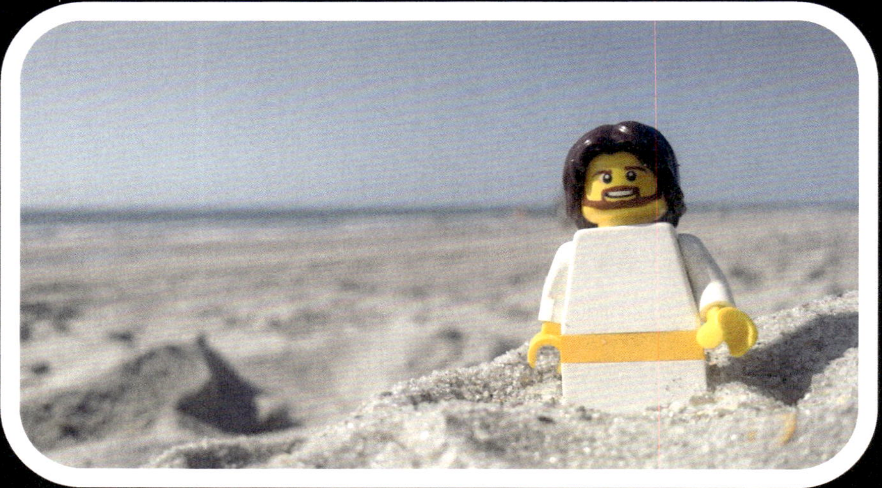

## Day 24

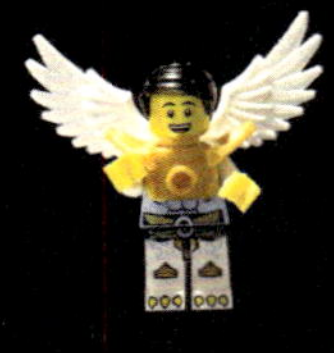

**BRICK BUILD: JESUS CHRIST LOVES YOU! BUILD A BRICK HEART THAT CAN BE FILLED WITH GOD'S LOVE!**

Epheshians 3:16-19

And [I] pray that, He will strengthen you with His power by breathing His Spirit into your inmost soul, so that Christ, through your faith, may make his home within your hearts in love; And I pray that you, now firmly rooted and established, may, with all Christ's people, have the power to comprehend in all its width and length, height and depth . . . the love of Christ; and so be filled to the full with God himself.

51968430R00031

Made in the USA
Middletown, DE
15 November 2017